D1422366

The Armburgh Papers

The Armburgh Papers

THE BROKHOLES INHERITANCE IN
WARWICKSHIRE, HERTFORDSHIRE AND ESSEX
c.1417–c.1453

Chetham's Manuscript Mun. E.6.10 (4)

EDITED WITH AN INTRODUCTION BY

Christine Carpenter

THE BOYDELL PRESS

First published 1998
The Boydell Press, Woodbridge

ISBN 0 85115 624 X

The Boydell Press is an imprint of Boydell & Brewer Ltd
PO Box 9, Woodbridge, Suffolk IP12 3DF, UK
and of Boydell & Brewer Inc.
PO Box 41026, Rochester, NY 14604–4126, USA

A catalogue record for this book is available
from the British Library

Library of Congress Catalog Card Number: 98–7954

This publication is printed on acid-free paper

Printed in Great Britain by
St Edmundsbury Press Ltd, Bury St Edmunds, Suffolk

CONTENTS

The publishers acknowledge the generous financial support of the Marc Fitch Fund in the production of this volume

PREFACE

My chief debt is to Dr Edward Powell, who not only provided notes for most of the technical legal terms (these are all marked (E.P.)) but, in reading through my typescript, saved me from several errors and omissions. I must also thank Dr Richard Davies for suggesting that Chetham's Library approach me after they had found this wonderful manuscript and for hospitality on my first exploratory visit, and the staff at the Library, especially Dr Michael Powell, for their help in all my dealings with them over the manuscript. Thanks are also due to Boydell & Brewer, especially Dr Richard Barber, for their alacrity in taking the manuscript when I found myself suddenly and unexpectedly without a publisher, and for considerable forbearance in not demanding more than some entirely reasonable changes to a text which had been completed for a different imprint. Finally, the fellow-scholars whose brains I picked while footnoting the manuscript are acknowledged at the points where their advice and information were decisive, but I must offer a more general thank you to Dr Benjamin Thompson for setting me on the right track initially with a host of queries relating to matters ecclesiastical.

Note that the general reference for writs discussed in notes by E.P. is *Registrum Omnium Brevium Tam Originalium Quam Judicialium* (London, 1687).

Where ambiguity may arise in the cross-referencing, footnote references are to be taken to refer to the text unless the cross-reference explicitly refers to 'Intro.'

ABBREVIATIONS

Cal. Close Rolls	*Calendar of Close Rolls Preserved in the Public Record Office 1396–1509* (19 vols., London, HMSO, 1927–63)
Cal. Fine Rolls	*Calendar of Fine Rolls Preserved in the Public Record Office 1399–1509* (11 vols., London, HMSO, 1931–62)
Cal. Pat. Rolls	*Calendar of Patent Rolls Preserved in the Public Record Office 1399–1509* (London, HMSO,1903–16)
Cat. Anc. Deeds	*A Descriptive Catalogue of Ancient Deeds in the Public Record Office* (6 vols., London, HMSO, 1890–1915)
CIPM	*Calendar of Inquisitions Post Mortem . . . Preserved in the Public Record Office* (20 vols., London, HMSO, 1904–)
Complete Peerage	*The Complete Peerage*, ed. V. Gibbs, H.A. Doubleday *et al.* (13 vols., London, 1910–40)
DNB	*Dictionary of National Biography*, ed. L. Stephen *et al.* (53 vols. with 6 supplementary vols., 1885–1912)
EETS	Early English Text Society
o.s.	original series
Feudal Aids	*Inquisitions and Assessments Relating to Feudal Aids . . . Preserved in the Public Record Office* (6 vols., London, HMSO, 1899–1920)
HMC	Royal Commission on Historical Manuscripts
HP	*The History of Parliament: The House of Commons 1386–1421*, ed. J.S. Roskell, L. Clark and C. Rawcliffe (4 vols., Stroud, 1993)
IPM Hen.VII	*Calendar of Inquisitions Post Mortem . . . Preserved in the Public Record Office, Hen.VII* (3 vols., London, HMSO, 1898–1955)
IPM Rec. Comms. Hen.V–Ric.III	*Calendarium Inquisitionum Post Mortem sive Escaetarum, iv, Hen.V–Ric.III* (Rec. Comms., London, 1828)
PRO	Public Record Office
VCH	*Victoria County History*
Wedgwood: Biographies	J.C. Wedgwood, *History of Parliament: Biographies of Members of the Commons House 1439–1539* (London, 1936)

INTRODUCTION

This is one of the most remarkable documents for the history of late-medieval England to have been discovered in recent years. First, and above all, it is the largest collection of private letters from the period to have been found since the four major correspondences, those of the Pastons, Stonors, Plumptons and Celys, were published in the nineteenth and early twentieth centuries.[1] Like all but the last of these, it comes from a gentry family, and the roll therefore adds considerably to our evidence for this social group, which is now acknowledged to be of crucial significance to our understanding of politics and society in late-medieval England, but which has left so little beyond the most formal evidence behind it.[2] In this case, however, it is a lesser and much less well documented family. Indeed, were it not for this roll, we would know very little about the complex and compelling litigation of the Armburghs.

This collection of letters is also different in covering a shorter period, and dealing mostly with a single dispute and with affairs in only one generation of the family, that of Robert and Joan Armburgh. Unlike the other correspondences, the roll therefore tells us little about gentry life beyond the impact of sustained litigation, although we shall see that this was wide-ranging. However, in many ways it is the concentrated focus of the document which makes it so especially informative, giving us a detailed privileged view of what it meant to be in one of these long-running suits. There is also the added benefit that its chronological focus is largely the earlier part of Henry VI's reign – the greatest concentration of letters comes from the later 1420s and early 1430s – followed by another clutch from c.1448–53. While the Paston letters at their fullest cover the period c.1440–80, the Stonor collection is at its richest for the period c.1470–83 and the Plumpton one does not really come into its own until after Bosworth. The roll is thus almost unique in giving us a close view of one of the most important elements in political society as the polity began to feel the stresses and strains of governance without a king, during the later

---

1 The references here are to the standard editions as used today: *The Paston Letters*, ed. J.G. Gairdner (6 vols., London, 1904, rpt. in 1 vol., Gloucester, 1983); *Paston Letters and Papers of the Fifteenth Century*, ed. N. Davis (2 vols., Oxford, 1971–6); *The Stonor Letters and Papers 1290–1483*, ed. C.L. Kingsford, (3 vols., Camden Soc., 3rd ser., 29, 30, 34, 1919–24, rpt. Cambridge, 1996, ed. C. Carpenter); *Plumpton Correspondence*, ed. T. Stapleton (Camden Soc., 1839, rpt. Gloucester, 1990); *The Cely Papers 1472–1488*, ed. A. Hanham (Early English Text Soc., 273, 1975).

2 The growing literature on the late-medieval gentry is listed and surveyed in C. Carpenter, 'Gentry and Community in Medieval England', *Journ. British Studs.*, 33 (1994), pp.340–80. See also, published since then, G.L. Harriss, 'The Dimensions of Politics', *The McFarlane Legacy*, ed. R.H. Britnell and A.J. Pollard (Stroud, 1995), pp.1–20.

stages of Henry VI's minority.[3] Then, like the Paston letters, it offers another look at the gentry at the time when the full import of the adult Henry's inability to rule was becoming all too plain.

But its significance goes beyond the merely historical. There are the love letters or poems in the middle of the roll. All but one of these is unknown elsewhere, and to find such poems apparently linked with a named and identifiable person is most unusual.[4] There are also the two most memorable letters, those to Thomas Bendyssh and John Horell, especially the second, which contain literary invective of a high order.[5] Indeed, there is a freedom of language in several of the letters which one meets relatively rarely in the more famous correspondences, concerned as they are for so much of the time with business affairs, even in the letters within the family. As I have suggested elsewhere, this is not because the writers lacked feelings but rather because they were usually writing business letters and the family servant who carried the letter would probably be furnished with more personal information, to be given by word of mouth.[6] Robert Armburgh, however, although he used servants to carry his letters, was writing less to manage a business than to assert his rights to the lands which were fundamental to that enterprise. Armburgh's correspondence as we have it, unlike those of the Pastons, Plumptons and Stonors, is not focused on a central routine of management of estate and family on which conflict may at time intrude, but is about conflict, and some of the letters are to personal enemies. And so we have the direct invective by and about his supposed allies and the personal attacks on his foes. These are not only significant additions to the corpus of fifteenth-century English prose, but, like the lively account of the fates of those who opposed the Armburghs,[7] and the description of Warwickshire men in general and the Armburghs' farmers at Mancetter in particular as 'sturdy fellows . . . strange, sly and mighty with subtle words',[8] they serve as a reminder, which historians would do well to take to heart, that, even if these people lived centuries ago, and if many of their concerns were alien to ours, they were real people, possessed of as powerful emotions as anything we are likely to find today.

---

3   C. Carpenter, *Locality and Polity: a Study of Warwickshire Landed Society, 1401–1499* (Cambridge, 1992), p.394; R.A. Griffiths, *The Reign of King Henry VI* (London, 1981), pp.144–8.
4   For more on these, see below, pp.58–9.
5   See below, pp.90–1, 120–3.
6   See C. Carpenter, 'The Stonor Circle in the Fifteenth Century', *Rulers and Ruled in Medieval England*, ed. R. Archer and S. Walker (London, 1995), p.178.
7   See below, pp.61–7.
8   See below, p.139.

(i) The document

The document was found in Chetham's Library amongst some miscellaneous papers donated to the library by Raines, the nineteenth-century Lancashire antiquary, a substantial benefactor of the library, who had himself referred to the document in one of his own writings.[9] It consists of a roll, written on both sides, containing copies of papers written between about 1417 and the early 1450s. These are nearly all letters and most of them concern a dispute over the Brokholes/Roos properties in Hertfordshire, Essex and Warwickshire. The roll arrived in the north-west in error, 'Mancetter' in eastern Warwickshire, the focus of much of the dispute and subject of many of the letters, having been mistaken for 'Manchester'.

The top of the verso gives us the history of the document but does not explain why it was thus misconstrued. This part is badly torn, but there are, in a seventeenth-century hand, the remains of a summary of the contents: 'To Mild of Clare and Bernard Willi . . . erne etc Harpo, and Barbo, the Lady Chartile, Thom . . . Bendisch Rick Ketford, John Rigges . . . Abbat of M[erivale] . . . tenants of the Manour of Manchester'.[10] Underneath, in Raines' writing, is written, 'F R Raines MA Milnrow, To the Chetham Library, Manchester, 1850'. In the same writing, the word 'Manchester' in the summary is crossed out and 'Mancetter Co. Warw.' substituted beneath.

The origins of the document and how it reached the north-west are explained further down by Raines, who writes, 'This roll was in the possession of Sir Wm. Dugdale & was lent by him to his friend Dr. Theophilus Howorth of Howorth in Rochdale about the year 1660 and was given to me by Mr. John Elliott, attorney of Rochdale in 1835'. Underneath this is written 'F.R. Raines' and underneath that, in the same writing, 'See Dugdale's Hist. of Warwicks: Vol. 2 p.1077. Ed. 1730'. Dugdale had a large collection of Warwickshire material, much of it from local gentry families, built up with the help of Sir Simon Archer, a member of the Archer family of Warwickshire, which he used to write his exceptionally detailed and accurate history of Warwickshire.[11] It was not unusual for antiquaries to lend each other papers and, in at least one other instance, this turned into permanent ownership.[12] Howarth was a Manchester physician and an antiquary. He was a friend of

---

9   I am most grateful to Dr Michael Powell, librarian at Chetham's, for his help in tracing the origins and for information on its early history and north-western owners. On Raines, see *DNB*, xlvii, pp.177–8. Raines made reference to the roll in F. Gastrell, *Notitia Cestriensis*, ii I (Chetham Soc., 1849), p.100 n.5 (quoted in *VCH Lancs.*, v (London, 1911), p.175 n.8b), although for inexplicable reasons he dated it to Henry VII's reign.

10 All these are recipients of letters.

11 William Dugdale, *The Antiquities of Warwickshire* (2 vols., London, 1730, rpt. Manchester, n.d.); P. Styles, *Sir Simon Archer*, Dugdale Soc. Occasional Papers, 6 (1946).

12 Styles, *Simon Archer*, pp.43–4. Chetham's Library Mun. A.4.89 (11371) had a similar history: Dugdale to Howarth to Raines.

Dugdale and was in extended communication with him, mainly over his attempt to establish that he was related to the Howards of Norfolk. His interest was probably aroused by the role in the affair of the Holt family, one of the claimants to the Brokholes estate, for they were also a Rochdale family and the Howarths had had dealings with them in the fifteenth century.[13]

It seems probable that the error of 'Manchester' for 'Mancetter', which led to the document's eventual deposit in the north-west, was perpetrated by Howarth. Although Dugdale did not make use of the document in his 'Warwickshire' for genealogical or historical purposes, he would have been well aware of the identity of the Warwickshire manor at issue, not to mention of the people involved, and he was far too good and careful a historian to be guilty of such an egregious error. Moreover, the seventeenth-century hand describing the document, which contains the error, does not look like Dugdale's.[14] There are two possible scenarios. One is that Howarth was shown the document by Dugdale, perhaps because he thought Howarth might be interested in the reference to the Holts; intrigued by this, Howarth borrowed it, forgot that it referred to Mancetter, not Manchester, mislabelled it and never returned it, thinking perhaps that it was better for it to remain near the supposed geographical location of the dispute. The other more sinister one is that Howarth saw the document lying amongst Dugdale's papers, made the mistaken identification and 'borrowed' it. That would at least explain why Dugdale made no use of the document and perpetrated errors in his account of Mancetter that he could have avoided had he used the roll:[15] had he already examined it, it seems probable that he would have made use of the contents, even if the roll was no longer in his possession. Ironically, the loss of the document for more than three centuries, perhaps by an act of collector's vandalism, almost certainly saved it from permanent loss. Had Dugdale kept the roll, it would presumably have ended up with most of his other original sources in the Archer Collection and gone up in flames with the Birmingham Reference Library and the rest of the collection in 1879.[16]

(ii) The dispute

The dispute which dominates the roll focused on three different inheritances, of Roos, Brokhole and Mancetter, which had come together in the persons of the daughters and coheiresses of Geoffrey Brokhole. The Roos inheritance lay in Hertfordshire and Essex. In 1375 the male line ended and the property

---

13 Chetham's Lib. Raines xi, f.30; *VCH Lancs.*, v, pp.174–5; H. Fishwick, *The History of the Parish of Rochdale* (Rochdale and London, 1889), pp.413–21.

14 Compare the writing in the document in n.12, above, which is Dugdale's hand.

15 Dugdale, *Warwickshire*, pp.1077–8.

16 Styles, 'Simon Archer', p.10; *Catalogue of the Birmingham Collection*, edd. W. Powell and M. Cashmore (Birmingham, 1918), p.ix.

went to Ellen, aunt of the last John de Roos.[17] It consisted of Great Brockholes or Roos in Radwinter, Giffards, or Stanley Giffards, in Great Sampford (both Essex), Roos Hall in Sarratt and Over Hall in Gedelston or Gilston (both Hertfordshire).[18] Ellen married Geoffrey Brokhole, who owned New Hall in Asheldham (Essex) and Brokholes in Great Munden (Hertfordshire).[19] Geoffrey also owned a third of the manor of Mancetter in eastern Warwickshire. This had come to his family by the division among three daughters of the de Mancetter inheritance in 1365, one of whom Geoffrey's father, another Geoffrey, had married.[20]

The precipitating event in the dispute was the death in 1419 of Ellen, leaving two daughters, coheiresses to the entire inheritance. These were Joan, wife of Thomas Aspall of Essex (Aspall was dead by early July 1420) and Margery, who had been married to John Sumpter of Colchester but was already dead; her heir was their son, John Sumpter the younger, who was still within age.[21] In December 1419 custody of the young Sumpter's part of the inheritance was awarded to the Hertfordshire esquire and Duchy of Lancaster official John Leventhorpe.[22] By January 1420 there were already difficulties, when an arbitration awarded that John Sumpter (presumably the elder) should deliver to Joan by midsummer half of the manors of Sampford and Gedelston, together with the evidences for them, an agreement that was apparently not performed.[23] On 10 July the escheators in Warwickshire and Hertfordshire (which was a joint escheatorship with Essex) were ordered not to interfere with the estates in their jurisdiction to which Joan and John Sumpter the younger were heirs, as none of them were held of the king. This was presumably intended as a prelude to the final division. An undertaking to the king on Joan's behalf, made five days before, that she would not remarry without permission was probably not unconnected with the relinquishing of any royal claims to custody of the lands. That it was made by John Sumpter senior and Thomas Mylde, both of whom were to be on the opposing side to Joan, suggests that, despite the need for the earlier arbitration, there was not yet any serious dissension among the heirs.[24]

What the chancery officials who made these orders were ignorant of was

17 *VCH Herts.*, iii (London, 1912), p.320.
18 P. Morant, *The History and Antiquities of the County of Essex* (2 vols., London, 1768), ii, pp.526, 536; *VCH Herts.*, ii (London, 1908), p.439, iii, p.320.
19 Morant, *Essex*, i, pp.367–8; *VCH Herts.*, iii, p.127. See also *The Place-Names of Essex*, ed. P.H. Reaney (English Place-Name Soc., 12, 1935), pp.208, 513.
20 *VCH Warks.*, iv (London, 1947), pp.119–20. The Brokholes third was called Rose Hall, which suggests a Roos origin, but this was apparently not the case.
21 *Cal. Close Rolls 1419–22*, pp.82, 116; *Cal. Fine Rolls 1413–22*, pp.274, 275, 304; *IPM Rec. Comms. Hen.V–Ric.III*, 7 Hen.V/19; below, text pp.87–8 and n.87.
22 *Cal. Fine Rolls 1413–22*, p.304; *HP*, iii, pp.591–5.
23 See below, text, p.194.
24 *Cal. Close Rolls 1419–22*, pp.82, 116.

that John Sumpter the younger had died on 4 July 1420.[25] This was the real beginning of the dispute, for, according to Joan's side of the story, he left no siblings, a devastating blow to John senior's hopes of acquiring half the Roos/Brokholes inheritance for his family: the property should now have devolved in its entirety to Joan.[26] However, two alleged sisters to John the younger were produced: Christine and Ellen, aged respectively fifteen and fourteen in October 1426.[27] According to Joan, these were not proper heirs but illegitimate daughters of Sumpter senior.[28] All the same, at the delayed Essex IPM on Sumpter junior held in early October 1426, they were declared to be his heirs.[29] In May 1427 it was said that Joan was already in possession of her part of the inheritance and it was ordered that the Sumpter half in Essex be divided and that Christine, the older daughter, who had already proved her age, be given her part of it. The following November it was announced that Ellen had proved her age. The surviving proofs of age for both daughters are from Essex and date to March 1427 for Christine and July of that year for Ellen.[30] It is reasonable to assume that they were done in the joint escheatorship of Hertfordshire and in Warwickshire at about the same time. Certainly, according to Joan's party, the two girls were found heiresses and of age, and allowed to sue out their inheritances in all three counties.[31]

In Warwickshire they may have had the help of the escheator, who was in fact the crucial local official in these matters of inheritance;[32] his involvement on the Sumpter side relates to a substantial change of personnel on both sides in the 1420s. At Michaelmas 1420 Joan remarried.[33] Her husband, Robert Armburgh, seems to have had no property beyond what his wife brought him. He was the brother of William Armburgh, presumably the one who is listed among the Huntingdonshire notables who took the oath to maintain

---

25 PRO C139/21/6; below, text, pp.88–9. It is very improbable that there was any kind of chicanery in this time-lag, merely that the wheels of central officialdom ground too slowly to take cognisance of this crucial event.

26 According to a statement in the roll, John's sisters died about Lammas (1 August). If this was true it is possible that they died immediately after their brother (see below, p.193 and n.491 there for discussion of dating).

27 Below, text, p.89; PRO C139/21/6.

28 Below, text, pp.61, 193.

29 Below, text, p.88–9; PRO C139/21/6.

30 *Cal. Close Rolls 1422–9*, pp.299–300, 357; PRO C139/31/72, 73.

31 Below, text, p.92.

32 H.M. Jewell, *English Local Administration in the Middle Ages* (Newton Abbot, 1972), p.101; Carpenter, *Locality and Polity*, pp.355–6.

33 See below, text, p.79. This is unequivocal, as is PRO C1/4/65 (which shows that they were married by 3 May 1422) and the entry in the Feet of Fines (*Feet of Fines for Essex*, iv, 1423–1547, edd. P.H. Reaney and M. Fitch (Essex Archaeological Soc., 1964), p.3 (Hilary Term 1424)), despite the fact that Joan is still referred to by the crown as former wife of Thomas Aspall as late as 1427 (*Cal. Close Rolls 1422–9*, pp.299–300). Armburgh's wife is called 'Margaret' in the chancery record of the dealings that he and his wife had over the marriage of Margaret, daughter of Joan by her first husband, Philip Kedington, in July 1421, but this is clearly an error (*Cal. Close Rolls 1419–22*, p.206, verified in the original: PRO C54/271 m.14d.); below, pp.9–11 for the Kedingtons and their role in the case).

the peace in 1434: this would fit with the later designation of Reynold, Robert's nephew and probably son of his brother William, as 'of Hemingford Grey' and 'of Huntingdon'.[34] Robert may well have been a younger brother of William, in which case it was this marriage which made his fortune, and his anxiety to defend all parts of his wife's inheritance at any cost is made more explicable.

On the other side, by the time the order for the division of the lands in Essex was made in May 1427, Christine, the older daughter, was married to Thomas Bernard of Clare in Suffolk and Northamptonshire.[35] By about early November 1427, a new participant had arrived: James Bellers, the son of Ralph Bellers of Leicestershire and of Brownsover in eastern Warwickshire, not far from Mancetter, who had married Ellen.[36] It appears that Ralph Bellers and his friends were pulling the local strings that made the recognition of the Sumpter girls as legitimate heiresses possible. It was implied by Robert Armburgh that Ralph Bellers had used his powers as escheator of Warwickshire and Leicestershire to advance the cause of the Sumpter daughters. As Bellers was escheator in 1426–7 this would fit with the timing of the proofs of age and liveries for these two. Ellen was still unmarried in May 1427, by which time much of the groundwork in establishing the girls' rights had been done, so it would seem that Ralph lent a hand before the marriage to his son, in the expectation that the marriage would be a suitable *quid pro quo* once the lands had been secured.[37] The role of William Flete, escheator of Hertfordshire and Essex at this time, who oversaw the IPM for John Sumpter the younger, seems

34 *Cal. Pat. Rolls 1429–36*, p.376; *Cal. Close Rolls 1447–54*, p.448, *1454–61*, p.33; Wedgwood, *Biographies*, p.19; below, nn.to text 391, 461. William may also be the husbandman of Godmanchester (see below, n.391 to text; also Carpenter, *Locality and Polity*, p.75 for the continuing use of this term even for minor gentlemen at this time).

35 *Cal. Close Rolls 1422–9*, pp.299–300; *The Visitations of Essex*, ed. W.C. Metcalfe (2 vols., Harleian Soc., 13, 1878), ii, p.617; *VCH Northants*, iv (London, 1937), p.66. Bernard, a younger son, may also have had family in Cambridgeshire and even been from that county. There is a Thomas Bernard of Eltisley in the oath-list for Cambridgeshire of 1434 and, more significantly, a Robert Bernard (the name of Thomas' father) of Isleham in the same county; the parson of Isleham, Master John Bernard, is singled out as one of those who was a 'grete labourer' on the part of Armburgh's enemies (*Cal. Pat. Rolls 1429–36*, pp.385, 387; below, text, p.62). Furthermore, Bernard's office from the duke of York was steward in Cambridgeshire and Huntingdonshire (see below, n.135 to Intro.). For a suit between Bernard and Sumpter on the marriage agreement, see PRO C1/10/18.

36 Below, text, pp.66, 92, 145 and see n.139 to text for the date of the marriage; *Cal. Fine Rolls 1422–30*, p.214; PRO CP40/670 rot.414d; PRO KB27/669 Coram Rege rot.22 for Bellers as 'of Brownsover', which the family sold in 1471–2 (*Cal. Close Rolls 1468–76*, p.225; Warks. Rec. Off. CR162/75, 76). Ralph, described as 'of Leicestershire' in 1428 (*Cal. Fine Rolls 1422–30*, p.214) was presumably a member of the Bellers family of Leicestershire (E. Acheson, *A Gentry Community: Leicestershire in the Fifteenth Century c.1422–c.1485* (Cambridge, 1992), pp.218–19). He also had lands in Warwickshire, at Wappenbury and Eathorpe, which he had sold by 1437/8 (Dugdale, *Warwickshire*, pp.294, 296). See also Carpenter, *Locality and Polity*, p.648 (where James II does not feature because he had clearly died in his father's lifetime and, before the discovery of this document, seemed not to have played a significant part in Warwickshire affairs).

37 Below, text, p.92; A.C. Wood, *Typescript List of Escheators for England and Wales*, in the PRO (List and Index Soc., 72, 1971), p.170; *Cal. Close Rolls 1422–9*, pp.299–300; PRO CP40/670 rot.414d.

to have been equally equivocal, for he was part of the circle in these counties to which Sumpter and Bernard belonged and which was to act influentially on behalf of the Sumpter heirs. So was Edward Tyrell, the escheator before whom the proofs of age in Essex were done. Another actor in these events, John Horell, a man brought up by Ellen and her mother, seems to have played a dubious role in this, perhaps in giving the Sumpter girls privileged information which, had they really been imposters, they would not otherwise have had.[38] Similarly, the officials at Colchester, friends of Sumpter, were said to have 'stolen out a record under the town seal of Colchester' attesting the girls' legitimacy.[39]

Bellers' arrival on the scene had even worse repercussions for Armburgh and his wife, for he was a close servant of John Kempe, archbishop of York from 1425 and, most significantly, chancellor from March 1426 to 1432. Thomas Bernard was also said to be 'a squire of the chancellors'. This gave Armburgh's opponents obvious advantages when it came to petitioning the chancellor, but also less obvious but equally pronounced ones in getting writs out of chancery, possibly including those to the escheator which had enabled the Sumpter daughters to inherit, and certainly including judicial writs, which could then be concealed from their rivals. It is surely not pure coincidence that, when nothing had been done since John Sumpter the younger's death in 1420, Kempe's arrival set in train the processes that were to ensure the Sumpter heirs' succession: the writ for Sumpter's IPM was issued in April 1426, not long after Kempe became chancellor.[40] In fact, chancery was one of the several areas of interest controlled by their antagonists with which Robert and Joan had to contend.[41] The most unbiased follower of the events related to the securing of the Sumpter half of the inheritance has to admit that they seem all a little too pat: the Sumpters acquire two friends in chancery, Bernard and Bellers, the latter becomes escheator in one of the counties at issue, Warwickshire, while another associate, Flete, already holds the office in the other two counties, Hertfordshire and Essex, and is followed by another, Edward Tyrell. A considerably delayed IPM on young John Sumpter and proofs of age for the girls follow, all arranged to be during the tenure of Bellers, Flete and Tyrell, and, when all is well on the way to completion, Bellers' son is married to the unmarried heiress.[42]

After the orders of 1427, which left the Sumpter daughters in possession of

---

38 PRO C139/21/6, /31/72–3. Tyrell was younger brother of Sir John Tyrell, who was specifically named as one of the Armburghs' enemies (*HP*, iv, p.683) and see below, pp.16, 88, 120–3.

39 See below, text, p.62.

40 For Kempe, see *DNB*, xxx, pp.384–8, and *Handbook of British Chronology*, ed. E.B. Fryde, D.E. Greenway, S. Porter and I. Roy (3rd ed., London, Royal Historical Soc., 1986), p.87; PRO C139/21/6.

41 *Cal. Pat. Rolls 1436–41*, p.497, *1441–6*, p.42; *Cal. Fine Rolls 1422–30*, p.214, *1430–7*, p.340, *1437–45*, p.43; below, pp.1, 88, 107, 115, 117, 141–2.

42 See also the accusation that influence was brought to bear on the IPM jury by 'Baynard of Essex' (below, text, p.62).

their half of the inheritance, even though the formal division with Joan Brok-holes had yet to occur,[43] there seems to have been a relative lull. There was some trouble over woods at Mancetter, probably during the 1420s, which Harpour and Barbour, Armburgh's farmers at Mancetter, were requested to deal with.[44] These men, who feature prominently in the letters, were probably William Harpour of Mancetter and Richard Barbour, probably the yeoman of Atherstone next to Mancetter.[45] About the same time Ralph Beauchamp, a kinsman of Armburgh and vicar of 'Scharnyffeld' (perhaps Sharnford, Leices-tershire one of the advowsons owned by the priory at Monks Kirby in east Warwickshire?), who also seems to have had some part in the farm of Man-cetter,[46] was arrested at Colchester. The cause of the arrest was burning houses, but is likely to have been connected to the Essex wing of the dispute. John Sumpter was a leading resident of Colchester and Simon Mate, the bail-iff of Colchester in 1427, to whom Armburgh wrote about Beauchamp's arrest, was one of those cited by the Armburghs as a particular enemy. Two other Colchester citizens, John (more probably Thomas) Godestone and Wil-liam Notyngham, were similarly singled out and two of these three, Mate and Notyngham, had been feoffees to Ellen Brokhole, mother of Joan Armburgh and Margery Sumpter, while Notyngham had also been her executor.[47]

Another matter which complicated Robert Armburgh's life at this time was the fate of Joan's children by her first marriage. Before Aspall, she had been married to Philip Kedington of Suffolk and Ashdon, Essex. It was from this marriage that there came the surviving children of whom we hear, a son Robert and a daughter Margaret.[48] Robert gives every indication of having

---

43 See below, pp.12, 113–14, 119.

44 Below, text, p.89. This is in a clutch of letters which seem all to date to the 1420s: see below at indi-vidual letters for dating.

45 William Harpour of Mancetter, husband of one of the coheirs to the de Mancetters, seems the obvious recipient (*VCH Warks.*, iv, p.120; *HMC Report on the Hastings Manuscripts*, i (London, 1928), p.149; *Cal. Pat. Rolls 1446–52*, p.302). Sir John Barbour, the priest, had the farm later on (below, pp.34–5) but at this stage, when the farmer is given a forename, it is Richard (below, text, pp.134, 139); for Richard Barbour yeoman of Atherstone, see *Cal. Pat. Rolls 1436–41*, p.456.

46 J.G. Nichols, *The History and Antiquities of the County of Leicester* (4 vols., London, 1795–1811, rpt. Wakefield, 1971), iv, p.919, and see below, n.155 to text; below, text, pp.134–7.

47 Below, text, pp.93–4, 194; P. Morant, *The History and Antiquities of . . . Colchester* (2 vols., London, 1748, rpt. East Ardsley, 1970), i, p.99; *The Red Book of Colchester*, ed. W.G. Benham (Colchester, 1902), pp.46, 47. For Godestone and further information on the others, see below, n.14 to text.

48 Below, text, pp.90–1, 126–7, 178; F. Haslewood, 'The Ancient Families of Suffolk', *Procs. of the Suffolk Institute of Archaeology and Natural Hist.*, 8 (1884), p.176; Morant, *Essex*, ii, p.541. See also below, nn.144, 145, 147, 149 to Intro. for difficulties in determining what exactly Philip owned in Ashdon. Robert implies that there were other sons and there is later evidence of three other sib-lings (see below, n.144 to Intro.). However, one of these may well have been the parent of Joan's eventual heirs, the Palmers (see below, p.30). An additional complication is that Joan's IPM, which gives the details of Philip's settlement of Ashdon, names these children as offspring of Philip, not of Philip and Joan. This makes Armburgh's reference to Robert as 'my wife's son' odd, and I have found no evidence that Philip was married before his marriage to Joan (below, text, pp.90, 112; PRO C139/115/28; see also below, n.148 to Intro.). There is a curious alternative version in H. Chauncey, *The Historical Antiquities of Hertfordshire* (2 vols., 2nd ed., Bishops

been a difficult young man with a gift for invective equalled only by his mother's. Philip Kedington died some time after 1406 and before 1410/11, leaving Robert still underage. Just before his death, Philip apparently enfeoffed at least some of his lands to perform his last will, and amongst the feoffees was Thomas Bendyssh of Steeple Bumpstead in Essex, Robert's godfather. The Bendyssh family had a long history of association with the Kedingtons, so this feoffment was a further mark of their trust.[49]

According to Robert, writing in the later 1420s, this trust was betrayed and Bendyssh stole him away and gave him to the earl of Oxford, who, as lord of Ashdon in Essex, the Kedingtons' most substantial property, had the right of guardianship. Oxford so mistreated him that he still bore the scars and the earl also 'hindered and undid' his mother; this appears to have been financially, for it deprived her of the ability to help her son. Bendyssh refused to hand part of the land back to Robert's mother and her fellow executors so that they might perform his father's will, as he was supposed to, but sold the land and kept most of the money from the sale, so that the will remained unperformed and Philip's soul unredeemed. Robert accused Bendyssh of trying to keep the Kedington estate of Chevington in Suffolk, in which Bendyssh had no rights, and which Kedington's widow was supposed to have for life, with remainder to Bendyssh and the other feoffees, and of having entailed the Kedington estates, against Philip's wishes, with remainder to himself and his heirs. Bendyssh also failed to sell the land that was supposed to provide the marriage portion for Robert's sister, Margaret, taking the profits for himself instead.[50] To cap it all, Bendyssh was now, according to Robert, assisting Sumpter in establishing the *bona fides* of the latter's supposed daughters, to the ultimate disinheritance of Robert, who was Joan's sole male heir.[51]

Robert Armburgh had already had to deal with the repercussions of his wife's first family in 1421, when he and Bendyssh submitted to an award on the demand for the £40 for Margaret's marriage.[52] By 1429 Kedington was quarrelling with his mother and Armburgh over his inheritance: Armburgh

---

Stortford, 1826, rpt. Dorking, 1975), i, p.369, which, besides getting Kedington's name almost entirely wrong, seems to have no basis in the evidence.

49 Below, pp.90–1; Morant, *Essex*, ii, p.348; *VCH Cambs.*, v (London, 1973), p.150; PRO PCC Wills Rous f.58v.; *Cal. Fine Rolls 1399–1405*, p.54, *1405–13*, p.63; *Cal. Close Rolls 1396–99*, p.499; *A Calendar of the Feet of Fines for Suffolk*, ed. W. Rye (Ipswich, 1900), p.282; *Visitations of Essex*, p.317. But see n.144 to Intro. for problems concerning Philip's children. For Joan's invective abilities, see below, text, pp.120–3.

50 Below, text, pp.90–1, where dating is considered, and pp.10–11; Morant, *Essex*, ii, p.541; *CIPM*, xviii, p.60; PRO PCC Wills Rous f.58v. for most of the Suffolk properties mentioned in this letter; also *Cal. Close Rolls 1447–54*, p.473. Armburgh was almost certainly in possession of Chevington in 1438 (*Cat. Anc. Deeds*, iv, A9099). Bendyssh was a feoffee for the Kedingtons in Ashdon but for which lands is not clear (see below, nn.144, 149 to Intro.). If they were the manor in Ashdon, this was certainly in Joan's hands at her death (see below, n.144).

51 Below, text, p.91. *Essex Feet of Fines*, iv, p.1 shows that he was friendly with at least one of the Armburghs' opponents, John Godestone (above, p.9).

52 *Cal. Close Rolls 1419–22*, p.206. See above, n.33 for comment on the probable error in this.

wrote that Robert and his wife 'ben parted from us in great wrath'.[53] Kedington was given an annuity from Mancetter, perhaps in settlement of his demands during his mother's lifetime.[54] Meanwhile there was also the problem of his sister. She was married some time during 1428–9, an event which put still more strain on the increasingly precarious Armburgh finances.[55] Her husband was called 'Walkerne' and may have been William Walkerne of Baldock in Hertfordshire. Not long after the marriage, she was asking Armburgh for more money so that she could lie in in sufficient dignity to be visited after the birth of her first child.[56] Perhaps Armburgh was not entirely sorry when his step-son died in May 1430, although the question of allowing his farmers in their accounts the annuity charged to Kedington on Mancetter remained a bone of contention for some time after.[57]

It was towards the end of the decade that affairs in Warwickshire began to take a more serious course. In about 1429 Harpour and Barbour, Armburgh's farmers at Mancetter, were assailed from a number of directions.[58] The first case in the roll was brought by the duke of Norfolk – this must be the second duke, who died in 1432 – against them and six neighbours from the nearby village of Atherstone and from Mancetter itself. They were alleged to have beaten tenants of his at 'Wytherle': Witherley, Leicestershire, just over the border from Mancetter. This is particularly interesting as there has been some debate about whether this duke involved himself in Warwickshire affairs at this time.[59] The next entry is an action of debt brought by Ralph Bellers against Harpour and Barbour in chancery, where, as we have seen, Bellers was notably influential. It was argued by Armburgh that, since the two had never had any financial dealings of any sort with Bellers, there could be no basis for such a plea. Unfortunately for Armburgh's farmers, when the writ of arrest for the two was sent out, it was alleged on the return that they had resisted arrest in force and broken the king's peace by assaulting the bailiffs sent to make the arrest. This put them in danger of prison and Armburgh had to offer advice on evasive action.[60] At about this time the two farmers were

---

53 Below, text, p.112.
54 Below, text, pp.124, 129–30, 134.
55 Below, text, p.127; for Robert's finances, see below, pp.47–9.
56 Below, text, pp.126–7; *VCH Herts.*, iii, p.285. Note that Philip Thornbury (see below, p.30) was involved with the Walkernes in 1421–2 (*Cal. Close Rolls 1419–22*, pp.251–2). There is a possible objection to this identification of Margaret's husband, for which see below, n.181 to Intro.
57 Below, text, pp.124, 129–30, 134. The letter referring to his death was written in July 1430, so the reference to Saint Dunstan's Day (19 May) in relation to Robert's last illness would suggest it was St Dunstan's day of that year.
58 For the dating of these, see below, text, pp.104–9, 114–18. This is a group of cases which seem to belong to the same period and the reference to the impending coronation held on 6 November 1429 (text, p.112; B.P. Wolffe, *Henry VI* (London, 1981), p.48) seems to put it firmly in 1429.
59 Nichols, *Leicestershire*, iv II, pp.1007–8; Carpenter, *Locality and Polity*, p.318 n.147; also below, p.15.
60 Below, text, pp.106–8, 115; text, pp.117–18 probably also refers to this case. Bellers' petition was addressed, not surprisingly, to his patron the archbishop of York i.e. Kempe, a fact which

indicted for some further offence, apparently at the instigation of an unknown Warwickshire prior.[61] At this point Armburgh expressed the hope that the chancellor, who had consistently favoured his servant Bellers, would soon be changed.[62] There is no more information on any of these cases, but things were soon to take a still more ominous turn in Warwickshire.

However, before we follow further events there, we must direct our attention first to Hertfordshire and Essex and then to the steps that Armburgh was taking to secure his position in Warwickshire. At about this time there was a move to divide Roos Hall in Hertfordshire, and Armburgh wrote an anxious letter to his agent telling him how to avoid being cheated by the division.[63] It was apparently this attempt at a partition which led to judicial proceedings which were concluded by a *nisi prius* – the process by which King's Bench and Common Pleas cases could be heard before a jury by delegation in their county of origin – at Ware in Hertfordshire in 1429. Here, according to the story told later by the Armburghs, the justice, John Cokayn, would not allow them to present their evidence and the jury was full of men in the livery of the archbishop of York, the chancellor and patron of Bellers. The account is not explicit but we must assume the case was lost. At least the losing party had the satisfaction of seeing Cokayn smitten with a fatal illness within a couple of days: one of many enemies whom they asserted to have met their just deserts as a direct result of their intervention on the wrong side.[64]

No more is heard of this but a great deal is heard of an episode at Radwinter in Essex. Here there was also the expectation of a division. In November 1427, in what must have been a response to the royal order for division made the previous May, Bernard and Bellers and their wives had begun litigation in the Common Pleas against the Armburghs over their right to divide the lands in Essex. The latter denied this, on the grounds that their opponents were not tenants of the land. Towards the end of 1428 a verdict was given for Bernard and Bellers by *nisi prius* at Chelmsford and the following Trinity Term the partition was ordered in the Common Pleas.[65] In expectation of a partition, Bernard and Bellers had sold their part of the woods, apparently without regard for what we would now call issues of conservation, especially in dis-

---

substantiates this approximate dating. Barbour came to chancery but Harpour escaped by pleading illness. Although the original petition does not survive, a subsequent one of unknown date, requesting a new writ to William, does (PRO C1/9/335). The reference to a *sub poena* and an attempted arrest in the case may connect it to the unspecific remarks about a *sub poena* and arrest against the Armburghs at the beginning of the roll (below, pp.63–4).

61 See suggestions below, n.231 to text.
62 Below, text, p.112.
63 Below, text, pp.113–14.
64 Below, text, p.65 and see the whole section, text, pp.61–7 for the record of God's judgements. The case can be dated by Cokayn's death, in 1429 (see below, n.30 to text); I have not found the record in the Common Pleas.
65 PRO CP40/670 rot.414d. See also the comment on text, p.62, which implicates Baynard (see above, n.42 and below, p.16) in attempts to influence the jury.

posing of the wood in the garden that gave cover to the house. This drew four letters in response. One was to 'Constabal', who must have been Armburgh's agent here, asking him to sell the timber on the Armburghs' own part in all haste, in case the partition should deprive them of any of the timber that was still standing.[66] Two were to the purchasers of some of the wood, threatening them with legal action.[67]

The fourth was the most extraordinary outburst from Joan Armburgh to John Horell, the Essex landowner who seems to have been brought up at Radwinter by Joan and her mother and repaid them by giving intimate and allegedly false information to establish the legitimacy of the Sumpter heirs. This is the gem of the whole collection and would more than hold its own in any of the fifteenth-century correspondences.[68] Not long after, Thomas Bernard and his brother-in-law, Thomas Mylde of Clare in Suffolk, offered to bring Bernard's wife to Munden in Hertfordshire, where Robert and Joan could come and view her and decide on her ancestry. The invitation was accepted with characteristic grudging rudeness but no more is heard of the proposal.[69] Also about this time, there was trouble in Sarratt in Hertfordshire. One John Carter had entered on 1 January 1428 and was still holding the land, by the assent of Robert Armburgh, at Easter 1429. This must have been Armburgh's farmer, who had presumably been told to take over the other half of the still undivided manor.[70]

By early 1430 Robert was becoming seriously embarrassed financially by the costs of the case and by various other entanglements, family and otherwise. The details of the obligations that have yet to be discussed and the implications of Robert's wider financial situation will be considered later.[71] The unfortunate effect was to force him to put pressure on his farmers and tenants at Mancetter to produce their rents, something that was to be a constant thread in his dealings with them thereafter. This was not necessarily an easy matter for either farmers or tenants, especially when they began to receive counter-demands for the money. It was also not a good way to hang on to their loyalty, so essential when there was a rival attempt on their allegiance and their purses.[72]

Nevertheless by the late 1420s Armburgh had at least found some effective political support in Warwickshire, where he had initially been a complete

---

66 Below, text, pp.118–19.
67 Below, text, pp.119–20, 123–4.
68 Below, text, pp.120–3 and see above, p.8 for speculations on what Horell had actually done.
69 Below, text, pp.61, 130–1. For more on Mylde, see below, p.16.
70 PRO C1/69/348. There is no means of dating this petition, but it is not likely to have been entered long after the date mentioned.
71 See below, pp.47–9.
72 Below, text, p.126. For the significance of his relations with his tenants, see below, pp.24–5, 34–5, 48–9.

stranger. In fact he had acquired some powerful allies there.[73] Foremost amongst these was William Mountford, the greatest gentry landowner in the county and a close servant of the ruling power in the shire, Richard Beauchamp earl of Warwick.[74] Mountford's helpful influence went further still, for with him came two other powerful figures in Warwickshire politics at this time. One was Sir John Cokayn of Pooley in north Warwickshire, the other John Malory.[75] Malory was a particularly significant acquisition because he was one of the more prominent gentry in eastern Warwickshire, where Mancetter lay. Malory and Mountford had held all three major local offices in Warwickshire – sheriff, MP, JP – while Cokayn, although now more active in Derbyshire, had been sheriff and JP. Mountford and Malory were still on the commission of the peace. All three became feoffees for the land, probably in the late 1420s, possibly earlier, and this gave them an obvious role in its protection.[76]

Although Cokayn now saw Derbyshire as his real centre of activity[77] and Mountford's residence and many of his lands were further west, more important still was the fact that these three landowners represented the remains of what had once been a powerful political connection in northern and eastern Warwickshire, under the aegis of William Lord Astley of Astley in central northern Warwickshire. To some extent this connection had devolved upon Reginald Lord Grey of Ruthin who had married Astley's daughter and heiress as his second wife, but, with his wide-ranging interests, including of course those in Wales, Grey was not really in a position to involve himself much in Warwickshire afairs.[78] However, in this instance he did have some sort of involvement, for Mancetter was held of Grey, as part of the Hastings of Pembroke inheritance, and it was possible for him to interfere in the destiny of the lands, as indeed he did in about 1428–9. It was then that he announced that he wanted to keep the lands in his own hands until the issue had been resolved. Armburgh responded with some justice that, once livery had been awarded, however improperly, the overlord had no more part to play.[79] He argued also that it was not Grey's intention to block the granting of livery but rather the work of his receiver in Warwickshire, Thomas Rokesdon, an official inherited from Lord Astley.[80]

It may well be true that Grey did not know what his men were up to in

---

73 The larger problem of the role of local influence here and elsewhere in the dispute is considered below, pp.41–6, 52, where fuller references will be found.
74 Carpenter, *Locality and Polity*, esp. pp.65, 687–8. For Warwick, see below, n.13 to text. For references for the careers of Armburgh's principal allies in Warwickshire, see below, nn.213–15 to text.
75 Below, text, pp.106–7, 111, 139, 143–4, 147–8, 151–2.
76 Below, text, pp.138–9 and n.33 to text for discussion of the date when they were enfeoffed.
77 Carpenter, *Locality and Polity*, pp.314–16.
78 For the extent of his concerns elsewhere, see *The Grey of Ruthin Valor*, ed. R.I. Jack (Sydney, 1965). For Grey, see also *Complete Peerage*, vi, p.158; Carpenter, *Locality and Polity*, p.314.
79 *VCH Warks.*, iv, p.119; below, text, pp.74, 108–9, 115–16, 118.
80 Below, text, pp.109, 115.

eastern Warwickshire[81] but, whether he did or not, it seems that the Mancetter affair was getting drawn into a larger power struggle in this part of the
county in which Grey's men played a role. It is not easy to establish what was
going on in this part of the county but an attempt has been made elsewhere to
construct a narrative, which goes as follows.[82] During the mid-to-late 1420s
the rule of Richard Beauchamp earl of Warwick in eastern Warwickshire,
where he was territorially at his weakest and had established his authority
most recently, came under challenge, notably from nobles and gentry who
had interests in both eastern Warwickshire and Leicestershire. The core of the
opposition seems to have consisted of part of the old Astley connection,
which may have been actively urged on by Grey of Ruthin or may have been
acting independently, and the following of a newcomer in this part of the
county, Warwick's energetic widowed aunt, Joan Beauchamp Lady Bergavenny.[83] Hitherto she, and her husband William before her, had been a useful ally in west Warwickshire and Worcestershire but, from the time that she
acquired the Botetourt/Burnell properties, which included lands in Leicestershire and north Warwickshire, in about 1420, she appears to have decided to
challenge her nephew for control in northern and eastern Warwickshire. Both
of these were relatively recent adjuncts to Warwick's west midland power
base. The second duke of Norfolk, whom we have just observed impleading
Armburgh's farmers at Mancetter, may also have been involved in this
attempt to undermine Warwick in eastern Warwickshire.

If one looks at the personnel engaged in the Brokholes case at this time,
there is considerable support for this suggested explanation of affairs. Because
of local geography and the structure of noble and gentry estates, eastern Warwickshire was always more susceptible to control from Leicestershire than
from west Warwickshire.[84] While several prominent members of the Astley
connection had, like Mountford, either remained or become close to the earl
of Warwick, it was the families with cross-border connections, some from the
Astley connection, others not, that gave Warwick most of his greatest problems at this time. Amongst these were Ralph Bellers, described by Armburgh
as 'chief labourer in all manner matters against us', and another who was
shortly to reveal himself as an antagonist, and allegedly a great friend of Bellers, Sir Richard Hastings. Hastings was an east Warwickshire/Leicestershire
landowner of rather greater prominence, who served the second duke of Norfolk and was associated with Lady Bergavenny. It is also worth noting that
among the associates of this east Warwickshire/Leicestershire grouping at this
time was John Leventhorpe of Hertfordshire and Essex, another owner of an

---

81 A point considered in Carpenter, *Locality and Polity*, p.384.
82 For what follows, see Carpenter, *Locality and Polity*, pp.360–2, 363–4, 369, 373–90.
83 For Lady Bergavenny, see below, n.13 to text.
84 Carpenter, *Locality and Polity*, pp.299–300, 307, 360–1.

estate in east Warwickshire, the man who had been awarded custody of the Sumpter part of the estate some years earlier.[85]

Moreover, Lady Bergavenny was also active in the Hertfordshire and Essex region. Her husband, Lord Bergavenny, had inherited estates in Essex from the Hastings of Pembroke, which she held in full as his widow, and she herself had acquired lands in Cambridgeshire as part of the Botetourt estate.[86] The gentry here were linked to a variety of local nobles, but several of the most important had served Joan Bohun, countess of Hereford, and some of these, along with other local men, were transferring at least some of their loyalty to Lady Bergavenny. Amongst them were a number of the key players on the Sumpters' side: the people who were identified as particular enemies by Armburgh included Lady Bergavenny's associates: Richard Baynard, Robert Darcy, John Tyrell and Richard Fox. Indeed Baynard is said to have met his deserved end while hunting with Lady Bergavenny. By 1443 Thomas Bernard and his brother-in-law Thomas Mylde, another who was singled out by Armburgh as a supporter of the opposition, were linked to the connection, which had now been inherited by Joan's son-in-law the earl of Ormond. Leventhorpe had dealings with Robert Darcy; William Flete, the escheator who had administered the IPMs in Hertfordshire and Essex which had pronounced the Sumpter girls heirs to their alleged brother, also belonged to this local network, as did Thomas Godestone and Sumpter himself.[87]

In Warwickshire itself, Hastings was amongst Joan's closer associates. As we have seen, another noble who has been tentatively identified with opposition to Warwick in eastern Warwickshire at this time was the second duke of Norfolk. He had estates and overlordships in both east Warwickshire and Leicestershire and employed Richard Hastings in the late 1420s. His action for trespass against the Armburghs' farmers at Mancetter in about 1429 substantiates the hypothesis that he *was* active in east Warwickshire at this time. That this probably coincides with the pleas brought against the farmers by Bellers and others lends significant support to the idea that his involvement was linked with a wider attempt by powers in east Warwickshire and Leicestershire, including Lady Bergavenny and some of the former Astley connection, and with or without Grey's approbation, to make life difficult for the earl of Warwick and his followers here.

---

85 Above, p.5; below, text, pp.66, 142, 143–4, 145; HP, iii, pp.591–4; Carpenter, *Locality and Polity*, pp.381 (Leventhorpe is here erroneously said to be of Leicestershire and Brownsover: the author was clearly and inexplicably confusing him with the Bellers: Leventhorpe had Newnham Paddox in Monks Kirby until he sold it in 1433: *VCH Warks.*, vi (London, 1951), p.175), 314–15, 381–2, 385–7; *Cal. Close Rolls 1441–7*, p.171; *HMC Hastings MS*, i, pp.7, 83–4.

86 'Exul', 'Cases from the Early Chancery Proceedings', *The Ancestor*, 8 (1904), pp.173–8; *CIPM*, xvii, p.357, xix, p.304.

87 Below, text, pp.61–3; HP, ii, pp.150–2, 199–200, 749–52, iii, pp.88–91,114–16,198,592–4, iv, pp.683–6; *Cal. Pat. Rolls 1441–6*, p.241; *Cat. Anc. Deeds*, ii, B3752; *Complete Peerage*, x, p.125; Carpenter, *Locality and Polity*, p.373; PRO C1/16/111; *Cal. Close Rolls 1399–1402*, p.147, *1413–19*, p.381, *1422–9*, pp.196, 397–8, 399–400, 408. For Mylde's relationship to Bernard, see below, p.61.

A further examination of the Armburghs' protectors in Warwickshire pro-
vides still more evidence that this was the case. Following the arrangement of
the letters, it seems that the first person there to be approached by the
Armburghs was Edmund Lord Ferrers of Chartley, a rising power in north
Warwickshire and south Staffordshire. This approach was made through his
wife, a kinsman of Joan's, and can probably be dated to February 1428.[88] During the 1420s, especially as Warwick's relationship with Lady Bergavenny
cooled, and his participation in north Warwickshire grew, he had forged an
alliance with Ferrers which led ultimately to a confrontation between Ferrers
and Lady Bergavenny in north Warwickshire. Among the north Warwickshire gentry who gravitated, either formally or informally, towards Ferrers,
several of whom were also the earl of Warwick's men, was William Mountford. Thus, the connection with Mountford, and through him to his old associates in the Astley circle, Cokayn and Malory, could well have come initially
through the Ferrers of Chartley.[89] All this places Armburgh in a circle linked
to Warwick and Ferrers.

Furthermore, it has been suggested that Ferrers himself was drawn into the
power struggle in east Warwickshire, on the side of those who were under
attack from the associates of Lady Bergavenny and their allies.[90] Armburgh's
extended appeals to him and his wife, and the reassurance to Harpour and
Barbour of c.1429 that they would be safe against Bellers' writs if they spoke
to Lady Ferrers of Chartley, now place what was a rather speculative hypothesis on firmer ground.[91] To complete the evidence of the roll which supports
the version of east Warwickshire affairs in the 1420s suggested before and
reiterated here, the earl of Warwick himself can be directly associated with the
defence of the Armburgh interest. In 1433 Armburgh expressed the belief that
jurors who were the earl's tenants could be influenced on his behalf, and there
is also the matter of the identity of the recipient of this letter. It was addressed
to Laurence Sutton, one of his feoffees, whose son he apparently had either in
his care or in his employ; as he began to lose faith in his farmers Armburgh
increasingly relied on Sutton, and Sutton was warrener to the earl of Warwick
at Warwick.[92] It is indeed possible that the payment of an aid made to the earl
in the late 1420s by the farmers at Mancetter, which infuriated Armburgh

---

88 But the dating may need adjustment (see below, n.149 to text).
89 Below, text, pp.91–2; Carpenter, *Locality and Polity*, pp.314–17, 319, 377–8, 686, 692. An alternative avenue could have been Anne Prilly and her husband John Waver, owners of one third of
Mancetter (see below, n.111 and n.67 to text). In 1433 the Wavers' leading feoffees in their part of
Mancetter were William Mountford and his servant and near neighbour Richard Haversham –
although this connection could of course have resulted from the Armburghs' connection with
Mountford (PRO CP40/688 rot.322; Carpenter, *Locality and Polity*, p.335 and n. for Haversham).
90 Carpenter, *Locality and Polity*, pp.383–5.
91 Below, text, pp.107, 114–16, 117.
92 Below, text, pp.138–40, 150; British Library, Egerton Roll 8775. For this case and for Armburgh's
later relations with Harpour, the Barbours and Sutton, see below, pp.20, 24–5.

because Warwick was the tenant-in-chief of the land, whereas the immediate overlord was Grey, was designed to encourage protection from the earl.[93]

The letters also shed some light on the ambiguous position of Lord Grey in eastern Warwickshire: were his men in Warwickshire, notably his receiver Rokesdon, acting independently or under instructions from above? At the time that Grey was supposed to be trying to keep Mancetter in his own hands, Mountford was ready to be used as intermediary to Grey, to explain the legal position and, as feoffee, to warn him off.[94] Whether there was a misunderstanding or deliberate intent on Grey's part, Mountford, as the close ally of the most powerful man in Warwickshire and a former member of the Astley circle, was an ideal person to use. Certainly in about 1429 Grey's council in London, to whom both Mountford and Armburgh spoke, said 'that my lord meddled not thereof, nerhand this two year'.[95] That however does not exclude, and positively suggests, 'meddling' earlier, at the height of the tension in east Warwickshire. The verdict on whether Grey deliberately involved himself in east Warwickshire at this time must therefore remain open, but the Armburgh case at least endorses the opinion, derived from less direct evidence, that he was doing nothing to stop his followers attacking the Warwick connection there.

The single objection of substance to the belief that the light shed by the roll on the rather murky politics of east Warwickshire in this period firmly supports earlier speculations is the position of John Malory. If there was a showdown in east Warwickshire between Warwick and Lady Bergavenny and her allies in the middle to late 1420s, there is no denying that in 1427 Malory must be placed on the side of Warwick's opponents.[96] Yet here we have clear evidence that by c.1428 he was believed to be an unequivocal ally of the Armburghs, who were undoubtedly being supported by Warwick's allies the Ferrers of Chartley and possibly by the earl himself. There is no obvious solution to the problem, but it could be argued that it is easier to believe that Malory came over to Armburgh's side in about 1428 than to disregard all the evidence, from both the roll and elsewehere, pointing towards the interpetation that has been offered, including that Malory was associated with obstructing the earl of Warwick earlier in the 1420s. It could indeed be argued that Malory's role in the discomfiting of Warwick in 1427 had more to do with a sense that east Warwickshire was being neglected, as the Astley interest waned and the Warwick interest, focused primarily on western Warwickshire,

---

93 Below, text, p.125; *VCH Warks.*, iv, p.119.
94 Below, text, pp.108–9, 118, 125. Unfortunately there is ambiguity on p.109 which leaves it unclear whether Mountford is to speak to Grey or to Rokesdon, but the separate mention of Rokesdon further on suggests that Grey is meant and the other entries refer unequivocally to Grey's council.
95 Below, text, p.125.
96 Carpenter, *Locality and Polity*, pp.385–7.

grew, than with a wish to involve himself in resistance to the major powers in the county.[97]

Malory had been linked earlier in the century with Mountford and Cokayn through the Astley following, as well as with those who seem to have turned against Warwick. What we seem to see in the 1420s is a political division of the old Astley/east-north-east-Warwickshire connection, in which the more substantial Warwickshire figures, notably Mountford, stuck firmly with the earl of Warwick or Ferrers of Chartley. Malory was the exception: he had been a central figure in Warwickshire affairs, whereas the other east Warwickshire men connected to Astley, Grey or Lady Bergavenny in the 1420s were rather marginal, in the sense of being either primarily Leicestershire men or very minor landowners. He had thus more reason to transfer his allegiance to Warwick than to stay with the rival group.[98] It may not have been too difficult for Mountford to convince him that he did not really belong with these peripheral figures. In March 1430 Malory appeared as witness to a deed concerning the abbey of Combe in east Warwickshire, which had been on the receiving end of some of the attacks which have been attributed to Lady Bergavenny and her allies. Among Malory's fellow-witnesses were the earl of Warwick, Lord Ferrers of Chartley and William Mountford. If, as is likely, Malory had earlier drifted away from old allies like Mountford – perhaps because he was not sure where to go after the Astley group had ceased to be more than a vestigial force – this deed makes it clear that he had found his way back.[99]

We now come to the first major confrontation in Warwickshire over the inheritance. Although Mancetter had yet to be formally divided between the parties, Armburgh had, perhaps unwisely, urged his farmers to enter the part claimed by his adversaries and pay him the farm owing from it. Possibly he felt impelled to do so both by the fate of the woods at Radwinter and by Ralph Bellers' attempt to suborn Armburgh's farmers at Mancetter: Bellers told them that he was on the verge of an agreement which would have given the whole of Mancetter to James Bellers, while the Armburghs would receive an equivalent amount of land elsewhere.[100] It was presumably in response to the farmers' entry that Bernard and Bellers brought an assize of novel disseisin against Robert and Joan. On 21 July 1432, at Warwick assizes, the Sumpter half of the Brokholes third of Mancetter was recovered from Robert and Joan by an assize brought by Thomas Bernard alone (which implies that Christine had died), with James Bellers and Ellen, and £40 damages were awarded against Robert and Joan.

Armburgh was now in the enormously fortunate position of having a friend as sheriff, namely William Mountford, but even so it seems that

---

97 Something of the sort is suggested in Carpenter, *Locality and Polity*, pp.385–7.
98 As an officer (above, p.14) and in his local connections (Carpenter, *Locality and Polity*, p.314).
99 Bodleian Lib., Dugdale MS 15, p.13.
100 Below, text, pp.108, 117.

Mountford's influence in Warwickshire was no match for what Ralph Bellers could achieve through his friends in chancery. The Armburghs claimed that the assize 'was stolen out against us': that they were not informed that it was to be taken and that, to keep the process secret from them, and ensure that they lost by default, no distraint was made of their property to summon them to court. The lack of a distraint was on the pretext that they had nothing to be distrained by, when in fact they had substantial real and personal property in their undisputed part of the manor. The Armburghs even alleged not only that neither the sheriff nor his deputy for Warwickshire, John Campion, had any record or knowledge of the writ for the assize, but that there was no record in chancery either and that Ralph Bellers must have obtained the writ secretly and improperly. Contradicting this defence, based on his possession of the land, Armburgh also stated that it was in any case in the hands of feoffees at the time of the assize, which invalidated the whole proceedings, since they had not been taken against the feoffees, the owners at common law. This assertion appears to have been true, for Armburgh had mentioned the existence of feoffees well before the assize.[101]

In Easter Term 1433 the successful plaintiffs obtained a *scire facias* in the King's Bench to recover the damages they had been awarded by the assize. Robert and Joan denied its validity on the grounds that a different writ for the damages, a *fieri facias*, had already been issued to Mountford as sheriff by the justices at the assizes, and this was the issue on which they chose to go to trial. An attempt was made to get a copy of the *fieri facias* from Mountford under his seal, although it seems that the copy was obtained without his co-operation, for Armburgh subsequently sent Mountford a copy and asked him to publicise the Armburghs' case. The problem was that, even if the writ had actually been issued, Mountford had not received it but it had gone straight to his under-sheriff.[102] In Trinity Term 1433 a *venire facias* was issued for the jury for the following Michaelmas and Armburgh made strenuous efforts to discover the identity of its members, especially whether any were disposed to favour their adversaries on grounds of loyalty or of financial benefit and whether any should be disqualified for any reason.

By this time there was a new sheriff 'which is full friend to Bellers', a circumstance which was making it especially difficult for Armburgh to keep

---

101 Below, text, pp.64, 132, 135–6, 138, 140–2, 144, 147, 150, above, p.14; PRO KB27/688 Coram Rege rot.43. For Mountford as sheriff (in 1431–2), see *List of Sheriffs for England and Wales*, ed. A. Hughes (PRO Lists and Indexes, main series, 9, London, HMSO, 1898, rpt. New York, 1963), p.145. For Campion, see below, n.209 to text. This was a double shrievalty (Warwickshire and Leicestershire) and Campion, as Warwickshire deputy, received all the writs for that county (below, text, p.141). According to the Common Pleas (see below, p.21), Christine did not die until October 1432 but in that case she should have been included as a party to the assize.

102 Below, text, pp.136, 142–4, 145–6, 147–8, 149–50; PRO KB27/688 Coram Rege rot.43. On the sheriff's subordinate officials and the difficulties of keeping track of the office's paperwork, see M.M. Condon, 'A Wiltshire Sheriff's Notebook 1464–5', *Medieval Legal Records edited in Memory of C.A.F. Meekings*, edd. R.F. Hunnisett and J.B. Post (London, 1978), pp.410–28.

track of what was going into the sheriff's office. This new sheriff was in fact Richard Hastings, so Armburgh had plenty of cause to be concerned.[103] He was all the same able to procure a list of jurors. Unfortunately for us the enrolled copy of the writ that he sent to an unknown friend goes no further than the first two names on the writ. These are two respectable minor esquires from the other side of the county.[104] About this time Armburgh was expecting a *nisi prius* at either Warwick or Coventry – he did not know which – on the *scire facias*. It was at this time that he asked Laurence Sutton to enquire whether any of the jurors named on the *venire facias* for the *nisi prius* was tenant to the earl of Warwick.[105] Then or slightly earlier Armburgh was proposing to go on the offensive by suing a writ of error and an attaint against the jury in the original assize, and he was making enquiries as to whether there were any unqualified jurors on the original panel.

The next major legal encounter, which overlapped with these continuing processes, is quite difficult to evaluate. By the time it was fully underway Christine Bernard was certainly dead – she died, it was said, in October 1432 – although she was involved in the initial proceedings, and her husband, who had her lands for life, continued on behalf of her side of the family.[106] In Hilary Term 1433 Richard Hastings initiated a suit in the Common Pleas against some of the co-owners of Mancetter over the Mancetter advowson.[107] He alleged, with some apparent justice, that it had been conveyed during the previous century to Drakenage manor in Burton Hastings, east Warwickshire, the Warwickshire residence of the Hastings family, and he was able to cite a case in which his father, Ralph, had established his claim against the Mancetter heirs.[108] According to the Armburghs, this was a collusive suit, designed to force them to acknowledge the Sumpter heirs' title to the property; Hastings was said to be Bellers' friend and was one of the people singled out in their account of the case as a particular enemy, who had also, they said, secured a biased jury for their opponents.[109]

This is a plausible interpretation of what happened. We have seen that Hastings was linked with the east Warwickshire/Leicestershire network which seems to have been the main source of allies for the Armburghs' enemies in

---

103 Below, text, pp.143–4; PRO KB27/688 Coram Rege rot.43; *List of Sheriffs*, p.145.

104 Below, text, pp.145–6.

105 Below, text, pp.147, 150.

106 PRO CP40/688 rot.322; see below p.30. There are problems in dating Christine's death (see above, n.101).

107 For the account of the case given below, see PRO CP40/688 rot.322, *Collections for a History of Staffordshire*, ed. by the William Salt Archaeological Soc., 17 (1896), pp.143–5 (an imperfect record) and *Calendars of the Proceedings in Chancery under Elizabeth I, to which are Prefixed Examples of Earlier Proceedings in that Court* (2 vols., Record Commissioners, London, 1827), ii, p.xiv; also below, text, pp.66–7, 145. In the account given in the roll, Hastings is called 'Ralph', but the legal proceedings show that it was Richard, who was the head of the family at this time, who brought the suit, and this is confirmed elsewhere in the roll (Dugdale, *Warwickshire*, p.53; below, text, p.66 and n.).

108 See also *HMC Hastings MS*, i, pp.149–50.

109 *Proceedings in Chancery under Elizabeth I*, ii, p.xiv; below, text, pp.66–7.

Warwickshire. Moreover, the timing and personnel of the suit are suggestive of collusion. The precipitating event was the death of the previous incumbent, William Brinklow, and the presentation of John Brokholes (presumably a cadet of the Brokholes family) in April 1432. While this would of course have been the occasion for Hastings to act if he believed his rights to be undermined by the presentation, the interesting fact is that Brokholes was presented by a group of Mancetter heirs who did not include the Sumpter daughters and their husbands, a circumstance that is strange because it was likely to invalidate the presentation. The writ to the bishop of Coventry and Lichfield to prevent the admission of any priest, issued on Hastings' behalf in June, naturally named only those who had made the presentation, but, when Hastings impleaded the Mancetter owners, he did name the Sumpter claimants as defendants.[110] Indeed, the defendants in the suit who actually appeared in the Common Pleas to answer the charges, apart from John Brokholes and the bishop, were the Bernards and the Bellers, along with only one other co-owner of Mancetter, Thomas Arblaster. All the others, including the Armburghs, were impleaded but did not appear.[111] Could it be that, by the connivance of some of the heirs to Mancetter, the presentation was deliberately made in such a way that Hastings could challenge it, with the ultimate intention that the Armburghs would be forced to act as co-defendants and thus acknowledge the Sumpter heirs' claim?

The Armburghs certainly thought something odd was going on. The grounds for their absence from the Common Pleas are probably lodged in their chancery plea. They complained to the chancellor that this suit, initiated while the legal aftermath of the assize was still pending, effectively forced them to acknowledge the rights to the estate of the Sumpter heirs, or to lose their rights to the advowson. They alleged that their position had been further undermined by a manoeuvre recommended to the Sumpter heirs by Ralph Bellers and another clerk of the chancery, Nicholas Wymbysh, who was later to be a feoffee for Ellen Bellers. Each of the parties concerned had taken out an independent *quare impedit*, the writ for advowson cases, but, the Armburghs claimed, six months earlier, Bernard and the Bellers had secretly secured a writ which named the Armburghs jointly with them. This ploy obliged the latter to recognise the others' rights in the property, unless they were simply to default and be non-suited, incurring more damages and losing

---

110 *HMC Hastings MS*, i, pp.149–50 (this gives the name of the former priest as Robert Brinklow, but it is William in the plea roll); PRO CP40/688 rot.322 gives the date of death for Brinklow.

111 The defendants from the other thirds of Mancetter were Arblaster, a Staffordshire esquire, and his wife Alice, Agnes widow of Nicholas Rowley, William Harpour and his wife Joan, and Thomas Mulso and William Weldon, feoffees of Anne, sister and heir of Peter Prilly, married to John Waver of Warwickshire (the last is not named as a defendant) (*VCH Warks.*, iv, p.120; *Colls. Hist. Staffs.*, 17, pp.143–5 (which does not list the defendants fully); PRO CP40/688 m.322; *Cal. Pat. Rolls 1429–36*, p.284, *1446–52*, p.302; *VCH Leics.*, v (London, 1964), p.232; Carpenter, *Locality and Polity*, p.669; see also above, p.9 for Harpour).

the advowson.[112] It is also a fact that, after endless delays, Hastings finally defaulted in Easter Term 1436 – by which time, significantly, Bernard and Bellers were well on the way to establishing their right to their half of Mancetter – and that the victorious defendants remitted their damages to him.[113]

On the other hand, if Hastings was engaged in a collusive suit, he was putting a lot of effort into it. According to his story in the plea roll, not only did he try to prevent the lords of Mancetter presenting, he himself presented a candidate to the bishop, one John Swalwell, and he did it within two days of the death of the previous incumbent. His rivals and the bishop alleged that the other presentation had been made 'long before', but it had in fact been effected only the day before, that is the day after the incumbent's death, a fact which might well imply haste in the face of an unwelcome impending presentation from Hastings.[114] Moreover, because of the uncertainty, six months elapsed without a presentation and the bishop was consequently able to present his own candidate, Thomas Heton, in November 1432 and it was Heton who seems to have kept the benefice.[115] Perhaps Bernard and the Bellers thought this a worthwhile price to pay for establishing their rights to Mancetter and managed to persuade the other owners, apart from the Armburghs, to support them in this. Perhaps the most likely explanation is that Hastings began the proceedings, on his own initiative, to prevent the presentation by

---

[112] *Proceedings in Chancery under Elizabeth I*, ii, p.xiv; below, p.66; J.H. Baker, *An Introduction to English Legal History* (2nd ed., London, 1979), p.46. For Wymbysh, see M. Richardson, 'Early Equity Judges: Keepers of the Rolls of Chancery, 1415–47', *American Journal of Legal History*, 36 (1992), pp.441–65, esp. 459–61, A.B. Emden, *A Biographical Register of the University of Oxford to A.D.1500* (3 vols., Oxford, 1957–9), iii, pp.2120–1 and below, n.21 to text. In 1418 Wymbysh was described as clerk of the Petty Bag (*Calendar of the Signet Letters of Henry IV and Henry V*, ed. J.L. Kirby (London, 1978), 823. This was probably the same office as clerk of the rolls. In the sixteenth century the clerks of the Petty Bag were particularly concerned with the common law jurisdiction of chancery, including the supervision and custody of records and the preparation of documents relating to litigation involving chancery officials (W.J. Jones, *The Elizabethan Court of Chancery* (Oxford, 1967), pp.156–7). See also PRO KB27/669 Coram Rege rot.21 and Warks. Rec. Off. CR162/66 for his links outside chancery with Ralph Bellers. It may be that the writ was taken out at the same time as the others but backdated by six months. (Note compiled by M.C.C. and E.P.)

[113] PRO CP40/688 rot.322. The proceedings against the bishop seem not to have come to any conclusion at all (*ibid.*). It may also be significant that, the case against the Mancetter lords having reached a *nisi prius* at Coventry in February 1434, part of the jury defaulted, a rather unusual occurrence at this stage; maybe, before the assize case had gone right through the King's Bench, the parties did not want a verdict at this point and the jurors were discouraged from turning up. This *nisi prius* at Coventry is mentioned in a letter (text, p.145). The jurors, who are named in the plea roll, included Thomas Hugford, a close servant of the earl of Warwick, and William Parker of Tanworth, a Ferrers of Chartley man (Carpenter, *Locality and Polity*, pp.313, 687, 692). These two did turn up but I would be reluctant to read too much significance into this, especially as the political conditions in Warwickshire in the late 1420s no longer obtained by this time (see below, p.26). The Armburghs claimed later that they had lost their share of the advowson by default (below, p.66) but Robert undoubtedly had it in 1449 when he was a party to the grant to the abbey of Merevale (see below, p.34).

[114] PRO CP40/688 rot.322; *HMC Hastings MS*, i, p.149.

[115] PRO CP40/688 rot.322; Dugdale, *Warwickshire*, p.1078; P. Heath, *Church and Realm 1272–1461* (London, 1988), p.131.

the Mancetter owners, and was then prevailed upon to turn it into a collusive suit. There is certainly a strong aura of collusion by the time the plea in the Common Bench was well under way. Given that Hastings was sheriff in 1432–3, none of this looked very promising for the Armburghs.[116]

But there was a chink of light. The chancellor had at last been replaced, as Kempe gave way in February 1432 to John Stafford. This made it possible for Robert and Joan to submit a petition to chancery. The petition covered both the assize with its related suit for damages and the plea over the advowson, and it was submitted in late 1432 or early 1433. Ralph Bellers' undertaking in chancery not to harm Joan or Robert, given in February 1434, may well relate to the new regime there.[117] Even so, Armburgh was being vexed with a *sub poena* (cause unknown) from the chancery, and the other proceedings continued.[118] On the *scire facias* concerning the damages from the assize, so far the jury had failed to appear at Westminster, but in November, perhaps 1434, a distraint on the *scire facias* was given against Armburgh.[119] In Hilary Term 1435 the proceedings in the King's Bench on the damages from the assize were still hanging and a *nisi prius* was ordered at Warwick for February. There seems to have been further delay, for later that year there was a new writ of *venire facias*, which the Armburghs' opponents were hoping would lead to a *nisi prius* the following July: it had indeed been scheduled for Warwick for 18 July. Armburgh's earlier determination to get a writ of error against the assize verdict seems to have backfired here; he claimed that the writ of error had been entered without his knowledge and that it had opened the way for this new *venire facias* by his opponents.[120]

Indeed in Warwickshire things were far from well. First Armburgh was falling out badly with his farmers. The root cause was clearly his increasingly desperate need for money on the one side and the farmers' uncertainty about the future ownership of the land on the other, complicated by the other financial demands on the land (mainly family ones) which led the farmers to claim that they had already paid some of the money elsewhere. Harpour and Barbour were worried about the damages that might be distrained from the manor, and this seems to be the main reason for their alleged withholding of money, while Armburgh consistently and unconvincingly dismissed their concerns and insisted that profits they had taken from the manor before the assize were legitimately to be put towards the part of the farm which was still

---

116 *List of Sheriffs*, p.145. During the proceedings, Hastings, as an interested party, quite properly declined to do the sheriff's duty of summoning the jury and it was done by the coroner, but that of course would not have prevented Hastings bringing influence to bear on the jury or on any other parts of this or any other legal process (PRO CP40/688 rot.322; Carpenter, *Locality and Polity*, pp.263–4). There are also rather confusing accusations against Hastings as sheriff in the roll, which are considered below (p.26).

117 *Cal. Close Rolls 1429–35*, p.313; *Proceedings in Chancery under Elizabeth I*, ii, p.xiv.

118 Below, text, p.149 (this may be the *sub poena* referred to in general terms below, p.64).

119 Below, text, p.151.

120 PRO KB27/688 Coram Rege rot.43, /695 Coram Rege rot.2v; below, text, pp.150, 155.

owed him. He pointed out that, if his opponents' damages were collected while the unpaid farm remained in the farmers' hands, the money owed to him would end up in his enemies' pockets rather than his own. Furthermore, Armburgh was still demanding the money for his woods as well as the instalments of the farm that he said were unpaid. By c.1432–3 he was claiming that over £40 was owing, and he began to round on his farmers, calling their agreements with him to their attention and reminding them how keen they had been to take the land, how they knew it was in dispute and how they had promised him to set about getting local men on their side. Richard Barbour was accused of coming to Westminster and ignoring Armburgh while speaking to his adversaries, as well he might have done if he was worried about the possible repercussions for himself. Bellers' promise to 'save him [Barbour] harmless' was dismissed by Armburgh. Finally, it was alleged that Barbour had positively assisted the enemy over the assize. These accusations may not have been entirely without foundation, for in 1436 both Richard Barbour and William Harpour were in a consortium which leased the disputed part of the manor from James Bellers. Reading Armburgh's letters to them, one has some sympathy.[121]

The man he used to chivvy the farmers was Laurence Sutton, the earl of Warwick's warrener, and this man was increasingly being used as Armburgh's access to local support.[122] That of course says an awful lot about how his Warwickshire allies had fallen away. Malory, although he was still alive when most of these letters were written, died some time between November 1433 and June 1434.[123] But even before then, the fact that his last known transaction, of November 1433, brought him together with John Leventhorpe and Ralph Bellers cannot have been reassuring.[124] Before then there were suggestions that at least one of Armburgh's feoffees, apparently one from Warwickshire, was turning against him and an urgent letter gave a minutely detailed account of the meeting when the feoffment had been made, to remind Mountford, Malory and Cokayn of their obligations in the case.[125] It is more than probable that Mountford's inability to find his copy of the missing *fieri facias* was strategic, and the lack of obvious response to the direct and indirect pleas to him c.1432–3, together with his fading from the case, suggest that he was no longer available as an ally.[126] Similarly, there are no more letters or references to Lord and Lady Ferrers of Chartley after this time.

---

121 Below, text, pp.132–7, 148–9; Derbyshire Record Office D505M/D14. For the family obligations and for the implications of Armburgh's difficulties, see above, pp.10–11 and below, pp.47–9.

122 Below, text, pp.138–9, 149–51.

123 Bodleian Library Dugdale MS 13, p.343; *Cal. Close Rolls 1429–35*, p.313. He was probably dead by February 1434, when the Commission of the peace was reissued without him (*Cal. Pat. Rolls 1429–36*, p.626).

124 Bodleian Library Dugdale MS 13, p.343.

125 Below, text, p.139.

126 See also below, text, pp.151–2, which suggest an element of desperation in further appeals to Mountford.

There must indeed be a question mark over Mountford's demeanour as early as 1432, when he was still sheriff. The Armburghs complained later that the jury for the recovery of the land had been rigged by Richard Hastings, who had taken it to 'the farther side of the shire', next to the his own 'livelihood'. This was not an uncommon ploy, but the difficulty is that this could really only be done with ease by the sheriff or one of his officers, and the sheriff at the time of the assize was Mountford, not Hastings. Moreover, Hastings' property in Warwickshire, centred on Burton Hastings, was close to Mancetter; it was Mountford whose residence, Coleshill, was more distant. The accusation could conceivably refer to a different recovery, taken while Hastings was sheriff the following year, but there is no record of a second verdict on this issue, and the statement that the Recorder of Coventry, 'which was their chief counsel in all this matter' was dead within a year fits with the death c.1433 of John Weston, then Recorder. Accordingly, if we are to believe the substance of this statement, it must be Mountford, not Hastings, who manipulated the assize. Even if the story is as inaccurate regarding the packing of the jury as it is concerning the identity of the sheriff, which it could well be, Weston's role itself calls in question the enthusiasm at this stage of the Armburghs' allies of the previous years. Like Mountford, he was a central figure in the Warwick affinity. The fact that Armburgh and Joan made new feoffees in Warwickshire about this time may support the hypothesis that they were becoming unsure of their erstwhile friends.[127]

What was happening was that circumstances in Warwickshire were turning against Armburgh. By the early 1430s Richard Beauchamp was back in control, having seen off Lady Bergavenny and the remnants of the Astley connection. Norfolk, if he had played any part in this, died in 1432 and even Hastings was absorbed into what had become an all-embracing political alliance, encompassing the whole of Warwickshire and much of the surrounding counties. The east of the county was no longer a contentious area, not least because the greatest territorial power here, the young earl of Stafford, had come into many of his lands and been absorbed into the Warwick connection.[128] No one had any interest any more in protecting the land of a man of no local significance who was not even resident. Thus, Armburgh's allies were now John Campion, quite an influential man in his immediate vicinity but no match for the many greater men in the county, Laurence Sutton and another

---

127 Below, text, pp.66, 140–1; above, n.116 for Hastings as sheriff; Carpenter, *Locality and Polity*, pp.293, 327–8, 377, 690, and p.453 for an instance of moving judicial proceedings; *The Coventry Leet Book*, ed. M.D. Harris (4 vols. in one, EETS, o.s., 134, 135, 138, 146, 1907–13), pp.44, 144, 157. It should be noted that Hastings, who is also said to have died within a year of the verdict, did in fact die in 1436 (PRO C139/83/58), but this does not mean there must have been a second recovery in 1435, because Weston was almost certainly dead by 1434 and certainly no longer Recorder by then. This could perhaps be a garbled version of the jury for the advowson, which had certainly been summoned during Hastings's shrievalty, although he had not himself been responsible (see above, n.116). For discussion of the means of influencing juries, see below, p.46.
128 Carpenter, *Locality and Polity*, pp.320–1, 390–3; *Complete Peerage*, ix, p.606.

of similar lowly status to Sutton, [Thomas] Cokkes. It is most improbable that Sutton's aid after 1433, the year when he was asked to influence tenants of the earl of Warwick, indicated the implicit assistance of the earl of Warwick: there is no other evidence of any member of Warwick's entourage taking any interest in the case. Even in 1433, Armburgh's hopes of using Warwick influence via Sutton may be more a reflection of the political situation of a couple of years before than of any realistic hopes now.[129]

He was also trying to obtain the help of 'Starkey'. There were several members of this minor gentry family of east Warwickshire but this one was almost certainly Thomas, who was named as under-sheriff in a petition to Kempe's successor as chancellor. He and Edmund Starkey, probably his brother, were receivers to Mountford some time before late 1444. The Starkey in question was also under-sheriff at the time of the 'stolen' assize and was later held responsible by the Armburghs for the alleged return of the writ: it was recorded with some pleasure that he 'was smitten with a palsy and his mouth set aside and his eyen drawn and so taken in every joint of his body' within days of his misdeed. One supposes he had recovered sufficiently by about 1433–5 to be appealed to. Whatever his state of health, neither by status nor by connection nor by inclination does he seem a very promising person to solicit.[130] In 1435 Armburgh was rather desperately trying to ingratiate himself in addressing an unknown man and the 'gentlemen of [his] kin' in Warwickshire on the grounds that 'a young gentleman the which is kin to them' would eventually be heir to his wife. He was also especially anxious that the recipient of the letter should speak with Thomas Erdington, sheriff of the county and ask him to 'be good master and good friend to us'. As Erdington was feed by Warwick, while his recently deceased father had been closely associated with both Warwick and the Ferrers of Chartley, this was a logical step to take but, in the new circumstances, it was not a very hopeful policy and there is no indication that it produced any results. Similarly, an attempt to bribe an unknown lord and lady – perhaps Lord and Lady Ferrers – into offering assistance about this time seems to have been fruitless.[131]

Indeed this was the beginning of the end, as far as credible attempts to secure the full Brokholes inheritance were concerned. In July 1435 the jury at Warwick finally rejected Armburgh's story about the second writ and affirmed that the damages should now be executed.[132] As the lease to Richard

---

129 Below, text, pp.149–52, 155. For Campion, see below, n.209 to text. 'Cokkes' is referred to (below, text, p.155); there are two possible candidates from this time, both called Thomas, both of similar status, probably yeomen, one of Ilmington in southern Warwickshire and one of Barford in south-west Warwickshire (*The Register of the Gild of the Holy Cross . . . of Stratford-upon-Avon*, ed. J.H. Bloom (London, 1907), pp.39, 52; *Cat. Anc. Deeds*, iii, A4248, 4488).

130 Below, text, pp.64, 152; *Proceedings in Chancery under Elizabeth*, i, p.xxxvi; *Handbook of Chronology*, p.87; *Cal. Close Rolls 1441–7*, pp.277–8; Carpenter, *Locality and Polity*, pp.220–1, 667. This family's criminal propensities would also not have made it a very suitable choice as an intermediary to Warwickshire landed society.

131 Below, text, pp.154 and 193–4 and n.361 to text.

132 PRO KB27/688 Coram Rege rot.43.

Barbour shows, by early 1436 James Bellers was in possession of his part of Mancetter. The witnesses to the lease included the abbot of Merevale, a powerful neighbour and friend of the Ferrers of Chartley, who was later to feature more prominently in the case. His participation on this occasion, not to mention the fact that the lessee had been one of Armburgh's own farmers, shows that the Bellers were beginning to establish themselves in Warwickshire.[133] In Essex things were no better. In July 1436 Armburgh wrote a letter to an unknown person or persons at Sampford complaining of the way the recipient(s) had perpetrated assaults (presumably on Armburgh's tenants or servants) and had prevented his servants distraining the property of his farmer, and that men from Thaxted nearby had attacked and imprisoned his servant.[134]

This was another affair arising from efforts by the other side to get the land formally divided, for Armburgh maintained that their claims that the partition had taken place were false. It is also another indication that Armburgh was failing by this time to get the local powers on his side: he reminded the recipient(s) that they shared a lord. This is most likely to have been the duke of York, who had had livery of his lands in 1432. He owned Thaxted and much of the surrounding area and was moreover personally lord of some significant participants in the affair, notably Thomas Bernard, who may indeed have been the recipient of the letter; also Robert Darcy, Thomas Mylde and John Tyrell. York, who was in France at this time, may have played no part in Armburgh's discomfiture but the letter suggests that Armburgh was unable to make headway with those who mattered locally in Essex, as in Warwickshire.[135] Indeed, from the evidence we must conclude that by the mid-1430s Robert and Joan Armburgh had been comprehensively defeated in their efforts to obtain the other half of the inheritance.[136]

At least Armburgh had the comfort of knowing that all was not well with two of his adversaries. John Sumpter died an allegedly horrible death in 1432 or shortly after.[137] By February 1436 James Bellers was in debt. Accordingly, at her husband's request, Ellen joined him in conveying their part of the inheritance to feoffees, presumably as security for a loan. Worse was to follow, if we are to believe the tales of the Armburghs. Bellers went to Normandy,

---

133 See above, n.121; Carpenter, *Locality and Polity*, p.385.

134 Below, text, pp.152–3.

135 Below, text, pp.152–3; P.A. Johnson, *Duke Richard of York 1411–1460* (Oxford, 1988), pp.10, 20, 29–30, 228, 230, 235, 239; J.T. Rosenthal, 'The Estates and Finances of Richard, Duke of York', *Studies in Medieval and Renaissance History*, 2 (1965), p.194. Note that of these, only Tyrell is known to have been in his service by 1436.

136 This rests on the fact that in February 1436 James Bellers was able to convey his part by a fine in Common Pleas, which he could not have done without proper title (see immediately below). The fine refers to halves of the manors owned by Bellers and Bernard, which might imply that they had managed to obtain the Armburgh part as well, but the Armburghs remained in possession of their part (see below, p.30) and it must mean halves of their half of the inheritance.

137 Below, text, p.61 and n.5 to text.

with the intention, one must assume, of restoring his fortunes there. But he did so against the wrong side; he got into bad company and attacked 'an English pile', and killed and wounded some of the soldiers inside. For this he was taken and beheaded. In March 1437 Ralph Bellers persuaded James' widow into a scheme for getting the debts paid. She agreed that the first feoffees should pass the lands on to another group, in return for the sum of £35 and, if necessary, payment of debts of James and Ellen totalling 40 marks. The lands were to be held as surety until the sums had been paid off. The actual creditor in the second group was William Russell, probably a citizen and draper of London, but his associates and witnesses very much represented the chancery interest, led by Ralph Bellers and Nicholas Wymbysh, another chancery official. The principal recipients of the first conveyance were William and Thomas Pekke of Bedfordshire. William was shortly to be a leading participant on Lord Fanhope's side against Lord Grey of Ruthin in the disturbances in Bedfordshire of 1437 and 1439. Whether one should read any significance into this relationship is a moot point. If there is evidence that Reynold Armburgh, Robert's nephew, was serving the Greys of Ruthin in the 1450s, it is stretching the evidence to suggest that for this reason their enemies had made common cause with the Greys' enemies as early as the 1430s. Given Bedfordshire's propinquity to Hertfordshire, the Pekkes may simply have been trusted near-neighbours of James and Ellen Bellers or have had access to a source of loans. In any case, according to Ellen, the men used in these conveyances were very much Ralph Bellers' friends, rather than hers or her husband's.[138]

By November 1439 Ellen had married Ralph Holt of Gristlehurst in Middleton, Lancashire[139] and she and her second husband were petitioning the chancellor for return of their lands from Ralph Bellers, William Russell and the other feoffees. When the two were due to come to chancery to claim Ellen's inheritance, Joan Armburgh seized the opportunity to raise the old claims to the lands. Despite the change in chancellor, Bellers' credit with the chancery staff was still good, as the conveyance of 1437 demonstrates, so it is not surprising that Joan's petition is not known to have had any results, although Ellen's was in fact withdrawn on 1 November 1439.[140] Indeed, it must have afforded the Armburghs some satisfaction that their opponents were now at odds with each other. In July 1441 Holt and Bellers made mutual

---

138 Below, text, pp.64–5, 188–91; *Warwickshire Feet of Fines*, iii, ed. L. Drucker (Dugdale Soc. Publs., 18, 1943), 2592; *Cal. Close Rolls 1435–41*, p.127; PRO C1/9/356. The second conveyance names James as if he were still alive, but his widow's petition explicitly says that he was dead by then. I have found no other evidence for the fate of James Bellers, but I have no reference for him after these two settlements. For Russell, see *Cal. Close Rolls 1441–7*, p.387. For the others, see notes to the text, below pp.190–1. For Armburgh and Grey, see *Cal. Close Rolls 1447–54*, p.448, where Armburgh is called 'of Hemingford Grey', one of the Greys' properties in Huntingdonshire (Jack, *Grey of Ruthin Valor*, pp.1–2, 6). For Pekke and the Bedford 'riots', see P. Maddern, *Violence and Social Order: East Anglia 1422–1442* (Oxford, 1992), pp.206–25, 247.

139 *VCH Lancs.*, v, pp.174–5; PRO C1/9/356.

140 PRO C1/9/356; *VCH Herts.*, iii, p.127; below, pp.87–8.

recognisances to accept the arbitration of John Stopyndon, a clerk of chancery and one of Bellers' cofeoffees. This might indicate that Bellers had been able to put Holt at a disadvantage, but Holt was certainly the only claimant from the Sumpter side in 1453, a fact which implies that the feoffees for the debt no longer had any claims on the land by then.[141]

That Holt emerged the victor against Bellers was perhaps simply because Bellers died – there is no reference to him after December 1441[142] – and during the next few years other participants disappeared for the same reason. Thomas Bernard's son had already died by 1436, when the reversion to Ellen of Thomas' dead wife's lands was included in the fine of that year, and we must presume Thomas himself to be dead by 1453, when he failed to join Holt in litigation over the inheritance. Although there is an IPM for a Thomas Bernard of the same family in 1463/4, it is likely that the last certain mention of our Thomas Bernard is a life appointment by the duke of York dating to 1447.[143]

The most significant death in these years was of Joan Armburgh. This occurred in November 1443. It was immediately preceded by a settlement of her property. By this, all her estates in Hertfordshire, the Essex property of Stanley Giffards in Sampford and the Kedington lands in Suffolk were to go to John Palmer, Joan's nephew, and his heirs, with remainder to his sister Joan and her heirs, and remainder after that to a group of feoffees, who included Robert, his nephew Reynold (who was then or later married to Joan Palmer) and Sir Philip Thornbury of Hertfordshire, to whose heirs the lands were ultimately to come. Mancetter and the Essex properties of Brokholes in Radwinter and Asheldham (confusingly called 'Ashdon' here) were remaindered to the same group of feoffees, excluding Reynold but including Joan Palmer, for ten years and thereafter entailed in the same way as those which were to go straight to the heirs. In making her dispositions Joan Armburgh said that these feoffees 'had been to her true, trusty and special friends and wellwillers in all such causes and matters as she had desired them, and that of long time continued by her at that time unrewarded or recompensed . . . and the said Philip Thornbury most special, for she declared at the same time that he was to her at all times true and faithful kinsman and friend'. As a kinsman, Thornbury was in some sense her heir in blood as well as in law. He had earlier connections with some of the personnel in the case and their associates, and may well have been involved with the Armburghs and their associates for many years.[144] Armburgh also claimed, more contentiously, that Joan decreed

---

141 *Cal. Close Rolls 1435–41*, p.489, *1447–54*, p.473 (and see below, p.38). For Stopyndon, see below, text, p.190.

142 *Cal. Pat. Rolls 1441–6*, p.42.

143 Below, text, pp.188–9; above, n.141 to Intro.; *IPM Rec. Comms. Hen.V–Ric.III*, 4 Ed.IV/11; Johnson, *Richard of York*, p.228. He was certainly dead by November 1449 because he did not participate in the Mancetter heirs' conveyance of the advowson (see below, p.34).

144 Below, text, pp.183–4; PRO C139/115/28; *Warks. Feet of Fines*, 2619; *Essex Feet of Fines*, iv, p.34;

that all her fee simple lands should be sold to provide for her soul and those of her family, and that Armburgh should have them at a special low price. Unfortunately the will has not survived but the version offered by Armburgh does not seem to square with the fine, although the provision about the fee simple lands was allegedly in a copy of the will that Armburgh showed to a man called Bastard. As Bastard pointed out, since Armburgh was both feoffee and executor, there was a sizeable conflict of interests here.[145]

The identity of the Palmers has been almost impossible to establish. John seems to be son of Sybil Palmer, who appears twice in the letters. At some point, perhaps after Joan's death, he and a brother of Robert Armburgh, probably William, had dealings with property in which Robert had an interest.[146] From the fact that the guardianship of the earl of Oxford, overlord of the Kedington family's estate at Ashdon, Essex, is referred to in a letter to Sybil from one of her children, probably John, the Palmers are likely to have been heirs to the Kedington family, that is, the family of Joan's first husband. And indeed, although the evidence is far from clear, a Palmer family seems to

---

Cal. Close Rolls 1447–54, p.474 (the quotation is from the original roll (PRO C54/304 m.28d), which was probably quoting Joan's will, or alternatively her verbal death-bed dispositions, if her husband's rather different account of her last wishes was untrue: see immediately below, p.30). The fine for Mancetter and Stanley Giffards, as printed in *Essex Feet of Fines*, does not include the remainder to Joan but it is there in the version printed in *Warwickshire Feet of Fines* and in the IPM (PRO ref. as above). An additional complication is that the IPM also mentions a settlement made by Philip Kedington of his property in Ashdon, 'Berklowe' (untraced) and Chelveston (in Sturmer), held of four different lords, including the earl of Oxford, and this is the settlement which refers to Kedington's children as if they were not Joan's (see above, n.48 to Intro.). It is the only evidence for Kedington's two other sons, John and Thomas, and his other daughter, Eleanor, apart from Robert's mention of 'my brethren', who were dead by the time he wrote (see below, p.90) and contains the successive remainders to them and their heirs referred to below, p.32. One can only suppose that the IPM jurors, trying to remember an earlier settlement, perhaps with inadequate written evidence before them, forgot that these children were Joan's as well. If they were not, it is very difficult to explain how they could have any rights to inherit the Brokholes/Roos lands (unless, of course, the relationship that has been traced here between Joan and the Palmers is entirely in error). Robert Kedington, in his invective to Thomas Bendyssh (below, pp.90–1), mentions an entail with remainder to Bendyssh which is presumably the one registered here, but alleges that Bendyssh forged it. That is, of course, possible. For Thornbury, see Chauncey, *Hertfordshire*, i, p.91; *HP*, iv, pp.589–91; PRO PCC Wills Stokton f.85; *Cal. Pat. Rolls 1429–36*, p.461; *Cal. Close Rolls 1419–22*, pp.191–2, 251–2 (a participant in this conveyance is William Walkerne, perhaps Margaret Kedington's husband: see above, p.11), *1429–35*, pp.159–60. For Reynold, see below, pp.33, 36, 49–50, 59 and below, n.461 to text and, for his marriage to Joan Palmer, see below, p.33.

145 Below, text, pp.176–7, 183–4. The land in question may be the land in Chevington (see above, p.10) which Kedington and Joan were later said to have bought together, even though it too featured in Joan's settlement. But this statement seems to conflict with the fact that Philip's father mentions land there in his will (*Cal. Close Rolls 1447–54*, p.474 (here called 'Palmer': see below, n.148 to Intro.); PRO PCC Wills Rous f.58v).

146 Below, text, pp.67–8, 184–5. Even this simple matter is complicated by the fact that, writing to Sybil Palmer, Robert Armburgh (the probable writer of the letter) refers to what 'John Palmer bequeathed his mother your wife' (below, text, p.67) and we have to guess that, by this slip of the pen, he momentarily forgot that he was writing to Sybil herself and not to her husband, rather than that he substituted 'wife' for some other female relative of Sybil who really was John Palmer's mother.

have had an interest in Ashdon, Essex, although this could be a separate estate, also held of the earls. A tenement called 'Palmers' in Kedington, Suffolk could be another connection with a Palmer family, either that of Ashdon or another.[147] An additional point of confusion is that on one occasion Joan's first husband is called 'Philip Palmer'.[148]

What confuses the issue further is that the second letter to Sybil Palmer, which refers to 'my sister' and therefore must be from John Palmer (unless Sybil had any further surviving children) mentions the writer's grandmother and the grandmother's husband in terms that make it most probable that these are Joan and Robert Armburgh: the recent death of this grandmother is mentioned, as are the consequent dealings of her husband (who is clearly not the writer's grandfather) with the earl of Oxford over the writer's inheritance. Unless we are dealing with an entirely different family, this can only be the land of the Kedingtons in Ashdon, Essex, mentioned earlier, of which Oxford was overlord, and this land had been given to Joan for life by Philip, with successive remainders to his children.[149] Although there may be doubts arising from Joan's IPM as to whether these children were also Joan's,[150] the Palmers must have been the heirs of her body to have had her own inheritance left to them and so, if they were indeed Philip's grandchildren, then they were also hers.

How then can the Palmers have been simultaneously Joan Armburgh's nephew and niece and her grandchildren? There are two possible solutions, both of which may be correct. First, at this time, and for some time to come, 'nephew' and 'niece' could be used interchangeably with 'grandson' and

---

147 Below, text, p.185; above, p.10; Morant, *Essex*, ii, p.541 (where a John Armburgh is also mentioned as having land here temp. Henry V, which may or may not be significant); *IPM Hen. VII*, i, p.435. See also comments in nn.148, 149 to Intro.

148 This was in 1453 and referred to the man with whom she bought land at Chevington (*Cal. Close Rolls 1447–54*, p.474: confirmed in the original: PRO C54/304 m.28d). That she had yet another husband, also called Philip, with land in the same place as the Kedington family, would surely be straining coincidence too far, and in any case Armburgh refers to Philip Kedington as Joan's first husband (below, text, p.178), but it is just possible that this was an alias of the Kedington family; the Palmers do crop up in some guise as tenants in two of the places where the Kedingtons had land. See further comments below, p.33.

149 See below, text, p.185; PRO C139/115/28. A major difficulty in tracing Kedingtons and Palmers, in the absence of any coverage of this part of Essex by the VCH, has been Morant's confusion over the history of their manor in Ashdon and my inability to discover who ended up with the Kedington manor here. There were several manors in Ashdon, and Morant seems to have muddled the descent of some of them, notably those of Kedington et al. and of Hotoft (Morant, *Essex*, i, pp.540–1; *HP*, iii, pp.115, 429; see also above, n.147). According to Philip's settlement, on the failure of all his heirs – something which seems to have occurred – some part at least of Ashdon was to revert to the feoffees (but see above, n.144). The leading one of these was Thomas Bendyssh and, since this family too had a manor in Ashdon, it may well be that they simply absorbed the Kedington property into their own estate (PRO C139/115/28; Morant, as above; PRO PCC Wills Wattys f.101).

150 For the IPM's (PRO C139/115/28) confusing reference, in its account of the Kedington lands in Ashdon and elsewhere, to Philip's children as sons and daughters of Philip, rather than as Joan and Philip's children, see comments in nn.48 and 144 to Intro.

'granddaughter'.[151] Secondly, although Joan is referred to as 'Palmer' throughout these settlements and dispositions, she married Reynold Armburgh, Robert's nephew, and could well have been betrothed, if not married, by then.[152] That would also make her Joan Armburgh's niece. As it was not uncommon for a brother and sister to marry a brother and sister, John could well have married a sister of Reynold and therefore have been Joan's nephew. Although John's mother-in-law may later have been referred to as 'Thornhill's wife', there is no evidence that William Armburgh, Reynold's probable father, was still alive in the early 1450s, when this mention is made, and 'Thornhill's wife' could thus have been William's widow, now remarried to a Mr Thornhill.[153]

There are then two possibilities. If Palmer was indeed an alternative name of Philip Kedington, then these are the children of either Robert or his younger brothers named in the settlement of Ashdon, John and Thomas, all of whom were dead by this time. The second possibility is that they were the children of Philip's other daughter, Eleanor, who would have to have married a man named Palmer and then died. Sybil would therefore be Palmer's second wife, John and Joan's stepmother. Alternatively, it is just possible for the mother of John and Joan to be the other daughter, Margaret, if she had failed to have any children by her marriage to Walkerne, if the latter had died, she had remarried a man named Palmer, had then died herself after giving birth to John and Joan and her husband had then married a Sybil. On the whole, Eleanor seems the more likely of the female candidates.[154]

Some time after this, probably during the later 1440s, John Palmer died without direct heirs, apparently after his sister Joan, who also had no heirs.[155] Nearly all the remaining letters, insofar as they can be dated, come from the years 1448–51. They cover five principal areas of concern to Armburgh, mostly interlinked. It will come as no surprise that the major part consists of letters resulting from Armburgh's continuing financial problems, of which most are increasingly abusive letters to his farmers and tenants at Mancet-

---

151 A. Macfarlane, *The Origins of English Individualism* (Oxford, 1978), p.147.
152 See below, text, p.184. Reynold was a lawyer and son of one of Robert's brothers, almost certainly William (see below, n.461 to text); like William, he came from Huntingdonshire (pp.6–7, above; *Cal. Close Rolls 1447–54*, p.448, *1454–61*, p.33).
153 See below, text, p.67 (where the ambiguity of the reference to 'Thornhill's wife' is considered). 'Mother-in-law' could mean stepmother but that would not be possible as the letter in which Thornhill's wife is mentioned is addressed to John's mother, or stepmother.
154 PRO C139/115/28; see above, p.11. If Margaret's husband was indeed William Walkerne, then, remarried to Justice Prisot, she was still alive in 1455; moreover, the evidence does not suggest that she had an additional husband between Walkerne and Prisot (*VCH Herts.*, iii, p.285; and see below, n.181 to Intro.).
155 Below, text, p.67, where the dating of this letter is discussed. Both John and Joan were certainly dead by the time of the alienation of the Merevale advowson in November 1449, because they did not participate in it, although Joan's husband did (see below, pp.34, 71). There are problems concerning the order of the Palmers' deaths (see below, p.36).

ter.[156] A smaller number of letters under this heading deal with the ramifications – mostly in London – of the execution of John Palmer's will and with farmers in other counties.[157] In 1439 the farm of Mancetter had been taken over by Clement Draper of Atherstone, one of the de Mancetter heirs. He was a yeoman of some substance, who farmed the royal manor of Atherstone or acted as bailiff, or both, while it was in the possession of both the duke of Bedford and the duke of Buckingham. He held the Mancetter farm until 1448, but not without the usual financial wrangles, for in 1446 'a reckoning' was made at Westminster between Draper and Armburgh. This, the latter maintained, was still unfulfilled by Draper in 1449.[158]

The story of the farm thereafter brings in the next matter of these years, the grant of the advowson to the neighbouring abbey of Merevale. At this time the abbot was a forceful man, John Ruggeley, who had already had some involvement in the affair in witnessing the lease of the Bellers part of the manor in 1436. He was later to found a gild and chantry in the church, the chantry to include Henry VI and his queen in its prayers, for which this acquisition was the necessary prelude.[159] In November 1449 all the heirs to Mancetter gave the advowson to the abbot.[160] The *quid pro quo* was to be land for them all in Peatling and Bruntingthorpe in south Leicestershire, and in November, probably of that year, the other heirs to Mancetter had assembled at Merevale, without Armburgh, where the abbot allocated the land amongst them. This led to complaints by Armburgh to the abbot that he had received no money from these lands, accompanied by a request that the abbot write to the tenants of the new lands, where neither Armburgh nor his servant were known, to encourage them to pay their rents, and a letter from Armburgh on the same theme direct to the bailiff and tenants there.[161] But it raised a more serious problem which was the question of the farm of Mancetter.

The abbot proceeded to use the abbey's ownership of the advowson to interfere on the manor and tried to force Armburgh to make his own man, John Atherstone, farmer there. The abbot's concern was not entirely for the interests of his servant, for the man to whom Armburgh was proposing to give the farm was Sir John Barbour, who had been presented to Mancetter by

156 Below, text, pp.68–9, 72, 74, 76, 171–2, 182.
157 Below, text, pp.67–8, 187.
158 Below, text, pp.69, 71, 74, 171–2; *Rotuli Parliamentorum*, iv, p.411; *Cal. Pat. Rolls 1446–52*, p.302; C. Rawcliffe, 'The Staffords, Earls of Stafford and Dukes of Buckingham 1394–1521' (unpubl. Sheffield Univ. Ph.D. thesis, 1974), p.372. Draper may have been part of the consortium to which Bellers had leased his part of the manor in 1436 (see above, p.25): one of the lessees was 'Clement Alen, draper' and other evidence shows that Clement Alen or Aleyn was of Atherstone. Draper was certainly one of those who delivered the *scire facias* on the damages, on behalf of the Sumpter heirs, in 1433 (Leicestershire Record Office DE 2242/3/(unnumbered); see above, p.20; PRO KB27/688 Coram Rege rot.43).
159 See above, p.28, below, n.56 to text; Dugdale, *Warwickshire*, p.1079; *Cal. Pat. Rolls 1452–61*, p.475.
160 *Cal. Pat. Rolls 1446–52*, p.302; Bodleian Library Dugdale MS 9, p.334.
161 Below, text, pp.69–70, 71–2, 74–5, 76.

the bishop of Coventry and Lichfield in February 1449, that is just a few months before the abbey acquired the benefice. Barbour's presence as the sitting tenant seems to have infuriated the abbot, who was also anxious about the glebe lands, which were now the abbey's but were occupied by Barbour.[162] In the event, the lease was given at Ladyday 1450 to Barbour, a man called William Barkby and Robert Grey.[163] The latter is an interesting choice. He was the younger brother of Edward Grey Lord Groby, eldest son of Reginald Grey of Ruthin by his second marriage, to the Astley heiress. He was also, like his older brother, an annuitant of the duke of Buckingham.[164] Both Grey and Buckingham had come to have some influence in east Warwickshire during the 1440s, a period when, for most of the time, there was no adult earl of Warwick. If their power there had waned towards the end of the decade, it was beginning to recover in the early 1450s. Thus, in appointing first Draper and then Grey as farmers, Armburgh was taking some care to see that he was choosing men who would be able to defend the land. This may also have been insurance against the abbot, for the abbey had retained its links with the Ferrers of Chartley, now represented by Edmund's son William, and during both the 1440s and the early 1450s, even after William's death in June 1450, there was tension between Grey and Buckingham on the one hand and Ferrers of Chartley and his followers, much of it centring on the area near Mancetter.[165]

The problems encountered by the farmers were perhaps to be expected. They were harassed by both Ralph Holt and John Atherstone, and Barbour, who seems to have had the major responsibility for the farm, was unable to keep up with his payments and continuously hounded for them by Armburgh. By September 1451 Armburgh was owed eleven marks by Barbour.[166] It all seems to have come to a head eventually, in about 1452, with Barbour, in classic Victorian novel fashion, collapsing under the weight of debt, and having his life saved by an unknown lady (who may have been Lord Ferrers' widow), who not only nursed him but encouraged him to negotiate personally with Armburgh. At this point Barbour apparently gave up the farm, urg-

---

162 Below, text, pp.68, 70, 180–1; Dugdale, *Warwickshire*, p.1078. Barbour was alias Mountford, which suggests an illegitimate origin, perhaps from the family of William Mountford. However, it is quite likely that he was the son of Armburgh's former farmer, Richard Barbour; he mentions the need to pay his father's debts but does not give his father's name (above, p.9; below, text, p.182). In the midst of all this, Armburgh did tell the abbot that he had let the farm to Atherstone, but this does not seem to have been the case (below, text, pp.74–5 and n.77 to text).

163 Below, text, pp.68, 188. The second of these, although oddly dated, shows that the decision was made about a month before Ladyday.

164 *Complete Peerage*, v, pp.358–9; Jack, *Grey of Ruthin Valor*, p.37n.; Carpenter, *Locality and Polity*, p.700.

165 Carpenter, *Locality and Polity*, ch.11 and pp.447–58; Bodleian Library Dugdale MS 9, p.334; *Complete Peerage*, v, p.320. It should also be noted that Arblaster had been retained by Buckingham in the 1440s (C. Rawcliffe, *The Staffords, Earls of Stafford and Dukes of Buckingham 1394–1521* (Cambridge, 1978), p.233).

166 Below, text, pp.68, 70, 74–5, 180–2.

ing Armburgh not to give it to any but Robert Grey.[167] What happened to the farm thereafter is not known.

The third of Armburgh's difficulties had a bearing on the payment of the farm. This was his nephew Reynold, probably son of his brother William, widower of Joan Palmer. This match must have seemed a good idea at the time, as a way of keeping the inheritance in the family, should John Palmer die.[168] On the assumption that Joan Palmer did predecease her brother John, Reynold had no direct claim on Mancetter, as, although he was one of the group to whom the Hertfordshire and Suffolk lands and some of the Essex property were remaindered after the deaths of John and Joan, he had no part in Mancetter. However, his wife had been one of the feoffees who were to hold Mancetter for ten years after Joan Armburgh's death, and this may have encouraged him to believe that, as her widower, he did have a claim both on Mancetter, including the advowson, and on the exchange lands in Leicestershire. Although Reynold's uncle would not accept that this gave him any right to the Leicestershire lands, Reynold was nevertheless made party to the alienation of the advowson. Furthermore, he was a lawyer: not the type to let go easily in property suits. Much of the trouble in getting the farm paid by both Draper and Barbour was due to the fact that they, and the tenants, had paid some of it to Reynold without authorisation from Robert, and the latter was not disposed to accept these payments against the farm.[169]

Reynold's role brings us to Armburgh's next concern, which was the ultimate destination of the estate. Armburgh's most pressing needs seem to have been to get his wife's will fulfilled and, as part of this, to secure the lands to which she had allegedly given him first – and cheap – refusal. To this end he needed a release from the feoffees. But some of them wanted to buy the lands cheap themselves, while Philip Thornbury, as the feoffee to whose heirs the estates were to pass in the event of the deaths of John and Joan Palmer, was, not surprisingly, equally reluctant to act. He may have been encouraged by 'Bastard' (perhaps Richard Bastard of Bedford), whose wife was Thornbury's niece and who therefore stood in line to inherit.[170] According to Armburgh there had been a death-bed request by both Joan Armburgh and John Palmer,

---

167 Below, text, p.183. For the dating, see below, text, p.182. Barbour refers to his saviour as 'my mistress your cousin' and we know from elsewhere in the document that William Ferrers' mother was cousin to Joan Armburgh (below, text, pp.92, 114).

168 See above, p.30; below, text, p.184.

169 Below, text, pp.70–5, 76, 172, 182; *Cal. Pat. Rolls 1446–52*, p.302; *Cal. Close Rolls 1447–54*, p.474; PRO C139/115/28; n.165, above. On lawyers, see below, pp.50–2. It seems fair to assume that Joan never inherited the lands, because otherwise, as her widower, Reynold would have made far more ambitious claims to the property.

170 Below, text, pp.173–8. See notes there for the identification of Bastard and above, pp.30–1. These discussions suggest that Thornbury was indeed the ultimate heir and was not fronting for someone else, as has been suggested (*HP*, iv, p.590), especially as an alleged late preference for the right heirs of John Roos on the part of Joan Armburgh and John Palmer (see below, text, p.177) was presented as a change of heart.

against Joan's settlement and will, that, if the specified heirs failed, the remainder to Thornbury's heirs should not stand and the Roos lands should go to the heirs general to the Roos estates. These were an interesting group, which included Edmund Bendyssh, son of Robert Kedington's hated godfather. They were from the Hertfordshire-Essex-Suffolk area, so, however honourable Armburgh's intentions towards the heirs of Roos, this was a clever means of acquiring a number of influential allies and keeping Thornbury out, while he got access to the fruits of his dead wife's lands.[171]

What made it all much more difficult was the fifth and last of Armburgh's problems, the claim to the estate made by the Chancys, two brothers, both called John. Both Roos/Brokholes and Chancys came from a younger branch of the Rooses of Helmsley and the inheritance in Hertfordshire had, through a rather complex descent, come to be divided between the families. Most of the Chancys' lands were in fact in the same villages as the Roos': Gedelston and Great and Little Sampford.[172] The Chancys must have deemed, not unreasonably, that they had as much claim to be the right heirs to these estates as anyone else, and that they certainly had more right to them than Philip Thornbury or his heirs. In late 1448 or early 1449 they entered the Roos manor in Sampford and a year or so later they did the same at Gedelston. As neighbours, these entries would have been simple for them. They attempted to force the farmers and tenants there to pay them their rents and were said to have their eye on the Roos manor in Radwinter, which they did indeed add to their spoils before long, and the rest of the Roos inheritance. What made things much worse for Armburgh was that the Chancys had extremely powerful friends in this region. Chancy the younger was described as an esquire of the duke of Exeter. In some desperation Armburgh wrote to Clement Spicer of Essex, one of the residual heirs to the Roos lands. He attempted to play on Spicer's interests in the lands, and implored him to speak with his lord, the duke of Buckingham, to get him to persuade Exeter both to exert some taming influence on Chancy and to arrange an arbitration to be performed by the lords of the participants.[173]

This effort to engage Buckingham's interest on Armburgh's behalf was hardly likely to succeed, for the Chancys, having indeed entered Radwinter, enfeoffed all three manors to the dukes of York, Exeter and Buckingham,

---

171 Below, text, p.177 and see below, n.418 to text for identification of the heirs. See above, p.10 for Bendyssh and immediately below for Spicer, another heir.

172 Chauncy, *Herts.*, i, pp.366–9.

173 Below, text, pp.173–5, 191–3; Wedgwood, *Biographies*, p.788; Rawcliffe, *Staffords*, pp.234–5. For more on arbitration, see below, p.51 to Intro. There had been some sort of confrontation between Armburgh and the Chancys long before, perhaps as neighbours but perhaps also over the Chancys' rights to the land. However, as one of the justices who indicted Robert and his servant was Richard Baynard, friend of the Sumpter heirs, and as the episode took place in 1427, when tension over the Brokholes estate was building up, it is possible that this alleged offence at Great Sampford was related to the main dispute and that the Chancys were assisting the Armburghs' opponents (PRO KB9/223/2/62; see above, pp.6–8, 16).

Henry Bourchier earl of Eu, Sir William Oldhall, Sir Edmund Mulso and 'other knights and squires'. That ensured them the support of not only the premier noblemen of England but most of the great local nobles and two of York's closest servants. Although Exeter was already regarded as a local influence, he was in fact still in the wardship of York, who had already married him to his daughter, and we must presume that Exeter had brought in York, that York had brought in Bourchier, his brother-in-law, and Bourchier Buckingham, his half-brother.[174] This was in any case not a good moment for presenting a case against intrusion, especially one which could not be laid directly at the door of the duke of Suffolk or a close henchman, for government and nobility had other things on their minds in 1449–50: a major parliamentary and political crisis and a series of violent uprisings by the lower classes.[175] Armburgh petitioned parliament, asking that the Chancys be made to come and show their evidence, but if the petition had any effect it was the reverse, for the next entry on the roll, which presumably post-dates the petition, is an agreement by Armburgh to show his evidences to John Chancy the elder, preparatory to the sale of Over Hall in Gedelston to Chancy. The sale may well follow on from an arbitration which does not survive but, if so, it does not look as if Armburgh got the deal he would have wanted.[176] It should be noted that Buckingham's participation against Armburgh did not enhance the latter's chances of making use of the duke's protection in Warwickshire.

And that, as far as Robert Armburgh was concerned, was really the end of the story. In July 1453, by which time Robert must have been dead, there was a settlement of the whole inheritance between, on the one hand, Philip Thornbury and Reynold Armburgh, representing the feoffees named in Joan's will, and, on the other, Ralph Holt and Ellen. It arose from a chancery plea brought by the Holts, in which it was rather disingenuously claimed that the lands had been entailed on Joan's heirs, now represented by Ellen. Their case concentrated on the feoffees' refusal to re-enfeoff the Holts, and no mention was made of the more complex remainders in the will. The complete

---

174 Below, text, pp.174, 191; *Complete Peerage*, v, pp.137, 212–13; Johnson, *Richard of York*, pp.235, 236; Rawcliffe, *Staffords*, pp.191, 193. Technically Bourchier's title was Viscount Bourchier from late 1446 but there can be no question about the dating of the letters. Although this feoffment may seem to cut across what have been considered deep divisions among the nobility in 1449–50, it is now clear that this was not so (J. Watts, *Henry VI and the Politics of Kingship* (Cambridge, 1996), chap.6).

175 Watts, *Henry VI*, pp.240–51, 266–78; R.L. Storey, *The End of the House of Lancaster* (London, 1966), chaps.2–3; I.M.W. Harvey, *Jack Cade's Rebellion of 1450* (Oxford, 1991). Spicer was written to by Armburgh just as he was about to depart for the April 1450 session of the 1449–50 parliament at Leicester (below, text, pp.174–5).

176 Below, text, pp.191–3. The parliament petitioned could well be that of 1449–50, if Armburgh had been quick, or of 1450–1. An attractive possibility is that it was the parliament of 1453, after York, Oldhall and Mulso had all been disgraced (Johnson, *Richard of York*, pp.113–22). But Armburgh was dead by late July 1453 (*Cal. Close Rolls 1447–54*, pp.473–4), so it would have to belong to the early stages of the parliament. The agreement with Chancy names 1 September as the date by which evidences are to be presented.

Roos/Brokholes inheritance was adjudged to the Holts, who now, by a strange reversal of fortune, themselves were sole representatives of the Roos/Brokholes line, as Joan Armburgh had earlier claimed to be. The fact that the award occurred during the period of York's discomfiture may explain why it ignored the claims of the Chancys. Nevertheless, although the Holts kept all the Warwickshire and Hertfordshire lands and the Radwinter property, the Sampford one may have come to the Chancys. It has not been possible to discover what happened to Asheldham.[177] Only in the case of the Suffolk land did the award accept Joan Armburgh's settlement of 1443, because, it declared, these lands had been purchased by Joan and her first husband, and so, it seems, it was acceptable to will them away from the heirs of the blood. In 1455/6 Philip Thornbury was in possession of this property.[178] Thornbury died in 1457 or 1458, leaving only a daughter to succeed him.[179] Reynold Armburgh was briefly a JP in Huntingdonshire in 1460–1, appointed just before the Yorkists returned, although he was quickly discarded by the new regime, and survived to at least 1475, when he was carrying on family tradition by litigating against the abbot of Merevale, in this instance over an unpaid legal retainer.[180] It is sobering to reflect that, without all this expenditure of time, money and effort, had Robert Armburgh and his wife accepted the claims of the Sumpter daughters right from the start, the ways of nature would have decreed that the inheritance ended up exactly where it did.[181]

---

[177] *Cal. Close Rolls 1447–54*, pp.448, 473–4; PRO C1/205/94; *VCH Warks.*, iv, p.120; *VCH Herts.*, ii, p.440, iii, pp.127 (an erroneous account of the events leading up to the settlement of 1453), 320; Morant, *Essex*, ii, pp.527 (Sampford, but Morant may be confusing the two manors at Sampford, the Roos one and the Chancy one), 536. He has nothing about the further history of the Kedington manor of Ashdon (see above, n.149). There is a gap between the Armburgh/Sumpter generation and the sixteenth century in his account of Asheldham (*ibid.*, i, pp.367–8). There is a curious judgement on Gedelston, for which the Holts did not have the evidences (because, one assumes, they had been handed to the Chancys as part of Armburgh's agreement with them: see above, p.38), in which it was agreed that they should nevertheless get this property too because 'God hath disposed specially for the said Ellen as experience hath often times showed' (see original: PRO C54/304 m.28d). For York, Mulso and Oldhall in 1453, see note immediately above.

[178] *Cal. Close Rolls 1447–54*, p.473; *Suffolk Feet of Fines*, p.306; above, p.30, and n.145 for doubts about this statement concerning the Suffolk estates.

[179] PRO PCC Wills Stokton f.85.

[180] *Cal. Pat. Rolls 1452–61*, p.667; PRO CP40/846 rot.327d, /856 rot.126.

[181] However, there is one remaining gap in our knowledge of the fate of the heirs to Armburgh, which is what happened to the Walkerne family. If, as has been suggested, William Walkerne was Margaret Kedington's husband, then Margaret and, it appears, heirs by William, were still alive when she remarried John Prisot, the chief justice in 1455, even though the eventual fate of the Walkerne lands implies that there were in the end no male Walkerne heirs, possibly no heirs at all (*VCH Herts.*, iii, p.285; Chancy, *Herts.*, i, p.96). But, on the assumption that the mention of heirs in 1455 was not to cover the possibility of a posthumous birth to Margaret, then their exclusion from any of the dealings with the Roos, Brokholes and Kedington inheritances between about 1443 and 1450 might invalidate the claims of this Margaret Walkerne to be née Kedington. John Prisot, Margaret's second husband, died in 1460, when Margaret was still alive (*DNB*, xlvi, p.402).

(iii) The importance of the document

At the start of this introduction it was suggested that what all the private letters from the fifteenth century offer us is a privileged intimate view of the
gentry world. Normally we are obliged to guess at what lies behind the impersonal and highly formulaic documents which make up almost the entirety of
the evidence which is left to us: governmental records, most usefully those of
the judicial system, and private records, mostly of property transactions, with
a smattering of estate papers. Without such guesswork, we really have no flesh
at all to put on the bare bones of this evidence, but we need to know whether
our speculations have any validity; the correspondences can help show us
whether they do. In this case we are offered prolonged and detailed scrutiny
of one particular dispute. We have the opportunity of judging the truth of
suppositions about the implementation of the legal system, and indeed the
whole panoply of royal government, in both outline and detail, and of deductions drawn from formal evidence about the gentry's response to litigation.[182]

The main interest of the case lies in its graphic account of how members of
the gentry went to law. In particular we can see, in both outline and detail, the
truth of all the accounts that emphasise the inseparability of private power
and private influence from the official public processes and the fact that this
was not seen normally as a form of 'corruption' but accepted as part of the
way the body politic functioned.[183] The need to exploit private power,
amongst both lords and fellow gentry – 'vertical' and 'horizontal' relationships – to expedite the public processes of law is summed up in the words,
probably of Armburgh, from near the beginning of the roll, when he says to
Sybil Palmer, 'The best counsel that I can give you is that ye get you lordship
and friendship.'[184]

Starting with lordship and the phenomenon for which the period is most
famous, if not notorious, we are given an insight into the working of 'bastard
feudalism' from the gentry perspective.[185] Perhaps the evidence for the

---

182 There has been a lot of recent work on this. The two most important late-medieval contributions
are E. Powell, *Kingship, Law, and Society: Criminal Justice in the Reign of Henry V* (Oxford, 1989),
and Maddern, *Violence and Social Order*. See also C. Carpenter, 'Law, Justice and Landowners in
Late-Medieval England', *Law and History Review*, 1 (1983), pp.205–37, and *Locality and Polity*,
Part II. Between them these works contain a full bibliography. On the interplay of formal evidence and letter evidence, see Carpenter, 'Stonor Circle'.

183 See especially, Powell, *Kingship, Law, and Society* and Carpenter, 'Law, Justice and Landowners'
and *Locality and Polity*, especially chaps.9i, 10i and 17.

184 Below, text, p.68: see also text, pp.89, 91. On horizontal and vertical relationships and the litera-
ture on these, see Carpenter, *Locality and Polity*, chap.9, 'Gentry and Community in Medieval
England', pp.356–65; S. Wright, *The Derbyshire Gentry in the Fifteenth Century* (Derbyshire Rec.
Soc., 1983), chap.5.

185 There is now a large literature on this. See G.L. Harriss, 'Introduction' to *England in the Fifteenth
Century: Collected Essays of K.B. McFarlane* (London, 1981) (a volume which also contains

protection offered to the Chancys by the major powers of Hertfordshire and Essex is fairly commonplace: we are used to petitions complaining of unfair interference by overpowerful protectors supported by deed evidence showing that powerful men were often made feoffees.[186] Nevertheless, it is useful to have the two facts put explicitly together so that we can be in no doubt that that was a major reason for the choice of feoffees who were locally irresistible.[187] What is more interesting here is the way horizontal bonds are deployed by the gentry to put pressure on the lords. In this case Armburgh tried, albeit unsuccessfully, to exploit his distant kinship to Clement Spicer, and the prospect of Spicer becoming an heir to the lands, to get him to persuade his lord, the duke of Buckingham, to encourage the Chancys' lord, the duke of Exeter, to tell the Chancys to leave Armburgh's property alone.

Equally instructive is the means by which the Armburghs gained access to the help of Lord and Lady Ferrers of Chartley and, through them, possibly to that of the earl of Warwick. What they did may be particularly characteristic of newcomers to an area. It would be nice to know whether they went through Mountford to the Ferrers or whether the approach was the other way round, but what we can say is that the Armburghs made the first contact and that, in order to do so, they exploited a kinship so distant that it has proved impossible to trace it. It would also be nice to know whether it was the Ferrers who were the unknown lord and lady to whom financial inducements were offered but, whoever it was, it is revealing that this could be done, even though, as we shall see, the outcome may indicate that this was neither normal nor necessarily useful. We can certainly conclude, on both these pieces of evidence, that, when a gentry family was making an approach to a possible lord, especially when it had few other local contacts, any means of introduction or inducement would be used.

Even though we cannot tell which approach came first, that to the gentry associate, or that to the lord, the Armburghs' affairs in Warwickshire tell us a lot about another key aspect of private influence, the role of horizontal networks among the gentry. It can be clearly seen that integration into these was vital to a gentry family's success. Mountford gave Armburgh access to Cokayn and Malory, through the remnants of the Astley connection, and also to the possibility of help from the groups in north and east Warwickshire to which Mountford and Malory respectively belonged. However, in Warwickshire, a county where lordship could be powerful and effective,[188] even if it was always at its most vulnerable in the east of the county, what we learn most about

McFarlane's classic essay on this subject) and Carpenter, *Locality and Polity*, Part II, which also give full guides to further literature.

186 See, for example, the instances cited in Carpenter, *Locality and Polity*, pp.284–9.

187 See also below, text, p.97: 'to give your estate to such lords that he should be wary to meddle with'. The nature and uses of deed evidence are discussed in Carpenter, 'Gentry and Community', pp.368–9. See also n.203 to Intro., below.

188 See the remarks in Carpenter, 'Gentry and Community', p.356.

from this story is the mutually reinforcing interplay of gentry networks with lords' affinities.

We have already seen, even if we cannot be sure of the order of events, that the Armburghs' links to the Ferrers, a noble family, and to Mountford, a fellow member of the gentry, complemented each other. The part that could be played by local connections at even the lower social levels in obtaining access to the help of the more powerful is exemplified by Armburgh's relations with Laurence Sutton. Because he worked for the earl of Warwick, Sutton was a means of bringing influence to bear on other men of his status, notably those who were to act as jurors. A reverse instance comes from Essex, where Armburgh tells Simon Mate of Colchester that, if he will not oblige him by offering protection against the law to Ralph Beauchamp, vicar and cousin of Armburgh, the latter will 'pray my lord to write to you himself'.[189] And at the highest levels, where lord speaks to lord on the affairs of their followers, Lord Ferrers of Chartley is asked to speak to Rokesdon, the troublesome receiver of Lord Grey of Ruthin, on the principle that this matter can only be sorted out by establishing what Grey's true purposes are.[190]

The negative side of lordship is shown in the fact that the Armburghs suffered in Warwickshire because their need there was at its greatest just at a time when the east Warwickshire group, the one that was most vital to their success, was proving unamenable to the control of the lords who, in one case (Ferrers), certainly befriended Armburgh and, in the other (Warwick), may have done so. What accentuated these difficulties was that they themselves were not in any way integrated into local society; they were hardly ever there. They could not drum up support amongst the local gentry in the teeth of the hostility of nobles like Lady Bergavenny and, since they had no local connections of their own which could be useful to a lord, once Warwick and Ferrers had dealt with resistance in east and north Warwickshire they had no interest any more in the fortunes of the Armburghs. That was why Armburgh was left with Sutton and one or two other Warwickshire yeomen; they had their uses but could not match the power of the middling and greater gentry, much less of the nobility.

In Hertfordshire and Essex there was a similar story, except that here the Armburghs had inherited what seems to have been a secure position in a network to which both of Joan's previous husbands had belonged. Thus, one result of the dispute was to split the network, and, as Armburgh was so rarely in the region, it is not surprising that it should soon exclude him. Two notable examples in the roll are the betrayals by both John Horell, a man brought up by the Brokholes family, and Thomas Bendyssh, feoffee and godfather to the family of Joan's first husband. This meant that Armburgh must also have lost the protection of the local lords – Bourchier, Fitzwalter, Bergavenny,

---

189 See text, below, p.93.
190 See text, below, p.116.

Holland of Huntingdon and Exeter, York and Stafford/Buckingham – with whom these groups were linked. Although we cannot be sure of the identity of the lord who was apparently protecting Armburgh's antagonists in 1436, we can be fairly sure that it was the same man who had once been Armburgh's lord as well. The later solidarity of the great local nobles against Armburgh and on behalf of the Chancys was the inevitable result.

Along with the need to be accepted in local society went the intense concern with repute that has been noted as a characteristic of the gentry. As ever the word 'worship' recurs, signifying this all-important quality.[191] It is even applied to a township and linked with the town's rights.[192] In this case the town was probably Mancetter and Armburgh was equating his own worship with that of his manor. An illuminating use of the word is in the context of Margaret Walkerne's lying in: if she lacks 'honest bedding' to show visitors, the worship of herself and her husband will be damaged. It is a rather endearing aspect of the almost obsessive preoccupation with status, reminiscent of a more modern bourgeois respectability, which shows how every form of display had to be carefully regulated. By the same token, worship could be damaged by revelations of indebtedness (which also of course encouraged opponents at law to more intensive attacks).[193] The local gossip that could affect standing for either good or ill is seen in the efforts to discredit the Sumpter heiresses by 'noising' their alleged low birth in the counties of the disputed lands, in the hope of turning against them local opinion, which could be reflected in a jury's verdict.[194] Another instance is Armburgh's assessment, based on alleged local knowledge and on what he had heard from 'a few cracking words' spoken by Reynold, of his lessee at Mancetter, Sir John Barbour, and of Barbour's willingness to pay his farm. It is more briefly but damagingly glimpsed in the report of John Horell's comments on the Armburghs which forms part of Joan's forcefully argued case against him.[195]

It is well known that reputation and local standing were intimately bound up with hierarchy but the clues to hierarchy offered by the wording of letters have hitherto been little exploited. In these letters they range from the unctuous address to Lady Ferrers of Chartley, through the 'worshipful sir' employed for the knightly Philip Thornbury and other gentry of standing ('right worshipful and reverent sir' for Sir William Mountford), 'reverent and worshipful sir' for the abbot of Merevale and 'friend' or 'wellbeloved friend' used for a variety of minor gentry, agents and yeomen, to the open contempt reserved for John Horell. Many of the letters that begin 'wellbeloved friend' do in fact express anything but love, and it is interesting that, except in the extreme case of provocation offered by John Horell, where the address 'bare

191 Carpenter, *Locality and Polity*, pp.198, 245.
192 Below, text, p.111.
193 Below, text, pp.127, 86, 128; Carpenter, *Locality and Polity*, chap.6.
194 Below, text, p.89.
195 Below, text, p.72; also text, pp.120–2 for reports by neighbours.

friend' is a play on the more normal mode, the outward forms of courtesy should be preserved. By contrast, 'worshipful sir' or 'worshipful and reverent sir' is never followed by any kind of invective, however provoked the writer may be, a fact which suggests that, on paper at least, such direct taxing of a superior could not be done. Similarly, John Barbour, Armburgh's unfortunate farmer at Mancetter in the early 1450s, addresses Armburgh as 'right worshipful and reverent master' or 'right worshipful and reverent sir' and always pleads rather than berates.[196]

One of the chief reasons for the acquisition of trusted associates and a reputation oneself as a man of worship was to obtain the necessary help in the settlement of estates. Again, the roll – like much other evidence – shows that those, like feoffees and executors, to whom such potential power over estates was given, could not be chosen at random. We have seen this already with respect to powerful local nobles. We have the explicit statement that Philip Thornbury was chosen to be a feoffee to Joan Armburgh's last will because Robert knew 'that she trust him well'. We can then see the consequences when trust was misplaced, in Thornbury's ambivalent behaviour after Joan's death.[197] The same is true of Thomas Bendyssh: both a trusted friend of the family and, allegedly, a betrayer of its interests.[198] In both these cases, the issue was the settlement of an estate after its owner's death, something that was of crucial importance to all these people, since on proper execution would depend the length of their suffering in Purgatory. The key role in this was, of course, the executor's: Bendyssh was both feoffee and executor.[199] This is not the only occasion when we get a close-up of the executors' ability to determine the outcome, for good or ill. Part of John Horell's act of betrayal was to prevent the proper execution of the will of Joan Armburgh's mother. Much of Robert Armburgh's business towards the end of his life was as executor to his wife. Although he had a vested interest in certain parts of it, there is no reason to doubt that he felt under a moral obligation to see that her last wishes were respected, and Joan, in her invective to Horell, mentions the works 'for [the] soul' of her mother that were to have been paid for from the goods that he stole.[200]

In the dealings with the Warwickshire feoffees can be seen the enormous political significance of the choice of associates, a broadly-conceived impera-

---

196 Below, text, pp.69, 92, 93, 104, 118, 120, 129–30, 138, 147, 173, 181, 182. See also Carpenter, 'Stonor Circle' pp.198–9. However, we should note that the abbot of Merevale himself addresses Armburgh as 'right worshipful sir' in his most threatening letter and 'right trusty and well-beloved friend' in a more friendly one (below, text, pp.179, 180). This may indicate a slightly different mode of address when a cleric writes to a layman; in this case, where the layman is of lower status than the cleric, the latter may choose to be particularly polite when he is exerting pressure.

197 Below, text, p.176. See also Carpenter, *Locality and Polity*, chap.9 and 'Stonor Circle', *passim*.

198 See above, p.10.

199 E. Duffy, *The Stripping of the Altars: Traditional Religion in England c.1400–c.1580* (Yale, 1992), chap.10; Carpenter, *Locality and Polity*, pp.222–5, 284–6.

200 Below, text, pp.122–3, 173–4, 176–8.

tive summed up by Armburgh's step-son Robert Kedington when he said that he hoped to overcome the hostility of Bendyssh 'through help of my friends'.[201] The Armburghs' three main supporters among the Warwickshire gentry, Mountford, Cokayn and Malory, were their feoffees: the linkage of the two capacities is explicit. So is the fact that they could be got at and persuaded to make a release to the Armburghs' enemies.[202] In the light of this and other evidence, there is no good reason for not using feoffments and similar documents of trust as evidence of political affiliation, however transitory. In this case there is some particularly nice detail in the account of the dinner party when the feoffment was made, when Mrs Armburgh offered home-made presents to her guests. This is a specific illustration of the mixing of business and pleasure which we can observe in a more generalised manner in the other correspondences and which underlay the growth of trust within a gentry network. The absence of Cokayn from the gathering does not undermine this point, since we know that he was one of those that Armburgh was later to call upon for help, but it does illustrate the known fact that individual grantors and grantees could add their seals to a deed at different times.[203] That was why Armburgh was so concerned that some of his feoffees might make releases to his enemies without his authorisation.[204]

The whole spectrum of the needs represented by lordship and friendship, from simple social intercourse to assistance in disputes, even to the point of bending or breaking the law, can be summed up in the Armburghs' concern with their standing with the 'country'. This is a most interesting word. It has been said that it was normally used for 'county' but to the Armburghs, in the administrative sense, it seems to have more to do with local juries, as in 'to put oneself upon the country'. While its non-administrative meaning to the nobles was as the region where they expected to be the directing authority, the Armburghs' use suggests a less overtly 'vertical' usage but rather the range of influential local people whose help might be sought.[205] This is an obvious extrapolation from the 'jury' meaning, as the latter would be drawn from the area of the disputed property and could be said to reflect local opinion. A good instance of this is Armburgh's retort to Bernard and Mylde that, once Bernard's wife has been viewed in Hertfordshire, 'the country . . . may be the more out of doubt that she came never of that blood'.[206]

Indeed, the necessities to ensure that the jury were well-informed of the

---

201 Below, text, p.91. 'Friends' appear on several other occasions e.g. text, p.92. Cf. e.g. *Paston Letters*, ed. Davis, ii, pp.4–5 for further evidence of this.

202 Below, text, pp.106–7, 109, 139.

203 Below, text, p.139; Carpenter, *Locality and Polity*, p.285. See also Carpenter, 'Gentry and Community', pp.368–9 and 'Stonor Circle', pp.176–86.

204 Below, text, p.139.

205 See below, text n.9; also R. Virgoe, 'Aspects of the County Community in the Fifteenth Century', *Profit, Piety and the Professions*, ed. M.A. Hicks (Gloucester, 1990), pp.4–6; Carpenter, *Locality and Polity*, pp.347–8, 'Gentry and Community', pp.375–6.

206 Below, text, p.130; also e.g. text, pp.147–8.

facts of the case and likely to be sympathetic, and to stand well in the neighbourhood were closely interlinked.[207] That local influence was of the first importance and of far greater significance than power over the workings of the central bureaucracy can be seen in Armburgh's statement that, with the help of the Ferrers of Chartley and their other friends in Warwickshire, the Mancetter farmers could be protected against all Bellers' machinations in chancery and other courts.[208] When a family lacked local friends, then it could be exposed not just to machinations in local administration but to the brutal reality that local power meant, in the last analysis, access to local force.[209]

That all these friendships, with both nobles and gentry, could be brought to play on the system of public governance is hardly news.[210] But we can see this happening in the Armburghs' affairs both in unusually detailed and in slightly unexpected ways. The efforts to influence sheriffs and under-sheriffs are a familiar phenomenon from other letters, notably those of the Pastons, and the roll confirms the suspicion that sheriffs did not always know what their deputies got up to.[211] An equally well known phenomenon is tampering with the jury but it is rarely as well illustrated as here. The deduction that gentry families at law wanted access to lists of jurors so that they could be not only 'laboured', or informed of the party's case, but also checked for men who might be friendly or inimical, or could be challenged as unqualified, is overwhelmingly confirmed. Names might also be needed for the same reasons after the verdict if an 'attaint' or action against the jury were contemplated.[212] In relation to juries, there is a most interesting use of the term 'labour'; it is not that the verb conjugates 'I inform, you labour' but that it has favourable implications when done on behalf of the writer and unfavourable when done on an opponent's behalf.[213]

As far as the records of the criminal law go, there are two particularly revealing points in the document. One is confirmation that indictment, far from being an impersonal legal procedure, could be used by an injured opponent, in much the same way that he or she would use a private suit: Armburgh, in threatening those who have felled his woods at Radwinter, says that 'I shall do you indicten of felony within a short time.'[214] Secondly, we have an instance where the accused party in a criminal indictment, alleged to have

---

207 Below, text, pp.89–90. On informing juries, see immediately below.
208 Below, text, p.117.
209 Below, text, pp.191–2; Carpenter, *Locality and Polity*, pp.283–7.
210 See references above, nn.182, 183.
211 See below, text, pp.115, 141, 143–4, and p.143 for independent behaviour by the clerk of assize; Carpenter, *Locality and Polity*, pp.354–5, 385.
212 Below, text, pp.138, 143–4, 150; also Carpenter, *Locality and Polity*, pp.356–7, 505. On juries and the important literature on them, see Powell, *Kingship, Law, and Society*, pp.66–74, 77–82.
213 Below, text, pp.62, 152.
214 Below, text, p.120; Powell, *Kingship, Law, and Society*, pp.66–71.

committed the crime of resisting arrest and assaulting the king's officers (which appears not uncommonly in the records of the King's Bench), is able to give his version of what happened, a warning if one were needed of the danger of taking these accusations at face value.[215] In many ways, this second point follows naturally on from the first.

If this is all obvious, albeit graphically illustrated, what may surprise some people is the way the case confirms beliefs about the 'hidden hand' in the most bureaucratic parts of government.[216] At the local level, even the clerk of the assize is suspect and susceptible to external control. The formal processes of Inquisition *Post Mortem* and proof of age are shown to be as crucial to the development of a case as any judicial plea. The chancellor and his officers are revealed as venal, in issuing legal writs, of chancery and of the common law; in allegedly concealing them; and in expediting IPMs and proofs of age. Even a royal justice is not above suspicion. Similarly, it is not just that people can be asked to put pressure on royal officials in an obvious way, but that the most formal processes of the law can be made to do one side's bidding: to prevent collection of damages by alleging a prior writ; to prevent arrest or to secure the release of an arrested man; to persuade the sheriff to ignore writs; simply to keep a careful eye open for the opponents' writs and, for the other side, to keep them hidden so that no formal response can be made; harassing mainpernors; the use of ecclesiastical courts to harass an opponent; in general, the use of litigation on several fronts as a form of harassment.[217] Some of this was just a matter of careful selection of a legal process but some went beyond, into the twilight zone where the outwardly high standards of the law met each litigant's need to make it work for him.[218]

Like the major Paston disputes, the Armburghs' affairs also show us very clearly why getting embroiled in a costly and lengthy conflict of this sort was not in the interests of a gentry family, especially if, as in this case, the suit was ultimately lost. Although there was almost none of the violence, to either persons or property, which disfigured the Pastons' affairs, the financial penalties were considerable. The Armburghs claimed to have been deprived of £40 worth of clear annual income from the lands, an estimate which may well be correct.[219] That is of course why they thought it worth their while to fight for it, but it was easy to reach a point of diminishing financial returns. The most basic bureaucratic processes, such as suing for livery and clearing up an estate on the death of the owner, required money, for administration fees and

---

215 Below, text, p.106; Carpenter, *Locality and Polity*, p.705.
216 Carpenter, *Locality and Polity*, pp.354–8.
217 Below, text, pp.61–6, 95, 107–8, 113–17, 140–2; and see the account of the case as a whole for further comments and examples.
218 Carpenter, 'Law, Justice and Landowners', *Locality and Polity*, Part II, *passim*, esp. pp.620–3.
219 Below, text, p.193. The fortunes of the Pastons at law are still best summed up in J.G. Gairdner's Introduction to *Paston Letters*, ed. Gairdner.

doubtless also for legal advice.[220] Above all, there was the cost of the suit. We have no figures, but we do have Armburgh's frequent requests for money, and other evidence that he was out of pocket, all directly attributed to the costs of the lawsuit. He may well have been a lawyer himself, but he still seems to have used expert legal advice, which would have to be paid for, and then there was also the cost of the writs. And the information about the progress of the case, sought in both chancery and county, may well have had to be paid for.[221]

This was on top of the ordinary costs of maintaining a worshipful life-style, aggravated in this case by the need to support at least two children from Joan's first marriage and the fact that the feoffees of Joan's first husband were not fulfilling the agreement to provide Margaret, her daughter, with a marriage portion nor maintaining her son from his father's estate. Another legacy of Joan's earlier history was the morass of debt and obligation into which she and her second husband, Thomas Aspall, had been drawn to finance his war service to Henry V. This was another expense to which many gentry families were exposed at this time and another reason why Armburgh could ill afford grandiose litigation.[222] Money was also required when owners died and heirs succeeded; there were not only, as we have seen, the costs of suing livery and establishing ownership but also the debts of the predecessor to be paid. All these burdens forced Armburgh to borrow. Borrowing within the family, as long as it could be afforded, at least minimised the loss of repute: the fact of borrowing need not generally be known and failure to pay would not normally end in the law courts. Public humiliation when an unpaid debt was called in by an outsider, which might even lead to imprisonment, was less easy to withstand.[223] The process was cumulative: the more that was owed, the more victory in the suit was needed and so the more had to be paid out in legal fees and was owed. Unless it was careful, a family could easily reach a point where it could afford neither to prosecute a case nor to give it up.

Even though, apart from the loss of woodland and its income and devastation of part of his woods, the property itself seems to have suffered little damage, there were nevertheless serious implications for the financial health of the Armburgh estate. Above all, there were the effects of the pressure on tenants and farmers and this at a time when neither was easy to come by.[224]

---

220 Below, text, pp.86, 185.
221 On the costs of litigation, see E.W. Ives, *The Common Lawyers of Pre-Reformation England* (Cambridge, 1983), chap.13; below, text, pp.112 and n., 137, 141, Intro. n. 229.
222 Below, text, pp.77–87. On the participation of gentry in war in the early fifteenth century, and consequent indebtedness, see Carpenter, *Locality and Polity*, pp.60, 120–1; C. Allmand, *Lancastrian Normandy, 1415–1450* (Oxford, 1983), pp.69–80, 246–9.
223 Below, text, pp.86, 127–8, 185. See also e.g. *Stonor Letters*, i, nos.111, 157, ii, no.260 and Carpenter, 'Stonor Circle', pp.188–90. See also the importance of debt to loss of worship, above, p.43.
224 For the fifteenth-century economy and a full bibliography, see J.L. Bolton, *The Medieval English Economy 1150–1500* (London, 1980), chaps.7–9. For the gentry economy in the fifteenth century and further reading, see C. Dyer, *Warwickshire Farming c.1349–1520* (Dugdale Soc. Occasional

Armburgh was ruthless with these, especially the latter, in his efforts to get them to pay the revenues which he so badly needed. But they themselves could easily get caught between demands for rent from both sides, particularly as the receipt of rent was itself an indication of seisin.[225] Furthermore, in this instance there was the issue of the damages; Harpour and Barbour, the farmers of Mancetter, knew that these hung over them like a sword of Damocles, but Armburgh refused to abate his demands on that account. What all this was apt to lead to was a loss of loyalty among tenants and farmers, the last thing that any litigant needed. Armburgh sensed it coming with respect to his farmers, and their defection seems to have been one of the turning points in the dispute. In this case, it was especially fatal because they were integral to the acceptance of their landlord within local society, a point to which we shall return.[226] Similar problems emerged c.1448–52. First Armburgh was pursuing the debts of Clement Draper, a man it was most unwise to offend, given his links with the duke of Buckingham, a nobleman whom Armburgh needed to palliate in Warwickshire and, above all, in Hertfordshire and Essex. Then Armburgh found that his need of the assistance of the abbot of Merevale in getting rent from his new tenants in Leicestershire exposed him to having a farmer forced upon him. Finally, although he was able to make his own choice of farmer, John Barbour, the combined pressure on Barbour of Armburgh, of John Atherstone, the abbot's nominee, of the Holts and of Reynold Armburgh forced him to give up the lease.[227]

Reynold's role in all this is another facet of gentry life well illustrated in the document: the function of the family, for good or ill, and its tendency to be thrown into sharper focus by conflict.[228] On the whole, the extended Armburgh family comes out well. William, Robert's brother, seems to have responded to the requests for monetary assistance and, although the context of the letters in which their business affairs feature is not always clear, they appear to have acted co-operatively. Another brother, John, was also approached for money.[229] Initially the same was true of Reynold, Robert's

---

Papers, 27, 1981); Carpenter, *Locality and Polity*, chap.5; Wright, *Derbyshire Gentry*, chap.2; A.J. Pollard, *North-Eastern England During the Wars of the Roses* (Oxford, 1990), chaps.2–3; Acheson, *Gentry Community*, chap.3; C. Richmond, *John Hopton: A Fifteenth-Century Suffolk Gentleman* (Cambridge, 1981), chap.2; C. Moreton, *The Townshends and their World: Gentry, Law, and Land in Norfolk c.1450–1551* (Oxford, 1992), chaps.4 and 5.

225 Below, text, pp.72–4, 134–7, 175; also p.108 for the dangers to them of outlawry proceedings; R.C. Palmer, *The Whilton Dispute 1264–1380* (Princeton, 1984), p.32; *Paston Letters*, ed. Davis, i, pp.301–2, ii, p.299. See also Armburgh's complaint that, through his farmers' alleged mismanagement, he had lost half the value of the part of the estate that was uncontentiously his (p.137). For a reference in another context to the importance of court roll evidence in establishing seisin, see p.187.

226 Below, text, pp.134–6, 148–9.

227 See above, pp.34–6.

228 See Carpenter, *Locality and Polity*, chaps.6, 7, 17 for discussion and bibliography. This subject is pursued further in Carpenter, 'The Stonor Circle'.

229 Below, text, pp.102–3, 110–11, 127–9, 187.

nephew and probably William's son, who apparently resided with Robert at one time, most probably while undergoing his training in the law, and who, it seems, was to be given something, perhaps an annuity, from Mancetter.[230] What turned Robert and Reynold against each other was their joint interest in the property of Joan's widow after her decease. This had arisen through the attempt to keep Joan's estate in the family, once it was clear that she would have no heirs by Robert, by marrying Reynold to one of her heirs. This, a good idea in theory, which suggests how cohesive the Armburgh family was at this time, foundered on the universal propensity for greed to bring about dissent in families and the Armburgh family's own particular inability to compromise in legal matters. On this evidence, the verdict on whether the extended family was a help or a hindrance to gentry at odds must remain an open one.

It can however be affected by the final question which needs to be asked which is how typical the Armburghs were of the ordinary run of gentry families. The answer must be 'not very'. There is certainly no reason to suppose that the methods used by Robert, within and without the law, were untypical. If his expertise with the actual processes of the law was of the sort found more commonly among gentry lawyers and administrators than amongst the normal run of families, this was one that could now be hired by any family with the means to pay for it. What was different was the scale of his actions and the responses they evoked. Armburgh was a man on the make.[231] Not only was he a younger son but, to judge by the fact that William Armburgh was more than once called 'husbandman', the family he came from was still at the bottom of the gentry hierarchy. He had the snobbery found among the Pastons, another family of this kind, and characteristic of the type. This is seen most clearly in Joan's lashing of John Horell, when she refers to her enemies as bondmen, unfit to live 'upon a lordship real', and makes grandiose and highly improbable statements about her ancestral rights to Radwinter, dating back to the Conquest and beyond.[232] Joan could be allowed a certain amount of social grandeur, since she was of genuinely lofty ancestry and had married beneath her and, like Margaret Paston née Maltby, could be forgiven for being a little twitchy about her status. Robert, however, in his put-down of his older brother William has the true snobbery of the social climber.[233]

Since the law was the main avenue of advancement, these men were often

---

230 Below, text, pp.112, 187. The first of these passages considers how Reynold, who must have been very young at this time, as the date is about fourteen years before he entered Lincoln's Inn (below, n.461), can be 'furthered'; as it is placed in the context of a letter to the Mancetter farmers on the subject of a plea concerning them and also mentions the need to offer something to Armburgh's stepson, Robert, the inference that an annuity is being contemplated seems justified.

231 On these, see Carpenter, *Locality and Polity*, *passim*; on the Pastons, see C. Richmond, *The Paston Family in the Fifteenth Century: The First Phase* (Cambridge, 1990).

232 Below, text, pp.121–2. Similarly, see Carpenter, *Locality and Polity*, pp.239–40.

233 Richmond, *Pastons*, pp.131–4; below, p.129.

lawyers, as Robert may have been. Those who were making their way as administrators usually had a smattering of the law.[234] When all this is put together, we have a group of men who were ruthlessly inclined to make their way, who had the expertise to exploit the governmental and legal machinery to do so, and who were often newcomers to areas where they had newly acquired estates, sometimes by purchase, sometimes by marriage and often, like Armburgh, by marriage to a rich widow.[235] An interesting insight into why widows were ready not only to remarry but to marry men of this sort comes in the account of the long-running saga of Joan Armburgh and her second husband's debts to Richard Ketford and others. The fact that Joan was a widow and felt vulnerable to the pressure of her creditors was clearly exploited by Ketford. It was in the midst of all this that she married Armburgh and he it was that went to prison, when she had been threatened with this fate before she married him.[236]

Certain aspects of Armburgh's litigation reveal this aggressive mentality. In almost any conflict at this time, especially one that went on so long and was proving so costly in money and time to both parties, there was an opportunity to compromise. Indeed, one of the objects in harassing an opponent with the law was, as in modern industrial action, to force him or her to compromise. We can see very clearly from this affair, with its successive appeals against verdicts and threats to attaint the jury, how litigation could never end a suit; only compromise could.[237] But the tone almost throughout on the Armburgh side is aggressive and uncompromising and at times almost obsessive. It is set by the rude reply to Bernard's and Mylde's rather reasonable suggestion of a meeting to determine the legitimacy of the Sumpter heirs. Although he stood to gain a lot by victory in the suit, Armburgh also stood to lose a lot in litigation, and the £40 of clear income, a satisfactory revenue for an esquire, that he and his wife had without dispute could be said to be an adequate windfall for a man who had started with very little. However, like the Pastons when tempted by the Fastolf inheritance, he seems to have found the sudden prospect of being twice as rich and powerful irresistible. Arbitrations to settle disputes by compromise were often performed by noble councils but when, in 1450, Armburgh was reduced to pleading with Clement Spicer for help in arranging an arbitration with the Chancys, he found all the

---

234 See Ives, *Common Lawyers*, *passim*, and references above, n.231. Although he used an attorney himself on occasion (see e.g. PRO KB27/688 Coram Rege rot.43), he was, despite his wife's lands, permanently resident at Westminster, and he seems to have had very full knowledge of the law and to have known his way around the law courts (see e.g. text, pp.95, 104–8).

235 Carpenter, *Locality and Polity*, esp. chap.4. For an instance of Armburgh's ability to use his familiarity with the law, note his ability to warn his lessees and others about the impending suit by the duke of Norfolk: information he had presumably acquired at Westminster.

236 Below, text, pp.83–4, 86.

237 The essential work on arbitration is by E. Powell: see *Kingship, Law, and Society*, where there is a full discussion and reference to his own and others' work. See also Carpenter, *Locality and Polity*, chaps.10–15, 17 and esp. p.624. For instances of appeals and attaints, see below, text, pp.132, 138.

significant nobles in the case ranged on his enemies' side. One of the reasons for this may well have been his normal implacability.[238]

At least the Pastons, although recently risen from bondmen, were natives of East Anglia. Armburgh, on the other hand, was trying to establish a claim in counties where he had no previous history, one of which, Warwickshire, was a long way from his native haunts of Huntingdonshire and Cambridgeshire. Moreover, not only was he unknown in these regions but, presumably impelled by the need to keep tabs on the processes of law and government at the centre (at which, it must be said, he seems to have been pretty adept), he was almost never out of Westminster. Even the agreement with the abbot of Merevale by the other co-owners of Mancetter, by no means all of whom were local, was effected in his absence. He was thus unable to make himself an indispensable part of local society, with the consequences that have already been described. His case was supported by influential local powers just as long as it suited them to do so. Once the stand-off between Warwick and Ferrers of Chartley and their rivals was over, there was nothing for anyone to gain by helping this absentee. Equally, in 1449–50, not a single member of the Hertfordshire and Essex nobility seems to have favoured Armburgh against the Chancys.

Intrinsic to this problem were the means by which the Armburghs tried to attract support, even when it proved easier to find. Although there are not many statements that make the point explicitly, the evidence we have, and deductions based on the course of local politics, give prominence to the idea of reciprocity among the gentry. Amongst people who had to rub along together as neighbours, agriculturalists, estate administrators, local officers and the leaders of local society, there was a strong sense of mutual solidarity, albeit breached at times by outbreaks of conflict. The conflict itself often resulted from a breakdown in local cohesion and could only be permanently resolved by its restoration.[239] But the Armburghs, as non-residents, had nothing to offer in this free market of returned favours. So they had to buy help: by direct offers of money, or by hinting at future possibilities of inheritance to distant cousins.[240]

This is the highly mercenary view of late-medieval landed society that we are often offered by historians. The obsessive litigation and willingness to play with the law which we see in the Armburghs' affairs is held to be part and par-

---

238 See below, text, pp.174–5, 191; also p.169: 'Get you all the friendship that ye can . . . ye shall pay me my money, every penny, with costs and damages'; *Paston Letters*, ed. Gairdner, i, pp.195–258; above, p.13. On noble councils' role in arbitration, see in particular C. Rawcliffe, 'The Great Lord as Peacekeeper: Arbitration by English Noblemen in the Later Middle Ages', *Law and Social Change*, ed. J.A. Guy (London, 1984), pp.34–54.

239 Carpenter, *Locality and Polity*, pp.621–5, 'Law, Justice and Landowners', pp.236–7, and 'Stonor Circle', *passim*. As in the other correspondences, the notion of reciprocity is made explicit in some of the letters requesting help e.g. text, pp.70, 128, 148, 155.

240 Below, text, pp.92–3, 154, 177, 193–4,

cel of this pattern of behaviour.[241] But the fact is that the Armburghs were not typical, except of a certain breed of late-medieval parvenus, of whom the Pastons are the most well-known instance, and, above all, that they failed. The precariousness of their position in Warwickshire is well illustrated by the fact that Armburgh chose his farmers because they promised to hang on to his lands for him and, with this in mind, to 'make the gentles and the country friendly to me'. He then most foolishly had differences with them over whether the payment to the steward of the neighbouring manor of Atherstone, made precisely to gain his support for Armburgh, should have been a recurring annuity or not.[242] That a gentleman of any standing should rely on his farmers to make a place for him in local gentry networks is astonishing, and it is hardly surprising that his farmers could be suborned and that all his efforts in Warwickshire failed. Similarly, in Essex, Armburgh and his wife fulminated over the damage to the woods at Radwinter but were able to do little other than utter horrible threats.[243] From this point of view, the actual process of litigation is instructive. Although he clearly knew his way round the courts, Armburgh made what seems surprisingly little use of the common law courts, especially of the King's Bench, where, considering the extent and prolonged nature of the conflict, relatively few traces have been left. On the other hand, we know that he appealed to both chancery and parliament and threatened to appeal to the king's council.[244] Such appeals tended to be employed by those who had too little support in the originating counties of their pleas to be able to guarantee them any success at common law: the essential help from sheriffs, JPs and juries and those whose power stood behind these officials was lacking; for a variety of reasons, the 'country' would not stand up for the Armburghs' rights.[245]

And so, throughout the roll, we must remember that, like the Paston letters, this is a one-sided view of a case and of the law. It is also, of course, a view of a case unfolding within the growing instability at the end of Henry VI's minority and the beginning of his majority and then at a time of real governmental breakdown in the late 1440s and early 1450s, when landowners were being forced to adjust to an increasing absence of governance.[246] It seems to reflect all the worst generalisations about abuse of the law in late-

---

241 Discussed in Carpenter, *Locality and Polity*, pp.3–7, and 'Political and Constitutional History: Before and After McFarlane', *The McFarlane Legacy*, pp.190–3, and E. Powell, 'After "After McFarlane": The Poverty of Patronage and the Case for Constitutional History', *Trade, Devotion and Governance: Papers in Later Medieval History*, edd. D.J. Clayton, R.G. Davies and P. McNiven (Stroud, 1994), pp.1–16.

242 Below, text, p.137; p.126 for the Atherstone annuity.

243 Below, text, pp.118–20.

244 See below, text, pp.153, 191–2 and above, p.24.

245 Carpenter, *Locality and Polity*, Part II, *passim*, esp. chaps.8, 9(i), 10(i) and Appendix 4; Powell, *Kingship, Law, and Society, passim*, esp. chap.4; above, pp.40–6.

246 See above, pp.15, 38, and Carpenter, *Locality and Polity*, chaps.10–12; Wright, *Derbyshire*, chaps.5–9; Pollard, *North-Eastern England*, chap.10; S.J. Payling, *Political Society in Lancastrian England: The Greater Gentry of Nottinghamshire* (Oxford, 1991), chaps.4–7.

medieval England, summed up in Armburgh's statement, 'For it is seld seen that a poor man hath favours there a lord is party.'[247] But that is by no means the whole story. We know from other evidence that 'worship' included the acceptance amongst neighbours that Armburgh was unable to achieve in either region of the dispute, and that it could be lost by over-zealous pursuit of personal interests by legal or extra-legal means.[248] In the roll itself we have the juxtaposition of 'conscience and worship', implying that a too insensitive conscience could lead to loss of worship, while 'law' and 'conscience' are also placed together. The statement that Armburgh's enemies 'will neither spare for dread of good nor for shame of the world to doon all the wrong that they mow' is, of course, a partisan one from a disgruntled party, who would doubtless have done the same things himself given the opportunity, but it does show a clear appreciation of the boundaries of acceptable behaviour.[249] And, while parties in any dispute are always apt to assume that they have God on their side, Ellen's confidence in providential direction of her affairs shows that lip-service, at least, was paid to religious morality. Meanwhile, the fact that so many other lesser landowners were struggling to stick to the norms in increasingly abnormal conditions is testament to the force of the more conventional modes of behaviour.[250] In a sense, the Armburghs' exceptionality vindicates this view of the norm: they did fail and we can see why, in intimate detail. That in itself is a major aspect of the document's significance. But, insofar as they were operating within societies comprising mostly the norm rather than the exception, their case also gives us the chance to look more closely at certain aspects of the gentry world. This has been a fairly cursory introduction to a rich new addition to the sources for the late-medieval gentry. The roll and its language will repay further careful scrutiny.[251]

(iv) The manuscript

The document appears to have been written in four different hands. It was apparently written in two separate sections, probably at different times, but possibly all at roughly the same time. With the possible exception of the love poems or letters, which comprise an intriguing and surprising interlude in the middle and will be discussed later, the whole roll consists of copies of letters,

---

247 Below, text, p.105.
248 See above, n.191; also Carpenter, 'Stonor Circle', pp.192–3, and *Kingsford's Stonor Letters*, ed. Carpenter, pp.29–30.
249 Below, text, pp.97, 136, 115.
250 See above, n.177; Carpenter, *Locality and Polity*, esp. Part II.
251 There are isolated pieces of information on other themes: for example, agricultural practice, including the use of manure (below, text, p.117), the use of silver plate as a pledge (below, text, pp.78–9, and see also Carpenter, *Locality and Polity*, pp.205–6, and 'Stonor' Circle', pp.188–90) and the cost of servants (below, text, pp.128–9).

apart from the occasional legal paper or property transaction. As already indicated, most of these concern the Brokholes estates and most appear to be from Robert Armburgh or his wife Joan. There are however a few letters to Robert, mostly to be found among the chronologically later entries. There are times when the copyist made errors, such as repeating or omitting words, and others where blanks had presumably been left by the original draftsman to be filled in at a later date. In these last cases one must suppose that the copyist was working from a draft still in the family's possession rather than from the completed original.[252]

It is not always easy to decide whether one is dealing with different hands or with the same hand using a different pen, but the hands seem to run as follows: Hand 1 from m.1 to m.4; Hand 2 from m.5 to the bottom of m.9, where Hand 3 is introduced for the last entry on that membrane (p.131). Hand 3 then continues on to the dorse, reading downwards from m.9, until part of the way down the verso of m.7, except for a series of entries by Hand 4, a completely different one, which uniquely uses pre-ruled lines and takes over for the bottom half of 8v (p.142). Hand 1 replaces 3 for the last entry of m.7 verso (pp.152–3) and continues for the first entry of m.6 verso (p.154). There Hand 2 starts again, with the love poems which continue into m.5 verso. When these end (p.168) there is a gap and the reader then has to turn the roll round and go to the top of m.1 verso, reading downwards, until this section, coming from the other direction, and all written by Hand 1, meets the gap after the last of the love poems.

The structure of the document suggests that it was begun by the scribe of Hand 2, that is at m.5 recto, and continued, perhaps immediately, by Hand 3. All the datable entries in this section come from the earlier part of the dispute, the 1420s and early 1430s. Hand 2 then returns to write the love poems and is essentially using spare space on the dorse of this part of the roll. The interpolation of Hand 4 amongst Hand 3's entries would therefore be by a scribe brought in temporarily, possibly a learner since this is the one with pre-ruled lines. The second part of the roll, probably compiled at a later date, was attached to the top of the first part and thus it begins at m.1 recto, with Hand 1. This starts with an idiosyncratic summary of the case up to about the 1440s (pp.61–7). Thereafter, most of this material deals with later events, in the late 1440s and very early 1450s. That these membranes were attached to the earlier part as soon as the recto had been written is suggested by the fact that the scribe, instead of turning over and continuing on the verso of m.4 when he had reached the bottom of the recto side of that membrane, went back to the top of m.1 (which is why it is the opposite way up to the rest of the verso) and that this part of the verso, unlike the recto of mm.1–4, which is entirely discrete, runs on to m.5, which it shares with the other part of the roll. Hand 1's

---

252 An example of blanks left to be filled in later is the sums to be paid to Armburgh by John Chancy for the purchase of part of the estate (see below, text, pp.192–3).

contribution ends with the adventures of the cleric, Sir Thomas Beek, which are apparently unrelated to the rest of the roll, except insofar as his sister served Robert Armburgh, but which are also datable to the early 1450s.[253]

However, there are two matters which complicate this relatively straightforward explanation. One is that there are a number of entries in Hand 1's section pre-dating the late 1440s and early 1450s. Hand 1's last entries on the recto are a lengthy section concerning the financial embarrassments of Thomas Aspall, Joan Armburgh's first husband,[254] and the effects of these on Armburgh, in the years 1417–23, followed by Joan's petition to chancery from the late 1430s and the IPM on John Sumpter the younger from 1426 (pp.77–89). Towards the end of the dorse of this section, on m.3v, at the letter to Sybil Palmer (p.184), the chronological sequence begins to be seriously disturbed. Although the previous entries seem not to have been made in exact chronological order, all the datable ones are from the late 1440s and early 1450s, but, from m.3v to m.5v, there are entries from the mid-1430s and 1440s – mostly records concerning the case – mixed in with letters and a chancery petition from c.1450 and concluding with Alison Beek's petition from c.1450–2. This need not detain us too long, for it is quite possible that, having copied out the documents relating to recent events, the scribe inserted others from earlier in the case, while continuing to make copies of the documents which were still being produced, as they were handed over to him. Apart from the Aspall material and the Sumpter IPM, all the chronologically earlier entries in this part of the roll date to the period between the chronologically last entry in the first part (1436) and the date when the later section was apparently begun, that is the late 1440s. The scribe was presumably using spare time and parchment by copying documents which had mostly been produced in this interim period and therefore not entered on the roll.

More difficult to assimilate to the theory of two separate rolls and two different periods of compilation is the fact that Hand 1 does in fact make an earlier appearance, in the part of the roll that was done first, for two entries at the bottom of m.7 verso and the top of m.6 verso (pp.152–4), following on from Hand 3 and just before Hand 2 returns with the love poems. As elsewhere in the roll, this scribe deals with material later than anything written by the others – these entries can be dated to 1435–6 – but they cannot have been interpolated later between the other entries, since they share membranes with both Hands 2 and 3. There is also the fact that these entries really bring Hand 1 and indeed the whole roll full circle, since this earlier section ends with documents from 1436, which, three entries apart, is the earliest date of anything transcribed by Hand 1 in the first, but later, part of the roll.

It is therefore possible that the whole roll was written at one time in the

253 See below, text, p.196.
254 See below, p.78 for Aspall.

late 1440s or early 1450s, by four different scribes, one of whom used some parchment that was left empty to copy the love poems. But, even if this was the case, the way the dorse of the numerically first four membranes is arranged still makes it virtually certain that these membranes were the last to be written and were attached to the later membranes during the course of composition. This being so, as they deal almost exclusively with events which postdate almost all the entries on the last five membranes, one may reasonably surmise that this was a later compilation. The fact that the only entries concerning the main dispute in mm.5–9 which belong to the period covered by mm.1–4 are by Hand 1, and are the last ones in the earlier compilation before the love poems, strengthens the case for Hand 1 being the last scribe to contribute to the roll as a whole.

There are other possible scenarios, but what is most likely is that Hand 1 was drafted in to compile the end of the earlier part of the roll and that the roll was then abandoned round about 1436, as the first phase of the dispute was being concluded. Hand 2 used the spare space at the end of the dorse for his love poems. Later on, probably in the late 1440s, Hand 1 started a new compilation which he attached to the first one. Indeed, after a lull from the early 1430s, the case took a new turn in the later 1440s, with the aftermath of the death of Joan Armburgh and then the settlement of the Mancetter advowson and the dispute with the Chancys, and this could well have been the impetus to restart the compilation. As is suggested below, the summary of the case with which the roll begins could well have been produced at this juncture.[255] Hand 1 seems to have entered the new material from the late 1440s and early 1450s, in a fairly unsystematic order, on the recto of the first two membranes. He then added the three entries from much earlier, using another two membranes (pp.77–89), attached these to the top of the earlier roll and continued copying contemporary material on the dorse of mm.1 and 2.[256] On mm.3 and 4 verso, he wrote out a mixture of recent and older material relating to the case and concluded with the Beek petition, which ran on to m.5, the first membrane of the original portion.

Most of the documents are directly related to Robert or Joan; letters to or from them or transactions concerning them. Sometimes their authorship of letters has to be inferred but this is usually quite easy to do. Sometimes there are doubts and occasionally a letter seems unrelated to their affairs. However, there is no reason to doubt that the roll was drawn up for them. The only documents belonging to the opposing side are the feoffments made by the Bellers in 1436 and 1437. Although these come late in the sequence of enrolments, it is highly improbable that the roll had by then come into the hands of the eventual winners of the suit, Ellen Bellers and her second husband

---

[255] Below, p.61.
[256] However, the entries at the top of m.1v cannot be dated and may be earlier (see below, text, pp.168–71).

Ralph Holt, because they are followed by enrolments which would only have been of interest to the Armburghs. It is more probable that, with access to governmental departments at Westminster, Armburgh was able to get copies of the Bellers feoffments out of the Common Pleas and chancery.[257]

There is no obvious reason for the presence of the poems, written by Hand 2, other than the one suggested: that the clerk was filling up spare parchment, after the roll, or its earlier part, had been compiled. Although the lines are mostly indicated, the poems are written out as if they were letters and, at times, they turn into prose. This might suggest that they were indeed meant to be letters, especially as, amongst these (semi) prose interpolations, is the rather plaintive request for a reply.[258] The first, pre-existing poem may well have been written out from memory, as it differs from the two known copies and misses out some of the verses. The lines after 'valete' seem to have been added by the writer, which adds force to the hypothesis that it was intended as a letter. So does the fact that elsewhere the poem appears with its 'Responsio', lacking here, which might suggest that a reply is awaited.[259] It would be nice to think that the next letter or poem, beginning 'En Jehan *roy* soueraine', is the expected reply, but it is otherwise very like the others in tone and reads much more like a man's letter to a woman than the other way round.[260] One must therefore suppose that the 'roy' is a slip of the pen.

A possible hypothesis – on the assumption that the rest of the poems were original compositions and not copies of lost lyrics – is that, having written out the first poem from memory, perhaps intending it to serve as a love letter, the writer went on to experiment with similar efforts, some macaronic, some not. The inventiveness and unusual quality of some of the vocabulary suggests that these are original compositions[261] and the amount of repetition might suggest successive drafts. So might the crossings out, almost the only occasion for these in the entire roll, suggesting the agonies of composition rather than the copying that is otherwise going on. It must be said that there is not much evidence of error or correction but that could be explained by the easy banality of the poet's muse. Much must depend on whether the 'Joan' addressed in these letters or poems is a real Joan and, if so, whether she was perhaps Joan

---

257 See below, text, pp.188–9.

258 Below, text, p.165.

259 Below, text, p.156. See W.O. Wehrle, *The Macaronic Hymn Tradition in Medieval English Literature* (Washington, D.C., 1933), pp.119–21; *Early English Lyrics*, edd. E.K. Chambers and F. Sidgwick (rpt, London, 1947), pp.15–19; *Medieval English Lyrics*, ed. R.T. Davies (London, 1963), pp.159–61. All these use the Cambridge University Library manuscript, Gg.iv.27 part 1a ff.10b–11a. Another copy is in Br. Lib. Harleian MS 3363 f.90b. The Cambridge manuscript, from the early fifteenth century, consists mainly of the works of Chaucer; the British Library copy is amongst a collection of miscellaneous rhymes and songs. I am most grateful to Professor Helen Cooper for her help with the poems, both comments and the identification of the known poem.

260 See below, text, p.156.

261 Pointed out to me by Dr Thorlac Turville-Petre, drawing particular attention to the author's use of suffixes and to 'reconsiler', 'securable', 'relever' and 'releser'. I am most grateful to Dr Turville-Petre for these comments.

Armburgh or Joan Palmer. Even then, we would not know whether the scribe was merely doing some playful exercises or really was the lover or husband of the addressee. At one point (p.160) the addressee is named as 'mine own lady and sister', which could suggest that they are the composition of John Palmer to his sister, Joan, or of one of Robert Armburgh's brothers to his sister-in-law, Armburgh's wife Joan. The reference immediately after to something done by 'my son' would indicate the writer to be Robert's brother, William, whose son, Reynold, lived with the Armburghs for a while (as we shall see shortly). However, if it was either of these, the poems would have to be copies rather than the scribe's original compositions, as it is extremely improbable that either of them would be the scribe of Hand 2: it is too early for Palmer and neither of Robert's brothers seems to have lived with him.[262]

Indeed, who actually wrote the roll remains a mystery. One of the hands could have been that of Ralph Beauchamp, who seems to have worked for Armburgh, and, as a cleric, should have a fluent hand, but if his parish was really in Leicestershire he would have been too far away to be in Armburgh's employ as a scribe. He is the recipient of some of the letters but, as the roll consists of copies, that in itself would not invalidate his claim to be the scribe of the roll itself.[263] Armburgh himself may have copied some of the documents. All four hands could simply have belonged to confidential and literate servants, lay or clerical. A pleasing hypothesis is that Hand 2 and the author of the love letters was Reynold Armburgh, husband of Joan Palmer, who lived with his uncle, perhaps while studying at Lincoln's Inn in the 1440s, and might well have helped him out by acting as secretary. If, as has been suggested, Reynold's sister married John Palmer, Joan would at that point have been Reynold's sister-in-law as well as his wife, but whether Reynold could already have had a son who could have troubled the recipient is another matter. More generally, as he did not enter Lincoln's Inn until 1443–4, and almost all the references to him belong to the 1440s or later, he seems too young to have been this scribe, unless the whole of the earlier part of the roll was copied out at one time, perhaps during the 1440s.[264]

A note on the text

The beginning and end of the roll are quite seriously damaged and this affects four of the entries, which are therefore incomplete. The fact that there are four scribes, none of whom uses spelling and abbreviations with any

---

262 For John Palmer, Robert's brothers and Reynold, see above, pp.30–3, 36, and below, n.461 to text.

263 See below, n.155 to text for Beauchamp and his benefice.

264 See above, pp.36, 49–50, and below, n.461 to text; also text, p.112. There is one possible indication that he was older than the other references to him might suggest; this is discussed above, n.230 to Intro.

consistency, allied to the notorious lack of method and consistency in much of the use of abbreviations in late-medieval English hands, has caused some difficulty in obtaining an accurate text. It is not always possible to tell, for example, whether a flourish, particularly at the end of a word, is no more than that, or whether it indicates a missing letter, usually an 'e'. The text here offered may therefore not always be absolutely accurate where spelling is concerned; however, any problems concerning meaning have been clearly indicated. All abbreviations have been extended and modern lettering used for thorns and yoghs. Modern capitalisation has been used throughout and modern punctuation has been added, at a minimal level, for the purposes of clarity, except in the Latin passages, which were already punctuated. Some of the English text was punctuated with strokes, but, as the use of this was both variable and inconsistent, it was employed as a guide to the meaning of the passages where it appeared, rather than taken as an absolute basis for punctuation.

Gaps and blanks in the text have been indicated, as have alterations, but inserts have not, since it is evident that these were simply the result of faulty copying and had no deeper significance. All quotations in the introduction and footnotes are given in modernised spelling.

THE TEXT

An anonymous account of the case up to c.1443/8[1]

[m.1] . . . ce that hath fallen amonges hem that haue holpen Cristin the wyf of
Thomas Bernard[2] . . . [Joa]ne the wyf of Robert Armeburgh[3] of xl li worth
lyflode. Atte the by gy[nyng] . . . that he had in the chauncerye and greet
steryng of lordschip and thoren grete supportacion and in the contre made
the same . . . Cristin and Elene by certayn inquisicions vnlavfully taken to be
found . . . somtyme hys wyf and coparceners[4] with Johane [the wyf] of Robert
Armeburgh a boveseyd . . . ole somtyme of Essex . . . to the seid Johane . . .
[d]yed seised of, where as of trou[the] . . . neuer kam of that blood, ffor . . .
[sa]me John holde diuers women by side his wyf which [?]is openly knowen
. . . by side, by the which he gat there [Cr]istiane and Elene and other moo.
Atte lest wey he fadryd hem but yit . . . were hys or noon, for a child that is
got[en] in suche maner women schuld be called *filius populi* that is for to sey
. . . peple and may clayme no manne to theyre fader. And a non after al this
vntrouthe i wrought the same John Su[mpter][5] . . . church in tyme of seruice
whanne there was most multitude of peeple went oute of mynde and wa . . .
[?]and . . . levyd xiiij wykes and so he dyed with oute howsill and schryft and
with oute ony manere of . . . koude a spye and a non after that Cristin his
elder doughter, the wyf of Thomas Bernard, dyed sodenly also with oute
how[sell] and sch[ryft]. Also Mylde of Clare[6] that hath [margination: John
Sumpter] weddid Bernard suster hadde the same Cristin in his kepyng two
yere after that sche was we[did] to the same Bernard and was a grete

---

1 This account of the case must have been written before the death of Robert Darcy in 1448 (see
   p.63 and n.19 below), but it may well have been written rather earlier, for it really only deals with
   the events of up to c.1436 and the others named as being dead by the time it was written, Baynard,
   Fox and Tyrell, were all dead by early 1437 (see below, nn.8, 17, 18). From the composition of the
   roll (see above, pp.54–9), it is perhaps most probable that this was written as an *aide-mémoire* after
   Joan Armburgh's death in 1443 (see above, p.30). On the other hand, there is a strain of lively and
   idiosyncratic vituperation which might suggest Joan as author (see below, pp.120–3) and it is also
   conceivable that Joan wrote this to remind herself and posterity how the lands had been lost, perhaps when she knew her life was coming to an end. It could then have been copied in by the writer
   of the second part of the roll when he began to assemble entries after Joan's death, as an account of
   the 'story so far'.
2 See above, p.7.
3 See above, p.6.
4 I.e. coheiresses: see above, Intro. p.5.
5 John Sumpter the elder of Colchester (*HP*, iv, pp.532–3; above, p.5). The *HP* entry suggests he
   died after Hilary Term 1432, when he participated in a fine. The document implies here that he
   died closer to the time when his daughters' claims were established i.e. 1426–7 (see above, p.6),
   but there is no escaping the fact that he was councillor in Colchester in 1428–30 (*HP*, as above).
6 Thomas Mylde: *Cat. Anc. Deeds*, ii, B3616; above, pp.5, 13.

supportour and mayntenour to hem in theyre vntrouthe, thorow a lasshe that he hadde on . . . nye [?]upon poynt of deth and stood in jopardye of hys lyf and so he is blynde of both eyen. Also Master John Bernard parson of Yeslam[7] in Cambryggeschyre was a grete labourer in this matere with the seid Cristin and Elene be cause of Thomas Bernard and bare moche of the cost and with inne a while after he was robbyd and mordrid with his owne neighbours. Also Baynard of Essex[8] was oon of the grettest mayntenour of heire partie for he with other assosid to hym labvored so the contres[9] that were taken by Inquisitions and by action of particion[10] that he made hem passe a yenst the said Johane and yit he wolde not cesse thereby but toke with hym gentill men of that contre ye which hadde no maner knowlech of ye trouth of this mater and recorded a fore the chaunceler in the chauncerye in hynderyng of the seid Johane that Cristin and Elene were millieriers[11] and coparceners with the same Johane of the lyfelode a boveseid[12] and with inne a while after as he went a huntyng with my lady of Bergeveney[13] sodenly he felle downe and dyed with owte howsill and shrifte and a non after he walkyd and yit doth and hath don moche harme as it is opynly noysed and knowen in the contre there a boute. Also John Godeston, William Notyngham and Simund Mate, thre of the byggesmen of Colchester[14] for love that they hadden to Sumpter for asmoche as he savyd that Godstones lyf and ellys he hadde be hanged for the erle of Arundell[15] goodes, they stalen oute a record under the towne seale of Colchestre that Cristin and Elene were doughters millieriers to the same John

---

7 Probably Isleham: see above, p.7 n.
8 Richard Baynard of Messing, Essex (c.1371–1434) (*HP*, ii, pp.150–2).
9 That is, the jury, from the expression for going to trial by jury trial: 'to put oneself upon the country' (A. Harding, *The Law Courts of Medieval England* (London, 1973), p.67). See also above, p.45.
10 A common law action, commenced by writ *de partitione facienda* to compel the division of an inheritance among coparceners. The Armburghs' defence against this action was of course that they were solely entitled to the inheritance: see pp.193–4, below. (E.P.)
11 A child born in wedlock.
12 See above, p.5.
13 Joan Beauchamp Lady Bergavenny (d.1435), sister and eventual heir (in some of his estates) to Thomas earl of Arundel (see below, n.15), widow of William Beauchamp Lord Bergavenny (d.1411), the younger brother of Thomas fourth earl of Warwick and hence uncle of Richard Beauchamp earl of Warwick (*Complete Peerage*, i, pp.24–6, 28, xii II, pp.378–82; Carpenter, *Locality and Polity*, pp.31–2; above, pp.15–16).
14 For Mate and Notyngham, see above, p.9. For John Godestone esquire of Essex, collector of the customs at Ipswich, an associate of Sumpter and Baynard, died 1441, see *Cal. Pat. Rolls 1429–36*, p.401; *Essex Feet of Fines*, iv, p.16; *Cal. Fine Rolls 1430–7*, p.37, *1437–45*, p.165. However, this may be an error for John's younger brother, to whom he was eventually heir, Thomas Godestone of Colchester, who, like Sumpter, Notyngham and Mate, held office in the town and was certainly friendly with Darcy, Baynard and others in their circle. Most significantly, his wife was godfather to Christine, the older of the Sumpter daughters. He died in 1432, which fits better with the tale that he died soon after his misdeeds, because these would seem to date to the process for finding the Sumpter daughters heirs i.e. 1426–7 (*Red Book of Colchester*, pp.46, 47; *HP*, ii, pp.199–200; *Cal. Close Rolls 1413–16*, pp.201–2; above, p.6; PRO C139/31/72).
15 This could be either Thomas earl of Arundel, d.1415, to part of whose estate Lady Bergavenny was a coheir, or his cousin and heir male, John, d. 1421, or the latter's son and heir John, d.1436 (but neither of these last two was universally recognised as earl of Arundel, although that would of

Sumpter and Margery his wyf and ryght heyrs to the ton halvyndele[16] of the lyflode a boveseid where that no suche record schuld be grauntid with oute assent of the baillefes and certeyn officers of the towne and with oute the assent of xxiiij of the thryftiest men of the towne that ben chosen to be of theyre counsell which wollen record yf they be examynd that they were neuer prevy therto. Also the same Godston and hys ffelauschip dede do make an ordinaunce in the towne in hynderyng of the seid Johane that what manne or woman diskured ony maner counseill of the towne shuld be committed to preson and make a ffyne. Which ordinaunce is cause that poore men and other, that haven verrey knowleche of thys matere and have knowleched to diuers persones a forn tyme, dare now no more speke ther of. The which Godston, Notyngham and Simound Mate, not withstandyng that they were lykly men and lusty to have lyven mony a yere, for theyre vntrewe labour, Godde schorted her lyfe dayes and dyede al thre with inne a while after. Also Ffox of Essex[17] laboured a yenst the seid Johane and hyndred her in the bygynnyng of this matere and afterward he, hawyng better knowleche of this matere, spak to Sir John Tirell,[18] Darcy[19] and Baynard to hadde this matere amendid, but they wolde not consent therto in no manere wyse and than Ffox seyde these wordes, 'In the peyne of my lyf, this gentile woman schall ouer lyve vs alle and have her lyflode maugre oure hedys, and we lyke fooles have put oure soules in jopardye for other mennes auantage'. And somme of this is fallen, for ther is non left a lyve saf Darcy, whom Godde is of power to punys- she as he punysshed hem whanne he seeth his tyme. Also Bagbyes,[20] that tyme dwellyng with the clerk of the rolles,[21] laboured alle that he koude to haue deceyved her of her evydence and bare her an hande that yf sche wolde delyuer hym her evydence that he wolde schewe it to men of counseill and make hys mayster, clerk of the rolles, good maister to her in her ryght. And he sawe that he myght not deceyve her in this wyse, he laboured after opynly a yenst the seid Robert Armebourgh and her and brought a writte

course not have prevented them being known as such in common parlance) (*Complete Peerage*, i, pp.246–8).

16 I.e. moiety.

17 Richard Fox of Arkesden in Essex and of Shropshire and Northamptonshire (d.1435), an associate of Lady Bergavenny and of several others from Essex and Hertfordshire active on the Sumpter side (*HP*, iii, pp.114–16; above, pp.7–8, 16).

18 John Tyrell of Heron, Essex (c.1382–1437), another of the Bergavenny etc. circle (*HP*, iv, pp.683–6; above, pp.7–8, 16). His younger brother was involved in establishing the legality of the Sumpter daughters' claims (see above, p.8).

19 Robert Darcy of Maldon, Essex (d.1448), also of the Bergavenny etc. circle (*HP*, ii, pp.749–52; above, pp.7–8, 16).

20 This is probably the William Bakepuz who was present, with clerks of the chancery, at the delivery of the great seal before Henry V sailed to Calais in 1416. He might be the same man as William Bakepuys esquire of Derbyshire but I have not established a clear-cut identification (*Cal. Close Rolls 1413–16*, p.368, *1419–22*, p.207). See above, p.8 for the opposing side's influence in chancery.

21 Nicholas Wymbysh, a close associate of Ralph Bellers (see above, n.112 to Intro. and below, p.190).

sub pena[22] at the request of her aduersaryes in to the abbey chirch of Westm[23] and, not withstondyng he delyuered non, he certefyed in to the chancerye that the seid Robert receyved the seid writte and threwe it in the dritte and trade it vnder his feete. And, with inne a while after, for his vntrouthe and specially for the offence that he dyde in the holy place, Godde chastised him and sent hym soche a dissease in hys bak, that he went stoupyng, that his shuldres were as lowe as his myddell and neuer recovered that dissease. Also Dirrayn,[24] somtyme of the newe inne and a clerk of the chauncerye, laboured besyly a yenst the seid Robert and Johane and toke a commission with xx persones therynne with him to a reste the seid Robert at request of his aduersaryes, and after that the seid Robert hadde founde suerte to kepe hys day in the chauncerye in the bygynnyng of the next terme, as the seid Robert went to the convers[25] to speke with the clerk of the rolles for to aquyte hys maynpersours, the same Dirrayn reryd al the Newe Inne vpon hym forto have slayn hym, which is opynly knowen a boute the Stronde. And with inne a while after that he hadde wrought al this malice he dyed sodenly withoute howsill and schryft. Also ther was a sise[26] stolen at Warwyk a yenst the seid Robert and Johane vpon the ton halyvndell of the thrydde parte of the manere of Mancestr withinne the same schyre, and   Sterky,[27] that tyme underschereve, at request of her aduersaryes, for asmoch as they wold have the assise passe by defaute, made a fals retourne the day of assise, seiyng that the seid Robert and Johane hadde nought with inne the schyre wherethorewe they myght be distreyned nor they hadde no baillefes, which was vntrew, for they were soole seised and in pesible possession of that other halvyndell of the thrydde parte of the manere of Mancestr, and yit wold they not cesse therby, for with inne a while after ther was a *nisi prius* at the seid Warwyk upon a *scire facias*[28] for xl li. damages which was recouered of the seid Robert and Johane by the assise

---

22 A writ of summons issued direct to the defendant to answer matters not specified in the writ but within the equitable jurisdiction of chancery, under threat of a specified penalty (see *Class List of Chancery Files* (List and Index Soc., 130 (1976), p.91). (E.P.)

23 Robert, who seems normally to have resided at Westminster (see above, p.52), was presumably at prayers there or perhaps transacting business. For this *sub poena* and the commission of arrest mentioned immediately below, see perhaps above, p.11 and below, pp.106, 134, 149.

24 This could be a member of the Warwickshire Durant family (Carpenter, *Locality and Polity*, p.654) but there are various other candidates (see *HP*, ii, pp.810–12 for some of these). None of the possible men is known to have had a legal training nor to have been employed as a chancery clerk. The New Inn was one of the Inns of Chancery (hence the reference to the Strand which was in the heart of the legal quarter of London) (Baker, *Introduction to English Legal History*, p.139 n.9).

25 This is the *Domus Conversorum* in Chancery Lane (on the site of the present Public Record Office), formerly the house of Jewish converts founded by Henry III. After the expulsion of the Jews by Edward I the *Domus Conversorum* was gradually turned over to use by chancery and became the headquarters of the department outside Westminster (Richardson, 'Early Equity Judges', pp.448–90. (E.P.)

26 An assize: see above, p.19.

27 Probably Edmund or Thomas Starkey of Stretton on Dunsmore, Warwickshire (Carpenter, *Locality and Polity*, p.667; above, p.27).

28 A judicial writ issuing from a court, in this case King's Bench, to enforce a judgement of that

a foresaid and there the same   Sterky yave a fals enformacion to the contre,[29] for they schulde passe a yenst hym and withinne a day or two after, the same   Sterky in reward of his vntrewe labour was smetyn with a palsey and his mouthe sette a syde and hys yen drawen and so i taken in euery joynte of hys body. Also Cokayn a justise somtyme of the comone place was commissioner in a *nisi prius*[30] vpon an accion of particion[31] atte Ware by twyxt the seid Robert and Johane and here aduersaryes and for asmoche as the issue that the contre schulde passe vpon was whether the seid Robert and Johane were tenauntz in free hold, that is to seyn weren soole seised or non of the maners of Ouerhall in Gedelston, Brokholes in Munden and of Rooshall in Soret with inne the schyre of Hertford, the seid Robert had with hym the same day a *nisi prius*, Walter Pegeon, a gentilman of Hertford schyre,[32] the which was feoffed in the seid maners with other and the dede of feoffament, the which the state was made by v or vj yere by fore the day of the *nisi prius*[33] and a xij tenauntz of the seid maners that weren present whan the feoffament was made and a clerk which had holdyn courtes in the feoffes names, which weren alle redy atte barre to gedyr forto have enfourmed the contre whan they hadde taken her charge. But the seid Cokayn, in hyndryng of the seid Robert and Johane and fortheryng of theire aduersaryes, charged hem to hold their pees and wolde not suffre theim to speke no word, ne wold suffre the said Robert hys counseill to enfourme the contre nor to take non excepcion to the writte nor to make no chalanges, notwithstandyng that somme of the jurrours that passed on the quest stode that same tyme in the bisshop of Yorkes clothing, which was that tyme, and yit is, good lord to thair aduersaryes[34] and had sent letres that same tyme to diuerses brasours[35] and jurrours, and for his vntrouthe God smote hym with sykenesses with inne a day or two atte most and was dede beryed with inne fourtenyght after. And a non after alle this

---

court. The procedure involved the summons of the defendant to show cause why execution of judgement should not be awarded. (E.P.)

29 See above, n.9.

30 John Cokayn of Bury Hatley, Bedfordshire JCP, died 1429, not to be confused, as the *DNB* entry does, with John Cokayn of Derbyshire and Warwickshire, for whom see above, p.14 and below, pp.106–7 (Payling, *Political Society in Lancastrian England*, p.81; J.H. Baker, *The Order of Serjeants at Law*, Selden Soc., Supplementary Series, 5 (London, 1984), p.505 (ref. from E.P.); *DNB*, xi, p.226). For the dating of this *nisi prius*, which seems to coincide with Cokayn's death, see above, p.12 and below, n.238.

31 See above, n.10.

32 Walter Pegeon or his wife may have had land in Munden (*Cal. Close Rolls 1429–35*, pp.159–60).

33 This may be the feoffment referred to below, p.139. Assuming the accuracy of the writer's memory, and that the Hertfordshire *nisi prius* did indeed take place in 1429, that means that Mountford and his fellow feoffees were acting for Armburgh from about 1423–4. That is not entirely plausible, given the absence at that time of the sort of threat that would lead Armburgh to approach such a distinguished body of men, and it intensifies the problems in relation to the role of John Malory, one of the feoffees (see above, pp.14, 18–19).

34 John Kempe archbishop of York 1425–52 and chancellor 1426–32 (see above, n.40 to Intro.).

35 I.e. embracers: persons who attempt to influence a jury. (E.P.)

James Bellers,[36] which had weddid Elene the yonger suster of the seid two wronge heires, went ouer in to Normandye and there, thorew infortune evyn after his forwrought malyce and vntrouthe, thorew temptacion of the devill, he assosid hym vnto soche as he was hym selfe and of his owne condicions and robbed an Englyssh pyle and slewe and hurt many of ys Englyssh sowdyours that were therinne and a non forewith the Capteyn of the place sewed[37] hym and toke hym and smote of hys heede and slewe many of hys felawes and be syde all thys many of the jurrours that passed vpon the Inquisicions and vpon the accion of particions felle to myschef, for somme of hem were brent and some the kanker brent a way her lyppes and fillen in dyuers sykenesses and somme her goodes wastyd a wey and felle to nowght and   Cristoffer,[38] on of the kyngys baillefs by syde Ware was a greet labourer amonges the jurrours a yenst the seid Robert and Johane and also, with oute ony other manere of warant saf a breve of attourne vnder her aduersaryes seales, streyned the tenauntz and fermours to don hem paye her aduersaryes, there as the kyngys officers schuld take no mayn tenaunce in no maner mater that stant by twyxt partie and partie and ys with inne a while after he was slayn a monges his neyghbours.

And the mene tyme the chirch of Mancestr fill voyde and the debate by twene Sir Ric Hastynges knyght[39] and the seid Robert and Johane and theire parceners for the avouson of the same chirch of Mancestr[40] the which Ric Hastynges and the aduersaries of the same Robert and Johane were confedrid and in soche wyse acorded that the seid aduersaries swedyn a *quare impedit* in thair owne name and in the seid Robert and Johane, hem vnwetyng, a yenst the seid Ric Hastynges, thorew which *quare impedit* the seid Robert and Johane lost the avouson of the same chirch by defaute for thei myght not joyne with the seid aduersaries in the seid writte with outen that they schuld have ben concluded of her enheritaunce[41] and the seid Ric Hastynges brased [*sic*] a false contre in the forthersyde of the schyre next to his owne lyflode, by which contre the seid aduersaryes recouereden the moyte of the thrydde part of the maner a foreseid[42] and therfor, for her false labour God schortyd her lyfe dayes with inne a while after, for the same Ric Hastynges,   the parson

---

36 See above, p.7.

37 I.e. pursued him. For comments on James' fate, see above, pp.28–9.

38 Forename omitted. This one may have been no more than a minor local officer, but there was a Thomas Christopher, king's serjeant and yeoman of the chamber in 1422, who had held this office since at least 1396–7 (*Cal. Pat. Rolls 1422–9*, p.19), and a John Christopher, groom of the chamber and armourer, active in 1437 and 1440 (*Cal. Pat. Rolls 1436–41*, pp.142, 433).

39 This is the older brother of Leonard Hastings and therefore uncle of the future Lord Hastings, Leonard's son. He was of Yorkshire, Burton Hastings in east Warwickshire and of Kirby Muxloe in Leicestershire (*Complete Peerage*, vi, p.370; *VCH Warks.*, vi, p.57; Acheson, *Gentry Community*, pp.234–5; above, p.15).

40 For this suit, occasioned by the death of the incumbent in April 1432, and the parties concerned, see above, p.21.

41 See above, pp.21–4.

42 See above, p.26.

which he presentid to the same chirch,[43]   recordour of Coventre[44] which
was her chief counseill in alle thys matere in her most prosperite weren dede
with inne a twelmonth after.

To Sybil Palmer: after 1443/8, probably c.1450–5[45]

*The letter concerns the administration of the will of John Palmer, probably
grandson and certainly heir of Joan Armburgh (see above p.00), and the unwill-
ingness of the executors to pay to Sybil the money bequeathed her by John in his
will.*

To Sibill Palmer [in margin] Dere and welbelouyd frende I grete yow well. It
is not unknowyn to yow how John Denton, ye and I comynd to gedir whan ye
were last at Westm of the xx marc that John Palmer bequethyd hys moder
your wyfe [*sic*] and how the seid Denton promysyd vs that as sone as John
Strodyr hys brother in lawe were come from be yende the see he wolde comyn
with hym and ordeyn so for the seid xx marc that ye schuld holde yow well
payd. Wherfor as sone as I hadde knowlech that Strodyr was come home I
sent for hem and comynd with hem of your matere but I felt by her comuni-
cacion, not withstondyng that Denton promised me by fore yow that he wold
be rvlyd as I wolde have hym, that he is in no wille to part fro the money, for
in the by gynnyng of oure trete he desyrid that I schuld speke with Thornhill
his wyfe, John Palmer is moder in lawe and with alle Thornhill is executours[46]
and wete yf they wold consent that ye schulde be payd of this xx marc, and yf
they wolde not, he desired that I schulde swe the seid executours in the
bisshop is court of London or in the Archys,[47] the which schewyth well that he

---

43 This was John Swalwell (see above, p.23).

44 Probably John Weston of Warwick (see above, p.26).

45 On Sybil Palmer, and problems with the identification of the Palmers, see above, pp.31–3 and
notes there. This letter must postdate the death of John Palmer, between 1443 and 1448 (see
above, p.33). The dates associated with the others mentioned in the letter (see note immediately
below) suggest a date in the early- to mid-1450s, which would probably make it the latest entry in
the roll.

46 In identifying these, *William* Denton, citizen and mercer of London, is the most likely candidate,
as he was executor of the will of William Thornhill, also citizen and mercer of London, along with
Thornhill's widow, Joan, Robert (not John) Strother, also citizen and mercer, and others: all these
were active as executors in 1453–5 (*Cal. Pat. Rolls 1452–61*, p.185; *Calendar of Letters Books of the
City of London*, ed. R.R. Sharpe (11 vols., London, 1899–1912), Letter Book K, pp.352–3). If these
identifications are correct, as is probable, then Strother's presence overseas would be due to trade
rather than war service. In 1444 William Thornhill witnessed a London gift of goods to, amongst
others, Robert and Reginald Armburgh, which strengthens the case that it is William Thornhill's
executors who are at issue here (*Cal. Close Rolls 1441–7*, p.235). It is not clear whether 'John Palmer his mother-in-law' is meant to qualify 'Thornhill his wife' or is another item on a list of people. For the possibility that 'mother-in-law' here means stepmother, see above, n.151 to Intro.

47 The provincial court of Canterbury. Wills were subject to ecclesiastical courts, and Thornhill's
will, being that of a London citizen, would be in the jurisdiction of the bishop of London, unless
he had substantial property outside the diocese, in which case, since London was within the Canterbury province, the archbishop of Canterbury's prerogative jurisdiction would come into play

wolle kepe still the golde as long as he may, for he wote well I have no power to swe the seid executours, for I have no specialte for to schawe for me, that is to sey I am not John is executour, wherfor the best counseyll that I can yeve yow is that ye gete yow lordschip and frendschip to swe the seid executours and ye schul have record I nowe, for I and alle thoo that ye spake with alle whan ye were last at Westm and other mo schull be redy to record with yow at alle tymes.

Robert Armburgh to Sir John Barbour (priest) of Mancetter: c. 20 September 1451[48]

The letter demands payment of the rent for the lease of Armburgh's part of Mancetter from Ladyday 1450 to Midsummer 1451.

To Sir John Barbour [in margin] Dere and welbelouyd frende I commaunde me to yow. It is not vnknowen to yow that ye occupyed my part of the thrydde part of the manere of Mancestr and Darsthill[49] v termes, that is to sey Seynt Mary terme and middesomer terme in xxviij yere of the kyng that now is, Mighelmasse terme, Saynt Mary terme and midsomer terme in the xxix yere of the kyng that now is,[50] which termes drawen to the somme of xv marc, of the which I have resceyvyd iij marc with alowaunce of xj s. that ye payed Reygnold my cosyn,[51] which was not my wille, for I prayd yow that ye schulde paye no man but me. Wherfor consideryng the greet frendschip that I have schewed to yow and to your fadyr[52] by cause of yow and also the grete necessite and nede that I have of money, as I certefied you by letter the last tyme that my servuant was with you, I have greet merveyll that ye aquyte you no better to me. Therfor I pray you yevyth credens to the brynger of thys letter William Lenton my servaunt and payth hym my hole ferme that is behynde, hit drawyth to the somme of xj marc with oute Myghelmas terme which is litill more than sevnyght hens.[53] I have right greet nede ther to for I am and schall be put to importable cost or I schall lose xx li. of gode lyflode, the which

---

(R. Swanson, *Church and Society in Late Medieval England* (Oxford, 1989), p.160; B.L. Woodcock, *Medieval Ecclesiastical Courts in the Diocese of Canterbury* (OUP, London, 1952), pp.73–4).

48 For Barbour, see above, p.35. From the references to the overdue payments in the letter, the mention that Michaelmas is just over a week away, and the reference in a subsequent letter (below, p.72) to the fact that Michaelmas was a week after Lenton's visit, and allowing for Lenton's journey to Warwickshire – probably from Westminster, which is where Armburgh usually resided (see above, p.52) – it must date from about 20 September 1451.

49 Dosthill in Kingsbury went with Mancetter (*VCH Warks.*, iv, p.106).

50 That is, the periods from Ladyday (25 March), midsummer and Michaelmas (29 September) 1450, and from Ladyday and midsummer 1451. See also above, pp.34–6 for the dates of Barbour's occupancy.

51 His nephew Reynold Armburgh (see above, n.152 to Intro. and below, n.461).

52 Probably Richard Barbour of Atherstone, Warwickshire, a former lessee at Mancetter (see above, pp.9, 35).

53 In fact, Barbour relinquished the farm at Michaelmas (see below, p.183).

I pray you beth no cause of. Fforthermore I have greet merveyll, so as ye and I were acordyd that ye schuld resceyve my part of the manere that cam in by eschaunge for the avoyson of the chirch of Mancestr,[54] that ye sende me no worde what is don therto. I can no more etc.

Robert Armburgh to Clement Draper of Atherstone: probably late 1440s[55]

Also a demand for payment for the Mancetter lease, to an earlier lessee, who held it from 1439 to 1448.

To Clement Draper [in margin] Dere and welbelouyd frende I commaunde me to you. It is not vnknowyn to you how I sent you a letter by William Lenton my servant by the which letter I schewed you by a clere rekenyng that ye owght me at that tyme xj marc, of the which ye sent me but iij marc by the same William, mervelyng gretly consideryng the grete profyte that ye have taken of my grovnde that ye make no better payment. Wherfor I pray you yevyth credens to the seid William brynger of thys letter and payth hym the remenant, for it hath be long be hynde and I have greet nede therof as the seid William can enforme you well I nowe. I can no more at thys tyme but alle myghty God etc.

Robert Armburgh to John Ruggeley abbot of Merevale: after November 1449; perhaps late 1449/early 1450[56]

The letter asks for a copy of the deed of exchange by the co-owners of Mancetter of the advowson of the church of Mancetter for lands of the abbey in Leicestershire, effected in November 1449, and for a letter giving credence to Armburgh's servant, so that the latter can collect the rents due from the new lands.

To the Abbot of Meryvale [in margin] Worschipful and reuerent sir I commaunde me to you and yf it please you I wolle put you in remembrans of a text of holy writte which is thys, *sic fient nouissimi primi and primi nouissimi.*[57]

---

[54] See above, p.34. This means that Barbour was being made responsible for the income from these lands, even though they were in Leicestershire.

[55] For Draper, see above, p.34. He held the farm at Mancetter from 1439 to midsummer 1448 i.e. his last payment was at Ladyday 1448 (see below, p.71), and money for this was still being claimed by Armburgh in 1449, so the letter is likely to date to the late 1440s.

[56] Ruggeley was abbot of Merevale in east Warwickshire from at least 1423 to at least 1449 (Carpenter, *Locality and Polity*, p.378 n.130; Dugdale, *Warwickshire*, p.1079; see above, p.34). For the grant of the Mancetter advowson to the abbey, see above, p.34. It occurred in November 1449, which is the *terminus a quo* for the letter, but the reference to another letter may give a more precise date (see below, n.59).

[57] This is a misquoted biblical reference: 'Sic erunt novissimi primi et primi novissimi' (*Matth.* 20 v.16).

I put you thys text in remembrans for this entent, ye be remembryd that I was the last that grauntyd that the chirch of Mancestr schuld be approprid and the first that put my seale to the dede of eschaunge and thowe I were the first that put my seale to the seid dede I was and am the last that resceyvyd ony money of the manere that cam in by eschaunge for the seid chirch, for I resceyvyd neuer peny in to thys day of the seid manere. Wherfor I beseche you of your gode faderhode that ye wolle foche safe to yeve credens to my seruant William Lenton brynger of thys letter and deliuer hym a copy of the seid dede of eschaunge vnder yor seale as ye promysed me in the [m.2] by gynnyng, and for asmoch as I and my seruantys be not knowen a monges the tenants and hom[58] that have the rule of the lordschip that cam in by eschaunge for the chirch of Mancestr forseid, that ye wolle foche safe to do wryte a letter under your sygnet to the seid tenants and hom that have rule of the seid lordschip and William Lenton brynger of thys letter my seruant and rent gaderer, to that entent that whan the seid William comyth a mongs hem thei schull yeve credens to hym be cause of your letteris and yf it lyke you to do thus moch at my simple request I trust to God to do you soche seruise that schall do you greet ese and fortheryng in tyme comyng. And as tochyng the letter that ye sent me for your welbelouyd seruant John Attherston[59] I schall do alle that I may to serve your entent. I can no more at thys tyme. The Holy Trinite have you in hys kepyng etc.

A remembrance by Robert Armburgh of moneys paid to Reynold Armburgh, his nephew, from Mancetter: late 1450[60]

This is part of the continuing friction with Reynold over the latter's claims on the Armburgh lands (see above, p.00), in this instance rent from Armburgh's part of Mancetter manor.

A remembrauns what Reynold Armeburgh hath resceyn at Mancestr [in margin] Here is a remembraunce how Reygnold Armebourgh hath resceyvyd ij yer the ferme of my part of the manere of Mancestr, that is to sey of Seint Mary terme the Annunciacion and midsomer terme in the xxvj yere of Kyng Harry the vj and Mighelmas terme, Seynt Mary terme and midsomer terme in the xxvij yere and of Mighelmas terme in the xxviij yere of the same kyng[61] and thowe it were so that the seid Reygnold resceyvyd no money there in to Twesday next after the fest of Seynt Andrew the xxvij yere,[62] he resceyvyd

---

58 I.e. homage: the tenants.
59 See above, p.34. This may be the letter below, pp.180–1, which probably dates from late 1449 or early 1450.
60 The reference in this statement to the first year's income from the lands received in exchange (see below, n.66) would give a date in late 1450. For Reynold Armburgh, see above, p.36.
61 25 March, midsummer and Michaelmas 1448, and the same dates in 1449.
62 3 December 1448.

there the same day lij s of the tenants of ferme of the yere byforn, the which yere lay hole in the tenants handys, for Clement Draper was ffermour there ix yere as it aperith by his endenture, that is to sey fro Seynt Mary day the Annunciacion the xvij yere of Kyng Harry the vj,[63] resceyvyng at his first comyng in the ferme of the same terme in to Seynt Mary terme the Annunciacion the xxvj yere[64] and left the seid terme in the tenants hondys, for as moche as he resceyvyd Seynt Mary terme at hys first comyng he myght not resceyve Seynt Mary terme at hys goyng owithe, for he schuld than have resceyvyd the ferme of ix yere and an halfe, the which had ben a yenst hys endenture.[65] Fforthermore the seid Reygnold resceyvyd of my tenantys at Mancestr with inne Sir John Barbour ys terme xj s. vj d. and of the manere of Petlyng[66] which cam in by eschaunge for the chirch of Mancestr for the fyrst yere iiij marc.

Robert Armburgh to the coheirs to Mancetter manor: probably late 1451[67]

The letter contests Reynold's claim to part of the Leicestershire land that came by exchange for the Mancetter advowson and again makes a plea that Robert may receive his due from the income of the Leicestershire lands and also that nothing may be given to Reynold.

To the parceners of the manere of Mancestr [in margin] Worschipfull serys I commande me to you and, for asmoch as Reygnold Armebourgh my cosyn cleymeth to be parcener in the manere of Mancestr and in the londes that cam in by eschaunge for the avoyson of the parsonage of Mancestr therfor, I schewed myn evydences to Rafe Holt, John Attherston[68] and other which mowe well fele and knowe by the seid evydences that the seid Reygnold hadde

---

[63] 25 March 1439. All the payments listed here were made to Reynold in the period when it seems the farm was in Robert's hands (see above, p.35 for the next lease).

[64] 25 March 1448.

[65] This means that he was given the tenants' rents for the previous period of the year on his entry (from the preceding Michaelmas it seems, since Armburgh appears not to have divided the half-year between Michaelmas and Ladyday), and that he therefore did not take them for that period when he left.

[66] This refers to the lands at Peatling and Bruntingthorpe, Leicestershire which were given by the abbot to the heirs to Mancetter in exchange for the advowson (see above, p.34).

[67] The recipients are the other coholders of the manor, descendants of the last de Mancetter and their representatives, who alienated the advowson to Merevale; that is Thomas Arblaster of Staffordshire and his wife Alice; Anne, widow of John Waver and of Thomas Porter, both of Warwickshire, sister and heir of Edmund Prilly; Reynold Armburgh (included as former husband of Joan Palmer, Joan Armburgh's heir: see above, pp.30, 36); Clement Draper (see above, p.34: his descent is not known); Joan widow of William Harpour (see above, p.9); and Ralph Holt and his wife Ellen (see above, p.29) (*Cal. Pat. Rolls 1446–52*, p.302; *VCH Warks.*, iv, p.120; *VCH Leics.*, v, p.232). They assembled in Merevale to sort out the allocation of money from the Leicestershire lands in November 1451 (see above, p.52 and below, pp.178–9). See also n.111 to Intro.

[68] For Holt, see immediately above; for Atherston, a servant of the abbot of Merevale, see above, p.34.

neuer title nor ryght in the seid maner and londes. Wherfor I pray you whan ye comyn to gedyr that ye sette soche a rule that I may have my part of the londes that cam in by eschaunge after the rate, that is to sey after the halvyn-dell of the thrydde part of the manere of Mancestr of the which I am lavfully seised, and that the reuerent fader the abbot of Meryvale may have hit in kepyng to myn vse, for in to thys tyme I resceyvyd neuer peny therof. And yf the seid Reygnold my cosyn wolle make ony clayme in the seid manere and londes let hym swe the comyn lawe and with the grace of Godde he schall be answerd, for it is more reson that he which hath neyther title nor ryght nor evydens to schewe be put to hys accion rather than he which is lavfully seised and hath evydens i nowe to schewe for hym. I can no more at thys tyme but etc.

Robert Armburgh to Sir John Barbour: probably late 1451[69]

The letter concerns rent owed by Barbour as lessee of Armburgh's part of Mancet-ter. Armburgh suspects that Barbour is readier to pay Reynold than to pay him.

To Sir John Barbour [in margin] Dere and welbelouyd frende I commaunde me to you. It is not vnknowen to you how that I sent you a letter by William Lenton my seruant the last tyme that he was with you, in the which letter I schewed you by a clere rekenyng that ye ought me at that tyme xj marc with owte Mighelmas terme which was but a sevenyght after, the somme of both is xiiij marc, and also I compleyned me to you in the same letter of grete neces-site and nede that I have of money for plee of londe that I have hangyng at the comen lawe,[70] but I fele well that ye sette that but litill at herte. Wherfor I se well now that it is trew that your neyghbours have seid of you, for summe have tolde me that I schuld be schrewdely[71] payd and summe tolde me that ye have made pondys and reperacion with my ferme and summe sayn that ye be well payd that ye have a colour for a fewe crakyng wordys that Reygnold my cosyn crakyd there for to withholde my money. And summe sayn that ye be in better wille to pay hym than me and that schewyth well, for as it is reportid ye seyd to Reygnold that he was be holde to yow that ye kept so moch money of myn still in yor hande and that are ye litill be holde to don, consideryng the gode wille that I have schewed you and therfor I pray you sendyth me the money that ye owe me for ther schall no man nor ther can no man, Reignold nor non other, discharge you nor aquyte you ther of but I and that can Holt, John Attherston and other mo which have seyn myn evydens telle you well I nowe. I can no more etc.

---

[69] This clearly follows on from the previous letter to Barbour, probably making it late 1451.

[70] The only possible plea for which there is evidence is that against the Chancys over the lands in Hertfordshire and Essex, although there is no evidence of this plea having reached the courts of common law (see above, pp.37–8).

[71] 'Badly'.

Robert Armburgh to the bailiff and tenants of Peatling, Leicestershire: probably late 1450[72]
The letter forbids the tenants of the Leicestershire lands exchanged for the Mancetter advowson to pay any more rent to Reynold.

To the bayly and tenants of Petlyng [in margin] Dere and welbelouyd frendys I grete you well and have grete merveyll so as ye have very knowlech that I am on of the parceners of Mancestr, that ye wolde pay Reygnold Armebourgh my part of the money of Petlyng and Brantyngthorp, that is to sey of the londes which cam in by eschaunge for the avoyson of the chirch of Mancestr, with oute that he hadde schewed you a letter of atorne in my name. I do you to wete that he may not discharge you nor aquyte you of the money that ye have payd hym, for he hath neyther title nor ryght in no part of the manere of Mancestr nor in the londes, that is to sey Petlyng and Brantyngthorp with the pertynans, which cam in by eschaunge nor no manere of evydens to schewe for hym, and that knowyth Rafe Holt, John Attherston and other which have seyn myn evydens well I nowe. And therfor I charge you as ye wolle be savyd harmeles that ye pay hym no more money, for yf ye do I schall streyne you a gayne for alle the hole bothe olde and newe. I can no more etc.

Robert Armburgh to the tenants of Mancetter: probably late 1450[73]
A similar ban addressed to the Mancetter tenants.

To the tenants of the maner of Mancestr [in margin] Dere and welbelouyd frendys I grete you well and have greet merveyll, so as ye have very knowlech how I am and have be lavfully seysed and in possession pesible alle thys xxij wynter and more of the on halwyndell of the thrydpart of the manere of Mancestr, that ye wolde pay Reygnold Armebourgh ony money with oute that he hadde schewed you my letter and my seale. I do you well to wete that he may not discharge you nor aquyte you of the money that ye have payd hym, for he hath neyther title nor ryght in no part of the manere of Mancestr nor evydens to schewe for hym, and that knowyth Rafe Holt, John Attherston and other which have seyn myn evydens well i nowe. And therfor I counseill you and charge you both that ye pay hym no more money in the peyne of the perell that wolle falle therof, for yf ye do I schall distreyne you a gayn for alle the hole both olde and newe.

---

72 Probably from some time after Michaelmas 1450 (see also n.60, above).

73 This was probably written at the same time as the letter immediately preceding, as they are very similar. That means that Armburgh had possessed Mancetter for rather more than the twenty-two years he mentions (see above, p.5).

To Clement Draper: probably c.1449[74]

Another letter concerning money owed from the lease of Mancetter, containing another denial that Reynold has any rights in the manor.

To Clement Draper [in margin] Dere and welbelovyd frende I commmaunde me to you. It is not vnknowen to you what money ye owe me and how it hath be a grete while owyng and how I compleyned me to you in the last letter that I sent you of grete nede of money for plee of londe that I have hangyng at the comyn lawe, wherfor I pray you to considre these thyngys and as I may do for you in tyme comyng that ye wolle sende me the seid money by the brynger of this letter, for I have greet nede therof. I can no more etc.

For astochyng the fyne that Reygnold schew you for hym, he may nought cleyme therby, for yf a lernyd man see hit he schall well knowen that hit is ayenst hym and also I toke Reygnold the fyne to delyuer hit to Clement Draper which was that tyme my fermour for to discharge me of an homage and a releef that   Grey[75] cleymed of me for my part of the manere of Mancestr that I holde of hym the which fyne was in Clement Draper ys kepyng ij yere and more.[76]

Robert Armburgh to John Ruggeley, abbot of Merevale: probably 1450[77]

A letter concerning the lease of Mancetter and the continuing problems with Reynold's demands in Leicestershire.

To the Abbot of Meryvale [in margin] Worschipfull and reuerent sir I commaunde me to you and, consideryng by a letter that ye sent me in Trinite terme that last was the affyans, love and gode wille that ye have to John

---

74 This is likely to follow on from the previous letter to Clement, dated to c.1449 (immediately above); although it does not specifically mention the need for money arising from the law, it does say that Lenton would explain the need, which would have given Armburgh the means to tell Draper about the legal situation.

75 Although the Astley estate, the Greys' principal stake in east Warwickshire, went to Reginald Grey of Ruthin's heirs by his second wife, the overlordship of Mancetter was part of the Hastings of Pembroke inheritance and so was inherited in the older line and came to Edmund Grey Lord of Ruthin and earl of Kent (1440–90), as grandson and heir of Reginald by his first wife (*Complete Peerage*, vi, pp.159–60; above, p.35).

76 Because of the mention of Draper, this cannot be a postscript to the letter immediately above, addressed to Draper, unless the copyist had had a brainstorm. The addressee is consequently unknown.

77 A letter from the abbot, asking Armburgh to give the farm to Atherstone (below, pp.180–1), may be the one mentioned in this letter. In fact, the lease was given elsewhere at Ladyday 1450 (above, p.35). The lease seem to have changed hands again c.1452 (above, p.35) but the mention of the letter to the bailiff and tenants of Peatling and Bruntingthorpe (which is presumably the one above, p.73) suggests an earlier date for this letter than that. However, it is highly improbable that it would have been written in Trinity Term 1449, several months before the advowson was alienated and therefore, we must suppose, before the exchange land had come in. The most likely solution is that the abbot's letter was written in Trinity 1450 and that, to get his favour and Atherstone's assistance, Armburgh was simply lying to both about the farm.

Attherston, I have lete hym my part of the manere of Mancestr to ferme in hope and very trust that ye wolle shewe hym and alle my tenantys your gode favour and supportacion. Also I sende a letter at thys tyme by John Attherston to the bayly and tenantys of Petlyng and Brantyngthorp[78] chargyng hem that they paye no more money to Reygnold Armeburgh but that they paye you my part, that is to sey the halvyndell of the thrydpart of the seid londes that cam in by eschaunge, besechyng you by avyse of John Attherston to sende to the seid bayly and tenantys a nother letter vnder your sygnet counselyng hem to don the same.

To John Rigges ?of London perhaps from Joan Armburgh: if so, before 1443[79]

This concerns the release of a prisoner of her husband – presumably of her first husband Thomas Aspall (see n.79 immediately above) – and the consequent loss of his ransom; against this threat, Riggs' help is requested.

To John Rigges [in margin] Worschipfull sir I commaunde me to you certefying you how that John Wessynham[80] with other of hys assent have by imagynacion remevyd Sir Gerard here Bomerys,[81] myn husbond ys presoner owte of the gate howse of Westm[82] in to the Kyngs Bench and a gaynst lawe of

---

78 See n.66 to text, above.

79 There was a John Rigges in London in 1443 and, perhaps the same man, John Rigges grocer of London in 1454 (*Calendar of London Letter Books*, Letter Book K, p.281; *Calendar of Select Plea and Memoranda Rolls of the City of London*, ed. A.H. Thomas and P.E. Jones (6 vols., Cambridge, 1926–61), *1437–57*, p.134). There is no obvious way of dating this letter, especially because of the problems in identifying the others mentioned in it (see notes immediately below). If the 'husband' referred to is Robert Armburgh, then it must predate Joan's death in 1443 (see above, p.30), although that would put it badly out of sequence with the surrounding entries. If it was not written by Joan, it is difficult to see who the writer might be. E.P. suggests that the letter refers to a French prisoner (see below, n.81) who would, in that case, have been captured by Thomas Aspall when in France. This could well be the case, but, even if Joan wrote the letter after Aspall's death, unless the man suffered a long captivity (which is to some extent implied by the text), that raises problems with the dates of the tentative identification of Rigges.

80 There was a Wesenham family in Huntingdonshire, but no head of that family called John in the fifteenth century (*VCH Hunts.*, iii (London, 1936), p.147). A better lead may be the assault led by the prior of the Augustinians, Bedford on the prior of the Friars Preachers and some of the friars of Dunstable, among whom was John Wesenham, perhaps a member of the Huntingdonshire family (*Cal. Pat. Rolls 1441–6*, p.287). E.P. suggests John Wesenham of Bishop's Lynn (d.1434) (see *HP*, iv, p.811). The only conceivable connection between such a man and a French prisoner of war (n.81) would presumably be that Wesenham had become involved either in the funding of the ransoming process or in the financial affairs of the prisoner's captor. If Aspall was indeed the captor, then this could be another element in his complex financial affairs (see below, pp.77–87).

81 I have been able neither to explain this strange name nor to identify the man who bore it. It could be a priest but E.P. suggests, more credibly, that this is a French prisoner, which would explain the reference to the law of arms. The reference to his friends 'beyond the sea' strengthens the case.

82 Westminster gatehouse was a prison with a dual function: as the abbot's prison for his fee and for the clerks of the bishop of London taken within the liberty of Westminster, a right of imprisonment claimed by the abbots by 1282–3 (R.B. Pugh, *Imprisonment in Medieval England* (Cambridge, 1968), pp.136–7).

armys and alle manere of lawes have delyuerd hym by a proclamacion, where as by the comyn lawe there schulde no presoner be delyuerd by proclamacion but yf he were brought in to the seid bench for dette, trespasse or suspessyon of felonye. And thus by vnlavfull menys the seid Wessynham and othyr which have hadde the seid presoner in gouernance many yerys and wolde not suffre myn husbonde by hys lyfe nor other that hadde interesse after hys dissease to speke with the seid presoner, but yf it were onys or twyse in theire owne presence, purposyng hem to have the presoner ys ffynance hem selfe with oute the helpe of your gode maysterschip, and to that entent ther hath ben a certeyn persons be yende the see thys quarter of a yere and more to tretyn with the presoner ys frendys, and thus they purposyn hem to avoyde you and me and other that have interesse but thys matyr be the sonner holpen. Wherfor I beseche you in reverence of Godde that ye wolle come hydyr in alle the hast that ye may, for yit throwgh gode lordschip that ye mey geete, we may sette hande on the presoner and have hym well i nowe, for he is in a worthy manne ys howse of London in gouernance tille the fynance by come. I can no more at thys tyme but for the love of Godde take thys matere to herte etc.

Robert Armbrugh to John Ruggeley abbot of Merevale: probably 1450[83]

Armburgh reassures the abbot that he will favour the abbot's nominee, John Atherston, rather than give John Barbour the lease of Mancetter.

To the Abbot of Meryvale [in margin] Worschipfull and reuerent sir I commaunde me to you and for asmoch as I feele by your letter that ye supposyn that I wolde yeve soche favour to Sir John Barbour vicar of Mancestr that schulde hurte you and me and my coparcioners of Mancestr, I put you oute of dowte, by the grace of Godde ye schul neuer fynde me in that defavte, for thowth I were the last that consentyd to the eschaunge made by twene you and vs, I was on of the first that sette my seale to the said eschaunge, and therfor it was neuer nor is nor schall be myne entent to werke nor consent to the contrary in no wyse. And astochyng John Attherston I trust to Godde he wolle aquyte hym so to me that he and I schull do well i nowe. I can no more to you etc.

---

83 This seems to be an equally dishonest letter to that above (pp.74–5), written about the same time.

Robert Armburgh, at Westminster, to Sir John Barbour: c.early to mid 1451[84]

Armburgh is about to come to an agreement with Reynold and wants full details, both of the money paid by the tenants of Mancetter to Reynold while Barbour was lessee, and of the tenancies and value of Armburgh's part of the manor.

To Sir John Barbour [in margin] Right dere and welbelouyd frende I commaunde me to you. And for asmoch as Reygnold Armeburgh my cosyn and I, as I suppose, are lyke with inne schort tyme to come to a rekenyng, I pray you yewyth credens to William Lenton brynger of thys letter and sendyth me wretyn how moche money the seid Reignold resceyvyd of my tenantes, that is to sey of tho termes while ye have hadde my lyflode yn your gouernance, and the names of the tenantes that he resceyvyd the money of and what he resceyvyd of ech of hem and forthermore I pray you sendyth me the names i writyn of alle the persones that occupyen ony parcell of my lyflode at this tyme, londe, mede, pastur, tenement or ony other thyng, and the names of the parcell that they occupyen and what they beere therfore yerely, and also I pray you sendyth me wrytyn what money wolle be made of my part of the wode growyng on alle the grownde and the names of the chapmen that ye mowe have therto and who wolle yeve most therfore, and, astochyng the money that is by twen you and me, I pray you sendyth me asmoche as ye mowe, I have grete nede therto. I can no more at thys tyme but I pray Godde have you in his kepyng and I pray you to helpe and supporte William my seruant in gaderyng of my ferme. Wrytyn at Westm etc.

Robert Armburgh's account of the financial dealings of Joan Armburgh and her second husband, Thomas Aspall esquire, with Richard Ketford, London citizen, from 1417 to 1420 and Armburgh's own subsequent involvement: written c.1420 or 1421[85]

These seem to be financial obligations incurred as a result of Aspall's need for ready money to finance his participation in Henry V's wars, which were then inherited by Armburgh as Joan's subsequent husband. They reveal a complex credit network operated by London citizens.

[m.3] Thys is the a counte of Robert Armeburgh vpon the obligacion in the which he was bounden to Ric Ketford, the which obligacion was made vpon ij

---

84 This is likely to date to a year or so after Barbour had been given the farm (see above, p.35), which would make it perhaps early to middle 1451.

85 For the dating – perhaps late 1420 or early 1421 – see below, n.103. E.P. notes that the documents and statements collected here were probably memoranda and pleadings for the debt action brought by Ketford against Armburgh in the London sheriffs' court in 1423 (see below, pp.86–7). Ketford was a London citizen and sadler (which explains his use of Caldwell, another sadler, in these undertakings), who seems to have specialised in financing expenditure in war (*Cal. Close Rolls 1419–22*, pp.229–30, *1422–9*, pp.270–1).

obligacions in the which obligacions Johane hys wyfe was bounde in her weduohode, of the which ij obligacions on was made vpon ij tailles, the which were made by twyxt the forseyd Johane and the forseyd Ric a boute midsomer twelfmonth after the kyng went to Kaue.[86] Of the which ij tailles in the first taille was tailled xvj marc that remayned of an obligacion of xxj li., in the which Thomas Aspall somtyme her husbond[87] was bounde to the forseid Ric Ketford longe by forn the seid Thomas went ouer the see with the kyng and afterward payd hym x li. of the same obligacion and hadde of hym aquitaunce the which we have to schewen, and vj s. viij d. Ketford for yafe the seid Johane to maken her the beter willed to taillen with hym the seid xvi marc, and ferthermore ther was taylled in the seid taille xiij s. iiij d. that the seid Johane borewed of the same Ric by the handes of a preste that is callyd Sir John Armeg[88] at Mighelmasse next folowyng after the forseid Thomas, that tyme her husbond, went ouer the see,[89] also vj marc the which the forseid Johane borewed of the forseid Ric by her owne hondes at midsomer next folowyng,[90] so that the somme tailled in the first taille was xv li. vj s. viij d., and after this sche borewed an hakeney sadell *pretii* of xl d. and a payr of molyns[91] *pretii* of viij d. and a reyne *pretii* of iiij d. and also he lent a seruant of her iiij d. and at Seint Nicolas day[92] next folowyng sche borewed of hym xl s. by the handes of John Hill[93] that tyme fforester of Ilford and leyde hym to wedde there for xij

---

86 This is probably Caux and almost certainly refers to Henry V's expedition to Normandy of summer 1417, which in fact landed near Honfleur, just to the south of the Pays de Caux. Alternatively, it could mean the naval victory off the Chef de Caux on 29 June 1417, although Henry V was not present on this occasion (Allmand, *Lancastrian Normandy*, pp.9–11). The dating of the subsequent sequence of events is not affected because of the proximity of the two events (see p.82 below for the dating of these agreements to 1417). There is a contradiction in the dates given here, in that the first tally mentioned would then date to midsummer 1418 but Joan was not a widow until two summers later (see n.87, below), but it does not seem that any other date is possible for the king's departure. All this clearly refers to the service overseas of Joan's second husband, Thomas Aspall, for whom see n.87.

87 Thomas Aspall, Joan's second husband, escheator in Essex in 1409. They were married by 1410/11 and he made his will at Mantes on 12 June 1419 and was dead by 10 July 1420, despite being listed as her husband in a duchy of Lancaster survey from c.1420–25/6. Although the text shows that he served abroad with Henry V, I have found no record of the nature and location of his service, other than the will, though it is quite probable that he could be found on an unpublished muster roll. There is a chancery plea concerning entry of his lands while he was in France with the king and it is not impossible that the entry resulted from his financial entanglements (*Cal. Fine Rolls 1405–13*, p.245; *Cal. Close Rolls 1419–22*, p.82; *The Register of Henry Chichele Archbishop of Canterbury 1414–43*, ed. E.F. Jacob (4 vols., Oxford, 1938–43), ii, p.167; *Suffolk Feet of Fines*, p.282; *Feudal Aids*, vi, p.584; PRO C1/68/124).

88 A squiggle at the end of this name could indicate 'er', in which case the priest could well be a member of the Armburgh family, but the same mark is to be found at the end of 'fastinggang' in this entry.

89 Michaelmas 1417.

90 Midsummer 1418 (but see comments above, n.86 to text).

91 Possibly 'molan' or 'mullen', a bit or horse's headstall.

92 6 December 1418.

93 There are several possible John Hills. Perhaps the most likely, given the London and commercial context, is the London customer of 1414, who may be the chamberlain of London in 1416, a fishmonger, who was dead by August 1422 (*Cal. Fine Rolls 1413–22*, p.5; *London Plea and Memoranda*

siluer spónes and a saltsaler of siluer i couered, and at fastynggang twelfmonth after[94] sche kam to London for to reken with hym and there he seide
that he hadde delyuered to her husband vpon the see syde at hys last goyng
ouer to Kaue iij li. in harneys and prayed her to have surete therof. And there
by twyxt hem both thei made the secunde taille, in which taille was tailled the
somme conteynyng the first taille and all these other sommes folowyng after,
and dede breke the first taille so that the somme of the last tayle drawyth to
the somme of a xx li. xj s. iiij d., of the which ij tailles we have the foilles[95] for
to schewe. And afterward the same Johane made the seid Ric an obligacion
vpon the last taylle and for asmoch as hit was founde by an endenture, the
which the seid Ric schewed forthe the same tyme that the iij li., the which he
seide that he schuld have delyuered her husbond in harneys at the seesyde was
but iiij marc, therfor ther was a bated vj s. viij d. of the somme tailled a fornseid, so that the seid obligacion was made of xx li. iiij s. viij d., the which obligacion was made at Ester next folowyng.[96] And at midsomer next folowyng[97]
sche dede borewe of hym xx s. and at lammesse[98] next sewyng the seid Ric
cam to the seid Johane and brought with hym the first obligacion of xxj li., the
remenaunt of the which obligacion was tailled in the first taill, and there, by
sotil ymaginacion and thretyng of presonement and thorowe the vntrouthe of
certeyn persones that were a boute her, he lent her an c s. and dede her seale
an newe obligacion of xxvij li. and brak the olde and afterward the seid Robert
Armeburgh wedded the seid Johane at Mighelmasse next folowyng.[99] With
inne a sevenyght after he was weddid the same Ric arestid hym in to the countour and there, vnknowyng of that deceit don to his wyfe, he brak the ij obligacions and bonde hym selfe in a nother obligacion of alle the hole.
Ric Ketford [in margin of previous section]

A record gaynes the a counte of Ric Ketford

Atte be gynnyng, as touchyng the xvj marc that remaynde of the olde obligacion the which he sayth schulde have ben fo [*sic*] a chevesans[100] of waxe by

---

Rolls 1413–1437, pp.44, 50; *Calendar of London Letter Books:* Letter Book I, p.269). There was also
a yeoman of the larder in 1414 but his only extant grant is in Oxfordshire rather than Essex (*Cal.
Pat. Rolls 1413–16*, p.169). I have found no reference to the office of forester of Ilford, but Great
Ilford was owned by a leper hospital which was subject to the abbey of Barking and Little Ilford
by Stratford abbey. Since Aspall mentions a resident of Barking in his will and Armburgh, after
his marriage to Aspall's widow, is referred to as 'of Barking', a connection with Barking abbey
might be the more likely (Morant, *Essex*, i, pp.7–8, 26; *Chichele Register*, ii, p.166; below, p.86).

94 Shrovetide i.e. 20 February 1420.
95 I.e. counterfoils.
96 Easter Day 1420 was 7 April.
97 Midsummer 1420.
98 1 August 1420.
99 Michaelmas 1420; and see above, p.6 and n.
100 Either 'provision of' or 'raising money for'; probably the latter, since 'cryans', which means
pledging or taking credit, is used as a synonym immediately below. The wax was presumably for
sealing the various obligations.

syde the obligacion, ther was a prest y called Sir John Wheteworth[101] and her owne doughter[102] and a yoman with the forsaid John, whan the ij^de taille was made by twyxt her and Ric Ketford, the which wollen record that the xvj marc which was a parcell of the first taille and after put in to the ij^de was the remenaunt of the olde obligacion, and thei wolle make hit goode, by what othe that any man wolle put hem to, that at the makyng of the ij^de taille the forseyd Ric schulde have delyuered to the seid Johane the olde obligacion and the endentur of the parcell the which were payed owithe. [The arrangement of the next segment is as set out here i.e. a new paragraph but without the gap found normally between entries.]

Ric Ketford [in margin] Item accordyng to this ther was a rekenyng made by twyxen Robert Armeburgh and the forseyd Ric at Westm in the cloyster by fore the chapitre dore on Seint Katerine ewyn was a twelfmonth,[103] by forn Sir John Thomas prest[104] and Ric Tibray[105] and Caldewell the kyngs sadeler[106] and there the first parcell that the forseid Ric rekend that schulde have be dewe of this obligacion of xlvij li. iiij s. viij d., the which the forseid Robert is bounde inne, was the xvj marc that remaynyth in the olde obligacion, as hit schewyth by the a counte that was write the same tyme, the which the forseid Sir John wolle recorde. Wherfor hit schewyth woll that he dede the seid Johane wronge for to make her to be bounde in the olde obligacion agayn.

Ric Ketford [in margin] Item in evydens that the recorde of Sir John Thomas and Sir John Wetewode schulde be trewe, there was an hosyer of London callid Whyte,[107] the which was with Thomas Aspall and the said Johane, that tyme his wyfe, at Seint Georges barre[108] atte the departyng of hym when the forseid Thomas went ouer the see to Caue. And there in audience of the forseid hosyer he rehersyd to hys wyfe alle the dettes that he owght in London. And amonges alle othere he rehersed that he owght to Ric Ketford xvj

---

101 John Wetwode chaplain was instituted to the vicarage of Chilham, Kent, of the Brigettines of Syon, in 1434 (*Chichele Register*, i, p.284).

102 Presumably Margaret, daughter of Joan and Philip Kedington (see above, p.9).

103 See below, pp.81–2 for the obligation itself; the Latin wording makes clear that it means the evening before the feast i.e. 24 November. The obligation may well have been made in the aftermath of Armburgh's arrest at Michaelmas 1420 (see above, p.79), which would date this whole account of the dealings with Ketford, with its reference to St Catherine's eve twelve months before to some time after November 1421, though it could have been made during the proceedings following a further arrest in February 1423 (below, p.86).

104 A John Thomas was ordained deacon in the Salisbury diocese in 1416 (*Chichele Register*, iv, p.321).

105 I have not been able to identify him, although there was a place called Tilbirey next to Clare in Suffolk, an area from which some of the people in the Roos/Brokholes case came, including Joan's first husband (*The Cartulary of the Augustinian Friars of Clare*, ed. C. Harper-Bill, Suffolk Records Soc., Suffolk Charters, 11 (Woodbridge, 1991), p.104).

106 William Caldwell citizen and sadler of London, whose will dates to September 1434 (*London Plea and Memoranda Rolls 1413–1437*, pp.277–80). Note also that the administration of the goods of Geoffrey Brokholes, Joan's father, was given in 1406 to Robert Caldwell amongst others (PRO PCC Wills Marche f.86).

107 I have not been able to find a London hosier of this name.

108 In Southampton. (E.P.)

marc and no more, of the whiche xvj marc he charged her to with drawe xl s. of vserye and thys wolle the seid hosyer recorden.

Ric Ketford [in margin] Item a nother evydens that his owne rekenyng is not trewe, hit may be prevyd by his owne evydence and his owne rekenyng. He hath seid ofte tyme that the xvj marc, the which we sayen is the remenant of the olde obligacion, schulde have be for a chevessaunce of wax by side the obligacion and a longe tyme by fore that the seid Thomas Aspall was bounde to hym in that same olde obligacion, of the which xvj marc he hadde no sewerte by his owne seying, til the forseid Johane made hym sewerte in the first taille that was made by twene hem tweyne, after that her husbond went ouer the see. Wherfor hit semyth vntrewe, ffor yf he hadde lent to hym thys xvj marc as he sayth hym self by fore the xxj li., he wold have take surete of hym for the xvj marc as well as for the xxj li., and in evydence that his owne rekenyng is soche we schull schewe the copye of the obligacion of x li. xiij s. j d. ob. in which the forseid Ric was bounde to Hanewell grocer with inne Ludgate for the seid Thomas Aspall and the date of the obligacion of xxj li., the which the forseid Thomas Aspall was bounde inne to hym.

Ric Ketford [in margin] Item that the x li. xiij s. j d. ob. of the cryans of wax was in the obligacion of xxj li. and not by siden may be preved by his owne endentur and his owne rekenyng, and the vserye wolle be founde in the somme, ffor he hath often tyme rekened that the parcelles of the olde obligacion schulde be xxvj s. viij d. at on tyme and vij li. at a nother tyme and xiij li. at a nother tyme, the which parcelles ben in the endentur the which he hath vnder Thomas Aspall seale, the which xiij li., be Ketford owne seiyng, schulde have be payed to Hanewell grocer within Ludgate,[109] the which is not soth, ffor hit schewyth by the obligacion that Ric Ketford was bounde in to the same grocer, that the seid grocer had but x li. xiij s. j d. ob. and hym self that other part, safe hit may well be demyd that the brocour hadde a noble for his travayle and here it semyth cam the xl s. of vserye, the which the seid Thomas Aspall chargyd his wyfe to withdrawen in audience.

Various evidences concerning Richard Ketford's financial dealings with Joan, Aspall and Armburgh, 1417–23

Ric Ketford [in margin] Memorandum de compoto Ricardi Ketford super obligacione Roberti Armeburgh hic coram domino Johanne Thomas capellano, Thomas,[110] Ricardo Tybray et Caldewell sellario Regis in vigilia Sancte

---

109 William Hanwell citizen and grocer of London, active 1415 and 1427 (*Cal. Close Rolls 1413–16*, p.201, *1422–9*, pp.344–5).
110 *Sic*: the Christian name only is given. Since this is clearly the 'reckoning' referred to above (p.80), and Thomas, Tybray and Caldwell are the only witnesses mentioned there, the insertion of the extra Thomas is probably a slip of the pen.

Katarine in introitu capellae Westm.[111] In primis predictus Ricardus compu-
tat de xvj marcis remanentibus de quadam vetere obligacione et de decem
libris tresdecim solidis denario et obolo solutis Willielmo Hanewell grocero
infra Ludgate pro Thoma Aspall viz pro cera et de v libris deliberatis Johanne
uxori dicti Thome pro placito de Traule et de xl s. deliberatis predicte
Johanne super vado de salsaro cum cooptero et cum duodecim collearis
argentis. Et de duobus marcis deliberatis Rogero Bright[112] pro predicta
Johanna. Et de tribus libris deliberatis in harnes supradicto Thome Aspall vt
patet per unam indenturam. Item de sex libris deliberatis predicte Johanne
eodem tempore quo ligata fuit in vetere obligacione de xxj libris. Et falsum est
totum istud compotum vt probari potest per testes fidedignos absque hoc
quod non concordat summae contentae in obligacione.

Copia obligacionis x li. xiijs. j d. et ob. in quam Ricardus Ketford obligatus
fuit Willielmo Hanewell grocero quam quidem copiam idem Willielmus tra-
didit Ricardo Tybray.

Noverint vniuersi etc. me Ricardum Ketford civem et sellarium civitatis
London teneri etc. Willielmo Hanewell civi et grocero dicte civitatis in decem
libris xiij s. denario et obolo solutis vltimo die Julii proximo etc. Datum
primo die Aprilis anno regni Regis Henrici quinti quinto.[113]

Memorandum quod hec est datum obligacionis xxj li. in qua Thomas
Aspall obligatus fuit Ricardo Ketford.

Datum obligacionis predicte sexto die mensis Aprilis anno regni Regis
Henrici quinti quinto.[114]

Copia indenture per quam Ricardus Ketford petiit allocari de summis
infrascriptis.

This endentur witnessyth that Thomas Aspall squier of the schyr of Essex
oweth to Ric Ketford citizen and sadeller of London xxvj s. viij d. of money
borewed. Item vij li. I payed to Rafe Silkeston grocer.[115] Item xiij li. of money
I borewed, of the which parcell the somme ther of is in an obligacion. Also for
j cake of wex I bought of Hanewell at Ludgate the which Ric Ketford is
bounde for the somme therof comyth to x li. xiij s. j d. ob., my wyfe to Ric
Ketford plegge. Item for harneys and sadelles iiij marc, to be payed therof at

---

111 24 November; see above, n.103 to text for the probable year.

112 A servant of Armburgh (see below, p.129).

113 1417. This shows that Ketford borrowed part of the money he lent to Aspall from Hanwell. The
sum in the obligation confirms Armburgh's story (above, p.78).

114 1 April 1417: this gives a firm date to help identify the expedition to 'Kaue/Caue' (see above,
p.78).

115 Ralph Silkeston citizen and grocer of London, probably son of Laurence Silkeston, skinner, will
dated October 1434 (*Calendar of London Letter Books*, Letter Book I, p.265; *Cal. Close Rolls
1429–35*, p.112; *Calendar of Wills . . . in the Court of Husting, London 1258–1688*, ed. R.R. Sharpe
(2 vols., London, 1889–90), ii, pp.277, 489.

Hampton.[116] In feith and trouthe to the payement of this endenture I bynde me, myne eyres and myne executors and my goodes on this half the see and be yonde wherso euer they may be founde to alle maner thyng with inne writen I have sette my seale.

[marginal note written down the side at right angles, bottom to top] And so hit apperith in the contryved endenture, safe a brocour had vj s. viij d. of the same parcellys as hit apperyth here after

Further replication of the defence of Joan and Robert Armburgh against Ketford's demands

This is the copye of the endentur in the which was entryd by Ketfordys seiyng alle the parcelles of the olde obligacion of xxj li. rehersyd in the by gynnyng and of other certeyn parcell the which he lent to Thomas Aspall, as he sayde, by side the obligacion, the which endentur euery man may well knowe is but feynyd, bothe by the makyng, by the sealyng and by the maner of lyvere that Ketford made therof to the seid Robert Armeburgh. By the makyng euery man may knowe that it was neuer of lerned mennys makyng nor of a common scrivenerys but a thyng feyned and of the said Ketford owne makyng and wretyn of summe yonge man that wrote his parcell, and he myght not excuse hym that he hadde no connyng man redy for to make it, for London lakkyth neuer lerned men nor comyn scryvenerys but he kept not that ony man schuld have hadde knowlech of his vntrouthe and, as by the manere of sealyng, euery man may well deme that seth it, that Ketford and soche other as were of his counseill hadde take of summe other dede which was made by twen hym and the seid Aspall a fore tyme and as hit semyth thei hettyn the baksyde of the seale so hote to make it cleve vpun the endenture that hit meltid throwgh the perchemyn. For hit scheweth well that yt was neuer sette on with a seale as the manere of doyng is. And, as tochyng the lyvere of this endenture, what tyme Ketford sawe that he was compellyd by the arbitrement of the abbot of Westm, which was chose arbitrour by assent of hem both, to bryng in this endenture by forn hym and in hys presens to make lyvere therof to the said Robert, he browght it forth and in the presens of the abbot and of diuers other which were present the same tyme, where as he was bounde by arbitrement to have delyvered it to the partie al hole, he rent of the seale and brakke the ethe ndenture on v or vj peceys and drew it downe in the floore a forn hem alle, the which he dede for that entent that no man schuld have hadde knowlech of his disceyt, nor how it was a contrevyd endenture. But the seid Robert Armeburgh, havyng very knowlech of his vntrouthe, gadryd vp alle the peecys and schewed to the abbot the makyng of the endenture and the manere of sealyng and to many other that were present the same tyme, and hath joyned alle the peecys and sewyd hem to gedyr, so that the endenture

116 Southampton (see below p.84).

may well be redde and hath it yit for to schewe. And by alle these causys euery man may well knowe that it was a contryved endenture and made for that entent to disseyve the said Johane in her wedowhode, for he wist well that sche wold yeve no ful credens to hym nor make hym surete in her wedowhode of soch parcell as he said that he hadde lent to Thomas Aspall her husbond by his lyve, with oute that he hadde schewed her sum scriptur vnder his seale, and therfor he contryved this endenture and rehersid certeyn parcell ther in, the which he bare her an hande he had lent to the same Thomas Aspall at diuers tymes, that is to seyn, ij marc at on tyme, vij li. at a nother tyme and xiij. li at a nother tyme, of the which parcell the same Aspall seald hym the olde obligacion of xxj li. And by side these parcell conteyned in the obligacion of xxj li. he rehersyd other certeyn parcell in the same endenture, the which he sayd he had lent hym at diuers other tymes also, that is to seyn iiij marc in harneys at on tyme and x li. xiij s. j d. ob. for a chevessaunce of wax of Hanewell grocer with in Ludgate a nother tyme, the which parcell are bothe vntrewe, for, astochyng the iiij marc in harneys the which Ketford seyd that he delyuered the said Aspall vpon the see syde, whan the kyng went to ward Caue, ther be iij or iiij yomen which were withholdyn with hym for that vyage and abyden with hym to his lyvys ende and summe of hem were dwellyng with hym in house long tyme by forn, which wolle recorde and make it gode, in what wyse ony man wolle devyse, that the seid Aspall hadde no manere harneys of the same Ketford at the see syde nor in no nother place in that tyme nor twelfmonth by fore that he went ouer with the kyng to Caue. And they wolle recorde also that the said Aspall had non other harneys in alle that vyage but the same harneys that he hadde whan he went ouer with the kyng to Caleys, which was twelfmonth by forn,[117] of the which harneys ther is summe therof yit to schewe, the which was neuer worth iiij marc, ij marc nor xx s. And astochyng the x li. xiij s. j d. ob. for the chevessaunce of wax of Hanewell grocer, the which Ketford seyd was dwe to hym by side the obligacion a fore seid, euery man may have very knowlech by the obligacion that Ketford was bounde in to the seid grocer for the same chevessaunce and by the olde obligacion of xxj li., the which Aspall was bounde in to the seid Ketford, that Ketford seiyng was vntrewe and that yit was a parcel of the olde obligacion and not by side, for the obligacion that Ketford was [m.4] bounde in to the grocer for the seyd chevessaunce beryth date primo die Aprilis anno regni Regis Henrici quinti quinto, and the date of the obligacion of xxj li. that Aspall was bounde in to Ketford was sexto die Aprilis anno regni Regis Henrici quinti quinto,[118] the which schewyth well that the seid chevessans was

---

117 That is twelve months before the 'four marks in harness' given Aspall in 1417, which is reiterated just before this additional sum is mentioned. The only visit by Henry V to Calais at about the right time would be that in October 1416 the king was in Calais for secret meetings with the Emperor Sigismund and the duke of Burgundy (A. Tuck, *Crown and Nobility 1272–1461* (London, 1985), p.253).

118 1 and 6 April 1417: for the former, see above, p.82.

made iiij or v dayes or Aspall were bounde in the seid obligacion of xxj li. to Ketford. So it must nedys be that it was a parcelle of the same obligacion, for it may not be demyd in no wyse that, whan Ketford hadde lent Aspall this summe of x li. xiij s. j d. ob. and afterward toke suerte of hym for other smaller parcell, that he wold not letyn this grett summe in his honde with oute suerte. No more he dide, for this x li. xiij s. j d. ob. was in the same summe of xiij li. the which was the chevessauns of wax that Ketford spake of and was a parcelle of the olde obligacion of xxj li. as the endenture makyth mencyon of, the which xiij li. Ketford was bounde to Hanewell grocer in x li. xiij s. j d. ob. for the seid chevessauns and hym self hadde the other parte, safe the brocour hadde a noble. And here cam in the xl s. in vserye that Aspall badde the forseyd Johane that tyme to withdrawen, in audiens of White hosyer, and that semyth well, for it is seld seen or neuer that a craftes man or ony other maner man wolde helpe a strangeman to make a chevessauns of soche a summe and be bounde therfor with oute that he schuld take a vantage therby hym self, no more wolde Ketford, but he wolde have take to moche a vantage, for his entent was to have hadde alle the olde obligacion of xxj li. therby, of the which obligacion this cevessauns of wax was but a parcelle, for, there as Ketford after the seid Johane hadde made hym suerte by taille of the xvj marc which remayned of the seid obligacion, as it is rehersyd in the bygynnyng, schuld have made lyvere to her therof, he serchyd alle coffyns with his evydences in her presens therafter and made hym as thow he coude not fynde hit and bare her on honde that as sone as he myght fynde it he wolde breke it or sende it to her. And a boute ij yere after and more,[119] suppo-syng by cause of the grete besynesse and entanglyng that sche hadde at the comyn lawe that sche schulde have foryetyn moche of this thyng, he cam a geyne to her and browght with hym this same old obligacion and tolde her that her husbond Aspall by his lyfe owght hym the somme therof and prayed her that sche wolde make hym suerte therof in her weduohode and, for asmo-che as he was in doute yf sche hadde in mynde the xvj marc the which sche tailled with hym, whethyr it was the remenaunt of the olde obligacion, and for the obligacion were so payed oute or no, he hadde with hym this contry-ved endenture and, for asmoch as he sawe well that ther was no more dif-ferens by twen these ij sommes, that is to seyn of thys xvj marc which remayned of the olde obligacion and of the x li. xiij s. j. d. ob. for the cheves-sauns of wax but ij d. ob., he bare her on honde and enfourmed her frendes and her counseill that this money of the chevessauns, which drawyth to the somme of xvj marc safe ij d. ob., was the same somme that sche tailled with hym and that the hole obligacion was due to hym dette, and in evydens therof he schewed hem the same parcelles for the chevessauns of wax in the contreved endenture vnder Aspall her husbondys seale, the which caused hem

---

119 Some time after April 1419. This could refer to Joan's negotiations with Ketford in London in February 1420, except that the sums do not tally (see above, p.79).

to yeve the more credens to hym, not conseyvyng the sealyng nor the manere of makyng of the contryved endenture. And thus, thowgh[120] vntrewe enformacion and schewyng of this contryved endenture and mede and greet promisses   he made   summe of her counseill and of tho that schulde have ben her frendys   hys frendys, and thervpun by avyse of hem he thretnyd her to arestyn her in to the countour[121] and went oute of her inne as thowe he hadde gon for a seruant and in the   mene   tyme   by   assent   of hym they comownyd with her and tolde her how that her aduersaryes, and they myght aspye her in the countour, wolde lay pleynts vpon her for dette that Aspall late her husbond owght hem and so kepe her in preson long i nowe, and tolde her also how greet nede sche hadde of money to swe lyvere of her moder ys enherytaunce, the which was falle to her the same tyme, and counseylled her for alle these causes to borewe sum resonable summe of hym and make suerte of alle the hole, for sche hadde moche nede of hys frendschip, and they wist well they seyde that he wolde not aske it withoute that he hadde ryght therto, and that the endenture schewith well, and thus throwgh vntrouthe of sum that were a bowithe her and of her counseyll sche borewed of hym v li. and, with xx s. borewed of hym but a litill by forn, sche sealyd hym an obligacion of xxvj li. and brakke this olde obligacion of xxj li.

Proceedings before the London sheriffs: Ketford versus Armburgh (February 1423), with part of the king's writ of *corpus cum causa* ordering Armburgh's release from the sheriffs' custody as he is litigating in the Common Pleas, a superior court

Ric Ketford [in margin] Nos Willielmus Estfeld et Robertus Tatersall vicecomites ciuitatis London[122] vobis significamus quod ante aduentum istius brevis Robertus Arneburgh infrascriptus per nomen Roberti Arneburwe nuper de Berkyng[123] in comitatu Essex gentilman die mercurii x⁰ die Ffebruarii anno primo interius specificato[124] captus fuit in comitatu Midd et ad prisonam domini regis in civitate predicta ductus ibidem ad saluo custodiendum virtute cuiusdam alterius brevis dicti domini regis nobis vicecomitibus comitatus Midd directi cuius brevis transcriptum vobis mittimus huic breve consutum. Et silicet[125] idem Robertus Arneburgh per nomen Roberti Arneburwe gentilman detentus est in prisona predicta virtute cuiusdam querele versus ipsum dicto die mercurii leuate ad sectam Ricardi Ketford civis et

---

120 Sic: 'through' is presumably meant.
121 The Counters were the prisons of the sheriffs of London and Westminster (Pugh, *Imprisonment in Medieval England*, pp.109–11).
122 For these two, see *London Plea and Memoranda Rolls 1413–37*, pp.100, 145, 160, 163, 168, 179, 1437–57, p.1.
123 See n.93, above for Aspall's connection with Barking.
124 This must be the first year of Henry VI i.e. 10 February 1423, which was indeed a Wednesday.
125 *Sic:* a variant on 'scilicet'.

sellarii London de placito debiti super demandum xlvij li. iiij s. viij d. Et unde prefatus Ricardus Ketford dicto die mercurii in curia dicti domini regis coram me prefato Willielmus Estfeld vno vicecomitum predictorum in Guihald ciuitatis predicte narrauit versus predictum Robertum Arneburwe et pertulit ad tunc et ibidem in eadem curia quoddam scriptum obligatorem debitum predictum testificans super quo prefatus Robertus secundum consuetudinem ciuitatis predicte examinatus fuit et cognouit xxj li. de summa predicta debita saluo quod predictus Ricardus Ketford recuperauit et execucionem habuit secundum consuetudinem ciuitatis predicte versus predictum Robertum de iiij li. v s. vij d. virtute processus vocati forinc attachm[126] quo [*sic*] cognicione predicta non obstante concessum est per me prefatum Willielmum Estfeld vicecomitem quod partes predicte habeant diem usque proximam curam dicti domini regis tenendam coram me prefato Willielmo Estfeld vicecomite in Guihald predicto causa examinationis premissorum predicte de residuo summe predicte in dicta querela contenta. Attamen ipsum Robertum Arneburgh coram justiciis interius specificatis ad diem et locum infra contentos habemus prout interius precipitur.

> London
> dimitatur per curiam et inuen[it]
> manuc[aptionem] essendi hic xvᵃ pas[chae]

Rex vicecomitibus London salutem ostensum est nobis ex parte Roberti Arneburgh de villa Westm in comitatu Middlesex gentilman quod cum ipse et quilicet legeus nostri in veniendo versus curiam nostram de Banco ad aliquod placitum ibidem prosequendum vel defendendum ibidem morando [breaks off]

Petition to chancery of Joan Armburgh: before November 1439[127]

This reiterates the Armburghs' claim that Ellen and Christine were not the daughters and heirs of Margery Sumpter. The occasion for the petition is Ellen's suit in chancery to be given her part of the estate by the feoffees, after the death of her husband James Bellers and her remarriage, to Ralph Holt.

Mekely besechith your poore suppliaunt Johane the wyfe of Robert Armeburgh, for asmoche as sche is enfourmed that Rafe Holt[128] is wyfe, late the wyfe of Jamys Bellers, which was brought in by inquisicions vnlavfully taken for on of the dovghters and eyrys of Margery Sumpter somtyme of Colchester

---

126 *Forinsecum attachiamentum*, i.e. foreign attachment, the process whereby the property of a foreigner (in this case a non-citizen of London) within a liberty could be seized to satisfy a debt to a citizen. (E.P.)

127 For the dating of this chancery petition – probably about 1437–9 – see above, p.29.

128 For Holt, see above, p.29.

and was neuer of that blode, which Margery was on of the dowghters and eyrys of Dame Eleyn Brokhole somtyme of Essex,[129] which Rafe Holt is wyfe doth calle her selfe Eleyn, which was neuer her cristen name, as hit may be preved by sufficeaunt record, schall come in to your court by fore you to requir the clerk of the rolles,[130] Rafe Bellers[131] and other to yeve her a state in xl li. of lyvelode in which they ben enfeoffed, of the which lyvelode your seid suppliaunt was wrongfully disherit throwh strengthe of lordeschip. Wherfor lyke it to your hygh and gracious lordeschip to examyne the seid Rafe Holt is wyfe whan sche comyth a fore you how holde sche is, where sche was born and in what place sche was cristenyd and who weren her godfader and god-moders and what was her cristen name and how many brethren and susters sche hadde on her moder syde and what were her names and in what paryssh thei were born and crystenyd. And that ye foche safe to examyne her forther-more of her auncetors, that is to say how was her grauntsyre and her graunt-moder of her moderside and what were her names and where they were born and where they deyden and were beryed and how many brethren and sustren her moder hadde and what were her names and where they were born. For, and sche be of that stokke, sche is of full age to have knowlech of all this. And that ye foche safe of your gracious lordeschip to take hede of her persone and deme by your wyse discrecion what age sche is of, for sche is moche elder thanne the inquisicion makyth mension by the which her age was preved.[132] And yit sche was made elder than sche schulde have be nerhand by ij yere and more. And that[133] wolle foche safe to charge the clerk of the rolles Sir Nicoll Wymbyssch[134] and her cofeffes that they make non a state to the seid Rafe Holt is wyfe vnto the tyme that sche be examyned in your gracious presens in maner and forme as a forn is rehersyd and this for the love of God and in the way of charite.

Part of the inquisition post mortem for John Sumpter jr.: 5 October 1426
This is the inquisition that established the legitimacy of the Sumpter heiresses.

Inquisitio capta apud Colchester in comitatu Essex die Sabbati proximo post festum Michaelis Archangeli anno regni Regis Henrici sexti post Conquestum quinto[135] coram Willielmo Flete escaetore[136] etc. vsque ibi. Qui quidem

---

129 See above, p.5.
130 Nicholas Wymbysh (see immediately below and above, p.22).
131 For Ralph Bellers, see above, pp.7–8.
132 See above, p.6.
133 'Ye' omitted.
134 See above, n.112 to Intro.
135 5 October 1426.
136 William Flete of Rickmansworth, Hertfordshire and London (d.1444), escheator of Hertfordshire and Essex from January to December 1426 (*HP*, iii, pp.88–91; above, pp.7–8).

predictus Johannes Sumpter[137] est ad huc superstes tunc sic. Et quod predicta Cristina est etatis quindecim annorum. Et quod predicta Elena est etatis quatuordecim annorum etc. ut in cancellaria.[138]

Robert Armburgh to William Harpour of Mancetter and Richard Barbour [of Atherstone]: c. late 1427[139]

The letter concerns wastes done to the woods at Mancetter by Richard Power, who has taken more than was allowed in the agreement with him. Harpour and Barbour are also asked to help with the case against the Sumpter heiresses.

[m.5] To Harpour and Barbour [in margin] Dere and welbelouyd frendys I grete yow wele and as touchyng the distresse that ye tokyn of Richard Power[140] I pray that ye woll take half a dosen of youre neghburghys and as many of hys and goth and ouerseyth the wodys that he hath hewyn, the which were not in hys comenantys, as yt schewyth be a payre of endenture made be twyxt me and hym. And seyth be youre discrecions what summe hyt drawyth to, the harmys and the wast that he hath done and deliuereth not the distresse in to the tyme that he haue leyd downe a resonable summe of money and till he haue fonde sufficeant suerte to me of the remenant aftyr that conscience and reson will aske. I can no more at this tyme but I pray yow bothe to make vs all the frendys in the cuntrey that ye may in auenture of that eny sise be take a yens vs and that ye woll wochesaue to noysin in the contre that Bellers wyf and here sistre be no rythfull heyrs to that lyflode ne my wyves sistre childryn as ye haue herd your self while ye were here, and more ye schull here yf ye come a gen.

---

137 This must be Sumpter senior.

138 The original IPM is PRO C139/21/6.

139 For these two, see above, p.9. The instructions at the end of the letter suggest it was written not that long after the Sumpter girls were found heirs to their brother (October 1426: see above, p.6) but it must post-date Ellen's marriage to Bellers. The instructions sent to the escheator on 21 May and 4 November 1427 imply that she was not yet married but it appears from other evidence that she had married by 5 November 1427 (*Cal. Close Rolls 1422–9*, pp.299–300; PRO C.P.40/670 rot.414d).

140 There were Powers in the Stratford Gild, and Walter Power, possibly of the same family, served Richard earl of Warwick and his father and possibly his uncle, William Beauchamp Lord Bergavenny, but I have not found a Richard in the right period (*Stratford Register*, pp.17, 74; British Library Egerton Rolls 8769–70; *Cal. Pat. Rolls 1399–1401*, p.123; for the Beauchamps, see above, n.13).

Robert Kedington, son of Joan Armburgh, to Thomas Bendyssh of Essex: c.1427–8[141]

The letter concerns frauds allegedly practised on Kedington and on his estate by Bendyssh in his capacity of feoffee and executor to Kedington's father, culminating in his support of the rival claimants. He is accused of betraying the family's trust and depriving Kedington, his mother and his sister of both money and landed property.

To Thomas Bendysch [in margin] Dere and welbeloued godfadyr, I comaunde me to yow meruelyng gretly that ye will take suche feyned and wrong accions a gens my fader and my moder, specialy in Cheuynton[142] there as ye know wele ye haue no londe, for it is opinly knowyn in the cuntre that ye toke neuer none astat in no parcell therof and yf ye schuld euer a take eny astat therin, ye wyte well hyt must haue bene of trust and not to your owne eus, and also thei must a yeve yow astat that hade never astat therin, for hyt is well knowin that my fader ne my graunsire[143] were neuer feffyd ne sesid therin, but it is done me to undirstonde that youre sayng is that ye schuld take this accion to myn eus and profyt, the wyche contrary is soth, and that ye han oft tyme preued a gens my fader, God haue mercy of ys soule, and my mother and me and all my frendes a fore this tyme. For there as my fader of hys trust that he had to yow, a lytill a fore that he deyde, fefyd yow with other in all the londys and tenementis that he had, to that entent that ye schuld a refeffyd my moder and my bredern, yf thei had leued, in certain parcelles therof and a youen vp youre a stat of the maner of Hancheche[144] what tyme that ye had be required be my faders executours, of the wyche my moder was principall, to that entent that thei schuld haue sould hyt and done for hys soule and parformed hys last will, the wyche ye wold not do but kept your astat and aftryward sold hyt and kept stille the most part of the goold in to this day, so that my faders will mygth neuer be parformed in forderyng of hys soule. And there as my fadyr was neuer in other will but that I sculd a stonde as frely in my lond whan I schuld come ther to as he dede be hys lyue, ye han made aftyr hys decess a taile ther vpon and made the remayndre to yow and to youre eyres of all my lyuelode, the wyche was neuer hys last will, but I hope in tyme comyng,

---

141 For Bendyssh and this letter, see above, p.10. The letter is from Joan Armburgh's son and heir by her first marriage, Robert Kedington (see above, p.10). For problems concerning the identification of this wing of Joan's family and its property, see above, pp.31–3 and notes there. The letter must postdate the IPM verdict and the Bellers marriage (see above, pp.6–7) and is likely to be roughly contemporary with the previous letter. If this whole sequence of letters is in datal order, then these two should belong to c.1427–8 (see next letter).

142 Chevington, Suffolk (see above, p.10).

143 Philip and Robert Kedington (see above, p.10).

144 This property is mentioned in Robert Kedington senior's will but, unless it is an unusual variant of Hargrave, Suffolk, which is listed as a Kedington property elsewhere, in a list which has nearly all the places listed in the will but not 'Hanchach', I have not been able to identify it (PRO PCC Wills Rous f.58v; *Cal. Close Rolls 1447–54*, p.473). 'Hanchach', who is addressed below, p.176, presumably came from this place.

thorgh helpe of my frendys, I schal a mende that wele ynowgth. And forder-more aftyr the decces of my fader ye stale me fro my frendys and delyuered me vp to the erle of Oxinford,[145] vndyr whos gouernance I was so euylly kept that I schall fare the werse of my body all the dayes of my lyef. And there, saue reuerence that ye be my godfadyr, thorgh youre vntrogth the erle hyndud and vndede so my moder at that tyme that sche was neuer in power to helpe ne fordere me ne none of here childryn in to this tyme. And there my fader had deuysed be hys last will the halfyndele of the tenement of landys[146] be sold and xl li. of the golde comyng ther of be youe to the mariage of Mergrete my sistre,[147] ye kept hyt still many yeres aftyr and toke vp the profytes therof to youre owne eus and aftyr that ye toke a gret summe of gold and let wronge heirs recuuer hyt be youre assent, the wyche is gret hyndring to me as wele as here. For into the tyme that my frendys haue gadered gold to mary here with all, hyt schal not lye in here power to rofresche ne fordere me but a lytill. And now there as my frendys han bene about to wythstonde the malyce and the vntrogth of theke fals cherle John Sumpter, the wyche wold make wrong heirs to enheriten xl li. worth of lyuelode, the wiche schall falle to my moder and aftyr here decces to me, ye han made a fret with hym and with Bellers and Bernard, the wyche han weddyd hys to bastard dougthers, and promytted hem all the forderyng and help that ye mow do in hyndryng of my moders rygth. Wherfore I wot wele ye han take these accions nother to my profyt ne to myn eus but, and ye mygth preuen youre fre hold vndyr colour of this accion, ye wold han hyt to yow and to youre heirs. But that schal neuer lye in youre power for I schal so labour in this mater with the help of my frendys that ye schul mowe syng as for ony profyt that ye schul take be these accions that songe that Dauid spokyth of in the sauter, '*Innanum laboraverunt*',[148] for youre labour I wote wele schal be suche and euer hath be to me and all my frendes be fore this tyme, that I schal haue no cause to bydde non other bedys for yow, were neuer that ye be my godfadyr but '*Deus laudem*'. I can no more at this tyme but I pray God yf yow grace to gouerne yow so now a gens youre last ende that ye mow come to the blisse that he bowt yow to.

---

[145] See above, p.10. This must be Richard the eleventh earl (d.1417) (*Complete Peerage*, x, pp.234–6).

[146] This is inserted in a gap that was left for it and appears to be the second half of the name of the tenement i.e. the omitted first half would have the name identifying these 'lands'.

[147] See above, p.11.

[148] This is another quotation from the Vulgate: 'Nisi dominus aedificaverit domum in vanum labo-raverunt qui aedificant eam' (*Psalms*, 126 v.1). It, and the following Latin tag, are inserted in a larger hand, which, on closer inspection, and when compared with the similar but smaller hand of 'gouerne yow', immediately below, turns out to be Hand 2 writing in a larger format.

Joan Armburgh at Westminster to Ellen, Lady Ferrers of Chartley: February 1428[149]

The letter plays on an alleged kinship with Ellen to ask for the help of Ellen's husband, Edmund Lord Ferrers of Chartley, in establishing Joan's claim against Bernard and Bellers in Warwickshire.

To the Lady Chartley [in margin] My rigth worschipfull and graciouse lady, I recomaunde me to yow as lowly as I am or may deuyse, desiryng of yowr honurable estat and prosperite plesant tydynges to here, wiche almygthy Jeshu yow grant so good as ye for youre self best can desire. My graciouse lady lykyt yt to youre ladyschipe to knowe that John Sumpter of Colchestre, the wiche was husbonde to my sistre and had be here to dowgthers the wiche ben dede and schuld haue departyd with me my modres Dame Elyn Brokholes enheritance, sumtyme the wyf of my fader Sire Geffrey Brokhole, heire to the thredde part of the maner of Mancestre in Warwyk schire, hath kept vp too bastard children of hys owen and defiled the deth of tho to muliereris and maketh the cuntre beleve that thei ben the same childryn that he had be hys wyf, and now late had writtes out of the chauncery directe to the chetour of Essex, of Hertford schire[150] and of Warwykschire and thus vnknowen to me or ony of my conseyle hath proued hem rygth heires and of ful age and hath sewed out lyuere of the to moyte of myn seyd enheritance and to strengthe hym a yens me in hys wrong hath maried oon of this seyd bastardes to Thomas Bernard a squyer of the chauncellers,[151] a nother to the sone of Raulyn Bellers, the laste yere eschetour of Warwykschire,[152] in disherytyng of me and of myn heirs with out help of youre graciouse ladyschip and socour. Weerfor lyketh it to youre rygth worthy and graciouse ladyschipe to consideren this gret wrong done to me youre meke and pouer kynneswoman, so as I am enformed be my frendys, and to se the disheriticion that mygth falle to yow yf I and my parceners deyd with out yssue[153] and that ye wochesaf so to stire my gracious lord yowr husbond that he schew hys gracious lordschipe and help in this cas that my rygth may be saued at the reuerence of God. And yf ony seruice be that myn husbonde and I may do to my lord youre husbond and yow in ony wyse, we sculle be alwey redy to fulfille it wyth all oure hertes and

---

149 Ellen (d.1440), wife of Edmund Lord Ferrers of Chartley (d.1435) (*Complete Peerage*, v, pp.317–19; above, pp.16–17). The letter, as the contents makes clear, is from Joan rather than Robert and must be February 1428 (see the date given at the end) because it speaks of Ralph Bellers as Warwickshire escheator 'last year' (see below, n.152). The first approach to her may be the petition below, pp.193–4.

150 A single escheatorship, held by William Flete (see above, Intro. pp.7–8 and n.136 to text).

151 For the influence of the Sumpter side in chancery, see above, p.8.

152 He was escheator in 1426–7 (*PRO List of Escheators*, p.169).

153 Ellen was daughter of Thomas Roche of Castle Bromwich, Warwickshire and heir general to the Bermingham family of Birmingham, Warwickshire (*Complete Peerage*, v, pp.318–19; Carpenter, *Locality and Polity*, p.377). I have not been able to trace any kinship connection between her and Joan Armburgh. For the importance of playing on this kind of relationship, see above, p.41.

pouer. My rygth wurschipfull and gracious lady, that blyssed sone of oure lady yow haue euermore in hys kepyng. Writen at Westmynster the viij day of Ffeuerer.

Robert Armburgh to Simon Mate of Colchester: c. late 1420s[154]

The letter asks for help for Ralph Beauchamp vicar of ?Sharnford, ?Leicestershire, who has been arrested in Colchester.

To Symon Mate [in margin] My dere and welbeloued frend, I grete yow wele and for as moche as Rauf Bechamp[155] my welbeloued hath compleyned   to me that he was arestyd and prisoned a mong yow for suerte of pees vnreson-ablelyche at the instance of certein persones the wyche had neuer knowleche in hys persone a fore tyme and also somond to chapeter[156] and entangled with out any laufull cause, I pray yow with all myn hert, consideryng that the mater and causys that he laboured about ben lawfull and resonable for euery ys bonde to seche and enquere for hys rygth, that ye will seke no weyes vndyr colour of law for to entanglyn hym and holdyn in daunger otherwyse than good feyth an [*sic*] conscience will, as ye wolle that I do for yow a nother tyme. And yf ye will not do so moche for me at this tyme I schall pray my lord to wryte to yow hym self.

Robert Armburgh to Ralph Beauchamp: c. late 1420s

The letter concerns further attempts to have Beauchamp released from prison in Colchester. Armburgh wonders why he has not yet been released and asks him to make further enquiries concerning John Sumpter.

To Bechamp [in margin] Oure welebeloued cosyn we grete yow wele and pray yow send vs y wryten the cause that oure aduersaries kepe yow stille in

---

154 There is no obvious date for this letter, other than the fact that Mate was bailiff of Colchester in 1427 (see above, p.9) and that John Sumpter, who was still alive when the letter was written, is not known to have been alive after Hilary 1432 (see above, n.5). It is in a sequence of letters which are not easily datable but all seem to belong to the 1420s.

155 Vicar of 'Scharnyffeld' and 'cousin' of Robert Armburgh (immediately below, and p.134). See above, p.9 for possible identification of the benefice with Sharnford, Leicestershire. However, examination of the Sharnford entries in the Lincoln bishops' registers from the period has not produced any references to Beauchamp, although he could have been the immediate predecessor of Thomas Watton, whose resignation enabled John More to be given the benefice in February 1432. Watton's predecessor and date of appointment are not given. The last occasion before this when a new incumbent was put in was 1417 (Lincoln Dioc. Reg. Repingdon, f.194v, Reg. Gray, ff.37v, 38v). The information in the last two entries is confusing and contradictory, but the point that the history of the benefice is unknown between 1417 and 1432 still holds. However, it should be noted that Chichele's register (*Chichele Register*, i, p.321) calls Sharnford a rectory, which may put the entire identification in doubt (and see immediately below, n.156).

156 From the next letter, it appears that the chapter was of the bishop of London. That might suggest that the benefice was within the London diocese but I have not been able to identify any likely place there.

prison, sythen that ye haue founde surete of pees and haue out a *supersedias*[157] the wyche is notified by the sheryue to the bayles of Colchestre and fordermore send vs word be the same lettyr yf your aduersaries take ony accion of dette, of trespas or disseyt or ony other maner a gens yow in here owne name or in ony other mannys and yf thei done send vs word what day and in what place and by what persone the accion is take, for this moste nedys be know, wheder we bryng yow out of here courtes by a *corpus cum causa*[158] or a *supersedias* and ferdermore send vs wordes by the same lettyr yf my lord of London or hys commissarie or ony other of hys officers vndyrneth hym haue ougth a temptyd a yens yow or vexyd yow by hys indiccion in here courtys sythyn thei were inibit[159] and sythin John Sumpter was somond, and, yf thei han, send vs word in the same wyse what day and what place and by what person hyt was done and with the grace of God we schul bryng yow out of here daunger with in ryght a [*sic*] schort tyme. And also enquere how longe John Sumpter hath dwellyd in Seynt Botolfys parysche and how many yerys it is sythyn he purchasyd the place that he dwellyth in, for he purchased that place with the gold that he toke for the place that he sold in Caxton Wekinne.[160] No more at this tyme but we han so ordeyned for yow and schul that with the grace of God ye schul a byde ther but a lytill while and therfore be of a good chere and drede yow no thyng at all.

Robert Armburgh to Ralph Beauchamp: c. late 1420s
Further efforts to secure his release from gaol in Colchester. Armburgh explains why the previous ones failed and hopes that Beauchamp will soon be freed on recognisance.

To Bechamp [in margin] My velebeloued cosyn I grete yow wele and as touching the *supersedias* that ye desyren, be cause of the surete that youre

---

157 A writ ordering the stay of legal proceedings or the release of a prisoner held in gaol. (E.P.)

158 A writ directing the sheriff or other keeper of a prison to produce the body of a prisoner, together with the cause of his imprisonment, before the king in chancery on a specified day. The attraction of this procedure for the prisoner (as indicated in the following letter) lay in the good prospects of obtaining bail upon appearance in chancery (see *Class List Chancery Files*, p.83). It appears from the following letter that it was not possible to obtain a writ *corpus cum causa* out of chancery until the record of the matter had been called into chancery by writ of *certiorari* (for which, see n.161, below). (E.P.)

159 This was the process by which the archbishop's court – in this case it would be the court of the Arches of Canterbury province, because the threat was of legal action from the bishop of London – inhibited proceedings in lower courts while an appeal was made to Rome (Woodcock, *Medieval Ecclesiastical Courts*, pp.7, 65–7; Swanson, *Church and Society*, p.161). Beauchamp must have been in trouble with the church authorities, as well as with the king's law.

160 Caxton is a village in Cambridgeshire; I have not been able to identify this particular settlement, which seems to be a sub-hamlet of the parish. St Botolph's was a parish in Colchester (*Red Book of Colchester*, p.91). Presumably the enquiries as to the length of Sumpter's residence there are designed to invalidate one of the charges against Beauchamp; for example that he did not reside there at the time of some alleged offence against him by Beauchamp.

aduersaries desiren of yow for brennyng of heir houses, ther may none be had but ye had founde seurtee be fore for the same cause, and the chaunsery wold no surete aunteyn but yf the party were present that schuld be bownde, and a *corpus cum causa* mowe we none han to brynge yow out of here courtes by fore the chaunceller in to that tyme that thoo causys that thei han a gens yow in here courtys ben brougth a fore hym be a *cerciorare*[161] and therfore I haue so labourd with help of my frendes that I haue getyn out a *cerciorare*, the wiche I send yow by the brynger of this letre, and hyt is retournable on Friday that next comyth and therfore, as soone as hyt comyth to yow, let hyt be deliuerd to the bailes forthwyth and loke ho that euer schal deliuer hyt to the bailes that he haue oon or too felowys wyth hym to bere hym record. Of the wyche *cerciorari* the bailes schal make retour hem self on Friday that next comyth as it is rehersed be fore and than we schul haue a *corpus cum causa* to bryng yow afore the chanceller and thorow help of good frendys we schul haue yow vndyr baily in to the next terme than to answere by fore the chan-celler to all the causys that youre aduersaries kan put to yow. And ferther-more as touchyng the seurtee of pees[162] that ye foundyn whan ye were last at home, your aduersaries han out a *cerciorare* for to do serche yf youre borowys han changyd here names or bene sufficient in the same tonnys and schires that thei seidyn thei were of. And hyt be founde the contrary, hyt schal be take for a disseytte done to the kyng and thervpon thei schul be punyschyd by prisonment and make fyne and raunson aftyr the fourme of the statute, and all thoo that were consentyng to hem, the wyche I hope to God schal not be foundyn for ther is nother ye nor I that knowyth no other but that thei ben sufficeant, and so thei bene hold a mong here negborowrys, and so ye mow say yf ye be examynd of this mater, and that ye wull put yow on the cuntrey yf ned be.

---

161 A writ of *certiorari*, issued out of chancery to call up the record of a case from an inferior court, after a party had complained that he had not received justice or that he could not obtain an impartial trial. In view of the power of Armburgh's adversaries in chancery, it is interesting that (as the letter makes clear) the effect of the execution of the writ would be for the matters to be heard in chancery. Armburgh could, for example, have arranged for the writ of *certiorari* to have been returnable in the court of King's Bench, although it does not seem that he was particularly happy about his influence in this court either (see above, Intro., p.53). (E.P.)

162 This is a surety to keep the peace, given before the JPs, sometimes as a condition of release from custody; the 'borowys' mentioned immediately below are his pledges or those who made surety for him, and his adversaries are using a *certiorari* to discover whether there was anything improper about these sureties, in which case the surety would be invalid (Powell, *Kingship, Law, and Society*, p.59).

?Robert Armburgh to John Coll bailiff of Huntingdon: c. early 1420s[163]
The letter, which is not obviously related to the Armburghs' affairs, concerns the execution of the will of John Herries, probably of Cambridgeshire.

John Coll of Huntyngd [in margin] My dere and welbeloued frende I comaund me to yow and am rigth glad that I haue herd of your prosperite and of youre welfare, doyng yow to wyte that of all maner maters the wyche be comprehendyd in youre letre I haue comynde with Richard Osberne clerk of the yeldhalle,[164] that is for to sayne as wele of the c li., the wyche ye desyren for to haue, as of the obligacion in the wyche Thomas Denyll of Walton[165] is boundyn to yow and John Chyksond,[166] youre sone, and I haue promittid hym, with that that Herry Hert[167] wole agree hym, to parfoorme youre desire in the foorme as it is in your lettre rehersyd, that ye schul make from yow to hym a relese as wele as ye and hys counsell can lawfully deuyse.[168] And ferther more I desired for to haue comynd with Herry Hertys owne   persone and

---

163 John Coll or Colles, bailiff of Huntingdon in 1423 and apparently merchant (*Cal. Close Rolls 1422–9*, p.73; PRO C1/11/179). All this seems to be related to the will of John Herries. Colles, described in the letter as a servant of Herries, was his executor, with Henry Hert and others, and was in some kind of conflict with the other executors by June 1424, when they made mutual recognisances (*Cal. Close Rolls 1422–9*, p.145). In May 1422 Richard and Thomas Osberne and John Carpenter, all three of London, and others mainperned in chancery for Henry Hert, citizen and draper of London, not to harm Colles, and in December John Vessy (see below, p.112) mainperned for Colles against Hert, while Thomas and Richard Osberne, John Carpenter and others did the same for Hert against Colles (*Cal. Close Rolls 1419–22*, p.258, *1422–9*, p.44). The nature of Armburgh's interest in all this is opaque, and he may not even be the writer, although the Armburgh family came from Huntingdon and may therefore have had some concern in Herries' will. There could be a connection with an unfulfilled will, with which Herries had been concerned, involving a grant of land to Ely cathedral (*Cal. Close Rolls 1419–22*, pp.113–14). The letter is likely to date from the time of the various recognisances concerning Herries' will, especially as it was just then, in the early 1420s, that Carpenter would have been clearing up Whittington's will.

164 Clerk of the chamber in London, agent and commissioner in London 1410–34, will dated January 1437. He and Hert had been co-executors earlier on (*Calendar of London Letter Books*: Letter Book K, pp.58, 111, 120, 179, Letter Book I, p.87; *London Wills*, ii, pp.484–5; and above, n.163).

165 There was a Thomas Danyell in Huntingdonshire, active in 1428 (with Vessy: see below, p.112, and described here as 'spicer of St Neots') and 1434 (*Cal. Close Rolls 1429–35*, p.39; *Cal. Fine Rolls 1430–7*, p.190), but there was also a Walton in Ashdon, Essex, the principal property of the Kedingtons (Morant, *Essex*, ii, pp.540–1; see above, p.10). In this context the Huntingdonshire man is perhaps the more likely.

166 John Chicksand was attorney to deliver seisin of some Hertfordshire lands in 1413. I have found nothing about Colles' relationship to Chicksand; he must have been a stepson or a son-in-law. Chicksand and a John Andrews of King's Ripton (also Huntingdonshire) were made feoffees in Colles' Huntingdonshire property in November 1424, when the latter went overseas (*Cal. Close Rolls 1413–19*, pp.93, 94; PRO C1/11/179).

167 Said to be of Stokkyngpelham, Hertfordshire, in 1424 i.e. Stocking Pelham on the Hertfordshire and Essex border, the region of the Roos/Brokholes estate, and described as a draper in 1405 (*Cal. Close Rolls 1422–9*, p.145; *Calendar of London Letter Books*: Letter Book I, p.42; and see above, n.163).

168 This letter has no indications of punctuation and moments of considerable ambiguity. Note particularly that an alternative reading of part of the sentence would be 'the obligacion in the wyche Thomas Denyll of Walton is boundyn to yow; and John Chyksond, youre sone, and I . . .'.

prayd hym that he wold a sent for hym and therto wold he not grauntyn, for he seyd he wyst wele that the foreseyd Herry Hert hath not so moche in hande of John Herryes[169] good ne wote not where for to haue with out youre enformacion, for he that a wold not a wayle for as touchyng the c li. that ye desyren he wyst wele [m.6] wote wele [*sic*] that ye that were John Herryes seruant were more preuy to hys dettys and bettyr knowin where thei ben owyng than the forseyd Herry Hert. And ferthermore I yaue hym enformacion how that Herry Hert and ye were boundyn iche of yow to other in gret sommes, that none schul make mynistracion of John Herries goodys with out othyr[170] and how that ye were fully disposyd, with out that the foreseyd Harry wold acorde with yow in the foorme a foreseyd, to geue youre astate to swyche lordys that he schuld be wery to medyll with. And thervpon he answered on this wyse and seyd as touchyng the c li., thowe it were so that Herry Hert had so moche in hande of John Herries good, he cowde not see how that consciens and worchip mygth be saued on iche side to graunte yow your askyng in that foorme withoute that it come in be a ward, the wyche a warde may not be had with oute that ye and the foreseyd Harry were bothe present, so that hys auise were that ye schuld come hedyr for the same cause, the wyche I seide to hym I wyst not whether ye wold or no. And yf ye schuld come I tolde hym, with outyn that ther were made good seurtee and sufficeant that ye schuld safe come and goo without ony maner entangelyng by [*sic*] made be the foreseyd Herry Hert or ony other in hys name be spirituel law or temporell, I wold not yeue yow conseil for to come. And ther vpon he grauntyd for to boundyn in what somme that the or youre counseil coude lawfully desiren yt, duryng the tyme of youre trete and youre comyng and your goyng be the foreseyd Harry Hert ne none other man in hys name, ther schal no thyng he temted a gens yow be temporell lawe ne sprituell. And Carpenter, Whytyngtons executour,[171] profird for to bounde in the same foorme with hym, the wyche Carpenter was present the same tyme, for he sent for hym while we weryn in trete, and therfore take good auisement of this letre, and how that ye wol be rewled in all these maters send me a clere answere in as schort tyme as ye can. And in the mene tyme, if I may haue any speche with Herry Hert and how that he wol be rewled in this mater I schal send yow word. And there as ye sayn in your letre that ye wol make from yow to hym a relese of all maner accions as law can deuise, send me word whether ye mene that ye wol relese vp to hym all the mynistracion of John Herries goodys or no.

---

[169] See above, n.163. He was of Cambridgeshire, although there was also a London skinner who could just possibly have been the same man (*Cal. Close Rolls 1413–19*, p.284; *Calendar of London Letter Books*: Letter Book I, p.247).

[170] These are likely to be the recognisances in n.163, above.

[171] This is John Carpenter, common clerk of London, executor of Richard ('Dick') Whittington (whose will was made in September 1421). He died between September 1440 and May 1444 (*Calendar of London Letter Books*: Letter Book K, pp.19, 76, 210, 242, 294; *London Wills*, ii, pp.431n, 432, 503n).

Robert Trenchemere of West Barry, Glamorgan to Sir Thomas Erpingham: probably c. 1417–22[172]

Another letter which does not seem to concern the Armburghs' affairs. The letter deals with Trenchemere's wife's claim to West Barry, thanks Erpingham for his assistance with it and asks for further help.

To Sir Thomas Herpyngham [in margin] My worschipfull and reuerent lord I comaund me to yow as enterly as ony creature best can and may effectualy,

---

172 Both this and the next letter seem out of key with the rest of the collection, in that they deal with affairs that cannot be easily related to the Armburghs, their associates and opponents and that they both concern south Wales, specifically the lordship of Glamorgan and the diocese of Llandaff. The previous letter is also not immediately relevant to Armburgh's interests and, like these two, may not even be from him. It may be significant that these three, which seem to belong to earlier in the decade, or even slightly earlier, break into a sequence of letters which all appear to belong to the later 1420s. It is therefore possible that they were interpolated by the copyist and had more to do with his interests than with those of the Armburghs. Sir Thomas Erpingham is the famous soldier and servant of Henry IV and Henry V (*DNB*, suppl. vol., ii (London, 1901), pp.189–90). The writer of this letter, Robert Trenchemere, was husband of Joan, heiress to West Barry, originally held by the de Barry family (also of Lufton, Somerset) and then by Thomas Marshal of West Chinnock, Somerset, who died in 1387. After Marshal's own line died out, his eventual heirs were his sisters, who sold West Chinnock to John Stafford, the future bishop of Bath and Wells, in 1414, and Joan was daughter of one of these sisters. For more on the context of the letter, see below, n.178. I am entirely indebted to Mr H.J. Thomas FSA for this identification and I would like to express my deep gratitude to him for solving a puzzle which had completely defeated me and being so generous with his information and with references (*Feet of Fines for the County of Somerset Henry V to Henry VI*, ed. E. Green (Somerset Rec. Soc., 22, 1906), pp.45, 83; Thomas Gerard, *The Particular Description of the County of Somerset*, ed. E.H. Bates (Somerset Rec. Soc., 15, 1900), pp.84–5; *CIPM*, xvi, p.228). Trenchemere is described as 'of Erpingham' in 1399 (*Cal. Close Rolls 1399–1401*, p.41); if he were a tenant or household servant of Sir Thomas, that would explain the tone of the address. His family seems to have come from Bury St Edmunds (*Cal. Pat. Rolls 1429–36*, p.484) and that might explain how this letter came to be in the Armburghs' roll of copies: Joan Armburgh's first husband, Philip Kedington, came from near Bury; further evidence of the family's close connection with the area can be seen in a letter below, p.103. And so it could well be that either the Armburghs themselves, or their servant, if one of their employees was writing out their correspondence and its copies, agreed to write this letter for Trenchemere and kept a copy along with the family correspondence. The dating of the letter is problematical. Sir John St John, mentioned further down, died in 1424 but the letter alludes to his expected return from Bordeaux, where he was mayor and from which he returned for the last time in 1423 (*HP*, iv, pp.280, 283). However, the reference to Lord Despenser suggests an earlier date than this because Richard Beauchamp (son of Lord and Lady Bergavenny) ceased to be Lord Despenser in right of his wife in February 1421, when he was made earl of Worcester. Since the property concerned in the letter was a Despenser lordship, it is not impossible that the writer continued to refer to its lord in this way, but Richard died in March 1422 and it does not seem probable that his cousin, Richard Beauchamp earl of Warwick, who acquired the Despenser property by marrying Richard's widow, would have been called Lord Despenser, even in this context (*Complete Peerage*, ii, pp.427–8, xii II, p.382). It is in any case highly improbable that the date is later than April 1423, when the bishop of Llandaff, mentioned in the letter, died, since there was a vacancy until well into 1425, after the deaths of both St John and Erpingham's wife, who is also mentioned in the letter (below, nn.176, 180). Trenchemere had met Erpingham at Reading some time before he wrote the letter. There is no reason why the encounter should not have occurred in the normal course of their business, but it may be worth noting that the only occasion within the likely period for the letter when the king and his court were at Reading is May 1417 (*Cal. Pat. Rolls 1416–22*, pp.102–6, 112, 115, 129, 140, 141). St John appears to have been in England in June 1417, when he indented to serve the king in the Normandy campaign, but it is

desyring to here tydynges of your prosperite and worschip full estate wiche I pray God of hys grace he continue and entrete, humbely thankyng yow of the gret resute and consolacion that ye dede to me at Redyng in my sekenesse wyche was to me a gret comfort and an hye recreacion and for youre gracious letter that ye sent to my lord of Landaf,[173] for the wyche, God yelde hym of hys goodnesse, he doth me all the comfort and all the ese that he may goodly doon, and ferthermore I am so hyly y bounde to yow that my symple persone may neuer suffice to make a seche to yow for the gret comfort and the gret chere that ye dede to my wyf whan sche was last in youre presence and for the letter the wyche ye toke here to Nicholas Rede[174] for to delyuere here the munimentys of here heritage, with the wyche letre by cause of yow my lady of Salisbury[175] sent iiij of he [*sic*] squiers to the forsayde Nicholas and he gaf hem answere that he wold in reuerense of my lady and of yow lokyn lokym [*sic*] hem vp and send hem to here within a schort tyme. And for as moche as I haue conceuyd by summe of hys entendaunce that my Maister Sir John Seyn-iohn disposyth hym to come ouere from Burdeu with inne a while aftyr Mychelmasse,[176] I wold besche yow for the mercy of God for ye bene welle of my refute,[177] and to yow is my fynal recours and trust, passyng all lordys and erthely creatures, that ye wold wochesaf of your excellent bounte let write a letre to Sire John Seynt John preying hym that he wold hold yow couenaunt of that ye spak to hym of as touchyng Westbarry my wyf is heritage in the schire of Kerdyff[178] with inne the dioc of Landaff, that whanne he schal haue

---

not impossible that he was due to return from Bordeaux just before, as his time in Bordeaux was interspersed with several visits to England (*HP*, iv, pp.282–3).

173 John de la Zouche was bishop from 1407 to April 1423, after which followed a vacancy of more than two years (*Handbook of British Chronology*, p.293; *Chichele Register*, ii, pp.247–8, 685). As can be seen further on, his favour was sought because the land at issue was in his diocese.

174 This is probably the relative of Thomas Marshal, father of the then heir to Marshal (another Joan) mentioned in Marshal's IPM (*CIPM*, xvi, p.228).

175 This is either the widow of John, eighth earl (she died in 1424), or the wife of Thomas, ninth earl, who might have been acting on her own while her husband was overseas (*Complete Peerage*, xi, pp.391–5). The Salisbury lands included a fee in Somerset and Dorset held by John de la Mare, who may be the John Streame alias de la Mare who married Joan Trenchemere's aunt and previous coheir to West Barry, Isabel Marshal, and this may explain the reference to the help of Lady Salisbury (*Somerset Feet of Fines Hen. V–Hen. VI*, p.45; *Cal. Close Rolls 1405–09*, pp.455–6).

176 Sir John St John of Paulerspury, Northamptonshire and Fonmon, Glamorgan (d.1424), mayor of Bordeaux (see above, n.172) (*HP*, iv, pp.280–3). His interest in the affair was as lord of Penmark, Glamorgan, and hence of West Barry and also, it seems, because he had an interest in West Barry itself (see n.178, below).

177 'Refuge'.

178 West Barry in Cardiff was in Penmark in the Despenser lordship of Glamorgan. Penmark had belonged to the Umfravilles, a branch of the barons of Prudhoe, but during the fourteenth century it came by marriage from Henry, the last Umfraville, first to Simon de Furneaux and then to his daughter Elizabeth, wife of Sir John Blount, who had it in 1362. In 1370–1 Penmark was divided between Elizabeth and Sir John St John of Fonmon, who had married her aunt, the other daughter of Henry Umfraville, and eventually the whole of Penmark came to the St Johns (*Cartae et Alia Munimenta quae ad Dominium de Glamorgancie Pertinent*, ed. G.T. Clark, rev. G.L. Clark (6 vols., Cardiff, 1910), iv, p.1564, vi, pp.2381–2; I.J. Sanders, *English Baronies: a Study of their Origin and Descent 1086–1327* (Oxford, 1960), p.49 n.4; T. Nicholas, *The History and Antiquities*

seyen oure munimentes and oure euydencys, as I hope to God we schul haue rygth good, that he wold spare vs in reuerence of yow and not put vs vn to no gret cost in pursuyng of oure owen rygth. And ferthermore I beseche yow of youre benyngne grace that ye woll wochesaue in reuerence of God to lete write a nother letre to my Lord Spenser[179] that, in cas that Sire John of Seynt John wold not lete vs entre in to my wyues forseyd hertauge with out pursute of lawe, that he wold wochesaue of hys lordschip in reuerence of yow, chargyn hys officers that thei do vs all the rygth and all the fauour that thei mowe rygthfullyche doon. My weleworschipfull lord y haue no more to sey to yow at this tyme but that ye woll wochesaue of youre gracious lordschip to haue me recomaundyd to my reuerent lady your wyf.[180] And I pray God of hys infynit mercy he geue yow bothe mygth and grace to serue hym to hys plesaunce.

[written at right-angles in margin of next entry, running left to right] I pray yow enterlyche with all myn hert yf ye mow a [breaks off *sic*]

To ?William Swan: c. 1419–20[181]

Another letter concerning affairs in south Wales, this time those of the bishop of Llandaff (probably John de la Zouche), who is in financial difficulties, as a result of having to make payments to secure his see. The last phases of the papal schism are making things still more complicated for the bishop. Again, there seems no obvious reason for the presence of this letter in the Armburgh roll.

Worschipfull and my welbeloued frend I comaunde me to yow and am rygth glad of youre fortheryng and youre good presperite and welefare, the wyche I

---

of *Glamorganshire and its Families* (London, 1874), p.100; G.T. Clark, *Limbus Patrum Morganiae et Glamorganiae* (London, 1886), pp.463–4; J. Brownbill, 'St John of Bletsoe', *Genealogists' Magazine*, v (1929–31), pp.355–9: I owe this reference to Mr Thomas; J.S. Corbett, *Glamorgan: Papers and Notes on the Lordship and its Members*, ed. D.R. Paterson (Cardiff, 1925), pp.119, 220; *Feet of Fines for the County of Somerset 12 Edward III – 20 Richard II*, ed. E. Green (Somerset Rec. Soc., 17 (1902), pp.207–8; J. Collinson and E. Rack, *The History and Antiquities of the County of Somerset* (3 vols., Bath, 1791), i, p.262). Joan Trenchemere's appeal to St John as lord is therefore logical but it seems to have had a further urgency: the St Johns had acquired West Barry some time in the later fourteenth century and it had come into the possession of John St John's younger brother, Alexander. In c.1425, as a widow, Joan Trenchemere sued Alexander St John for West Barry, as heir of Marshal (PRO C1/6/322: information and reference courtesy of Mr Thomas; see also H.J. Thomas, 'Castle, Church and Village: Medieval Barry', *Barry: The Centenary Book*, ed. D. Moore (Barry Island, 1984), pp.59–61, which differs slightly from the story as told me by Mr Thomas).

179 See above, n.172.

180 A writ for her IPM was issued in January 1425 (*Cal. Fine Rolls 1422–30*, p.82). She was Erpingham's second wife, Joan, daughter of Sir Richard Walton and widow of Sir John Howard (*DNB*, suppl. vol., ii, p.190).

181 The letter probably has to be understood against the background of the ending of the schism and the early period of the papacy of Martin V, elected undisputed pope at the Council of Constance in 1417. Martin was unable to return to Rome until September 1420, although he left Constance with a view to returning in May 1418. The letter implies that it was written at a time when his

haue wele conseyued by the letres the wyche ye sent to my lord of Landaff.
And for as moche as I haue wele vndyrstonde by the entent of a strav [*sic*]

return was imminent, which would seem to place it in 1419–20, although it could possibly refer
to any place in which he stayed, including Florence, where he resided from February 1419 to September 1420. A limiting factor, however, is that the place be considered of sufficient importance
to the pope's plans for it to contain at least part of the curial administration before his arrival.
This does not necessarily rule out Florence, since Martin's decision to stay there pending the
return to Rome was a considered one. The curia had been absent from Rome since the sack of the
city and flight of John XXIII in 1413. From the time of his election, Martin was putting pressure
on the English church, notably by providing candidates to benefices, including to bishoprics,
sometimes by translation; although the change of bishops belongs more to the early 1420s,
awareness that it was pending would explain the interest in papal promotion of the bishop of
Llandaff. I am most grateful for the advice of Dr G.L. Harriss and Dr Patrick Zutshi on this letter
(M. Creighton, *A History of the Popes from the Great Schism to the Sack of Rome* (2nd ed., 6 vols.,
London, 1897), ii, pp.104, 116, 131–2, 142–3; M. Harvey, *England, Rome and the Papacy,
1417–1464* (Manchester, 1993), p.3 and chaps.7 and 8). The description of the bishop suggests
that, as in the previous letter, this is John de la Zouche, who was of aristocratic birth, a Franciscan
(former provincial minster in England) and a doctor of theology. The Vettori and Alberti were
bankers; it seems the bishop had been obliged to use money to secure his bulls when he was given
Llandaff, to which he was appointed by papal provision in 1407, because this occurred in the
middle of the schism – indeed at a particularly awkward time in the relations of England and the
papacy – and he would otherwise have been unable to secure his see (John le Neve comp. B.
Jones, *Fasti Ecclesiae Anglicanae 1300–1541, xi, The Welsh Dioceses* (London, 1965), p.22; A.B.
Emden, *A Biographical Register of the University of Cambridge to 1500* (Cambridge, 1963), p.358;
Harvey, *England, Rome and the Papacy*, p.81; Heath, *Church and Realm*, pp.239, 260–2; above,
n.173). Given the reference to the bishop of Llandaff, this may well be from the same writer as the
previous one i.e. Trenchemere, though the writer appears to be member of the bishop's household, and, while it is conceivable that Trenchemere, having his wife's inheritance within the diocese, served the bishop, as well as Erpingham, the two spheres of interest seem too far apart
geographically for this to be probable. The writer may well be a cleric of the bishop's household.
If Trenchemere wrote the letter, it cannot be addressed to Erpingham because of the much more
informal and less deferential address. It has been suggested to me by Dr Gerald Harriss that the
letter is addressed to a proctor at the curia and that the recipient could therefore be William
Swan. He was proctor in the early part of the century, was in England in 1418–19 (when he could
have been seen by the writer), began to be entrusted with particularly important business from
1419 and used both the Vettori and the Alberti. Moreover, he had a brother, Richard, who was a
London skinner and acted as his agent in England, who may well have known Thomas Halle.
Another possible recipient is another proctor at the curia, John Blodwell, an associate on occasion of Swan's, who also patronised the Alberti and could also have been in England at the appro-
priate time, and has the additional merit of being Welsh, though unfortunately from the wrong
diocese (St David's), and perhaps thus more likely to have the concern for the bishop of Llandaff's interests implied in the letter. An alternative dating is the period from 1407 to 1414 when
Gregory XII was travelling around Italy, especially if the recipient is Swan, who was closely associated with this pope. Swan was in England in 1411–12, when he could have been seen by the
writer, although he may not have returned to Gregory's curia until some time during the Council
of Constance: he was certainly active in the curia at Constance by 1416. Zouche was elected during Gregory's papacy and may therefore have looked to him for further preferment. Again, it
would be necessary for the pope to be returning to a place where his administration was already
in place. It is not inconceivable that the writer is referring to the arrival of one of the popes at
Constance itself (Emden, *Biographical Register of the University of Oxford*, i, pp.202–3, iii,
pp.1829–30; Harvey, *England, Rome and the Papacy*, pp.30, 82; Harvey, 'England and the Council
of Pisa: Some New Information', *Annuarium Historiae Conciliorum*, 2 (1970), pp.263–83; E.F.
Jacob, 'To and From the Court of Rome in the Early Fifteenth Century', *Essays in Later Medieval
History* (Manchester and New York, 1968), pp.58–78; *Cal. Close Rolls 1413–16*, p.265, *1422–9*,
pp.477–8, 481–3).

enclosyd in the same letre of the wyche I hade inspeccion that ye ben welewillyng to my lordys promocion and fortheryng and spien or haue knowyng of a voidaunce of ony see, that ye wol bene a good procuratour for hym and a good mene to oure holy fadyr the pope whan he comyth, or to the vycary generall or to hem that haue the gouernaunce in the mene tyme, wherethorugh, yf God wol wochesaue, he mygth be forderyd. For ye know wele he is an able persone bothe of byrthe, of gouernaunce and of degre of scole to be promotyd to ony dignitee of holychirche and yf it so be that ony grace of promocion wol falle, wherethorow with the grace of God he mygth be forderyd, that ye wol wochesaue to goon to the Albertynes, for I know wele by the last tyme he tristith more to hem than to the Victours, for thei southen out hys bullys the wyche Wyctours had resseyued gold for and ellys hade be lost be cause of the diuision that felle a non astyt, and wyth hem make chevysaunce of suche a summe of gold as ye knowen is nedfall to spede that cause and sendith ouer word to your brother or to Thomas Halle merser[182] on here be halue and thei schal haue boundys sufficeant to be paied at a day resonabelyche assyned, and thowe it so be that my lord send no word to yow as touchyng this mater, put neuer the lesse youre entent ne youre besynesse to speden and foderyn this cause yf that mow be, for I know wele hys concience is so strett that he wold not for an c li. yeuen ne spek ne make meene in this cas, for I haue oftyn tyme herde hem seye that it were symonye. But I dar wele take it vp on me, yf God wold vochesaue, that he mowe be promotid thorugh your good exitacion that is[183] schal be to yow the beste cause that euer ye sped daiis of your lyue, ad [sic] thow it so be that I haue had no gret queyntaunce of yow a fore this tyme, sauyng that I haue seye yow oftyn tyme at London and in other places with my lord, tak neuere the lese this letre to hert, for I hope we schul be betyr aquenyntid in tyme comyng. Also your brother and I be wele queyntid to gedyr.

Robert Armburgh to William Armburgh: c. 1428–9[184]

He asks to borrow money from William, as the costs of the suit and of his [step]daughter's wedding are proving too much for him.

To William Armeburgh [in margin] My dere and welbeloued brother I comande me to yow and for as moche as it is not vnknowyn to you that I haue be now a greet while grevously vexed at the comune lawe be myn

---

182 Citizen and mercer of London, active 1413–14 (*London Plea and Memoranda Rolls 1413–37*, p.33; *Cal. Pat. Rolls 1413–16*, p.87).

183 *Sic* recte 'it'.

184 William was brother – probably older brother – of Robert and probably father of Reynold, of Godmanchester, Huntingdonshire (see above, pp.30, 49–50 and below, n.461). The marriage referred to in the letter, below, occurred in the financial year from Michaelmas 1428–9 (see below, p.127) and so the letter is likely to date from about then.

aduersaries, the which been maintened thorough greet lordship, thorough the
whiche vexations as wel as be my doughters mariage[185] I put to greet cost and
haue borowyd moche good for the which I am lyke to be soule [*sic*] shamed
but yf it be paied withynne short tyme, the wiche may not be doon with out
help of your good brotherede, I pray yow with all myn hert as I may do for
yow in tyme comyng that ye woll wochesaf to lene me x or xij marc or summe
notable somme wherthorough I might be releuyd and my worship sauyd at
this tyme and loke what suretee ye wol haue therfore, be yt assignement in a
manere of myn or an obligacion, ye shul haue yt al redy. I can no more at this
tyme but God haue yow in his kepyng.

Robert Armburgh to an unknown abbot [?possibly of Bury St Edmunds]: perhaps c.1428–9[186]

*Armburgh asks for the abbot's support for a priest who was once in his wife's
household in securing the amalgamation of two parishes, one of them certainly in
Suffolk, the other in the presentation of the abbot.*

To a [*sic*] abbot [in margin] Worshipfull and reuerent sire I comande me to
yow, doyng yow to wete that a good frende of myne Sir William Englond
sumtyme dwellyng with my wyf now parsone of Chetbury[187] hath perunitid
his chirche with vekerage of your collacion[188] and purposith hym to come to
yow for a presentacion in all the haste that he may. I pray yow entierly of your
good faderhod that he may the rader be sped of that that he comyth for and
fare the better be cause of me, for he is sufficiently y letterd, of good conferna-
cion[189] and honest and with the grace of God an able persone to haue cure of

---

[185] Almost certainly the marriage of Margaret Kedington (see above, p.11).

[186] The abbot may well be of Bury St Edmunds (see below, n.188). There is no obvious way of dating
the letter, except insofar as it comes in the middle of a series of letters dating from c.1428–9. The
writer is most probably Robert Armburgh, since it concerns the rector of a parish where Joan's
first husband had land (see refs. in n.187, below).

[187] Chetbury or Chedburgh, Suffolk was a place where the Kedingtons had land. It was held in
1436/7 by Margaret widow of Sir John Pilkington and was probably a Mortimer overlordship,
owned from early 1425 by the young duke of York (PRO PCC Wills Rous f.58v; *Cal. Close Rolls
1447–54*, p.473; *IPM Rec. Comms., 3 Hen.VI/32, 15 Hen.VI/61*; *Complete Peerage*, xii II, pp.905–6;
VCH Lancs., v, p.90). I have not been able to identify the parson.

[188] What seems to be happening here is that Sir William has received papal dispensation to unite a
vicarage of the unknown abbot with his parsonage but now needs the agreement of the abbot to
the presentation (see Swanson, *Church and Society*, p.44). Given Chedburgh's proximity to Bury
St Edmunds, the abbot may well be of Bury and the vicarage one of the many parishes in the area
owned by the abbey and lying within the abbey's jurisdiction (*Feudal Documents of the Abbey of
Bury St Edmunds*, ed. D.C. Douglas (British Academy, London, 1932), pp.cli–clii, clvi).

[189] This word is not very legible; 'governation' i.e. governance would make more sense but is a less
likely reading. What may be meant is 'confirmation' i.e. confirmed in his appointment by a repu-
table authority.

soule and, yf ther be any seruice that I may do for yow or ony of youres, comande me and I shal be redy to do at all tymes as ferforth as that lyeth in my power. I can no more at this tyme but I pray God haue yow in his kepyng.

Robert Armburgh to William Harpour and Richard Barbour: probably c. 1427–9, written between 26 November and 19 January[190]

He warns them that they and other men of Atherstone and Mancetter have been impleaded by the duke of Norfolk for assault on his tenants at Witherley, Leicestershire. They are advised on how to proceed and especially to respond to the plea before proceedings of outlawry are begun against them.

[m.7] To Harpour and Barbour [in margin] Dere and welbeloued frendes I grete yow well doyng yow to wete that the Duc of Norfolk[191] suyth an accion of trespas a yenst yow and vj mo of your neghburghes of Adurstone[192] and Mancestre, seyyng that ye shuld haue bete tenauntes of his of Wytherle[193] and thervpon ther is awardid out a yenst yow an *alias capias*[194] the wiche is retournable at the vtas of Seint Illari[195] and the next writ is a *plurias capias* and

---

190 This is the first of a series of letters, mostly concerning pleas against Armburgh's farmers at Mancetter, which probably all date to the late 1420s or very early 1430s. It is clear that they all postdate the livery of the lands of May 1427 and some, if not all, postdate James Bellers' marriage to Ellen, which had occurred by 5 November 1427 (above, n.139 and n.36 to Intro.), while we have three firmer dates: the approaching coronation of Henry VI, in November 1429 and letters within the series dated respectively 8 July and 1 March 1430 (below, pp.112, 126, 128 and above, n.58 to Intro.). The fact that the last two are in that order shows that we cannot assume an exact chronological arrangement, even when letters belong, or seem to belong, to the same period. For the significance in local political terms of all these letters of the late 1420s and early 1430s concerning Mancetter, see above, pp.13–19. For more on the dating of this letter, see below, n.196.

191 John, twelfth earl and second duke of Norfolk (d.1432) (*Complete Peerage*, ix, pp.605–6). See above, p.11.

192 Atherstone, Warwickshire, next to Mancetter, a crown manor, held at this time by the duke of Bedford (*VCH Warks.*, iv, p.128).

193 Witherley, Leicestershire, close to Mancetter and owned by the duke of Norfolk (see above, p.11).

194 The letter offers a detailed account of mesne process (that is the process by which defendants were brought to court and judgements enforced) in cases of civil trespass (suits of trespass in which the king did not have an interest). The writ of *capias* or arrest was usually preceded in trespass cases by the less stringent process of distraint, but much depended on the status of the parties. In this case the fact that the duke of Norfolk was the plaintiff explains why process commenced with capias. The writs of *capias sicut alis* and *capias sicut pluries* were simply reissues of *capias* where the sheriff had made a return of *non sunt inventi* (not found) to the previous writ. As Armburgh here explains, once the *capias* writs had been exhausted, process moved on to the writ of *exigent*, which set in motion the procedure for outlawry. The defended was 'exacted', or summoned at five successive county courts (which in most counties were held monthly) and on the fifth occasion was outlawed if he had failed to appear. By the fifteenth century the penalties for outlawry were usually lenient but an outlaw did have to go to the trouble and cost of obtaining a pardon. See M. Hastings, *The Court of Common Pleas in Fifteenth Century England* (Ithaca, NY, 1947), pp.169–81; R.F. Hunnisett, *The Medieval Coroner* (Cambridge, 1961), pp.61–8; Powell, *Kingship, Law, and Society*, pp.74–6; below, n.203. (E.P.)

195 Law French for the Octave i.e. 20 January (I am most grateful to Professor John Baker for explaining this).

the next after that is an *exigent*. Wherfore I wold counsail yow to take all youre felawes with yow now in this vacacion tyme[196] and go to a justice yf ther be any dwellyng in youre cuntre and specialy yf ther be any of the comyn place, the which bene these: Babyngton chef justice,[197] Martyn,[198] Strang-ways,[199] Cotismore[200] and Pastone,[201] and take attourne with yow suche oon as ye knowyn that kepith Westmynster Halle all the terme tyme[202] and that wol not disseyue yow and recordith hym your attourne a yenst the next terme afore the same justice or ther be ony *exigent* awardid out a yenst yow. For yf ye abidyn till th*exigent* [sic] be awardid out ayens yow, ye shul stonde at a gret disavauntage for than ye may not chese but that ye shull abiden oon of these tweyne, eyther ye must lete the prosses ren a yens yow v shire dayes and be outlawed and thanne sue your charters,[203] the whiche wol drawen a greet cost and yet shal yt not be allowed withoute assent of the party, the whiche thei wol not assent to with oute a greet amendes made to my lord as wele as to hem, or ellys ye must come yn be a *supersedias*[204] and plete vnder bail, that is for to say ye must abiden in prisone til the ple be endid or ye must be main-prisid[205] to come ynansuere in propre persone from day to day till the ple be endyd, the whiche wol be to yow alle greet anger and also that wold drawen gret cost. And sendith me written the next terme in the begynnyng how ye haue done and sendith me also the mennys names that were betyn and what was the cause and, by your attourneys auis and myne, the *pluries capias* shal be poyntid and than shal ther none *exigent* be awardid out ayens yow and so ye shul pletyn be attourne and yt shal no disese be to yow nor to gret cost. I myght thorough fauour of the court recorde youre atourne in youre absens but it were not good to trust therto, for it is selde seyen that a pouer man hath fauours there a lord is party. Also I sende yow the copie of the writ closid in this letre. Schewith it to sum man of counsail and he wol telle yow what is best to do therto.

---

196 The letter must therefore have been written in the vacation between Michaelmas and Hilary terms i.e. between 26 November and 19 January.

197 William Babyngton CJCP (d.1455) (*DNB*, ii, p.315).

198 John Martin JCP (d.1436) (E. Foss, *A Biographical Dictionary of the Judges of England 1066–1870* (London, 1870), p.437).

199 James Strangways JCP (d.c.1442) (Foss, *Judges of England*, p.636).

200 John Cotesmore JCP (d.1439) (Foss, *Judges of England*, p.193).

201 Sir William Paston JCP (1378–1444), founder of the Paston family fortunes (*Paston Letters*, ed. Davis, i, pp.lii–liii).

202 I.e. one that is practised in the courts of common law, not a 'country solicitor'.

203 That is charters of pardon for outlawry. On the costs of obtaining these, see Hastings, *Common Pleas*, p.180. (E.P.)

204 A writ of *supersedeas* (see above, n.157) to suspend outlawry proceedings (Hastings, *Common Pleas*, p.178). (E.P.)

205 A mainpernor was the surety for the appearance of someone in court or for his future good behaviour and thus 'mainprise' the process of making such sureties (Powell, *Kingship, Law, and Society*, p.303).

Armburgh to Harpour and Barbour: probably late 1429/early 1430 or late 1430[206]

They are warned that they are in danger of arrest, as a result of their allegedly riotous response to the writ arising from a suit against them by Ralph Bellers. They are advised to seek the help of Armburgh's friends among the Warwickshire nobility and gentry, including Lord Ferrers. They are also to enter the other part of Mancetter, which Armburgh claims, and pay him the rent for it, notwithstanding the fact that the receiver of Lord Grey of Ruthin, who had the wardship of the land, refuses to allow them to do so.

To Harpour and Barbour [in margin] Dere and welebeloued frendes I grete yow wele doyng yow to wete that Rauf Bellers suyth an accion of dette a yenst yow in the chancery and hath out a writ *sub pena* and atachement[207] thervpon to areste yow by, the whiche attachement was retourned into the chancery at the quinzaine of Seint Martyn that last was.[208] And whether the retourne was made be the sherif or the vndersheryf or be Campion his depute,[209] it was to grevously made for thei haue made yow risers[210] be that retourne, for the seid retourne makith mencion that, there as Richard Hille and John Savage the kynges bailyes[211] dede here deuour to haue arestid yow, that ye shuld a rysen vp with force and armys with many other vnknowen brekers of the kynges pees and a made a saut to the kynges bailies and in that wise ye shuld a broken here arest. Wherefore, and ye be arestid here aftirward and come yn to the chancery be a *cepe corpus*,[212] ye shul be committid to prisone and make a fyn to the kyng and therfore hens foreward kepe yow out of arest for any thyng and gooth to my Lady Fereris Chartle and to my Maister Montfort[213] and to

---

[206] The same comments as to dating apply as in the previous letter, except that Bellers' involvement makes it almost certain that his son's marriage to Ellen Sumpter had occurred by now (see above, n.190). For more precise dating, see below, n.217.

[207] A writ directing the sheriff to 'attach', that is arrest one or more specified defendants to appear in chancery to answer specified charges. In this case the writ was an original writ initiating the action of debt brought by Bellers as a chancery official under the privilege of chancery (*Class List of Chancery Files*, p.89). (E.P.)

[208] 25 November.

[209] John Campion, a minor Warwickshire gentleman and lawyer (Carpenter, *Locality and Polity*, pp.294–5; above, pp.21, 26).

[210] I.e. rebels.

[211] These are the sheriff's lower executive officers ('Wiltshire Sheriff's Notebook', ed. Condon, pp.414–15). There was a John Savage of Tachbrook, Warwickshire in 1460, a John Savage senior of Kingston in Chesterton, Warwickshire in 1476 and another, of the same place, with no designation, in 1481 (Shakespeare Birthplace Trust DR 98/502, DR41/71/283–4). I have no information on Hill.

[212] The sheriff's return to the writ of attachment. (E.P.)

[213] Sir William Mountford of Coleshill, north Warwickshire (d.1452) (*HP*, iii, pp.797–800; above, pp.14–19).

my Maister Kokeyn[214] and to my Maister Malery[215] and to other good maisters of yours and prayith hem to speke to the sheryf that now is[216] and to the
sheryf that shal be the next yeere[217] and to here vndersheryfes and that thei
pray hem that thei do yow fauour and ther come ony mo attachementes out
of the chancery to hem a yenst yow, as I am siker ther shal, yat thei make no
warantes out to arest yow by. And loke that ye done thus for ony thyng in all
the hast that it may be do after this lettre is come to yow. For I haue spoke
with my Maister Montfort for the same cause and he hath grauntid me to
done his devour and desirid hym self to haue a remembrance therof, the
whiche I toke hym al redy and my wif spake with my Maister Cokeyn whan he
was last at London and he behyght here to done the same and desirid to haue
a remembrance therof also, the whiche is all redy made and I haue made
other tweyne mo, oon to my Lady Ffereres a nother to my Maister Malory so
that I haue made thre of hem, the whiche thre I sende yow with this letre, and
loke assone as this letre is come to yow that ye bere to eche of hem oon of
these remembrances and pray hem for to do for yow lyke as I haue rehersid
yow in this letre. And as the remembrance makith mencion in hym selfe, for,
and ye done thus and kepe yow out of areste from hens foreward, as yt shal no
maistry be thorough help of these worthi persones and other good maisters of
yours, be not aferd of no sute that Bellers or ony other can take a yenst
yow in the chancery for ther may no prosses be made out of that court,

---

214 Sir John Cokayn of Pooley, north Warwickshire and Ashbourne, Derbyshire (d.1438) (*HP*, ii,
pp.611–13; above, p.14).

215 John Malory esquire of Newbold Revel in Monks Kirby, east Warwickshire (d.c.1433–4) (*HP*, iii,
pp.673–4, above, p.14).

216 Probably William Peyto or Nicholas Ruggeley (*List of Sheriffs*, p.145; n.217 immediately below).

217 If the identity of the next sheriff was already known, that might suggest a date for this letter of
shortly before November. It also suggests that the letter dates to at least a year before Mountford
became sheriff in November 1431 (see above, p.19) because Armburgh would surely have known
this particular piece of good news by that month. However, in November 1429 the sheriffs were
not changed anywhere in England, probably because that was the date of Henry VI's coronation
and, to ensure that the new appointments remained valid, it was decided to wait until after the
coronation. The next general change was in February 1430 (see above, n.58 to Intro; *Cal. Fine
Rolls 1422–30*, pp.244, 297). Thus, with the context of the surrounding letters, we have a date of
either late 1429/early 1430 or of c. November 1430, more likely the latter (see below, n.251). An
additional complication is that John Harewell, the sheriff appointed in November 1428, died
right at the end of 1428 or in early 1429 (*List of Sheriffs*, p.145; W. Cooper, *Wootton Wawen: Its
History and Records* (Leeds, 1936), pp.14–15). However, there is no record in the Close Rolls of
his replacement. *The List of Sheriffs* (p.145) lists William Peyto as sheriff from Michaelmas 1428
but, curiously, places this after Harewell's later appointment. Harewell would indeed have had to
have been replaced and it could well have been by Peyto, who does indeed seem to have been
sheriff in 1429 (*HP*, iv, p.67, citing a return by Peyto of an election indenture for 1429). Whatever
happened, and whenever Peyto's appointment occurred, Harewell's death could not have been
predicted and so the anticipation of a new sheriff must surely date to a time when there was a
general expectation of changes in the sheriffs i.e. before February or November 1430. All the sheriffs of these years – Harewell, Peyto, Ruggeley (see above, n.216), Humphrey Stafford and of
course Mountford – were closely associated with the earl of Warwick, so, except insofar as
Mountford's appointment could be hoped to offer the Armburghs special favours, all of them
might be considered friendly (see above, p.17; Carpenter, *Locality and Polity*, pp.686, 687–8).

wherethorough a man shuld be outlawid or take any gret harme, with oute
that thei myght take his persone, and yf thei wol take any accion a yens yow in
any other court I shal poynt the writ and ye shul pletyn be attorne and not in
propre persone[218] and I shal saue yow harmles what euer yt cost me with the
grace of God. Ferthermore I sende yow the copie of this attachement and of
the retourne also for that that ye and youre frendes shuld see howe mali-
ciously the retourne is made, and I pray yow sendith writen to me in the
beginnyng of the next terme yf ther cam any writ *sub pena* to yow or no, for
thei myght not arest yow by thattachement with outyn that thei haddyn first
profird yow the writ *sub pena*, and yf thei dedyn thei dedyn a yenst lawe and,
yf yt be suyd a nother day, thei shul be chastisid therfore and, yf thei profird
yow the writ *sub pena*, sendith me word whether ye resseyued hit or no and
what ye deden therto word for word, and sendith me word also yf the kynges
bailyfs were aboute to arest yow by thattachement as the retourne makith
mencion or no, and what ye dede therto word for word and make sum frende
of youres to enquiryn sekerly whether the sheryf or the vndersheryf or Campion his depute made the retourne vpon thattachement or no, and sendith
writyn also for I sopose Bellers made hit by thauis of summe of his counsail
after yt was come in to the chancerie, and yf that myght be previd I shuld do
hym a veleny,[219] for I dede hym and summe of his counsail a smart velenye in
the last ende ende [*sic*] of the last terme for changyng of a ple the whiche was
ioynid to an issu betwene hym and me in the comyn place be fore all the justices.[220]

Ferthermore I pray yow entirth in to that other part that the bastardes
claymyn and occupiith yt and answerith to me of my ferme as ye be bounde
by the comenantes that were made betwene yow and me, for ye wot wele I
haue bore gret cost therfore and had neuer none auantage therof in to this
tyme, and there as Rokeston my Lord Greyes resseyuour[221] berith an hande
that my lord wold kepe yt in his owne handes in to the tyme that he haue full
knowyng whether of vs hath right therto, I am syker yt was neuer his entent
for yt ben termynd be the comyn lawe whether of vs right and not be my lord,
and also sithyn yt is so that oure aduersaries haue preued the seid bastardes
mulireres and of full age be comyn lawe, though yt be vnrightfully done and
be strenghte of lordship, and thervpon haue suyd lyuere out of the kynges
honde, my Lord Grey hath no lenger to done with all, nor he may not lettyn

---

218 One would expect this to be in Latin – *in propria persona* – but, if this is Latin, rather than English, it is grammatically incorrect.

219 Meaning to demonstrate a fact or circumstance bringing discredit. (E.P.)

220 Presumably the Common Pleas litigation over the partition of the estate in Essex (see above,
Intro., p.12).

221 Thomas Rokesdon, steward and receiver of Reginald Grey Lord Ruthin and, before that, agent,
probably servant, of William Lord Astley (Warwickshire County Rec. Off. CR136/C154, 156;
PRO E326/9103, 9045). For Grey himself, see above, pp.15, 17–18.

vs to occupie,[222] for lawe yffith vs an entre vpon oure aduersariis as for any thyng that thei haue done yet as be comyn lawe and with oute that thei had rekenerd yt of vs be a sise, the wiche with grace of[223] shal neuer ly in here pouer. But I am siker Rokeston doth but skorne yow and me bothe and playith parassent with Bellers and takith a reward of hym for to take vp the seide lyflode to Bellers and Bernard sones vse and berith yow an hande that he takith yt vp to my Lord Greyes vse, and therfore entrith and occupiith and sparith not for hym, for he hath no pouer to lette yow and, what that euer he say, lete hym done his beste, for I wol saue yow harmles. And also my Maister Montfort grantid me that he wold speke to hym that he shuld no more medlyn therof and telle hym that yt is his lyflode, for he ys enfeffid therynne and so yt [sic] writyn in the remembrance that I toke hym the whiche I redde by for hym and in alle the remembrances that ye shul delyuer to alle the other parties, and therfore remembre hem thervpon and pray hem to speke to Rokeston for the same cause and pray yow also to sende me my gold for the wode that I sold to yow by the next messenger that comyth be twene, for I haue right grete nede therto, and I pray yow ferthermore that ye stere Richard Power[224] fore that other part of the maner for the tyme that he hath occupiid, that is for to say fro the tyme that the bastardes had lyuere in to this tyme and sendith me word also how ye haue gouerned the stresse that ye toke of the same Richard for the wast and the harmes and the skathis that he dede in my wode.

---

222 This was because livery had already been granted and it could no longer be said to be in guardianship. Grey, although feudal lord of the manor, could not therefore claim any rights over it any more (see above, p.6).

223 *Sic.* 'God' omitted.

224 See above, n.140.

Robert Armburgh to William Armburgh: probably Nov. 1428 – Feb. 1430[225]

The letter is about securing the release of a servant of William, who is in prison in Huntingdon; Robert has taken pains to consult the sheriff and, with the sheriff's support, establish exactly which writs are required and how the process is to be managed.

To William Armeburgh [in margin] Here is a remembrance of the *replegiare*[226] and of the *alias* and the *plurias* the whiche Harry Thawytes,[227] the man of court that ye spak with in the Temple on Friday in the morwe, conseillid yow and me to take out of the chancery for to delyuer your man by out of preson. But at the begynnyng, there as he enformyd yow and me that the seid writtis shuld haue ben made to the baillyfs of Huntyngdon, the clerkis of the chancery wold none otherwise make hem but to the sheryfs, for thei sayn yt is the cours of here court and therfore thei wold none otherwise done and thervpon I haue spokyn with Sir Water of Poole sheryfe of Huntyngdon shire[228] and delyuerd hym alle iij writtis, whiche writtis, for as moche as he had not the seel of his office with hym, after he had broke hem and red hem he delyuerd me a yene with a letre vnder his prevy signet and special tokyn therynne made to his vndersheryf and a nother gentilman that haue his seel of office in here kepyng, chargyng hem to make a warant to the baylyfs of Huntyngdon to delyuer your seruant out of presone, the whiche letre with alle iij writtis I sende yow by John Karter your man, brenger of this remembrance. And as sone as the seid John comyth to yow, loke that ye take the sheryfs letre and alle iij writtis and bere hem to his vndersheryfe in to Cambryggshire. He shal fynde hym dwellyng in   and his name is   , and take hem hym and say that his maister grette hym wele and prayde hym to serue his lettre and,

---

225 This letter might be dated more precisely from the fact that Walter Pole is sheriff of Huntingdon-shire. He held the office Nov. 1417–18, Nov. 1423–4 and Nov. 1428–Feb. 1430 (*HP*, iv, p.103). Given the likelihood that all the letters in this sequence date from the later 1420s (see above, n.190), it is probable that this one belongs to his final period in office. The letter probably concerns the Armburgh family property in Huntingdonshire, although it could be related to the execution of John Herries' will (above, text, pp.96–7). However, the legal action discussed here may have been purely of interest to William and Robert's interest may have been solely by way of assisting his brother, in which case it would be a good example of the benefits of having a member of the family, familiar with the law, at Westminster.

226 A writ of replevin, which instructed the sheriff to release a prisoner. Writs of *sicut alias* and *cum pluries* might be issued if the sheriff failed to execute the first mandate (*Class List of Chancery Files*, p.80). (E.P.) Armburgh is anxious that his brother understands that no pledges, that is 'borowys' or 'mainpersours', are required to get his man released by this particular writ, whatever may be alleged to the contrary.

227 He is clearly a lawyer: there are references dating from 1430 to 1439 which could all be to a single man, of Terrington, Yorkshire, one of them a London transaction; if this really is one man, the last is evidence that he was active in London, as we would expect from a Westminster lawyer (*Cal. Close Rolls 1429–35*, pp.165–7, 186, *1435–41*, pp.236, 381).

228 Of Sawston, Cambridgeshire, nephew of Michael de la Pole, first earl of Suffolk (1371–1434) and sheriff of Cambridgeshire and Huntingdonshire on various occasions (*HP*, iv, pp.103–5; and see nn.211, above and 229, below, for bailiffs).

whanne he hath made yow out a warant, delyuereth hit to the bailyfs of Huntyngdon for thei must nedys serue hit,[229] and ellis the sheryf must appere in
propre persone at the quinzime of Seynt Illari in the chancery and telle the
cause why the writ was not execut, and that writ is suche, with oute that he
can the better excus hym, he wol be founde in a gret contempt and make a fyn
to the kyng and excusacion is ther none in the cas, for asmoche as your man
was arestid withoute warant. And loke that ye fynde no borowys, for this is
suche a maner writ that thei must makyn replevyn with oute any mainpersours, the copy of the whiche writ ye shul fynde writyn on the bak of this letre,
and yf thei wol of leudnesse or of evil will aske yow any mainpersours, ye
mow sayn that ye fonde the sheryf alle the mainpersours that ye ought to
fynde and ellis he wold not haue made yow out a warant.

Robert Armburgh to William Harpour and Richard Barbour: shortly before November 1429[230]

*They have been indicted of some unknown offence and Armburgh offers advice
on how to proceed. He is also concerned about family troubles – promotion for
his 'cousin' Reynold and conflict with his step-son, Robert Kedington, over Philip
Kedington's property – and about money; the continuing drain on him of these
difficulties and of his litigation may force him to break up his household.*

To Harpour and Barbour [in margin] My dere and welebeloued frendys I
grete yow wele and as touchyng the maters conteyned in your letre that ye
desirid I shuld haue done for yow at the begynnyng, I haue spoke with Montfort to wete yf the Priour[231] had ony writtis out a yenst yow vpon youre
enditement, and he seyth that he hath none out a yenst yow as yet nor none
shal haue but that ye shul haue warnyng therof, and ther as ye desiryn to
knowyn whether it were better to plete not gilty or put yow in the kynges
grace for the seyd enditement, as for the worship and specialy for the right of
the town,[232] yt were better plete not gilty and that shal the town wele fynde

---

[229] This is because Cambridgeshire and Huntingdonshire were a double shrievalty: if a writ for
Huntingdonshire was given specifically to the bailiffs for that county, there could be no excuse
that it had gone astray into Cambridgeshire. There was a similar situation with regard to the double shrievalty of Warwickshire and Leicestershire (see below, p.146).

[230] Some time before November 1429 because of the mention of Henry VI's impending coronation
(see above, n.190). The indictment could be for the alleged riotous conduct mentioned above,
p.106, but, given that the dating of that letter seems most likely to be late 1430 (see above, n.217)
and this one must be late 1429, this may be open to doubt. This is the earliest possible reference to
Robert's nephew, Reynold, and, as he did not enter Lincoln's Inn until 1443–4 and all the other
references to him date to the 1440s, either he was very young indeed and seeking a position as a
page or simply to find an education, or this is a different Reynold.

[231] Unidentified. Possible neighbouring priories or abbeys are Nuneaton, Merevale, Polesworth,
Alvecote and Arbury (see map in *VCH Warks.*, ii (London, 1908), at p.50).

[232] This reference to the worship and right of the 'town' (that is the township from which the trial
jury would be drawn) casts an unusual light on the local politics of jury trial. It reflects the desire

and ye do the contrary in tyme comyng, that is for to say and the enditement be sufficeant,[233] and yf the enditement be not sufficeant, ye mow make your fyn wele y nough and not hynder the town and moche lasse wol coste yow, none yt wold for to plete not gilty, but what your fyn shal be, that lyth in the discrecion of the justice the whiche shal not be known till yt be sesid. But, and the justices be spokyn to be forn, your fyn wol be moche the lesse be cause the kyng is partye with yow. And as touchyng your comyng heder, euer the sonner the better, for Vessi[234] and your attourneys han spokyn with me onys or tweys and haue moche merveile ye come not and therfore I consaile yow come be tymes that ye take none harme. And as touchyng Reynold my cosyn whan ye comyn hether, be yt oon of you or bothe, we shul comyn to gedyr and loke how he may best be ferderd. For as yet I am in ful purpos, withoute that the chanceller be changed, as yt is the comyn voys that he shal now at this coronacion,[235] to breke vp myn houshold. For yf he abide stille in offys yt shal not ly in my pouer to hold yt, I shall be put to so gret costes. And also Roberd my wyues sone and his wyf ben partid from vs in greet wrath and is in full purpos to hurle with vs for his fadirs enheritaunce withoute we yeve hym a gretter pension than yt lyth in oure pouer for to bere.[236] And also withoute my brother help me with sum resonable somme of money, as he behith me that he wold the last tyme that I sente to hym,[237] I am lyke for to be suyd of certeyn persones and soule [sic] shamyd and hyndrid for gold that I borwyd of hem the last yere, and therfore I pray yow with all myn herte to speke with hym and pray hym to releue me so in my greet nede that I haue at this tyme, that I may haue cause to do asmoche for hym a nother tyme. I can no more at this tyme.

of the local society to retain control over the determination of criminal indictments. By pleading not guilty to the offence in the indictment (which in this case would have been a trespass rather than a felony since the acused had the option of paying a fine), rather than putting themselves 'upon the king's grace', which means admitting the offence and asking for a pardon, the defendants opted for trial by jury drawn from the locality, if not in practice exclusively from the township in which the offence allegedly took place. (E.P.) See also above, p.43.

233 This means containing all the necessary details required at law to require the defendant to answer the charge; if not sufficient, or insufficient, the indictment could be thrown out (Powell, *Kingship, Law, and Society*, p.67).

234 This is likely to be the gentleman of Swavesey, Cambridgeshire, and possibly also of St Albans, who was an associate of Colles and was involved in the execution of John Herries' will. He was presumably one of the lawyers who was offering advice; although this could be a reference to Vessy's own business in relation to Herries, it is hard to see how Harpour and Barbour could have been involved in affairs so far away (*Cal. Close Rolls 1419–22*, p.259; *Cal. Fine Rolls 1422–30*, pp.33, 292; above, n.163).

235 See above, n.190.

236 Robert Kedington: see above, pp.10–11.

237 See the begging letters to William from this period (above, pp.102–3, below, pp.127–9).

Robert Armburgh to an unknown recipient in Hertfordshire: perhaps mid-1429[238]

Roos Hall, Hertfordshire is to be formally partitioned between the Armburghs and their rivals and Armburgh requests that the recipient familiarise himself thoroughly with the property so that he can make an informed choice when it comes to partition. He is advised not to accept a partition by lot as Armburgh is convinced that the sheriff will ensure that the Armburgh side comes off worst.

Dere and welbeloued frende we comandyn vs to yow, and for asmoche as the sheryf hath out writtes for to departe[239] the maner of Roos halle[240] betwene vs and oure aduersariis, we sende yow a letter of attorne to bene oure particion in oure name, prayng yow to take to yow a v or vj or as many as yow lust of your tenantes and of your neghburghs suche as ye soposyn that haue most knowyng of the erabil londys, of the medys and of the pasturys longyng to the seyd maner and of the rentys and the seruicys that comyn in to the seyd maner and of rentes and of seruicys that goon out of the seid maner to the abbot of Seynt Albanes[241] or to ony other and that haue knowyng also what feldys and croftys lyyng in clos longyng to the seyd maner and how many acres eche feld and croft contenyth in hym self and whiche ben of best soyl. And that ye wol wouchesaf to ouer see the maner with the purtenances as yt is beforn rehersid or the sheryf come or yf he be come whil he is aboute the particion, to that entent that whan thei haue departid the seid maner ye mow haue verry knowleche whether thei haue evyn departid hit or no, and whan the seid sheryfs and his ministres haue made the particion, yf ye see that the seid maner with the londys and tenementes medys and pasturys with the rentys and seruices that longyn ther to ben evy [sic] departyd on tweyn, and also that the rentys and seruices that goon out to the abbot and to all other lordys as before rehersid be leyd to eche part lyke muche and, yf the sheryf wol suffren yow to chese as custume and vsage and comyn cours of law ys and all wey hath be be fore this tyme,[242] we wol pray yow to chese the better part as ferforth as ye mow haue knowyng therof in oure name and that ye chesyn be youre owne syght and discrecion and by thavis of suche as ye wol take of youre counsaill and not be drawyng of lottys as many sheryfs vsyn. That is for

---

238 The recipient is not named but is likely to be a resident of Hertfordshire, since the letter concerns property in that county, perhaps a superior servant or agent, given the instructions and the address. Judging by the others around it, the letter dates from the late 1420s; the verdict which allowed the division of the Essex lands was given in October 1428 and the order for their division issued in the Common Pleas in Trinity Term 1429 (see above, p.12), so, if the Hertfordshire lands were subject to the same sort of time-table, it should belong to mid 1429: there is no surviving plea concerning their division but there was a verdict on this, probably in 1429: see above, p.65.

239 I.e. divide.

240 Roos Hall in Sarratt, Hertfordshire (see above, p.5).

241 The manor was held of the abbot (PRO C139/115/28).

242 This may refer to the right of Joan Armburgh, as the elder of the two daughters and coheiresses of Ellen (if that is what she was), to have first choice over the two halves of the manor. (E.P.)

to sayn some sheryfs vsyn whan thei haue departid a maner on tweyn, thei
wrytyn that oo part in a rolle and that other part in a nother rolle and rolle
eche part vp be hym self in wex and ley hem down be fore the parties and
makyn that oo party to take vp that oon and that other party that other, in the
whiche maner of drawyng lottes myght be greet deceyt be cause the sheryf not
frendly to vs but the full frend to oure aduersariis be cause thei be dwellyng
with the chanceller,[243] and therfore do yt not ne receyue yt not in no wyse,
whether the rollys be closid in wax or opyn, with oute that the sheryf wol suffre yow to ouer rede hem after thei be writen or thei be rollyd vp, and yet
takyth good hede of the rollyng vp and the leyyng down for changyng. For yf
yt happyd so, that by thassent of the sheryf and of oure aduersariis and of the
meters of the londe, were departid in suche wyse that that oo part were moche
better than that other and that wers part were entrid in ij rollys and the better
part but in oo rolle, alle iij lyke of letter, of parchemyn and of quantite, thei
myght after ye ye [*sic*] had ouer seyn the first ij rollys that shuld be shewyd
yow in the rollyng vp or in the leyyng down, chaunge hem and ley down thoo
too rollys that the wers part were entryd ynne and kepe stille the rolle that the
better part were entryd ynne. So that, whiche rolle that euer ye chesyn, we
must nedys haue the werse and thogh oure aduersaries take vp the mache
therof, the sheryf shuld afterward delyuer hym the rolle that the better part
were entrid ynne, and that other part shuld be cast a syde, and so for ought
that ye shul mow done thei shul haue the better and we the werse, and therfore withoutyn that ye make youre choys in this wyse as I haue rehersid here
and with that that ye se verrily that ther be no disseyt doon in the rollyng vp
and in the leying doun, drawith no lottys in no wyse nor, thowgh he wol
delyuer yt yow, resseyue yt not for yt myght be greet hyndryng to vs, but byd
hym leue yt with what tenant hym lust of the seyd maner and takith good
hede whan the londys ben departid and boundyd and whiche part ys leyd to
vs and whiche part ys leyd to hem that yt may be veryly knowyn a nother day.

Robert Armburgh to Ellen, Lady Ferrers of Chartley: probably late 1429/early 1430 or late 1430[244]

*The letter plays on the kinship to Armburgh's wife in order to ask for Lord Fer-
rers' help with the matters mentioned in the letter to Harpour and Barbour
(above, p.00) in which they were urged to seek Ferrers' assistance.*

To the Lady Charteley [in margin] Humbly besechith youre pouer suppliant
Robert Armeburgh, the whiche hath weddyd Johane youre pouer kynneswoman[245] doughter to Sir Geffrey Brokhole sumtyme heir to the thirde part

---

243 This is probably still Kempe (see above, n.40 to Intro.).
244 The great similarity of the wording (see nn.248, 250, below) suggests that this was written at the
    same time as the one to Harpour and Barbour, above, pp.106–9. Dr Powell points out that it is
    presumably the letter mentioned above, p.107.
245 See above, n.149.

of the maner of Mancestre, for as moche as Rauf Bellers dwellyng with the chanceller and marchal of his houshold[246] suyth an accion of dette a yens William Harper and Richard Barbour, fermours of the third part of the maner aforeseid and had out of the chancery a writ *sub pena* and atachement thervpon to arestyn hem, by the whiche atachement was retournyd at the quinzisme of Seynt Martyn that last was[247] and whether the retourne was made by the sheryf or the vndersheryf or be Campyon his depute, yt was made to grevously for thei haue made the seid William Harpour and Richard Barbar rysers by that retourn, for the seyd retourn makyth mencyon that there as Richard Hille and John Savage the kynges baillifs dedyn here devyr to haue arestid the seyd William and Richard, that thei shuld a resyn vp with force and armes with many other vnknowyn brekers of the kyngys pees and haue made a saut to the seyd baillyfs and in that wyse thei haue broke here arest,[248] wherfore, and thei ben arestyd here afterward and comyn to the chancery be a *cepe corpus*, thei shul be commytted to prisone and make a fyn to the kyng. And therfore I wold beschyn yow of youre right worthi and gracious ladyship that ye wold wouchesaf to sture my gracious lord youre husbond to spekyn to the sheryf and to hys vndersheryf whan thei comyn in to his presence or sende to hem and pray hem to doon hem fauour and, thow ther come any mo attachementes out of the chancerye to hem, that thei make no warantes out to arest hem by, for yt ys but a feyned accyon and an vntrewe, for the seid William Harpar and Richard Barbour nevir bought ne sold with the seid Rauf Bellers ne had for to do with hym be wey of ferme takyng, ne in none other maner wyse wherthorugh he myght of right askyn ony dette or dute of hem, but he suyth this accion a yenst hem, for that entent that he myght haue hem arestid and brought in to the chancery vnder colour of this accion, he wold entangil hem there and compellyn hem to paye hys sone, the whiche hath weddyd oon of the bastardes beforn rehersid, the moyte of the lyflode stondyng in debate betwene hym and Robert Armeburgh your suppliant aforeseid, not withstondyng that ther may none accion be mayntened in that court that is terminable at the comyn lawe and with oute that that oo partye were longyng to the same court, but he hath so gret fauour be cause he ys prevy with the chanceller that thoo that haue the gouernance of the chancery will neither spare for drede of good nor for shame of the world to done all the wrong that thei mowe done to aduersaries and serue his entent.[249] Ferthermore I wold beseche of your right worthi and gracious ladyship to sture my gracious lord your husbond to speke to Rokeston my Lord Grey Rythyns resceyuour, yf yt hap hym to come in my lordys presence or sende to hym, and pray hym that he lette not my fermours to occupym [*sic*]

---

[246] *Cal. Pat. Rolls 1441–6*, p.42; above, p.8.
[247] 25 November.
[248] See above, p.106; the wording is very similar.
[249] See above, p.8.

the moyte of the thirde part of the maner of Mancestre, the whiche ys holdyn of my lord and hys, and stont in debate betwene vs and oure aduersaries. For he wold not suffre hem to take no profit therof in to this tyme but berith hem an hande that my lord wold kepe yt in his owne handys in to the tyme that he haue full knowyng whether of vs hath most ryght therto [m.8], the whiche I am siker was neuer my lordys entent, for yt must determynd be the comyn lawe whether of vs hath right and not be my lord. Also sethyn yt is so that oure aduersaries haue prevyd the seyd bastardes the whiche thei pretendyn to be my wyfes partneres in the seyd lyflode mulirers and of full age by the comyn lawe, though yt be vnrightfully done and be strengthe of lordship, and thervpon haue suyd lyuere out of the kynges honde, my Lord Grey hath no lenger for to done withall, nor he may not lette vs to occupie, for lawe yffeth vs an entre vpon oure aduersaries as for any thyng that thei haue done therto as yet be comyn lawe and withoutyn that thei had rekeuerd yt of vs be a sise, the whiche with the grace of God shal neuer lye in here power[250] thorough help and supportacion of youre gracious ladyship and socour and therfore I beseche yow that ye lyke yow of youre worthi and gracious ladyship to haue this mater in remembrance, and whan ye haue leyser to remembre my gracious lord youre hosbond that, whan he spekith with Rokyston, that he pray hym that he medle nomore of the seyd lyflode, for I am siker he pleyeth parassent with Bellers and takith a reward of hym for to takyn vp the seyd lyflode to Bellers sonys vse, the whiche hath weddyd oon of the seyd bastardes and berith oure fermours an hande that he takith yt up to my Lord Greys vse.

Robert Armburgh to William Harpour and Richard Barbour: probably early 1430, possibly early 1431[251]

They are advised on how to avoid arrest on Bellers' chancery suit and to seek the help of Ferrers and of Armburgh's other Warwickshire supporters. They are urged again to enter the contested half of Mancetter manor and informed both that Armburgh has no intention of dividing it with his rivals and that Lord Grey of Ruthin has no further interest in it. They are to pay Robert Kedington an annuity from the manor.

To Harpour and Barbour [in margin] Dere and welbeloued frendes I grete you wel and there as ye wrot to me in your letter that I shuld make attorne in

---

250 Again, very similar wording to above, pp.108–9.

251 This seems to follow on from the previous letter, as it appears to concern further stages of the chancery suit against the farmers. If the previous one is of the same date as the very similar letter to Harpour and Barbour which was dated to late 1429/early 1430 or to c. November 1430 (pp.106–9), the reference to meetings before and *after* Christmas in this letter both confirms the suggestion regarding the time of year for these two (as long as the letter to Harpour and Barbour does not date to after Christmas 1430) and suggests that this one dates from early in 1430 or 1431; the date of July 1430 a few letters on (p.126) suggests 1430, if we can be sure that these letters are in sequence. The expression of hope for a change of chancellor in the letter, must, in any case, date it to no later than early 1432 (see below, n.253).

the chancerie to that entent that ther shulde no more prossesse be made out
ayenst you, that is for to say that ther shuld none attachement be awardid out
to arest you by, I haue attorne al redy ther ynne and haue had al this ix yeer
and more but notwithstondyng al that, we may not lettyn hem, for that court
is not lyke to the kynges benche or to the comyn place, for in thoo places a
man may poyntyn a wryt and answere be attorne, and in the chancerie he
must answere in propre persone. But ye dar not be aferd for ther may no
processe be made out of that court wherthorough ye shul be outlawed or take
ony harme, so that ye kepe you out of arest as it shal no maistry be for you
thorough help of oure good maistres and frendes that we haue in Warrwyk-
shire, on the which we hau do cost as ye wel knowe. And also I haue spoke to
my Maistres Montfort, Cokayn and Maleri bothe be fore Cristemesse and
sith, and thei grauntid me that thei wold speke to the sheryf and the
vndersheryf and to his depute, that though ther come any mo attachementes
to hem, that thei shul make no warantes out to arest you by, and loke that ye
speke to hem of the same lest thei foryete yt and to my Lady Fferrers Chartle
and to al other good maistres and frendes of ourys and yours and, yf ye wol
do this, ye shul mow sittyn in pees as for any arest or for any other thyng that
Bellers may do to you in the chancerye, and in al other courtes with the grace
of God I shal saue you harmles. And ther as ye sayen in youre letre that Bellers
bar you an hande that he and we were in suche maner of trete that his sone
shuld haue the hole of the thrydepart of the maner of Mancestre and we as
moche in a nother place therfore, safe reuerence he is fals, for we spak neuer
word of the mater til hym nor he to vs nor none other in his name. And
though he had, yt shuld not availlyd hym for we purpose not to parte no
lyflode with hem be assent, for, with the grace of God, with yn a short tyme yt
shal not lye in her power to lette vs vs [sic] to occupie al the hole, but he is fals
and vntrewe and euer hath be in al his werkyng that he hath wrought a yenst
vs from the begynnyng in to this tyme and that we han wel preued for al the
lordship and fauour that he hath, bothe in Michelmasse terme and in this last
terme. For we haue take hym with thre passyng fals turnys[252] for the whiche
he had be worthi to haue be commyttyd to prison and shuld haue be, had he
not ben fauouryd be cause of the chanceller, and yet he shal not fayle but that
he shal be chastisid therfore, were the chanceller chaunged, the whiche with
the grace of God shal be withyn a short tyme.[253] And there as ye sayn the
ferme lyth half vnocupied and that ther dar noman menure yt for fere that
Bellers wold steryn hem, ye wete wele yt may not be so, for, and ye wold suffre
hem, he myght distreyne on alle the hole for yt was neuer departid, and

---

[252] I.e. attornies.

[253] Kempe was replaced as chancellor on 26 February 1432 (for ref., see above, n.40 to Intro.). In
practice, while the change may have protected him against a recurrence of the worst abuses of
chancery, it does not seem greatly to have improved Armburgh's prospects within chancery,
probably because men like Bellers and Wymbysh, who had protected his opponents' interest,
remained on the chancery staff (see above, pp.8, 29, below, p.142).

therfore doth your profite with all, as I wot wele ye wol not lete yt lye vnocupied, and answerith me of my ferme as ye ar bounde be your endenture. For I must nedys saue you harmles for, what[254] I let yt you, ye behight me that yt shuld not lye in oure aduersaries power to make no maistries vpon the ground, and in trust of that, and for as moche as me thought ye were lykly men to helpe to maintene oure right, I was the better willyd that ye shuld haue yt. Ferthermore there as ye sayn that my Lordes Greyes conseil arestid vp half the wode for my Lord Grey, ye wot wel my lord may not haue to doon withal for many causes, the whiche writyn in the last letter that I sent you and also I dar wel say yt was neuer my lordes wil, for my Maister Montfort spak with my Lordes Greyes conseil at my request of the same mater and thei seide pleinly my lord nor his conseil had not for to done with al, ne had this other halfyere. And therfore I pray yow sendith me the money of all the hoole that is behynde be the next messanger that comyth betwene, for I haue grete nede therto, for ye wot wele I haue born gret cost for that maner and had neuer but lytil profit therof. Ferthermore I haue grauntid Robert my wyues sone an annuyte of vj li. to be takyn vp at the festes of Ester, missomer and Mighelmasse duryng certeyn of yeerys, as his denteure makith mencion, of the thirde part of the maner of Mancestre.[255] Wherfore I pray you whan your termys comyn, yf he come to you or sende, deliueryth hym redily for yt shal be a grete ese to you and sparyng of cost. For there as ye be boundyn be your endentures to make your paiementes at London, ye shul be dischargid therof as for the tyme and pay yt at home at your owne hous. I can no more at this tyme but I pray bothe that ye acquit you so to me whil I haue nede that I haue cause to thanke yow and reward hereafterward. Y writen etc.

Robert Armburgh to Constabal, probably bailiff of Radwinter: 1429/30[256]

He has heard that his rivals are taking the timber at Radwinter and are proposing to force a partition of the manor and then claim that all the woods were theirs. Constabal is urged to sell the remaining wood to prevent Armburgh's enemies getting away with all of it.

To Constabal [in margin] My dere frendes [sic] y grete you wele and for as moche as John my seruant hath warnyd me that myn aduersariis haue sold here part of al the wode that growyth on Radewynter ground, the whiche I am

---

254 Is this an error for 'when'?

255 This gives us an approximate date for the grant of the annuity referred to on p.124.

256 The final letter of the recipient's name is obscured by the entry itself. He is likely to be Armburgh's bailiff or other agent at Radwinter; I have not been able to identify him. This and the next three letters, all concerning the woods at Radwinter, give every indication of being written about the same time. There seems no reason to suppose that they do not belong to the same period i.e. some time in 1429 or 1430, probably the latter. The reference in the letter to an impending partition shows that they belong to the period when there was talk of partitions (see above, p.12) and before Bellers and Bernard were secure in their half of the properties i.e. before the mid-1430s

right sory fore and specialy for the tymbre that growyth in the gardyn the whiche was a grete couert for the place, of the which I take God to witnesse yt was neuer my purpos to haue sold stikke, and set in heverys to felle yt doonn [*sic*] and purpose hem to cary yt of the ground in all the haste that yt may be do, and purpose hem peraventure to go to a particion forthwith as the tymbire ys caried out and wol assay yf thei can getyn that that is now my part for here, thorough help of hem that shul make the particion, so that I were lyke to lese the profit of the tymbir and wode that growith on my part and, notwithstondyng that, the tymbre to be throwyn doonn with yn a while after, whiche were but a foly for me to put in aventure. Wherfore I pray yow that ye gete me chapmen therto in alle the haste that ye mow and that ye selle al that ouer growith on my part of the ground as wel in the grete wode as in the other tweyn smale wodys and in the gardyn and other places. For that that was feld in the grete wodes and in the tweyn smale wodes more than viij yeer goon, yt ought now for to make good fagot and though yt wold not be al the best fagot, loke that ye selle yt though ye selle yt therafter, for better yt is to take sumwhat therfore than nought, and as ferforth as ye mow that ye selle yt to a good company of felowys to gedir that thei mow the sunner deliuer her hande therof and lok that ye yeue no lenger dayes than oure aduersaries hau yoven that haue bought here part. And I pray you that ye slowthe yt not after this letter ys come to you til ye haue sped of youre chapmen for doute of comyng on of the partission.

Robert or Joan Armburgh to unknown recipients at Radwinter (perhaps tenants or lessees): 1429/30

The writer expresses surprise that they have allowed the depredation on the woodland to go unchecked and are warned that, if they have sold any to the Sumpter heirs, the Armburghs will take vengeance when they have secured the whole manor.

My dere frendis I grete you wele and for as muche as yt is do me to vnderstonde that ye haue bought summe of the houses and al the wode that growyth vnpon [*sic*] that oon halvyndele of the maner of Radewynter of myn aduersariis the whiche haue no ryght therynne but thorough a fals tale, the whiche thei claymyn be ij bastard doughters of John Sumpter of Colchestre the whiche thei han weddid, I haue greet merveile so as yt is no [*sic*] vnknowyn to you and is opinly knowyn in al the cuntre that the seid lyflode hath stonde and stont in debate betwene my seid aduersaries and me, thatt ye wold bargeyn with hem or makyn ony maner maistries theryn and do so gret

---

(see above, pp.27–8). There are also strong indications that John Sumpter the elder, who died some time after early 1432, was still alive when these letters were written (pp.119, 123 and see above, n.5 for the date of Sumpter's death).

strip and wast or desoule the maner as ye han do with oute that ye knowyn
that that thei haddyn a better title than thei han. For thei han profird the same
bargeyn to many tristier men than ye be, of the whiche some, whan thei had
spoke with me, left of, and other after I hade sent to hem wold no more medle
therwith. Wherfore I conseil you consideryng that, and I haue yt oonys in
pesible possession, as I hope to God with short tyme I shal, that yt shal lye in
my power to vndo you at the vtmost or fore hyndre you. And as ye wol saue
your self harmles and put your self out of jopardie of thynges that may be seid
to you therfore a nother day, that ye medle no ferther therof and, yf ye wol
sesyn be that that ye hau do I shal suffre, and yf ye wol not, be the trouthe that
I owe to God, I shal do you endityn of felonie²⁵⁷ with yn a short tyme and do
the worst that I can do to you be the comune lawe. For I had leuer ye stroyde
me x so moche wode in a nother place as the wode that stont aboute in the
gardyn, the which is a couert to all the place. With oute the which couert the
place is not able to stonde no while, ne yt is not able to be dwellyd in and therfore ye mowe fele by youre owne discrecions thei haue no title to the maner
that wol destroye that. I can no more at this tyme but I conseil you to do that
that wol be most profit to you here afterward.

Joan Armburgh to John Horell of Essex: 1429/30²⁵⁸

*A piece of sustained invective, in which images from the medieval bestiary are
strikingly deployed, against a man who is said to have been brought up in Joan's
family at Radwinter and to have betrayed her by giving his support to her rivals
for the property.*

To John Horelle [in margin] Bare [*sic*] frende in suche maner wise as thu hast
deseruyd I grete the, for as moche as yt is not vnknowen to the and oopynly
knowen in all the cuntre that thi chef makyng hath be thorough the maner of
Radewynter, first be my lady my modres day²⁵⁹ and sithern in my tyme and
notwithstondyng that thu, as a kukkowysbird devouryng the heysogge whan
she hath bred hym vp and as an vnkynd bird that foulyth his owne nest,²⁶⁰
hast labouryd fro that tyme in to this with myn aduersarie John Sumpter and

---

²⁵⁷ The indictment would be for theft of the timber. (E.P.)
²⁵⁸ The content shows that this was written by Joan. John Horell took a lease of the parsonage of
Radwinter with Joan and Robert in May 1422, when he was said to be of Great Sampford (PRO
C1/4/65). From the letter, he was clearly intimately connected to Joan's family. He is probably the
tax commissioner for Essex in 1463, although, given the time-lag between this date and the probable date of this letter, the commissioner could be another member of the family, perhaps a son
(*Cal. Fine Rolls 1461–71*, pp.102, 109). For comments on this remarkable letter, see above, p.13.
²⁵⁹ Ellen Brokholes.
²⁶⁰ 'Heysogge' is the hedge-sparrow, one of the three most common hosts for the cuckoo in England;
this is a pre-echo of *King Lear*: 'the hedge-sparrow fed the cuckoo so long that it had its head bit
off by its young' (I.iv, lines 238–9) (F. Klingender, edd. E. Antal and J. Harthan, *Animals in Art
and Thought to the End of the Middle Ages* (London, 1971), pp.536–7). Note also (from E.P.)

with hem that haue weddyd his tweyne bastard doughters, noisyng hem al
aboute the cuntre for mulirers and right heires, there as thu knowst wele the
contrarie is soth, so fer forth that thu as the develes child, fadre of falshode,
whos kynde is alwey to do evil a yenst good, hast forsworn the diuerse tymes
before chetours and justices to yeue the cuntres fals enformacion that shuld
passe betwene vs in disherityng of me[261] and of myn heires of the moyte of the
modres enheritance in al that euer in the is, the which with the grace of God
shal neuer ly in thi power nor in no javelys[262] that han weddid thoo fals bastardes. And beside this thu hast steryd myn aduersariis to do stripe and waste
with yn my ground and to throwe donn myn hegges and my wodes and specially the tymbre that growith aboute in the gardyn, the whiche grevith me
more than all the wronges that thei han do to me in to this tyme, and con-
seillest hem not to levyn so moche stondyng as peretrees nor appiltrees nor
no maner trees that berith frut and hast a reioisyng in thyn hert to se the place
at the vtmost devouryd and stroyd. In so moche that whan thu sittiste in tau-
ernys among thi felowys thu hast a comyn byword in maner as a fals proph-
ete, sayng that thu hopist to se the day to do an hare stirtyn vpon the herth
stone of of [*sic*] Radewynter halle,[263] but I trust to God, or that maner that
hath ben an habitacion and a dwellyng place for many a worthi man of myn
antiseters from the conquest in to this tyme and long tyme beforn be so deso-
lat as thu desirest, that thu shalt se be leue of myn husbond a peire galweys set
vp with yn the same ffraunchise[264] for thi nekke, for thou tho currys, the
whiche be more able to dewelle vpon a bonde tenement as here kyn askyth,

---

Geoffrey Chaucer, *Parliament of Fowls*, lines 611–13: 'Thow [cuckoo] mortherere of the heysoge
on the braunche/ That broughte the forth, thow reufullest glotoun!'

261 See above, p.13.

262 Worthless fellows.

263 E.P. was able to unearth the essential reference after M.C.C. had failed: the image of the hare on
the hearthstone as a symbol of devastation was a traditional one in medieval literature. It is used
to striking effect by John Rous in his polemic against enclosures. See J. Rous, *Historia Regum
Angliae*, ed. T. Hearne (Oxford, 1716), p.130: 'Praeparent ipsi locum antiquae prophetiae [the
prophecies of Merlin?] quod lepus pareret supra lapidem igne frequentatum, vulgari lingua dici-
tur le harthston: Water shall wax and wod shall wane/ No man shall be mane, and mane shall be
nane/ The hare shall kendyll on the harthstone/ My dere son than byld thy hows of lyme and of
stone.' See also the fifteenth-century doggerel burlesque poem: 'The hare and the harthestone
hurtuld together/ Whyle the hombul-be hod was hacked al to cloutus.' (*Reliquae Antiquae*, ed. T.
Wright and J.O. Halliwell (London, 1845), i, p.84). The same image appears in Walter Scott, *Guy
Mannering* (3 vols., Edinburgh, 1815), ch.8. M.C.C. adds: this striking image is very similar to the
famous one in *Women in Love*, when Birkin says, "... don't you find it a beautiful clean thought,
a world empty of people, just uninterrupted grass, and a hare sitting up?" (D.H. Lawrence,
Women in Love, ed. D. Farmer, L. Vasey and J. Worthen (Cambridge, 1957), p.127). Lawrence's
theme is the central motif of M. Innes, *Hare Sitting Up* (Penguin Books, 1964), p.17. In medieval
symbolism the hare, among other undesirable attributes, was said to be a harbinger of misfortune
(B. Rowland, *Animals with Human Faces* (London, 1974), pp.90–1).

264 This is a reference to the old franchisal right of infangenthef: to hang a thief caught red-handed
on one's lordship (F. Pollock and F.W. Maitland, *The History of English Law Before the Time of
Edward I* (2nd ed., 2 vols., Cambridge, 1898), i, p.577).

non vpon a lordship rial,[265] the whiche shewyth wel be the destruccion that
thei doon in the seid maner, levyn not a stykke stondyng vpon the ground, I
thanke God I am strong y nogh to by tymbre for a peyre galwys to hange the
vpon, and that thu hast wel deseruyd by the same tokne that thu robbest
tweyn women of Sampford, the whiche is wel knowyn, of the whiche oon of
hem thu settyst vpon a tre and that other thu laiest by a yenst here will in the
porters hous with yn the maner of Radewynter, for she shuld discuuere the.
Wherfore I trust to God that he wol vouchesaf to yeve me pouer to serue ye as
the egle seruyth his birdys whiche he fynt vnkynde and that wol smyte the
damme with the bylle and contrarie to his owne kynde, for whan the egle hath
kept vp his birdys til thei ben sumwhat myghty of hem self, he dressith here
hedys evene a yenst the sunne whan yt shyneth most bright and suche as hath
founde kynde to the damme and that loke werily in the sunne with oute eny
twynklyng or blenchyng of her ie as here kynde askyth, he bredyth hem vp til
thei be myghty i nogh of hem self to fle where hem lust. And such as he hath
foundyn vnkynd to the damme and that mowe not lokyn a yenst the sunne
with oute twynklyng of here ye, as here kynd wold, he drawyth hem owt of his
nest and drowith hem down a yenst the ground and brekyth here nekkys.
This egle in holy writ is lykned to Crist the whiche is fadre and modre to all
cristyn peple. Hes birdys ar lyknyd to the peple here on erthe, the which
ought to be alle his childryn, the sunne is lykned to rightwosnesse and trouthe
and, lyke as the egle seruyth his vnkynde birdys in maner and forme as yt is
before rehersid, ryght so the good lord shal serue the vnkynde childryn of this
world that wol not loke in the sunne of rightwysnesse ne goon in the wey of
his comaundementes but robbyn and revyn and doo extorcions and benym
men here goodes, here lyflodys and here lyves with fals forsweryng, he shal
shortyn here dayes and drawe hem out of here nest that thei haue be brought
vp yn, that is for to say out of this world and drowe hem in to the pytte of
helle.[266] And therfore by leve of that good lord I takyn example at the egle and
for as moche as thou lyk to the eglys birde that may not behold in the sunne
of rightwysnesse, that is for to sayn hast made thi self blynd as thorough brib-
erie and mede that thu hast takyn of myn aduersariis and woll not knowe the
trouthe, but as an vnkynd birde hast defoulyd thi nest that thu were bred vp
yn of a knave of a nought, that is for to seyn thu hast conceillyd myn aduersariis to streyn the maner of Radewynter as with ynne rehersid, the whiche
maner was cause of thi trist, and as a fals kukhowys birde hast labouryd to
devoure thi damme, that is to say my lady my modre and me, the whiche
haue be modres of thi trist and thi bryngers vp. For a none after the deces of

---

265 This contrasts bond or villein land with 'real property', that is immoveable property, but in this
   case it clearly implies also freely held land with lordship.
266 The image of the eagle and its young, sometimes with the Christian symbolism explained, was a
   commonplace in medieval bestiaries (F. McCulloch, *Medieval Latin and French Bestiaries* (2nd
   ed., Chapel Hill, 1962), pp.114–15; T.H. White, *The Bestiary: A Book of Beasts, Being a Translation
   from a Latin Bestiary of the Twelfth Century* (London, 1954), p.107).

my modre thu stalyst awey he [*sic*] mevible goodys fro Radewynter, that is to say nete and shepe and sweyn and hostilmentes of houshold that shuld haue be sold be here executours and doon for here soule, and afterward thu haddyst the gouernance of Radewynter and Thykho[267] and haddyst as moche of my good as drew to the value of xl markes and feyndist falsly a general acquitance vnder my husbondes seel and woldest neuer sesyn from that tyme in to this with thi fals recordys, in hope to haue disheryt me of my lyflode. And therfore I sure the my trouthe, yt shal not be longe, though yt shuld cost me xl li., but that I shal gete me a iuge to syttyn vndyr commyssion as ney the ffraunchise of Radewynter as I may and, yf lawe wol serue, with the grace of God thu shalt be pullyd out of that nest that thu hast gotyn yn thi trist and labouryd so sore to stroy yt and made to brekyn thi nekke on a peire of galwys. I can no more at this tyme but I pray God send the that thu hast deseruyd, that is to say a rope and a ladder.

Robert or Joan Armburgh to unknown recipients at Radwinter (perhaps tenants, lessees or the purchasers of the wood): 1429/30
This continues the theme of the despoliation of the woods at Radwinter and issues warnings to those who are profiting by it.

Dere frendys I grete you wel merveylyng gretly so as yt is[268] vnknowyn to you and opynly knowyn in all the cuntre that the moyte of the maner of Radewynter stont in debate betwene me and myn aduersariis, the whiche haue none other titil therto but thorough ij bastardes doughters of John Sumpter of Colchestre the which thei haue weddid, that ye wol takyn vpon you to entryn in to the said maner and hewe donn the wode or carye awey or makyn ony maistris therynne withoute my love and my leve, sithyn ye mow fele by your owne discrecion that, and I haue onys the seid lyflode in pesible poscescion, as I hope to God I shal haue withyn short tyme that yt shal lye in my power to vndo you at the vtmost and therfore I conseill you in savyng your self harmles to leve of be tymes, for I were loth to haue a cause to hurle with you herafterward or to do you ony disese, and also that were a gret foly to put your selfe in iupardie of that that myght be seid to you a nother day therfore, as for eny avantage that ye take therof, for at the most I wot wele ye take not past iij or iiij d. o the day and yet ye laboure right sore therfore, and yf ye wol sesyn and hold you be that that ye han doo, I shal suffren and, yf ye wol not, be my trouthe with the grace of God, I shal yeue you a cause with yn short tyme to wesshe that ye had laboured in a nother place. Task lugard,[269] that is to say

---

267 Thicko in Ashdon, Essex. Land there may have been linked to the Kedington manor in Ashdon (Morant, *Essex*, ii, p.541).
268 'Not' omitted?
269 Although this phrase might be an imperative, meaning some variant on 'take care', 'watch out',

meteles with oute hire, for be trouthe that I owe to God I shal do you ellys endityn and do the werst that I can do to you be comyn lawe.

Robert Armburgh at Westminster to William Harpour and Richard Barbour: 8 July 1430[270]

Armburgh contests in vehement terms the reasons given by his farmers for not paying him the full farm which he believes to be due from Mancetter, including sales of wood from the contested part. In passing, he mentions that his step-son Robert has died.

[m.9] To Harpour and Barbour [in margin] Dere frendys I grete you wel merueilyng gretly that ye wol deme me suche a fole to resceyue of you my ferme of myssomer terme that last was for the ferme of Michelmasse terme that next comyth, seyng that ye paide Robert my sone in lawe[271] myssomer terme in Ester weke beforn the whiche contrarie is soth. For ye wete wel ye wer neuer wont to pay me my ferme withynne a quarter my terme and other while half yeer at the leste. And also Robert sent me a letre, the whiche was writyn in Sonday next before Saint Dunstonys day, the which was but ij or iij dayes before he tooke his seknese,[272] whiche letre is selid with his owne seal and yt makith mencion that he was with you in the weke before and moche payne to gete of you Ester terme. And also I sent my man to you oporpos, the whiche was with you on myssomer euyn to that entent that ye shuld paye the seid ferme of myssomer terme to none other man but to me, and Robert day of paiement was not be his dede with ynne vj wekis after the terme. And therfore bryngith me or sendith me my Michelmasse ferme whan youre terme comyth, as ye ar bounde be your couenauntes, for trustith none otherwise to my curtasie. The gold that I haue resceyued at this tyme I resceyued yt none otherwise but for missomer terme. Fferthermore I merveille gretly that ye sende me word be my seruant that ye paide Robert in Ester weke also the money that is behynde of that oon halvyndele of the wode that I sold you, the whiche I am sekir ye wold not do ne han done, for I sent you word but a litil before that I grauntid hym his annuyte that ye shuld delyuer hym no money

---

the context implies that the word is 'task', as in 'job' or 'a set piece of work', and 'lugard' is, like the phrase which comes immediately after it i.e. 'meteless without hire' ('measureless, without reward'), a qualifier of 'task'. The *OED* does not have a medieval usage of 'lugard' but it was used in the early sixteenth century to mean sluggard or layabout. With a little adaptation of this usage, the phrase could therefore mean 'this is job for which you will receive no return' (as the next phrase in part reiterates). I must thank Professor Helen Cooper for her assistance with the phrase.

270 On the assumption that 'St John' means, as it usually does, St John the Baptist, this letter has a firm date of 8 July 1430 (see below, p.126).

271 I.e. stepson: Robert Kedington. For Robert's annuity from Mancetter and his financial relations with the Armburghs, see above, pp.10–11.

272 Robert died of this 'sickness' (see below, p.130), presumably a few days after the Sunday before St Dunstan, 14 May 1430.

though he cam to you, for as muche as he was departid fro vs in wrathe, nor to none other but yf he brouthe to you my lettre and my seel, and vnder the same forme I sent to all the fermours that I had, and in evidence therof, not withstondyng that yt was myn owne seruant that I sent to you at this missomer, I sent hym to you vndir a letre of credence and therfore I pray you, al maner of cancelys and excusacions put a side, sendith me the same money with the money of that other halfyndele of the wode that I sold you that the bastardys cleymyn be the next messanger that comyth betwene. And excuse you nought be my Lord Grey, for he may not, and I am sekyr he woldnot, byd you kepe the money stille in youre owne handys til ye knowyn hoo hath right, as ye sent me word be my seruant.[273] And also I haue spokyn with diuers of my Lord Greys conseill and so did my Maister Mounfort in my name also and thei ensuryd vs playnly that my lord medlyd not therof nerhande this ij yeer. Fferthermore I haue gret mervaille also of the word that ye sent me be my seruant, how that ye haue paide xxv s. for the maner of Mancestre to my lord of Warrewyk for a renable aide,[274] so as yt is not vnknowyn to you and to all the cuntre that it is holde of none other lord but of my Lord Grey as of the erledom of Penbroke, for though yt so be that the maner of Mancester be holdyn of a lordship or of a maner of my Lordes the Grey, whiche is holdyn of my lord at Warwyk,[275] we shul neuer the rather payen no renable aide to hym, for my Lord Grey shal acquite vs and al other that holde of hym be aunsyen seruice a yenst my lord of Warwyk, for yt may so fallyn that my Lord Grey wol withyn a short tyme askyn a renable aide of vs hym self, the whiche we most nedys pay yf it so be that he had neuer none of vs nor of oure aunseters before this tyme, and yt were a yenst reson that we shuld paye to hem bothene. And also though we shuld paye to my lord of Warrewyk, as I knowe wel we shul not, we shuld paye but for the quantite that we be possessid of, of a knyghtes fee, that is to say of an hoole knyghtes fee xx s. and of xx li. worth londe holdyn be sokage xx s. and of more more and of lesse lesse, and yet shuld he not haue yt but yf yt were to makyn of his sone a knyth or to the mariage of a doughter of his, and his sone must at the lest ben of xv yeer old and the doughter or of vij yeer old and, yf he haue yt to that oon, he shal not haue yt to that other, for he may not askyn yt but oonys al his lyue,[276] and as fer as I knowe he hath neyther sone ne doughter of that age and thus wol the statut and none other wyse. And therfore, yf yt be not paid, I concell you paye

273 See above, pp.108–9.
274 Sic: this is the word used all through; it is clearly meant to be 'reasonable', reflecting the term 're-
     asonable aid', as established in Magna Carta, caps.12 and 15 (*English Historical Documents, iii,
     1189–1327*, ed. H. Rothwell (London, 1975), pp.318–19).
275 See above, p.17.
276 These are the terms of the Statute of Westminster I (1275) cap.36, some of it given verbatim. The
     statute makes no mention of a prohibition on demanding an aid more than once but Magna
     Carta caps. 12 and 15 establish that an aid for the knighting of an eldest son and the marrying of
     an eldest daughter (two of the three possible conditions for levying it) may each be taken once
     only (*The Statutes of the Realm*, i (London, 1810, rpt. 1963), p.35; above, n.274).

yt not in none hope to be allowed of me, and yf ye haue payde aske yt ayene and doth no suche thyng with outyn conseil of hem that ye holdyn youre fermys of. Ferthermore as touchyng the xl d. the whiche ye sent me word that ye haue youen to the styward of Athirston,[277] pleynly ye shal not be allowed therof for me. For though I grauntid you at your desir to rewardyn hym as I dide other at the first tyme with xl d., to that entent that he shuld [*sic*] you and support you there in my right as touchyng that part that stont in debate betwene me and myn aduersariis, I grauntid yow nought that he shuld haue yt yeerly paid as an annuyte, neither for to help you ner support you in that part that haue alwey be in pesible possession of. For as touchyng that part I haue no nede to his help and as touchyng that part that stont in debate, ye dede neuer nought therto to myn availl as ye behight me ye wold doo in the begynnyng. For ye sent me neuer therof as yet the value of a peny neither of the ferme ne of the wode that I sold you, but ye haue take largely of that part that I stonde pesibly possessid of and rewardid youre frendes at your owne lust,[278] the which ye shuld not haue doo and I had knowyn youre condicions at the begynnyng, for I might haue had fermours y nowe, and haue gret magre[279] of some of youre partners of Mancestre, the whiche myght moche better haue maynteyned than ye mowe, for I woldnot lete hem haue yt. Wherfore, ye purpose you to haue youre comenauntes out to your termys ende, paieth me my money of my wode that ys behynde and kepith youre dayes of paiement and your condicions that ye ar boundyn yn in youre endentures. And doth so to me that I may haue cause to thanke you and rewarde you here afterward. And yf ye wol gouerne you in this wyse, I shal do so to you that ye shuld holde you wel paide. I can no more at this tyme but I pray God haue y [*sic*] in his keypng. Y writyn at Westm at the quinzime of Saint John the viij^e yeer of kyng h. the vj.

Margaret Walkerne to her step-father, Robert Armburgh: c.1430[280]

She is about to have a baby and, because of the financial demands on her husband and her friends, cannot afford 'honest' bedding which will pass muster before those who come to visit her after the birth. She asks Armburgh for a loan.

By Margaret Walkerne [in margin] My dere and welbeloued fadre I comaunde me to you, doyng you to wityn that I haue but a litill while to

---

277 Atherstone (see above, p.53). This could possibly be Clement Draper, although he was bailiff, rather than steward (see above, p.34).

278 Presumably a reference to the 'regard' to the steward of Atherstone mentioned earlier in the letter.

279 Ill-will.

280 Margaret is almost certainly Armburgh's stepdaughter, daughter of Joan by her first husband, Philip Kedington (see above, pp.9–10, 11). From the next letter we learn that she married during the year Michaelmas to Michaelmas 1428–9, so a date of 1430, possibly following on from the previous letter, would not be out of place.

goyng and am lyke withyn a short tyme with the grace of God to be delyuerd of child. And for as moche as ladyes and gentilwemen and other frendys of my modres and myn ar lyk to vysite me while I ly ynne childe bende [*sic*] and I am not purveyd of onest beddyng with oute the whiche myn hosbondys[281] oneste and myn may not he savid, and also my frendys haue be put to so grevous costes and inportable charges thorough entangelyng of here aduersariis and my husbonde ys newe comyn to his londes and is but bare and as yit hath lytill profit takyn therof and hath leyd gret cost on his husbondry that thei mow not aquityn hem to me as thei wolden, wherfor I wold beseche you of youre goode faderhode that ye wol wouchesaf in savyng of myn husbondes worship and myn to lene me ij marc or xx s. in to the next terme day that myn hosbond ferme comyth yn, and than with the grace of God ye shul be wele and trevly payd ayene. I can no more at this tyme.

Robert Armburgh at Westminster to William Armburgh: 1 March 1430[282]

Robert's own financial obligations, including litigation and the costs of Margaret Walkerne's wedding, have led him to borrow money which he cannot repay and so he asks his brother for a loan.

To William Armeb [in margin] My dere and welbeloued brother I comand me to you, and for as moche as it ys not vnknowyn to you that I haue be right grevously chargid and put to inportable costes this ix yeer and more thorough dettes paying and entangelyng of myn aduersariis and specialy fro Mychelmasse was twelmonthe in to Mychelmasse that last was thorough my doughters mariage and ij accions of particion, the whiche myn aduersariis suyd a yenst me,[283] withoutyn diuerse other grete accions the whiche thei haue suyd a yenst me from that tyme in to this, so that though I were endettyd more than I am yt were no gret mervaill, neuertheles I am right hevy that yt is so moche for I ought and Michelmasse that last was xxvj li., the whiche I borowyd of diuerse personys in London whiche be to me but strange men, of the whiche I haue paid but xij li. and yit owe xiiij li. to iij persones, of the whiche persones some haue weddys, the whiche shul be forfet withoute that the gold be payd be mydlenton, and for that other part I am boundyn be obligacion the whiche dayes were past out at Mychelmasse that last was. Wherfore the parties that I owe this gold to be right angry with me and hasty vpon me and haue warned me, with oute that I content hem betwene this and midlenton, that I shal borowe more of hem and that thei wol sue me and do the werst that thei can do to me, so that I am lyke to be shamed and soule [*sic*] hyndred

---

281 See above, p.11.
282 For dating, see end of letter.
283 I.e. 1428–9. This gives us the date for his daughter's marriage (see above, p.11). The action of partition for Essex was in 1427–9 (Essex) (PRO CP40/670 m.414d). The text refers to another partition in Hertfordshire (see above, pp.12, 113–14).

withoute that I haue youre help at this tyme. For, and myn aduersariis haue onys knowlech that I be endetted, yt wold be gret hyndryng to al myn other maters and also thei wold be moche the bolder vpon me. Wherfore I beseche you al this considerid, as I may do for you here afterward whan I am at more ese and better myn owne man than I am at this tyme, to lene me some reson-able somme of money for a twelmonth day and with the grace of God ye shul be wele and trewly payd at a day assyned, and loke what surete ye wol desire, be yt assynement in a maner of myn or an obligacion or bothe and ye shul haue al redy. I can no more at this tyme but I pray God haue you in his kepyng. Y writyn at Westm on Asshewenesday the viij yeer of kyng Herry the vj^e.

Robert Armburgh to William Armburgh: probably c. March 1430[284]

He asks him to intercede for him with their brother John for a loan and returns to him the carrier of the letter, a servant that William had lent to Robert who is sur-plus to the latter's requirements. He also requests the loan of some malt.

To William Armeburgh [in margin] Dere and welbeloued brother I comaunde me to you, doyng you to wete that I sende you a lettre for John my brother,[285] preying in the letre to lene me som resonable somme of money for certeyn causys the whiche I haue rehersid in the same letre. Wherfore I beseche you that ye wol wouchesaf to deliuer hym his lettre with your owne handys and, whan he hath vndon yt that ye wol ouerse yt with hym, and whan ye haue ouerseye yt and vnderstond my nede, that ye wol wouchesaf to stire hym to perfourme my desire at this tyme and, yf he wol not agre hym to the seurtee that I profre hym in the seid letre, that ye wol wouchesaf to profre hym to be bounde with me and sendith me word for he wol do so moche for me or no, for yf he wold don yt I wold sendyn a sekir messanger therfore. Fer-thermore I pray you whan John Sum[286] your seruant comyth to you with these letres, that ye consell hym to abide stille there and helpith hym to getyn a seruice among you, for I haue no nede to hym, for he shuld not haue bydyn so long with me as he hath doo but for be cause that he was youre seruant and that ye sent hym to me, for I myght better yeue a man v marc than yeve hym his boorde in this cuntre oo yeer. For whete and malt and other vitailles be passyng dere ouer that thei were wont to be.[287] And also he shal take gretter

---

284 There is no indication, but this must equally be to William and presumably dates to about the same time.

285 This is likely to be John Armburgh, citizen and girdler of London (d.1458). The identification is reinforced by John's appearance with two other men who feature in this document, [William] Denton and Robert Strother (*Cal. Close Rolls 1447–54*, pp.71, 239–40, 247, 498; PRO PCC Wills Stokton f.207; above, text p.67 and n.46).

286 Small space where letters appear to be rubbed out.

287 This remark helps reinforce the case for a date of 1430: the price of wheat, having been rather sta-ble during the 1420s, began to rise in 1428–9 and was particularly high in 1429–30 before

wagis with you than he shuld take with a gentilman to abyde with hym in housholde withoute that he coude doo moche better seruice than he can. And therfore I beseche you lete hym no more come to me as ferforth as ye mow, for yt is gret hyndryng to me and ne fertheryng to hym. And ferthermore I beseche you, as I spake to you whan ye were last with me betwene John my brother and you, that ye wol wouchesaf to lene me a vij or viij quarters of malt, for I wot wel I shal haue nede therto for certeyn causys that I told you, and lokith how the prys goth now, and with the grace of God I shal pay withyn twelmonth, and ye shal haue it. I pray you that I may haue good malt and that ye wol sendit be som man of youre owne cuntre etc.

Robert Armburgh to his tenants in either Warwickshire, Hertfordshire or Essex[288]

This letter requests payment of Armburgh's rents to his agents who carry the letter, because he is in financial difficulties brought on by litigation.

To my tenantes [in margin] Dere frendys I grete you wel, doyng to you wete that I haue be put to greuous costes now a while thorough diuerse sutys takyn a yenst me be myn aduersariis, wherfore I haue moch gretter nede of money than I had many a day be fore this. Wherfore I pray you yevith credence to Roger Bright[289] and John Rotour bryngers of this letre, and in fertheryng of my maters at this tyme paieth hem youre fermys, for I yeve hem ful pouer to resceyve the seid fermys with the rerages that ar behynde of old and to do that oght to be doo in this mater in to the tyme that I may do you ese hereafterward as I haue do herbore [*sic*], *vel sic*.

Robert Armburgh to [William Harpour and Richard Barbour]: c. mid 1430[290]

A further demand for their rent.

Dere frendys *vsque ibi* in fertheryng of my maters at this tyme *tunc sic* payeth hym the money that is betwene you and me and ferthermor, that I sent to you be my letre that ye paie Robert Kedyngton my wyues sone the annuyte

beginning to fall in 1430–1. Although fewer data make the pattern of malt harder to follow, it is similar, as is that for unmalted barley (J.E.T. Rogers, *A History of Agriculture and Prices in England* (7 vols. in 8, Oxford, 1866–1902), iii, *1401–1582*, pp.22–31).

288 Which tenants is not specified. The date is likely to be the same as that of the following letter.

289 Employed in the delivery of moneys from Richard Ketford (see above, p.82).

290 From the mention of Robert Kedington's death (see above, p.124) and of midsummer term, this must date from the second half of 1430, probably not much beyond midsummer, or Robert's death would be more generally known. From the reference to Kedington's annuity, the letter must be addressed to Harpour and Barbour, the farmers of Mancetter, from where the annuity was taken (see above, pp.124–5).

specified in his endentour, loke that ye paye yt no longer, for I haue werry word and ful knowleche that he ys ded and beried, but I pray you sendith me myssomer terme bothe partes[291] with the money afore seid be the same brynger of this lettre. I can no more at this tyme but I pray you spedith so the cause of my seruantes comyng at this tyme that I may haue cause to reward yow and thank you herafterward, for I haue bore more cost for that maner than I haue done for ony other maner touchyng the enheritance and lost avantage takyn therof.

Robert Armburgh to Thomas Mylde of Clare, Suffolk and Thomas Bernard: probably late summer 1430, possibly late summer 1432[292]

He agrees, very rudely, to come with Joan to meet Bernard and his wife at Munden, Hertfordshire, with the aim of establishing the true identity of Bernard's wife.

To Mylde of Clare and Bernard [in margin] Dere frendys comaunde [*sic*] me to you and for asmoche as ye and Bernard profird my seruantes to bryngyn his wyf to Munden in Hertfordshire and desirid that my wyf and I shuld come downe to the same place to se here, I wol not refusyn your profir but we wol come alredy, but not for that entent to knowyn whether she be my wyues sisters doughter or no, for I do you wel to wete we haue verry knowleche that she was neuer none of her childryn, and that with the grace of God shal be wel felt with yn a short tyme but we wol do yt to that entent that the cuntre after that she hath be seyn therynne may be the more out of doute, that she cam neuer of that blode and also to see yf she be lyke my wyf or no, as ye and myn aduersaris han noisid yt al a boute in the shire, and in many other places, the whiche contrarie after thei han ben onys sey to gedir I doubte not therof wol be founde soth, for gentilmen and other that haue seyn here commendyn here for a foule tame beste vngoodly of condicions and a naturel fool, and wel lyke in all manere semblaunce countenance and chere to the birthe that she is come of, that is to sayn to cherlys and kemsterys.[293] Neuerthelesse, yf ye wol

---

291   This may imply that Armburgh was putting pressure on them to pay the farm of the disputed part as well, but it may merely refer to instalments.

292   For Mylde and Bernard, husband of Christine, the older Sumpter girl, see above, pp.5, 7, 13 and n.6 to text. This letter probably predates the assize of July 1432 (see above, p.19 and below, p.132) because the absence of Bernard's wife as plaintiff from the assize must mean that she was dead by then. From the proposal for a meeting three weeks before Michaelmas, it probably dates from late summer and it could follow on from the previous letters and belong to 1430. If, on the other hand, she did not die until October 1432, as another source states (see above, nn.101 and 106 to Intro.), then the letter could belong to late summer 1432 but in that case we might expect some mention of Armburgh's intensive legal activity after the assize (see below, pp.132, 141).

293   A 'kempster' is a female comber of wool: Essex was a centre of the cloth industry in the later middle ages, and so this word must denote the occupation of low-class women, as the Sumpter girls are alleged to be (see L. Poos, *A Rural Society after the Black Death: Essex 1350–1525* (Cambridge, 1991), chap.3).

not bryng here to London, where as we shul fynde y nowe to sen here that had verry knowleche of al my wyues sister childryn, kepith your promysse and bryngith here down to Munden a thre wekys before Michelmasse next comyng at the leste and sendith me word by Roger my seruant a fourtenyght before at the leste what day ye wol be there and whiche of vs come sunnest abide other a day and with the grace of God ye shul wel see that I shal kepe comenauntes. I can no more at this tyme but God haue you in his kepyng.

Robert Armburgh at Westminster to an unknown recipient: probably 24 March 1431 or 22 March 1432[294]

Although not entirely legible, the letter clearly deals with demands on a tenant or lessee of some part of the disputed land, who has found himself at the legal mercy of the other side for payment of the rent from the land. Armburgh asks for the help of the recipient.

[Margination illegible] Oure dere and wel by loued frend we comande vs to you. And for asmoche as a ffermour of youres was broht in to the ch[auncery] . . . attachement in Illary terme that last was by our aduersaries, the which fermour thei wold a to impelled to paien hem the . . . of a certeyn parcell of the lyflode that stont in debate be twixt hem and vs. But for asmoche as thei myght nat come to . . . entent here counseill and thei desirenden to haue put hit in trete and so it was don, be the which trete yt was ordey[ned] . . . al the monaie that the fermour had in hande of theseid liflode shuld be put in the mene hande into the tyme that the trouthe . . . better knowen and aday assigned which ys in Mighelmasse terme that next comyth so that this money the which . . . to xx li. and more wer like to be lost with oute your help, the whiche vs wer riht lothe ffor we had . . . wer parted betwixt you and oder good frendes of oure and so that schall be youre good help, wherfor we besech you that ye wol fouche saff to laboure effectually aboute the matere that ye and we weren acorded of in the . . . of the last parlement and that ye wol yeve credence to the bringer of this letre. We kon namor at this tyme but God haue you in his keping. I writen atte Westm ye Saterday next aforn our lady day[295] . . .

---

294 Although the letters seem to continue in chronological sequence, we are very quickly at a date after the assize of July 1432, so it is not impossible that this and the next letters date from the second half of 1431 into 1432, rather than from the same dates in 1430–1. Although the same could apply to the previous four letters (see n.292, above for a possible later date for the previous letter), which give no indication of year, this is the letter where Hand 3 begins, so it is quite probable that there had been a lapse of more than a year in which no copies were added to the roll. If the letter is 1431, it would be 24 March, if 1432, 22 March.
295 Ladyday was 25 March: for a suggested dating, see immediately above, n.294.

Robert Armburgh at Westminster to William Harpour and Richard Barbour: 15 September 1432[296]

Further demands for their rent, including from the part of the manor in dispute, which Armburgh says must be paid to him even though his enemies have recovered the property by a recent legal action.

[m.9v] To Harpour and Barbour [in margin] Dere and well beloued frendes we grete you we grete you [sic] well and for asmoche as ye are be hynd of midsomer that last was with outen smale parcell of other termes be forn, and Mighelmasse terme ys now comen, we pray you that ye woll . . . vs bothen hole . . . be the bringer of this letre with the mony that is behynde of the wode [ye] bouht of vs, that is to seye of that part that we stonde in pesible possesssion off, of the whiche ye weten woll . . . [?]yeven neuer more of you but . . . viijs. whiche was atte midsomer in the vi^te yer of the king that now is[297] and furthermore we pray you that ye sonden vs som resonable somme onward of the tother part of the ferme and of the wode that oure aduersares claymen ffor . . . so be thei haven recouered of vs the londe by assise stolen oute ayenst vs vnlaufully with oute eny warnyng thei haue neuer the mor title to the land nor to the money whiche thei haue in hand. Nor ye be neuer the mor excused a yenst vs for many causes, and oon cause is this, the lond what tyme the syse was taken was in feffees handes and yit ys and not in oures, so that the recouerer stont voide, ffor ye wete well thei mowe nat recoueren another mannes lond by assise taken ayenst vs and also we purposen to sewen an error and ateynt ayenst the contre[298] in all the hast that we kon, and as touchyng the mony that ye haue in hande thei haue no title therto, no ye be nat exskused a yenst vs, ffor of the toon side, thow aman recouere lande of hym that is in possession by assise, wher as this caas is the contrarie, schall he resceiue no profites of the londe but fro the [sic] of thassise forward and yif ought be yn hande by [?]fore that longith to hym that was in possession a fore the day of assise. And also ye stonde y bounde to vs be an endenture and an obligacion and on the tother side our aduersariez hadden her damages graunted to hem by assise so that ye . . . nat bothe haue the profitz of the land befor thassise,

---

296 The reference to the assize means that the letter was written after July 1432, almost certainly later that year. As it refers to the approach of Michaelmas, the dating of Holy Rood Day must indicate *Exaltatio Sancte Crucis* (14 September) rather than *Inventio* (3 May), which would make the date 15 September 1432.

297 Since this must be Henry VI, the year is 1428.

298 These were two ways in which a limited form of appeal could be brought against a judgement under medieval common law procedure. An action of error, commenced by a writ of error, involved the summons of the record of the proceedings before a superior court in order to assess whether there was an error on the face of the record. An action of attaint was brought against the trial jurors (the 'contre') in the case for giving a false verdict: in effect the action involved the criminal trial of the jury for perjury. The penalties against attainted juries were draconian, involving imprisonment and forfeiture of land and property to the crown, although, in practice, these seem hardly ever to have been invoked. See Baker, *English Legal History*, pp.117–19; John Fortescue, *De Laudibus Legum Angliae*, ed. S.B. Chrimes (Cambridge, 1942), cap.26. (E.P.)

that is to seyn, the mony that ys haue in hand with the damages, for ye wete woll yif we had suffrid hem to take up the profitz of the londe, that is to seyn the money that ys have in hande that myht thei no damages have axed by thassise, and also yif eny man haue title to the mony hit most nedes be the feffees, ffor thei haven the possession of the land and alweies haven had from the first tyme that ye toke fe[rme] of vs and yit haven. Of which feffees we haue a letre of attourne be vertue of which letre we nowe take vppe [the] profitz and therfor paieth hem hem [*sic*] no parcell of the mony that ye haue in hande nor paieth hem neuer the rather from hennes forward the ferme of that part that stont in debate be twixt hem and vs, ffor in sothe yif ye don ye kon [?]not be saved harmeles a yenst the feffees and vs. We kon namore atte this tyme but yevith credence to the bringer of this letre and we pray God haue you in his kepyng. I writen at Westm the morn after Holy Rode Day.

Robert Armburgh at Westminster to Ralph Beauchamp: 15 November 1432[299]

The letter concerns Beauchamp's efforts to secure an exchange of parishes.

To Bechamp vicar of Scharnyffeld [in margin] Dere and wel be loued cosyn y comande me to you, doyng you to wete that my seruantes and frendes haven spoke with the vyker of Sampsons and thei seyn that he ys in ful will to resigne his vicrage to you but he wol have a pension of v marc, of the whiche he wol have riht sufficeant seurete of frendes of yours y bounden for you, for he wol nat trust to your owne seurete, and that y wote wel ys for fer of deth and of permutacion, and of al this he wold haue an answer befor Cristemasse or by Cristemasse at ferthest. Ffor there is a prest in the contre dwelling fast by hym that lith sor vppon hym to don resigne to hym but thorew our enformacion he is better will to resigne to you thane to hym. And therfor yif that ye thinke that hit be forthering to you, laboureth there aboute in al the hast that ye kan. And as touchyng the viker dwelling place, ye shal haue hit al holy to your self and he wol perveie for hym self in other place.[300] I kan namor at this tyme etc. I writen at Westm the Saterday after Seint Martyn day the xj yer of Kyng Henre the vj[te].

---

299 For Beauchamp, see above, p.93 and n.155.

300 At issue here is the resignation of the incumbent in return for a pension from the beneficiary; the incumbent is evidently driving a hard bargain (Swanson, *Church and Society*, p.56). It has not been possible to identify either the benefice or its holder; the latter may have been called Sampson, or this could be the geographical name of the benefice.

Robert Armburgh to Ralph Beauchamp, William Harpour and Richard Barbour: probably late 1432[301]

A diatribe on the non-payment of sums due to Armburgh from Mancetter, including the continuing issue of the payment for the wood. The arguments about money paid to Robert Kedington and the state of the legal action over the other half of the manor are again rehearsed. They are accused of letting Armburgh down and warned against consorting with his enemies.

To Bechamp [vicar] of Sh[irne]fford [in margin] To Harpour and Barbour [further down in margin] Dere and wel beloued frendes y grete you wel and for asmoche as ye sent me to seyn at Mighelmasse that last was by John Rotour my seruant[302] that y was paid of mydsomer terme next beforn and so sent hym ayen home daieles with outen eny ferme paid to hym of olde or newe, savng ij s., and in this wise forgoodly and vnresonably haven put me to costes to sende to you for my fermes as ye haven doon diuersez tymes toforen this where as ye are y bonde be your endenture to sende me the seid fermes at your owne cost, wherfor y send vnto you at this tyme Raf Herde another seruant of myne, doyng you to weten that y resceived no peny of you of theseid midsomer ferme, and so wote Ric Barbour riht well, and if ye woll seye the contrarie the acquitance of v marc and a half, the which he had of me in the Estre terme next before wol prove the trouthe, for the same xl s. that Richard paid me last was for the same terme of Estre and y resseyved hyt of hym the same day the quytance was made. And tho v nobles the whiche he payd me a boute mydlentyn alitil beforn that, whanne he kam first with the writt of *sub pena*[303] to appere to fore the chaunceller, was for Mighelmasse terme was a twelfmonth, and, if I had, Ric wold a desired acquitance therof, as wel as he dede of these other parcelles. And also y sawe neuer Ric sithen iij or iiij daies after mydsomer and your daies of paiemente come not til vj wykes after mydsomer, and ye wete wel ye be wont to make your paiemente a quarter or half yer after your day and nat before your day. And also Ric wold vnnethe speke with me whanne he was here last in Trinite terme, nor taken non avys of me nor of non of my conseill but, whan he had laboured what hym lust be thavys if myne aduersaries and of here counseill, he went his wey and bad me neither good day ne fare wel nor told me how he wold be gouernyd. And there for hit may wel be demed that he was in no grete wyll to paie me my ferme so fer before my day, and as tochyng the wode siluer the whiche ye sent me to seyn also by my seruant that ye have paid hyt to Robert of Kedyngton my wiffes son, y shal preven the contrarie by a letre vnder his owne seal, the which letre

---

301 As it is concerned with the Michaelmas rent, this letter is, like the previous one, likely to date from late 1432.

302 Named as delivery man for a letter, above, p.129.

303 The only *sub poena* mentioned so far is the one against the farmers concerning their debt to Bellers (see above, text, p.106). This may be the same one. There is also a rather unspecific mention of one against the Armburghs (above, text, p.64 and n.60 to Intro.). See also below, p.149.

was wreton but iij dayes beforn he toke his deth evyll, and by diuersez letres the which y sent to you my self of which y have the copies to schewen, and also by certeinez letres vnder your owne seel the whiche ye sent me, the which y have redy to schewe, be the which letres, yf y were of thoo condicions that som of you wold ben of and ye had me in the same plyte, ye were like to forfeten and renne in al the bondes that ye stonde bounden to me, for ye have broken al the condicions conteined in your endentures, as wel in brekyng of your daies of paiemente of your wodes siluer as of youre terme, and also in asmoche as ye have not sent me theseid ferme at your owne cost after the fourme y conteyned in your endentures, and therfor y merveil gretely, considering the resonable sommes that ye stonde y boundyn inne,[304] that ye kepe no better thos condicions conteined in theseid endentures. And also that ye wol send me to seyn that ye had paid me and other in my name mony the which ye payd nat and specially the wode siluer, ffor, and ye woll al thinges to leven, hold you in that wronge oppynyon, ye wol lese vj d. for the wynnyng of oon, for thow ye had paid to Robert my wiffes son, as ye dede nat, I wol preven by a letre vnder your owne seele that ye have broken your daies of paiemente and so forfend your bonde, ffor lokith your endentures and ye shul fynden that your last day of paiemente was past longe beforn the day that ye assigned in your letre that ye made your paiemente to theseid Robert, the which letre, and y were as evill willed as somme of you wold be to me, wold be in tyme comyng a ful record ayenst yow, that ye hau forfeted your bondes afornseid, and therfor yif ye lust to kepyn still your fermes and, that we shul ben oute of stress, sendith me by my seruant aboveseid my ferme of midsomer and Mighelmasse with other smale parcell that aren be hynde of olde and my wodesiluer and letith be hennes forward all suche sotel ymaginacions, canteles[305] and conjectyrs which mowe nat availl, for this is now the thrid tyme that ye haven ben aboute to serue me thus and that y avouche to record your owne letres. And ferthermore as touchyng the tother moyte of the lande the which my aduersariez claymen, thei haven vnlaufully recouered hit of vs by assise y stolen oute ayenst vs with outen eny manere warnyng or fyn made in the chancerie or writ or patent entred of record in the rolles, and with outen any manere of remembrance there of leften in the chauncerie or in the hanapere[306] where aman shuld serchen and haue knoweleche if eny sise were grauntid oute ayenst hym, thow the shreve were vntrewe and wold yeve no lauful warnyng, the which sise had neuer be taken nor past ayenst me, had nat some of yow be [*sic*], and yit my aduersaries haven neuer the better title to the

---

304 Fuller details of the obligations of Harpour and Barbour are provided in the following letter to Laurence Sutton. They were each bound in the sum of £20 to observe the terms of their indenture with Armburgh. (E.P.)

305 This is 'cautels': tricks or deceits. (E.P.)

306 The financial department of chancery, one of the functions of which was to take account of all documents sealed under the Great Seal and account for fees received for the issue of writs (A.L. Brown, *The Governance of Late Medieval England 1272–1461* (London, 1989), p.46). (E.P.)

land be lawe ne be consience be consience [*sic*], thei haven neyther tytle ne
riht, ffor thoo that thei claymen by ben bastardes and nat milleres, and that
som of you knowen wel y now by enfourmacion of worthi men and of other
meene folk, the whiche ye have herd spoken, and better knowyng with the
grace of God ye shul have with inne short tyme, and by lawe hath thei nother
tytle no riht. For we were not in possession of the land that day that thei toke
thassise ayenst vs, for ye wete wel yt was in feffees handes longe beforn, and so
the reouerer stant voyde as in lawe, and therfor y pray you sondith or bringith
me the gold that ye have in hand of that part bothe ferme and wode silver for
ye haven chaffrid[307] with all and taken the profit there of agood whyle and
there is noman hath tytle therto but y, for thoo causes beforn rehersed and
many other. For thou aman recouere land by assise laufully taken and by a
ioust title ayenst another, he shal take no profit of the land before the day of
assise but fro the day of assise forward and if he doo the sise shall be abatid.
And ye wete well the gold that ye have in hand bothe ferme and wode siluer
was dewe dette to me before the day of assise.[308] And a nother cause is this,
thei haven here damages y grauntid to hem for the wronges that thei submet-
tid vppon vs that we shuld a doon hem, and that ouergrete damages, thou
thei had had ioust title to the land. Ffor ye wete well ye toke neuer xl li. worth
profit of that part before the day of assise, vnnethes xl marc, and lawe wol nat
that thei shul haven here damages and the profitz of the land therto, and yif ye
kepen my gold, that is forto seyn al that ye haven in hand of bothe partes still
yn your handes, for that entent that my aduersaries shuld have execucion
there inne of here damages, do you wel to weten hit shal nat availl you nor
hem, ffor lawe wol nat that eny execucion shuld be taken in eny manere thing
that lith in accion as this doth, that is to seyn in dette or in eny manere thing
that stant in debate, that is to seyn that stant in plee or in eny thing that is
pletable be twixt partis and partis with oute that that the seid execucion shuld
be taken for the kyng. And y do you to weten also, because of the damages
that my aduersaries haven recouered of me in assise, thei mowe sewen no
manere accion neyther ayenst me no ayenst you, no doo namore to vs thanne
thei have doon for no profit that was taken for that part of the lande before
the day of thassise, for thoo damages weren grauntid hym for all manere
thinges that weren doon be forn and, yif ye leve nat me of suche thinges as
ben rehersed in this letre, scheweth this seid letre to whom that ye lest, so that
he be a lerned man[309] and nat my enemye nor frend to my aduersarez, and in
peyne of my lif he wol nat seye the contrarie of no poynt that is writen here
inne. Ffurthermore, all thinges rehersed before had in mynde, remembre yow
how, by youre owne desire longe tyme procured and be meenes made beforn

---

[307] Meaning to deal in merchandise.
[308] I.e. income from the estate that was due before the day of assize must belong to the person who
had the land at that time, regardless of whether it was actually paid over at that time or not.
[309] Meaning a lawyer.

and nat at my profere, ye toke the ferme of me and no thing vnknowyn to yow how that hit stood in debate and which were my aduersarez and what lordschip thei hadde. Remembre you also how large promesses ye made to me whan ye toke the ferme, seiyng that ye wold kepe my aduersariez oute of the grounde and that thei shuld nat be so hardy to come there on and ful trewely my ferme shuld be payd and sent to me with oute eny cost of me, and how ye wold so labour that ye wold make the gentiles and the contre frendly to me, the whiche promesse made me welwillyng to you, supposing thorew strengthe of you and of your frendes my riht shuld be better maynteyned. Remembre you also how at your excitacion and by your avys and conseill y dede grete cost on worthy persons and vppon other meene persones also of the same schir and, nat withstandyng this and alle the grete promesses that ye made me, how evyll ye have payd me my ferme in to this tyme so that thorew your bad paiemente and the grete cost that y have doon at your stering, I dar saveley seye hyt, y persed now clerely half the ferme of that part that y stonde pesible possessid of fro the tyme that ye toke hyt to ferme in to this day. And if y hadde ben as evil paid of al other as y have ben of yow, hyt shuld riht evill a leyn in my power to acquite me ayenst my aduersaries as y have doon and as y hope to God to doo in tyme comyng, consideryng the grete strength of lord-schip that thei haven, and therfor, al thinges considered and al manere vntrouthe y cast aside, schameth nat ne hyndre nat your self for covetise of a litil good and, thou ye have nat wel quyt you to me al this tyme after the large promesse that ye made to me at the by gynnyng, dothe your deu here after and aquyte you wel to me henes forward and by my trouthe y shal aquyte me so to you that ye shul hold you wel paid, and thou my aduersariez haven recouered that part of the lande that they clayme by assise, which recouerer stant voide as in lawe for certeinez causez before rehersed and many other, yif ye wol save yourself harmeles, paieth hem neuer the rather that part of the ferme from hennce forward, for douteth nat there of, yif ye doon ye shul paie that a yen. And thou Bellers be hote to save you harmeles, trustith neuer the better to hym, ffor with the grace of God hit shal nat lye in his power with inne a short tyme to save hym self harmeles. And as touchyng my ferme and my wode siluer of that oon part and also my ferme and my wode siluer that ye had in hande before the day of assise of that other part, I pray you that ye send hyt me by my seruant with oute eny more delays or comyth your self with hym and bringe hit and y shal quyte you so largely for your cost and labour that ye shull hold you wel paid.

Robert Armburgh to Laurence Sutton: probably late 1432[310]

Sutton is addressed as Armburgh's feoffee for Mancetter. The situation with regard to the land and to the money owing is again rehearsed. Sutton is asked to make enquiries concerning the jury for the assize that Armburgh lost, to urge Armburgh's feoffees for the disputed land not to release it to his enemies and to put heavy pressure on Harpour and Barbour for the money they owe Armburgh.

[m.8v] To Laurens Sutton [in margin] Dere and wel by loved frend y comande me to you, doyng you to vnderstande that my ffermours of Mancestre owen me xl li. and more for the maner of Mancestre, the which thei token hole of me to ferme by a paire of endentures and for a parcell of wode the which y sold hem for xiij marc of the which there were made a paire endentures be twene vs also and thei stonden bounden to me in ij obligacions eche of xx li. to perfourme the condicions conteyned in bothe endentures, the which bondes and endentures were made and enseled at Westm and, so moche the better for me, of which xl li. above rehersid xiiij li. and more is due to me for that moyte of the thrid part of the maner of Mancestre a fornseid that y stonde peisible possesed of, that is to seyn xl s. of mydsomer terme and xl s. of Mighelmasse terme that last weren and xl s. of wode siluer with outen other smale parcells that weren [be]hynde of olde, of som terms viij s., of som terms a noble, and of som terme xl d. and al the tother part of the xl li. a forseid, that is to seyn l mark and more, ys of that halvyndell of the thrid part of the maner of Mancestre a fornseid the which my aduersaries claymen and han recouered hit of me by assise, the whiche l mark is due dette to me also natwithstandyng that recouerer, and, for certeines causes which y have rehersed in a letre the which y sende to my fermours at this tyme by the bringer of this letre, for the recouerer stant voide in lawe for certeines causes which y have writen in this same lettre, and so y doute nat thereof that with the grace of God thei shul non auantage taken be that assise, but yit, forto stonden al cler, y purpose me to sewen a writte of errour and, with oute that thoo persones which weren enpaneld in thassise wollen trete with me, y pourpose me with inne a short tyme to sewen a teynt also, and therfor y sende you a copye of here names and pray you that ye wol fouche saf to enquerre and to maken other frendes of yours to enqueren also yf there be eny bonde man of hem or if eny of hem stonde outlawed, for if there be eny suche men amonges hem hyt ys errour good y now and if ye fynde eny outlawed man a monges hem, enqueren how longe thei haven stonde outlawed and, if thei haven eny chatres of outlawrie, how longe hit is sith thei gaten. And if ye fynde eny bonde man amonges hem enquerith of [*sic*] thei haven eny manumyssions and how longe thei haven had hem in the same wyse. Fferthermore y wol that ye

---

knowen how that Sir William Montfort, Sir John Cokeyn and John Malery of Warwyckschire with other certeines persones here of Hertfordschire[311] stonden enffeffed in that part of the londe that my aduersariez haven recouered of me longe before the day of thassise and yit don. Wherfor that recouerer stont voide as in lawe so that my aduersaries mowe non availl bere ther by, but it is doon me to vnderstande that some of my feffes aren turned a yenst me for, as y am enfourmed, the sise had neuer be taken ne past ayenst me had nad som of hem ben, and Ric Barbour oon of my fermours. And therfor y beseche you whan ye mete with eny of hem at Warwyk or in eny other place that ye wol comande my wife and me to hem and seyn that we praied hem to kepe still theire estates and that thei relesse nat vppe to oure aduersaries, for we ben enfourmed ye mowe seyn that theseid aduersariez haven laboured there aboute that thei wold fouche saf to acquyte hem to vs after the promesse that thei maden to vs at the by gynnyng and that we be nat deceyved of the trust that we had in hem whan we yoven hem astate in the lande and yif eny of hem wol seyn that thei knowen non astate that thei haven in oure lande, ye mowe seye this be the same token that thei dyned ws[312] at Westm and that we had twyes ordeyned for hem but at first tyme thei kam nat and that eche of hem had a purs of my wyves makyng and gold thereinne, but of the gold speketh nat for it was but litil, savyng Cokyn dyned nat with vs. And be the token ye mowe seye also that y have a letre of attourne selid with here signettes the which is made to certeinez persones to receyue the ferme of the land that thei ben enffeffed inne here names. And ferther more for asmoche as my fermours of Mancestre sent me to seyn by John Rotour my seruant[313] at Mighelamasse that last was that y was paid of mydsomer ferme next be forn, which ys not sothe, and that ye shull wel sesen by the letre that ye sende hem atte this tyme and so thei senten hym home ayen dayles with oute eny ferme paid to hym of old or of newe, savyng ij s. and, for asmoche also as the bringer of this letre hath no knoweleche of my matter nor ys aquenyted with my fermours and thei ben sturdy felawes here, strange, slye and myghty with sotil answers, senden hym home a yen withouten ony mony, and beren hym an honde that thei wolen with inne short tyme comen and speken with me and bring here ferme hem self as thei haven serued other seruantz of myne dyuersez tymes, the whiche was but avoidauns for the mene tyme, and therfor y beseche you, yif ye mowen tente in ony wyse, that ye fouche saf to riden to Mancestre and takith my seruant with, you and spekith with my fermours and askith hem the mony above seid and if thei wolen nat paie hit al or sum resonable somme there of, y make you myn attourne and yeve you ful power be vertue of this

---

311 This may be the feoffment referred to earlier in the roll (above, p.65); see comments there (n.33) for possible dating. Sutton's status as feoffee (see immediately below) seems to be for the half of the manor which was incontestably Joan's and Robert's.

312 *Sic*: error for 'w' vs'?

313 Mentioned above, p.134.

letre to streyne[314] hem therfor in euery parcell of the ground and to dryven the stresse in to what place of the schire you lust and to kepen still in to the tyme ye be paid of theseid mony or of sum resonable somme there of. And also ye haven power y now with outen this letre to streyne hem and doon what ye list but yif thei wolen make better paiemente hennes forward, for ye ben feffed in the lande and, for asmoche as ye shuld have good avysement of all thing that ye shullen seyn to hem, ye haven here acopye of the letre that y send to hem bothe, which ye mowen take aful enformacion of alle manere maters and therfor y pray you late sum kunnyng man rede it to yow ones or twyes or twyes [sic] that ye mowen have yt the better in mynde and, what cost that ye doon, takith hit vppe of the same mony that ye receyve of my fermours and, when ye have kauht of hem asmoche as ye mowen with fayr wordes, streynyth hem or doth what ye lust best for the tother part. Also your son farith well and comande hym to yow.

Robert Armburgh to an unknown recipient: perhaps early 1433[315]
This is a statement of why the assize of 1432, which found against the Armburghs, was not properly conducted – primarily that, because of improper influence in chancery, it was possible to bring the suit without the Armburghs being given proper warning.

[Margination illegible] For asmoche as worthi men and alle other thoren your enformacion shuld be the better willed to helpen vs in oure riht and the worse willed to supporte oure aduersaries in here wronges, therfor I have made yow here aremembrance of the sise that past a yenst vs atte Warwyk about Seint Margarete tyde that last was,[316] how hit was stolen oute ayenst vs and how and in what wyse we laboured to have had knoweleche there of in alle the places where as aman, be lawe, be consience or by reson shuld have had knowleche. At the bygynnyng the scheryve yaf vs no manere warnyng therinne, art lauful no vnlauful nor non other in his name and that we wol southe vs to record, and the processe of assise, the which makithe mencion that the shryve made his retourne the day of assise that we had not with inne the schire wherthorerewe [sic] we myht be distreynd nor we had no baillife, the which retourne was nat trewe, for we were in peisible possession the day of assise and ner hand a quarter after of the toon halvyndel of the thrid part of the maner of Mancestre in the which we enfeffed you and other at

---

314 I.e. distrain or distress, meaning to take property as a means of coercion, usually to get a debt paid or bring someone to court (Baker, *Introduction to English Legal History*, pp.52, 312).

315 From the reference to the assize, this must have been written before 21 July 1433, as 21 July was the date of the assize (see immediately below, n.316). It may be an *aide-mémoire* for a new feoffee (see contents of letter).

316 The assize took place on 21 July 1432 (see above, p.19).

Mighelmasse that last was,[317] and was occupied and xl li. worth katell with inne the ground, the whiche retourne was made vnder the fourme afornseid thorew brokage and made of oure aduersaries for that entent that thassise shuld be take be defaute of answere, and so it past a yenst vs but lawe but lawe [*sic*] and good consience wold that the schryve or the vnderschryve or here deputees shuld a taken a stresse openly vppon the ground and that stresse shuld nat abeen delyuered in to the tyme that we or oure baillif or oure fermour or thei that occupied the ground in oure name hadden y founde suffisant seurete that thei or we shulden a come to the cise, but oure aduersariez wost wel, and thei had do thus, thei shuld nat have had here purpoos for, and the contre had had ioust enformacion, the cise had nat past a yenst vs. Fferthermore we spak with Campyon the which was that tyme and longe beforn and yit is the schryves depute of Warwyk schyre and receiueth alle hys writes and makithe al hys retournes, and we askid hym yf there was eny cise ayenst vs and he knoweleched to vs that he had born vppe al the sises that shuld be at Warwyk at that terme and seid pleinly there was non a yenst vs atte all. Werby ye mowe wel felen thei weren in no wyll that we shuld have eny warnyng. Also we askid the clerk of the rolles[318] the same and he swore by his trouthe that there was neuer sise nor non other manere of thing oute ayenst vs of that court and there vppon the clerc of the hanaper at oure request serched his remembrances the which makithe mencion of all sises, and he seid pleinly there was non at all and ferther more we made oure attourne to serche the rolles in the chancerie for the writ that went to the schryve and the patent that went to the iustices of assise a forn the fine that oure aduersariez shuld a made to the king or thassise had be grauntid hem, so as the lande goth for ix mark to ferme erly with outen certeyn casueltes reserued to vs, for it hath nat be seyn a forn this tyme that eny sise went oute of the chancerie saf this sise, nor there shuld noon goon oute of theseid chancerie til thei had made a fyn therefore yif the land passid the value of xl s. yerly, and in to that tyme also that the writte and the patent and theseid fyn weren entred of record in the rolles, and oure attourne seid pleinly that he had serched twyes the rolles bothe beforn the day of a sise and after and he fonde neither writte patent ne fyn entred of record in the seid rolles nor no manere of remembraunce there of left in the chancerie, and there vppon, as sone as we had knoweleche that thassise was past eyenst vs, we compleyned vs to the chanceller and told hym how we were serued and he seid pleynly there was non grauntid oute for hym and was passing wrothe with the manere of doyng and seid yt shuld be so remedied that we shuld hold vs wel paid, and vnder this fourme, thorew the falssehede of oure

---

317 If the statement that Mountford and the others were enfeoffed several years before is true (see above, text, p.136), then this must be a new feoffment. This might suggest that, although Mountford, Cokayn and Malory are still named as potential allies in the letter, the feoffees had recently been changed; this may be a reflection of Armburgh's weakened position in the county (see above, pp.26–7).

318 This is presumably still Wymbysh (see above, n.112 to Intro.).

aduersaries and specially of Raff Bellerys the which is chef labourer in all manere maters ayenst vs and of other certeynes persones in the chancerie which ben frendly to hem, the sise was stolen oute ayenst vs, vnwetyng the chanceller or the clerc of rolles, wher as there hathe noman pouere to graunten oute assise but thei, and therefor y be seche you enformyth Montfort, Cokeyn and Malery and other worthi men that ben frendly to you of al this vntrouthe and praieth hem to be good maistres to vs and makith vs alle the frendes that ye mowen in the contre. Ffor we arn like to have somwhat to doon there or ought longe and, yif ye vnderstande nat what y mene be the moyte, that is to seyn be the halvyndell of the thrid part of the maner of Mancestre aboveseid, I shal declare hit to you here. Thic maner of Mancestre was many yers goon depertid of thre betwene iij susters,[319] the iij partes after the disses of oon of the iij susters, the to part fel to Sir Geffrey Brokhole my wyves fadir, the which thrid part after the deth of the same Sir Geffrey and Dame Elene his wyf which was my wyves modir shuld a ben departid in two be twene my wyf and ij susters, doughters of here, yif thei had leved to thei came to age, and for asmoche as thei ben dede, we askyn all the hole thrid part, but oure aduersaries bringen forth other ij girles and seyn that thei ben the same that weren my wyves susters childryn and by hem thei clayme the ton halvenden and so the striff that is by twene vs ys but for the toon halvyndell thei mowen make no clayme.

Robert Armburgh to an unknown recipient: probably between 8 July and 6 October 1433[320]

The letter summarises the progress so far of the suit against the Armburghs on the damages awarded on the assize and asks the recipient to speak to the previous sheriff, Sir William Mountford, sheriff at the time of the writ, concerning the writ at issue and to discover the identity of the jurors who are shortly to be summoned to decide the case.

Dere and well belovyd frende we gret yew well doyng yow well doyng yow [*sic*] to wetyn that oure aduersariis swyn a *scire ffacias*[321] ayenst vs in the kynges benche and aseid ffor to han had out an execucion ayenst vs ffor the xl li. damagz that thei recurid off vs yn thassise at Warwike amonday after the fest

---

[319] See above, p.5.

[320] The contents of the letter suggest a day between Trinity and Michaelmas Terms 1433.

[321] The *scire facias* was issued in Easter Term 1433, ordering Robert and Joan to appear before the bench at the quindene of Easter (29 April: see C.R. Cheney, *Handbook of Dates for Students of English History* (2nd ed., London, Royal Hist. Soc., 1970), p.68 on this). Both parties were then given another day to appear, the quindene of Trinity (21 June). It was then that Armburgh, appearing in person with Joan, put forward the defence that a writ for damages had already been issued at the assizes. The 'country', or jury, referred to here was summoned for the quindene of the following Michaelmas (13 October), although the verdict was not in fact given until July 1435, by *nisi prius* at Warwick (PRO KB27/688 Coram Rege rot.43).

off Seynt Margaret the x yere off the kyng that now ys, to the wheche we mad oure answere vnder this fforme, denyng that thei ought tohan [*sic*] non execucyion ayenst vs in the kynges benche, ffor asmoche as thei hawyn execucion a ffore the iustyces off the same assyse, the same day thassise was holden that ys to seyen a *fieri facias*[322] [*sic*] directe to Sir William Mountfort that tyme scherywe off the same schire retournable vppon Ffriday next be fforn the fest off Seynt Petyr in the chayere next ffolouyng[323] beffore the iustisis off the same assise, to the wheche answer vr [*sic*] aduersariis replyid and seid ther was no *ffieri facias* delyueryd to Sir Welyam Mountffort that tyme scherreve and that thei woldyn averryn be the contre[324] and we seiden yes that we woldyn put vs vppon the contre also and thus the yssu was ioynyd and the *venire facias*[325] out to make the contre and so the issu that the contre schall passe vppon this, whether this wret, that ys to seyn the *fieri facias*, was delyuered to Sire William Mont ffort, that tyme sherreve, or non. And therfor we hau ryght gret nede off my mayster Mountffort ys record in this cas ffor the clerke off assyse that ought be lawe at oure request to makyn vs arecord vndir his sell, he is so confedrid with oure aduersariis, what thorgh lordeschepe and thorogh mede, that he wol non makyn vs nat withstondyng that he was the first that gaff vs warnyng that the iustise off the same assyse had awardid out a *fieri ffacias* ayenst vs and not withstondyng also that his owne clerke[326] vs acopy off the same *fieri facias* with his owne hand, the whiche we hau al redy to schewyn, off the whiche *fieri facias* the copy ys wretyn in this bille word ffor word. Wher ffor we pray yow to spekyn with oure master Sir Wolyam Montffort and prayn hym that he wol vouchesaff to makyn vs arecord vnder his sell off this *fieri facias*. Ffor he thare no more doon bot don hit writtyn word ffor word as yt ys in this bille and rehersyn whon that that was dirette to hym in maner and fforme as the wret makythe mencyion and set to his sell. Fferthere more ffor asmoche as we mow hau no knowleche off the contre that ys enpanellyd betwene vs and oure aduersariis into the tyme the *venire ffacias* beretourned, the whiche schal not ben ther to the quynsym off Seynt Mighell,[327] we pray yow to enquier and to makyn other ffrendys off your to enqueryn, also off the contrie that ys enpanelyd, whiche ben just men and well consyenssyd and whiche woln takyn mede. And as nyghe as yt may ben enquerid iff ony off hem haue taken mede off oure aduersariis or etyn or drokyn [*sic*] withhem or withholdyn with hem off fees or off clothyng or kyn to hem or be to wardys ony that ys kyn to Bellers or to ward the scherreve whiche ys fful ffrend toBellers [*sic*] or withholdyn with ony off al thes off ffees

---

322 A judicial writ which lay on a judgement of debt or damages, by which the sheriff was ordered to levy the damages on the goods and chattels of the defendant. (E.P.)

323 'St Peter's Chayere' means St Peter *in cathedra*, so the Friday before is 20 February 1433.

324 See above, n.9.

325 The writ of summons for a trial jury. (E.P.)

326 *Sic*: a word is presumably omitted.

327 See above, n.321.

or off clotyng, or yff ther ben ony bond men or outlawod [*sic*] men off hem amd yff eny seche be, to whom thei arbond and be whom thei wern outlawid and what yere, and enqueryth all so yff ther be ony off hem that ys not suffysant off ffrehold, that ys to seyn that maynot spendyn v marc or xl s. ayere at the lest and where stond [*sic*] sesyd theroff or yt in feffes hondys. And all this mater whiche best ben enquerid be summe off that ben enpanellyd, iff yt so be that ony off hem ben ffrend to yow and yff this materis thorgh your good labour comyn to ony effecte, I be seche yow that ye wol vouchsaff to makyn a letter theroff and sendit doon to your sone, but yff ony off seruantes off myn come to yow in the meane tyme [seems to break off]

Robert Armburgh to Sir William Mountford: probably about the same date as the immediately preceding letter[328]
A direct request to Mountfort for a copy of the writ.

Vel sic here is aremembraunce whow oure aduersaris suen a *fieri ffacias* ayenst *vtsvpra usque ibi* thei might to hav non execucion ayenst vs ayenst vs [*sic*] in the kynges benche *tunc sic,* ffor asmoche as thei hadden a *ffieri facias* dirette to yow that tyme scherrewe *usque iby* that ther was no *ffieri ffacias* delyueryd to yow *tunc sic* and that thei wold averene etc. *usque ibi,* this *ffieri facias* was delyueryd to yow orno *tunc sic* and therffor we hau gret nede to your record etc. *usque ibi.* Wherffore we prey yew *tunc sic* to spekyn to Sterky[329] off this mater so that be his avis we myght haue arecord off this *ffieri facias* vnder your sell and yff ye woll seyn that ther cam no suche *fieri facias* to hym, ye mou schew hym the copy theroff and enfforme hym in what wyse y cam therto and also, yff hit lyke yewe to seyn so moche to hym, ye mou seyen that, yff he had youen vs lauful warnyng and amade a iust retourne the day off assyse, we had nat lost oure lond, ffor theras he made his retourne that we had none with inne the schire wherevppon we myght be distreynyd, nor we had no balyvis e we weren ~~inposs~~ sesid off the othere moyte off the thirde part off the maner off Mancestre and in pessyble possessyoon whiche was ocupied, and ye with other ware enfoffyd in that moyte that oure aduersaris recurid off vs be thassyse aboue seyd and therffore, yff hit lyke yowe, ye mou counsel hym to a quyte hym so to vs at this this [*sic*] tyme, that we han no cause to swyn non accyon off desset ffor the wrong retourne that thei made at that tyme.

[328] The recipient is indicated by the contents, which indicate also that the date is about the same as the previous letter. The phrases *tunc sic* and *usque ibi* are scribal abbreviations, indicating, in the case of the first, how the wording should be varied from the very similar previous letter and, in the case of the second, that the wording should be followed until the specified phrase (with thanks to E.P.).

[329] See above, p.64.

Robert Armburgh at Westminster, perhaps to either William Harpour or Richard Barbour: 15 [December 1433][330]

In view of the costs concerning the plea on the Mancetter advowson, the recipients are asked to give money to Thomas Arblaster, one of the co-owners of the manor and advowson, if he requests it.

Dere ffrendis I gret yow well and ffor asmoche as there ys atte yssw yoynyd betwene Raff[331] Hastynges knyght and vs, parceners of Mancestre, vppon the doyson[332] off chirche off Mancestre and a *venire facias* oute to makyn the contre, the wheche contre ys lyk to passyn about myssomer or with thyn awhil after, and so that there ys lyke gret cost to ben don to the wheche we must ben alle contrebutariis, wherefor I wol that yff Arblaster[333] come orsend to yow that ye delyuer hym xl s., and this letter schal ben your discharge. No more etc. I wretyn at Westmyster the xv isme day off [breaks off]

Robert Armburgh at Westminster, perhaps to either William Harpour or Richard Barbour: 18 December 1433

A similar letter.

Dere frendys I gret yow well. Ffor asmoche as there schal ben a*nisi prius* [*sic*] at Covyntre a Twysday next after Seynt Hillary betwene Raff Hastynges knyght and vs, parceners off Mancestre,[334] ffor the avoyson off this chirche off Mancestre, so that ther must nedys gret cost ben don, to the wheche we must alle nedys ben contributariis, where ffor I wol that yff Arblaster come sende to yow, that ye delyueryn hym xxvj s. viij d. and this schal ben your discharge. I wretyn at Westmynster the xviij day off Desembyr the xij yere off the kyng that nowys.[335]

Robert Armburgh to an unknown recipient: probably c. same date as the immediately succeeding letter

He encloses a copy of the writ for the jury, with their names and a copy of the writ for damages which is at issue, and asks the recipient to make the Armburgh version of the facts concerning the writ known to the jurors.

[m.7v] Here is acopy of the *venire fac* and of the contre that is enpaneld be twene Thomas Bernard and James Bellers and Elene his wif and Robert

---

330 This may well have been written just before the next one. For the background to these two letters, see above, pp.21–4.
331 *Recte* Richard (see above, n.107 to Intro.).
332 I.e. advowson, ownership of the right to present to a living.
333 One of the coheirs to Mancetter and hence a defendant against Hastings (see above, p.22).
334 For details of the defendants, see above, p.22 and n.111 to Intro.
335 This must be Henry VI and so 1433.

Armeburgh and Johane his wif and therfor y beseche you that ye wolen souchesaf to enfourmyn as many as ye mowe spekyn withall of the seyd panell what schall ben here issue in manere and fourme as the seid writt makith mencion. Rex vicecomiti Warr salutem praecipimus tibi quod venire facias etc. Thomas Sidenhale, Johannes Ffulwode etc.[336]

This *venire fac* makith mencion what schall ben the issue that the contre schall passen vppon, the whiche issue ys, wether the *fiere fac* that this *venire fac* makith mencion of were deliuered to William Montfort that tyme scherif a Monday after the feste of Seint Margarete the mayden the x yere of the kyng that now is or no. And, thow it so were that this *fiere fac* were deliuered to the vnderschreve and not to the hye scheriff,[337] ye mowe safly enfourmyn the contre that thei nede not to ben in doute therfore, for all maner writtes that ben deliuered to the vnderscheriff, lawe demyth hem deliuered to the hye scheriff, soo al manere writtes ben directe to hym, and by his auctorite thei ben serued and in his name his vnderscherif makith the retourne.

Also here is acopy of the *fiere fac* that the *venire fac* makith mencion of, the which was awardid ayenst the seid Robert and Johane the same day, and there as theseid writ makith mencion in self and was deliuered to Sir William Montfort that tyme scheriff the same day and yere as the *venire fac* makith mencion, and in evidens that this ys soth, Breen the clerc of assise[338] warned theseid Robert and Johane therof withhys owne mouthe in the begynnyng of Mighelmasse terme next folewyng and his owne clerc wrote hem a copye therof with his owne hand which thei hau to schewen, and thus, and ye fouche saf, ye mowe iustly enfourmyn the contre, and so y be seche you that ye doon. And thus thei mowe wel felyn, bothen be the *venire fac* and be the *fiere fac*, that thei hau aclere issue to passyn with theseid Robert and Johane yif thei wollen save here consiences and he [*sic*] owne soules.

Rex vicecomiti Warr salutem praecipimus tibi etc.[339]   + ye being the same tyme scherif and Sterky your vnderscheriff

---

336 This is the beginning of the list of jurors that would be on the writ. For the two men named, see Carpenter, *Locality and Polity*, pp.67–73, 655, 667.

337 This is the same problem in a double shrievalty as was mentioned in relation to Cambridgeshire and Huntingdonshire (see above, p.111).

338 There was a Robert Brene, attorney in a Devon case in 1441 (with thanks to Professor John Baker for this information). I have not been able to trace any other possible candidates. The clerk of the assize was the clerk who assisted the justices of assize on their biannual circuit. For the clerk of assize in the early modern period, see J.S. Cockburn, *A History of English Assizes 1558–1714* (Cambridge, 1972), pp.70–85 (addition by E.P.).

339 The gap is presumably for Mountford to insert his name in attestation.

Robert Armburgh to Sir William Mountford: probably late 1433 or c. July 1435[340]

A further request to Mountford for a copy of the writ, because of the impending verdict, with a copy of the jury writ and a request that he inform the jury of the strength of the Armburgh case.

To Sir Will Mounford knyght [in margin] Riht worschipful and reuerent sir y comand me to yow. And for asmoche as myn aduersariez pourposyn hem to have a *nisi prius* [sic] ayenst my wif and me abouten the last ende of the next terme at Warwyk or at Coventre, I wote neuer whethir, vppon the *scire fac* that thei hau a yenst vs in the kynges benche for the xl li. damages that thei receyveden of vs in the assise at Warwyk abouten Seint Margaretes day was twelfmonth +[341] y wold beschyn yow of your good maisterchip as ye be hight me the last tyme that y spak with you in your in atte London that ye wolde fouche saf that y myght hau arecord of the *fiere fac* that y spak to you of the same tyme, the which *fiere fac* was awardid a yenst my wif and me the same day of assise be the iustice of the same assise and directe to you, but y suppose that it was deliuered to your vnderscherif, for vppon this *fiere fac* is oure issue taken. For, whan thei askid an execucion in the kynges benche a yenst vs vppon the *scire fac* that thei han ayenst vs in that court, I seid thei ought non execucion to han ayenst vs in that court, for asmoch as thei haven a *fiere fac* a warded ayenst vs in to Warwyk schire the same day the assise was holdyn be the iustise of the same assise, the which *fiere fac* y seid was deliuered to yow the same day of assise was holdyn, and therto theireplyed [sic] and seid that there was non deliuered to you and that thei wolden averen be the contre and y seid this and that y wold put me vppon the contre and thus was and issue ioyned, the which issue ys whethir this *fiere fac* was deliuered to you or non in maner and fourme as hit is aforn rehersed, and theron this issue be whether this *fiere fac* were deliuered to you or non the contre dar not be in doute, for al manere writtes that ben deliuered to the vnder scherif, lawe demyth hem deliuered to the hye scheriff, forto hym thei ben directe and in his name the vnderscheriff makith his retorn. And in evidens that this *fiere fac* was awardid and delyuered in manere and fourme rehersed Breen the clerk of assise warned me there off with his owne mouth in the begynnyng of Mighelmasse

---

340 The reference to the assize and to the impending *nisi prius* would suggest a date leading up to July 1435, when the case for damages was finally heard by *nisi prius* at Warwick (PRO KB27/688 Coram Rege rot.43), but this would put the letter badly out of sequence with those that follow immediately. However, it is possible that Armburgh was confusing it with the *nisi prius* on the advowson, which was due to be heard at Coventry in February 1434 (see above, p.145), which would place the letter in late 1433, where it fits better into the sequence. Alternatively, Armburgh could have heard a rumour about an impending jury on the damages which turned out not to be true, a credible interpretation, given his uncertainty about the place. An earlier *nisi prius* on the damages was scheduled for February 1435 but that is also rather late for the positioning of this letter (PRO KB27/695 Coram Rege rot.2d).

341 Inserted above 'twelfmonth'.

terme next folewyng, of the which *fiere fac* also y schewed you a copy of his clerkes owne writyng. And all this may iustly ben declared to the contre be whom that euer ye southe saff and, for asmoche as ye schuld hau ful knowe-lech that yt ys soth as I have rehersed here, y send you a copy of the *venire fac*, and it liked you of your goodnesse that the contre myht ben enfourmed of this issue and of this *fiere fac* thorgh som seruant of yours, in suche wyse that thei myht felyn that ye wolden be good maister to me in this mater, I wold aquyten me to you in maner and fourme as y made promys to yow in your in[342] and rewardyn hym wel for hys travaill.

Robert Armburgh to William Harpour and Richard Barbour: probably late 1433 or early 1434[343]

Armburgh demands the money they owe him yet again, and with still more threats, and chides them for failing to secure him sufficient support in the 'country' and for allegedly consorting with his enemies.

To Harpour and Barbour [in margin] Dere and welbeloued frendes y grete you wel merveilling gretly so as ye owe me agrete somme of mony that ye send me no parcell there of, ffor lawe wolde that myne aduersariez shuld haue execucion of here damages in that good that ye hau in hande of myne as y knowe wel lawe ys expres the contrare, yet schuld ye not with holdyn me my good in to the tyme the issue that ys joyned wer tried be xij men and execu-cion awardid be the iustys,[344] ye mow not with holdyn me my good in to the tyme that it were arestid in youre handes be the scherif be a warraunt from the same iustice after execucion ys awardid, the which with the grace of God schal neuer comyn so ferforth, for no labour that my aduersariez hau made or euer schull maken.[345] For y have a spyed thinges that schull a voydynt with the grace of God wel y now, and also ye wete wel ye stonden bounde to me in resonable sommys to perfourmyn the condicions conteyned in your enden-tures, of the which condicions oon ys that ye schuld kepyn your daies of paie-ment so that, thou lawe wold yeuen my aduersariez execucion in that good that ye hau in hand of myne, yit myht y sewen my obligacion and recoueryn asmoch of you for brekyng of your daies of paiemente, and that ye mowe felyn be youre owne discrecion. For, had ye kept your daies of paiemente, my aduersariez schuldyn no good of myne a foundyn in your handes where inne

---

342 I.e. inn.

343 The verdict on the damages was still awaited when this letter was written (see above, n.340 for the date of this verdict). In view of the date of the next letter, this is likely to be another from late 1433 or early 1434.

344 See immediately above, n.343.

345 I.e. Armburgh says they must not withhold their payment to him due from the period before the assize and, if they do, the execution of the damages in favour of his adversaries will take from the farmers what is legitimately his.

thei myht a taken execucion, and also good consience and curtesyse bothe wold that ye schulden paiyen me my good, thou lawe were the contrarie, considering oon the toon side how that my aduersariez nor noon other han no knoweleche of the good that ye owen me but yf be oonly thorewe your enformacion, and consideryng oon the tother side hou grete menys ye maden to had the ferme not vnknowyng that it stood in debate, with large promysses how goodly ye wold aquyten you to me if ye hadden the ferme and also the good wyll that y have schewed you from that tyme in to this. For wel ye knowen y have doon grete cost at your excitation and have alowyd large rewardes that ye maden in the contre to getyn you supportacion, of the which y had neuer enformacion but of youre owne mouthes, and therfor y have no merveill, thou moche poeple [*sic*] labour ayenst me and thou y have ben kept fro my riht, sithen ye labouryn ayenst me and kepyn fro me my gode wherthoren my maters myghten a be sped. Alle these thinges considerid but y se wel ye ben ruled al by my aduersariez and by here conseill and no thing be me and that hath hindrid me thus ferforth, but yit hit is like to be more hindring to you in tyme comyng. And therfor y conceil you to levyn here conceil be tymes lest ye be deceyved and ouer moche hyndrid there by, for oon of you was but late desseyued of oon of my aduersariez conceil as the last letre that ye sent me makithe mencion, but he that dyde that disceit schal be taught vnder what fourme he schall sewyn a writ *sub pena*[346] oute of the chauncerie and how he schall deliuere hit and not to disseyven bothe the kyng and the partye. And seris,[347] demyth not that y send you this lettre nor that y sent you no letre afor this tyme for no wrath that y have to you but for oure bothes auantage, for y kept to have no cause to hurlyn with yow in tyme comyng for my good and so to puttyn vs bothe to cost, and therfor y pray you sendith me my good or som resonable somme ther off and aquytith you to me sum what after the promys that ye made to me in the be gynnyng and yet y wol do so to yow that ye schul hold you wel payd.

Robert Armburgh to Laurence Sutton: between 25 November 1433 and 20 January 1434[348]

Another letter concerning the forthcoming jury on the writ for damages arising from the assize of 1432. Armburgh sends the list of jurors, as well as a copy of the disputed writ, and asks Sutton to use his influence with the jurors, especially if any are tenants of the earl of Warwick. He is also requested to speak to John Campion, the deputy-sheriff of Warwickshire, on the subject of the jurors, including the addition of any further names.

To Laurens Sutton [in margin] Dere and welbelouyd frend y comaund me to you and for asmoche as there is acontre be twene myn aduersaries rerine

346 This could be the vexatious *sub poena* referred to above, text, p.64, but see also above, p.106.
347 I.e. 'sirs'.
348 This is another letter that refers to the assize as being at St Margaret's day 'was twelfmonth' and

vppon a *scire fac* which thei hau ayenst me in the kynges benche for the xl li. damages the which thei recouered of me in the assise at Warwyk at Seint Mararete tyde was twelfmonth, of the which contre as y am enfourmed some ben tenantes to my lord of Warwyk,[349] wherfor y sende you a copy of the pan-ell, besekyng you to comoon with as many as ye mowe haue knoweleche of and declaren to hem is the issue that thei schullen passen vppon, and enformyn hem in the manere and forme as this letter makith mencion and that ye wolen steryn other frendys of your to do the same and that ye wolen southe saf with help of your frendes to makyn vs alle the frendes that ye mowe ayenst the last ende of Illare terme that next comyth.[350] For at that tyme oure aduersaries wolen han a *nisi prius* a yenst vs for the same mater at Warwyk or at Coventre, y wote neuer wether, and y sende to you here acopy of the *venire fac* wherby ye schuln knowe the issue that the contre schal passen vppon and y send you also a copy of the *fiere fac* that was a wardid ayenst my wif and me be the iustyses of the same assise the same day the assise was holdyn, and vppon this *fieri fac* the issue is taken. For what tyme myn aduersariez asked yn execucion ayenst me in the kynges benche be the *scire fac* that thei hau a yenst me in the same bench, y answerid hem and seyde they ought non to hau, for asmoche as thei hadden a *fiere fac* a wardid a yenst vs be the iustice of the same assise, the which y seyd was deliuered to Sir William Montfort that tyme scheriff of the same schire at Warwyk the same day the assise was holdyn, and thei seiden that were noon deliuered to hym, that thei woldyn averen be the contre and we seyden this and that we wolden puttyn vs vppon the contre also and thus an issue was joynd, the which issue is whethir this *fiere fac* was deliuered to Sir William Montfort that tyme scheriff or no, and tho it wer so that this writt were deliuered to the vnderscherif, ye mowe seyn that thei nede not to ben in doute therfor, for all that euer is deliuered to the vnder scheriff, lawe demyth hit deliuered to the hye scherif, for al that the vnder scherif doth, he doth it be auctorite of the hye scherif, for al manere writtes ben directe to the hye scheriff and not to his vnderscheriff and in the hye scheriffes name al maner retourn ben made. And in evidens that this *fiere fac* was deliuered to Sir William Montfort in maner and fourme as aforn is rehersed, Breen, that tyme clerc of assise and yet is, warnyd me there of yn the begynnyng of the next Mighelmasse terme next folewyng. Of the which *fiere fac* y haue acopye to schewyn of his owne clerkes writyng and so ye mowe iustly enfourmyn the contre. And y be seche you to labouryn diligently for me atte this tyme for I haue grete nede to your help, and that ye wolen fouche saff to spekyn with Campyon the scheriffes depute of Warwyk schire which dwellith in Warwyk,

that must therefore also belong to the period between St Margaret 1433 and 1434, but in this case the date can be fixed more precisely by the reference to the coming Hilary Term, so it probably belongs to the period between the end of Michaelmas and the beginning of Hilary (25 November 1433 to 20 January 1434).

349 See above, pp.26–7.
350 Hilary Term ended usually some time in February (Cheney, *Handbook of Dates*, p.67).

and praieth hym to be good frend to me, ffor he hath be hight me frenship, but at your request he wol be moche the better willed and pray hym to enquere also yf there be eny tales made be the *distringas*[351] and that he wol fouchesaf to enformyn hem also.

Item vnam aliam de eadem tenura mittitur etc.

Robert Armburgh to John Campion: c. November or December 1433[352]

Armburgh makes a direct approach to Campion, both to discover the identity of any further jurors and to state his case so it can be given to the jurors.

To Campyon [in margin] Dere and welbyloued frend y comand me to you, doyng you to wete how the *distringas* awarded a boute Martynmas, vppon the *scire facias* the which hangith be twene my aduersariez and me in the kynges benche, was not entred the sameday the seid bench brak vppe which was the last day of the perlement. Neuertheles frendes of myne which y have in the-seid bench supposyn verily that hit is ovte. Wherfor y be seche you to enque-ryn yf there be eny tales made, for Hore which is now vnderscherif[353] was Bellers attourne and hath be myn ful enemye in al this matere, and he wol makyn these tales in the most favourable wisse that he kan for myn aduersar-ies, and there for y beseche you if ye mowen hau knowleche therof that ye wol fouche saf to enfourmyn hem and as many as ye mowen spekyn withall of the panell what schall ben here issue and how the *fiere fac* was deliuered the same day the assise was holdyn to Sir William Montfort that tyme scherif, or to his vnderscherif which is oon in effect, and so knoweleched Breen the clerk of assise to me in the begynnyng of Mighelmasse terme next folewyng after the same assise, of the whiche *fiere fac* his clerk wrote the same copy that y

---

351 The writ of *distringas* was the writ of distraint for the summons of jurors and the 'tales' were the *tales de circumstantibus*, that is men present in court who were called to serve on juries when insufficient numbers of jurors named on the panel appeared to serve. By the fifteenth century talesmen could be named on the bottom of the jury panel, and this is what Armburgh is asking that Campion be requested to invesigate. (E.P.)

352 This letter, with the enquiry to Campion on the distraint, which Armburgh asked Sutton to make at the end of the preceding letter, must belong to the same time. The reference to the bench 'brea-king up', at what must be the end of the Michaelmas term, does indeed suggest a similar date. However, the reference to the 'breaking up' coinciding with the last day of of parliament confuses the issue. This must be the parliament of July 1433, prorogued to October of that year: there was no further parliament until October 1435, by which time the *scire facias* was no longer impending but had been heard (see above, p.27). But, although the exact date of the ending of this parlia-ment is not known, it was still in session on 18 December, well beyond the normal ending of the Michaelmas Term, 25 November (*Handbook of Chronology*, p.568; *Handbook of Dates*, p.67).

353 This could be a member of the numerous family of Elmdon, Warwickshire and its various branches, which produced a Robert at about this time. Robert Hore was a filazer (clerk) of King's Bench during the reigns of Richard II, Henry IV and V (*Select Cases in the Court of King's Bench*, ed. G.O. Sayles, vii, Selden Soc., 88 (1971), pp.lxvii, lxix–lxx) (reference from E.P.) and thus a lawyer and could be the man in question. I have not found a reference to any of the Bellers using anyone of that name as attorney in the King's Bench rolls for this period.

schewyd yow withhis [*sic*] owne hand, of the whiche y send you a copy with a copy of the *venire fac* and of the panell be the bringer of this letre, which *fiere fac* ye mowe schewen and yt lyke you to hem that ben enpanellyd, and y be seche you that ye wol fouche saf to labouryn this matere a forn the begynnyng of the terme or ye comyn hedirward, ffor y am sekyr myne aduersariez schullyn hau suche favour in the benche that y schal have to schort a warnyng that there schall no man mowen labouryn abouten to enfourmyn the contre be twene that and the day of the *nisi prius*. And yf ye wolen fouchesaf to labouryn this matere for me atte this tyme, y woll acquyte me to yow in manere and fourme as y made promys to you and there of y wol make you good surete what cost ye doon at this tyme y wol paye yt yow whan ye come to London. And if ye mowe speke with my Maister Montfort or with Sterky y beseche you that ye wol fouche saf to asseyen if ye mowe hau a record of this *fiere fac* vnder here sealys, for my Maister Montfort grauntid me hym self that he wold spekyn vnto Sterky of the same mater. I kan nomore etc.

Robert Armburgh at Westminster to unknown recipients in Essex, probably Sampford: 26 July 1436[354]

They have attacked Armburgh's houses and his servant and prevented his servant distraining on Armburgh's lessee for his rent. Some of the leading men of Thaxted were involved in the assault and they are warned that Armburgh will have them brought to law by means of a recognisance to keep the peace that the town made under Henry IV.

Right dere and welbelouyd frendys I commaunde me to you mervelyng gretly, so many wyse menne as ben a monges you, that, thow hit were so that my lord and yourys[355] prayd you to supporte, stondby and helpe his seruant in his ryght, that ye wolde take vpon you to maynteyne him in his wronge and specially in brekyng of mennys howsys and betyng hem therinne and lettyng my seruantes to streyne my fermour for my owne lyfelode, of the which I am vnpayd therhond for iij quarters of a yere, the which I deere well say was neuer my lordys entent, for, not withstondyng that I have title by the right of my wyfe to alle the hole, I askyd not by fore this tyme nor yit do, but the on halvyndell, for the which halvyndell I may lavfully and wolle streyne on alle

---

354 There is no addressee; on the possible identity of the recipient and the context, see above, p.28. The letter clearly refers to events at Sampford, Essex and is dated 26 July 1436. In terms of the structure of the roll, this is the first appearance of Hand 1, so, as with the first appearance of Hand 3, there seems to be a gap of a year or so during which no entries were made (see above, n.294). The next entry – the last before the love poems or letters – is quite badly out of chronological sequence, which may indicate that there was some catching up, in the form of enrolling a copy of an important letter that had been written in the period when letters were not being enrolled.

355 This may well be the young duke of York (see above, p.28).

the hole in to the tyme hit be lavfully departyd, the which was neuer yit doen, as I enfourmed you whan I was last with you at Sampford. For yf hit hadde be lawfully departyd as I tolde you the same tyme, ye schulde fynde hit of record in the chauncery or in the comyn place, of the which particion ye schull fynde no record in the seyd placys that euer hit was put in execucion, seke ye whan ye leste. And serys, tho that beete my seruant did hit[356] only of here owne hedys but throwht mayntenance and stiryng of summe of the worthyest of the same towne, and that schewed well, for, whan they hadde caryed hym and vnlavfully with ovte ony officer or warant presoned hym in a mane ys hovse of the same towne of Thaxstede[357] there a monges you, summe of the best of the towne came to hym and rebukyd hym and seiden hit was well don that he was so servyd and justifyid well the dede. And therfor beth avysed what ye have don and how your towne was bounde in a grete somme at the exitacion of my lady of Hertford in Kyng Harry is tyme the iiij to kepe the pece,[358] and seth that thys mater be remedyid a yenst my seruant and me and chastise the persones that dide this dede with in your selfe, ye mowe lavfully do hit, and also ye have very knowlech what persones dide hit for hit was opynly doen, or by the trowthe that I owe to God, yf ye wol not do hit nor sese of your mayntenans to hyndre me thus in my lyflode, holdyth me excusyd I schall labour alle the wayes that I can lavfully to hyndre you a yen. And what ye wol do to this mater sendyth me word with in schort tyme for, as sone as I may fynde the chaunceler and the kynges counseill at leyser, in gode feyth I purpose me fully to certefye hem of the bonde and how and in what wyse ye have broke the peece at this tyme and many other tymes, the which I were right lothe to do, for ther be many goode menne and worthy menne within you which I wold be ryght lothe to displese or hyndre with that ye wolle remedye this mater with in your self. I can no more at this tyme but God have you alle in his kepyng. Writin at Westm on Saint Anne day the xiiij yere of Kyng Harry the vj.

---

356 'Not' appears to be omitted here.

357 Thaxted, Essex, owned by the duke of York (see above, p.28).

358 Hertford was part of the barony of Essex, owned by Edmund earl of Stafford who died at the battle of Shrewsbury in 1403, in right of his wife, Anne, daughter of Thomas of Woodstock earl of Gloucester. 'My lady of Hertford' in the time of Henry IV is therefore Anne, probably as a widow (*Complete Peerage*, xii I, pp.180–1; *CIPM*, xviii, p.272). It is possible that the scribe did in fact mistranscribe 'Hereford' as 'Hertford', in which case the person referred to is probably Joan, widow of Humphrey Bohun, earl of Hereford (d.1373), who died in 1419 (*Complete Peerage*, vi, p.474). It is not particularly likely that the undertaking to keep the peace, so long before the inheritance came into question, was related, but it did mean, if the undertaking was couched in general as well as specific terms, as they usually were, and was still in force, that the townsmen could lose the money pledged against their good behaviour.

Robert Armburgh to an unknown recipient in Warwickshire: June or July 1435[359]

There is a new writ for a jury on the damages in Warwickshire and Armburgh seeks the help of the recipient's family and friends, and especially of the sheriff, Thomas Erdington, who is referred to Armburgh's friends in the county who know the details of the affair.

[m.6v] Right dere and welbelouyd frende I commaunde me to you and sende you as ye desiren a bill in the which is rehersid a grete parte of the wronges that myn aduersaryes have doon to me but nouernye all besechyng you whan ye be at Coventre that ye go not oute of Warwyk schyr till ye have spoken with gentilmen of your kynne and of your alliaunce and enfourmyth hem of my matere and schewyth hem this bille besechyng hem that thei wolle be gode maisters and gode frendis to vs in oure right, consideryng that a yong gentil-man[360] the which is kyn to hem schall enherite the seid lyflode after the deces of my wyfe, but I pray you specially or ye go oute of Warwyk schir that ye speke with Erdyngton the squyer that ye tolde me of whan I spake last with you and enfourmyth hym of this matere and schewyth hym this bille and prayith hym that he be gode maister and gode frende to vs, for he is thys yere scheref of Warwyk schire[361] and hit lyeth in hys power for to do vs moste ese at this tyme of any other, for oure aduersaries have oute a new *venire facias* vpon the *scire facias* the which they have a yenst vs in the kyngis benche for the xl li. damagys that they recouered of vs in assise at Warwyk the which was stolen oute a yenst vs, unwetyng the chaunceler or the clerk of the rolles[362] and with oute eny ffyne made therfore, not withstondyng the londe is worthe ix marc a yer, the which is well knowen in Mancestr ther the londe lyeth. The which *venire facias* is retournable at the Octoes of the Trinite terme next

---

359 This is dated by the fact that it was written during the shrievalty of Thomas Erdington, November 1434–5 (see above, p.27) and by the date of the impending legal actions. The case was indeed put before a jury at Warwick by *nisi prius* at the St Margaret assize in July 1435 and so the letter most probably belongs to the period between the start of the Trinity Term (mid-June in 1435), in which the writ was probably issued, since it set a day in the following Michaelmas Term, and 18 July when the *nisi prius* took place (PRO KB27/688 Coram Rege rot.43).

360 This is presumably Joan's eventual heir, John Palmer, but I have had as little success in identifying his Warwickshire kin as in identifying the man himself, unless he came from the Leicestershire/Northamptonshire Palmers, who were connected by marriage with the Catesbys of Warwickshire and Northamptonshire, but there is no indication otherwise that he did so (Acheson, *Leicestershire*, pp.245–6; Carpenter, *Locality and Polity*, pp.97, 117–18; above, pp.31–2).

361 Thomas Erdington of Erdington, Warwickshire, son of a prominent local man, who held several local offices in Warwickshire and Leicestershire, where he also had land, and died, a knight, in 1467 (*HP*, iii, pp.33–4; Acheson, *Leicestershire*, p.228; Wedgwood, *Biographies*, p.302; there is quite a lot about his role in local politics in Carpenter, *Locality and Polity* and see also above, p.27).

362 This version, which exonerates both the chancellor and the clerk of the rolls from deliberate fraud, is a variant from Armburgh's normal assertion of full complicity on the part of the chancery officials (see text above, e.g. pp.63–5, 107–8).

comyng[363] and purposyn hem to have a *nisi prius* ayenst vs at Saynt Margaret
is tyde next folowyng.[364] And therfor prayeth hym that he saye to hys
vnderscheref that oure frendys, that is to say Campyon, Cokkes[365] and Laurens Sutton, mow be prive to the makyng of the panell as well as oure aduersaries and sayth to hym that the same Campyon, Cokkes and Laurens Sutton
kan enfourme hym well i now how and in what wyse the sise was stolen a
yenst vs and how the record of the assise was browth in to the kynges bench
by a writte of errour at oure suyte, and we neuer preve therto, with oute the
which writte of errour this *scire facias* mthere might not have be brought a gayne vs
in the kynges bench, and they kan enfourme hym well i now also how that
oure aduersaryes wolde disherite vs of this lyvelode and of much more
thorow ij bastardys, the which they pretenden to be my wyfys suster children
and come neuer of the blode. And therfore prayeth hym to be gode maister to
vs in oure right and we wolle deserve hit a gayns hym as hit lyeth in oure
power and better.

A sequence of love poems of unknown date

A[366] celuy que pluys ayme de mounde
Of all that I haue founde
Carissima
Salutez ad verray amour
With grace joie and honour
Dulcissima.

Sachez bien plessaunce and bele
That I am in good hele
Laus Christo
Mon amour done vous aye
As youre man nygyh and day
Consisto.

Dishore serray joious and fayne
Yf ge will me in certaigne
Amare
Assech serra ioiouz and lele
Ther were nothing that mygth me
Grauare.

---

363 19 June in 1435.
364 20 July 1435.
365 See above, pp.26–7.
366 This is the one poem of the sequence that is known to exist elsewhere. For references and further
discussion of the whole sequence, see above, pp.58–9.

Mis tresdouce and tresamez
Euer stedfast that ye will be
Suspiro
Soiez parmaneuant and lele
And in youre hert loue me wel
Requiro.

Jeo vous pray en toute manere
Theise wordys that be writyn here
Tenete
Ore a dieu que vous garde
And turne youre hert to me ward
Valete.

He that is youre man
I ensure yow to his laste
Sendyth to yow as he can
A rude letre y writen in haste.

* * *

En Johan roy [*sic*][367] souereigne
My dere loue faire and fre
En fyn amour certeigne
As reson tellyth me
Come a mon coer demesme
Swetyng I grete the
Vnquore duraunce en peyne
But ye my bote be
Care enfoy vous dye
I hold none youre pere
Desore en vous affye
As in my trewe fere
Tresbone tresdoute amy
Myn owen derlyng dere
De vostre loiall vie
Gladly wold I here.

Tresdout creature
Myn hert ys wonder wo
Pur vostre long demour
That is so ferre fro me
Or swetyng lele and pure
Let not oure loue goo

[367] See above, p.58.

Car certeigne and sure
I loue yow and no mo.

Si ieo le ose dire
That a gayn skyll
Que chast coer desire
But ye hyt fulfill
De vous quant ieo remembre
As faire as flour on hill
Souent face supprie
I sighe and morne ful still
Ne poit estre a taunt
As I wol wyth rigth
Mais Johan tout puissant
Yf yow me sene a sygth
A luy ieo vous comaunde
As he is most of mygth
Quil vous soit ardaunt
To loue hym day and nygth.

    * * *

Goodlyest[368] of all as semeth me
In myn hert
And of all other born also the gentilest most womanly
Yow ye do me smert
And to euer haue be the frendliest
Sethyn the first tyme of youre goodnesse
That yow lyst to youre seruice yeue hardynesse
To a teyne
Of my prayer haue tendyrnesse
And not disdeigne
Besechyng yow of youre goodnesse and benygnite
Myn hertys ioie and yerthely goodnesse
Of youre bontevous grace and mercyfull pete
Benyngly to helpe and redresse
And thow it so be that I can not wele expresse
The feerefull thougthis wiche I fele in myn hert
Haue ye not the lesse mercy of me smert.
On is that I dare not come in youre sigth
Til it plese yow asigne me a tyme of youre plesaunce

---

[368] In the next three poems/letters, the lines are uneven and there seems to be a certain amount of movement between verse and prose.

No withstondyng youre presence makyth me glad and lyth
To all myn heuynesse is souerain alligeance.
Wherfore sythin in youre seruice I
Contynue and schall with outyn variaunce
As ye me brougth in to maledy
Now beth gracious and schapyth remedy
Conseyuyng full that I nothyng desire
But fully yow to serue feythfully
To my lyues ende
With outyn change souerainly yow chere
And I yow ensure whil I haue lyef and mende
And ye luste now suche grace me sende
Of my seruice nougth disdeigne
Sithen yow to serue I may not in no wyse me refrayne
And sithyn hope hath yeue me hardinesse
To loue yow best and neuer to repent
While that I leue.
Withall my besynesse
To drede and serue
My will is holy ment
And here vp on God knowyth myn entent
Now I haue fully vowyd in my mynde
Souerainly yow to serue thow I no mercy fynde
But this is the effect of my preyere finall
Of you benyngne mercy grace for to fynde
For hert, body, lust, lyf and all
With all my reson and my full mynde
And my v wittys of on assent I binde
To youre seruice withowtyn ony stryfe
To make yow princesse of my deth and lyf
For lak of speche I can now say no more
To expresse my mater as I wolde I may not playnly [*sic*]
My wytte is dulle to telle half my sore
And nougth I haue yit for all my payne
For want of wordys I may not now atteygne
To telle half myn hertes hevynesse
Til it plese yow schewe me sume gladnesse.
By youre own suget and seruant and euere more wil be
Wyth all lowlynesse yow to serue
Humblement magre.

* * *

O princesse of womanhode enkyinnyd with all beaute
Youre excellence is fully replete with humilite
Youre gentilnesse passyth all other in dignite
Youre nobles[369] enncrowynd is with all benyngnite
I am youre seruant and suget with all obeisaunce
Wilfull to fulfille youre hertis plesaunce
Yow to comende in special remembrance
Is my trew entent with oute variaunce
Ye be lady of ladyes, ye floure of gentilnesse
Ye be sonne souerne of beaute, ye enlymyn all derkenesse
Ye be princesse gracious of all nobilnesse
Ye surmount all creaturs in worthinesse
Ye be welle of grace, the spring of goodnesse
Ye be medicine and cure, helere of all sekenesse
Ye be comfort and solas of all heuynesse
The beginner and causer of all gladnesse
Ye be fairest of fairer, ye be penacle of fairnesse
Ye be that ymage in whom is figurid all stedfastnesse
Ye be habundaunt in vertu and all mekenesse
Ye be graunter of grace and gracious of forgeuenesse
Ye be securable and fauorable in all distresse
Ye be loser and lisser of all duresse
Ye be reconsiler of all unbuxomnesse[370]
Ye be my lady rith full of erthly goodnesse.
This bref commendacion of my lady soueraigne haue I made with hert
    pensiff and payne
Besechyng yow that ye audience therof not disdeigne
But consider the trew entent of my hert in euery veyne.
Honour, estate, joie and reuerence
Encres of loue, vertu in dignite
Rychesse, wysdom, grace, hele and prudence
Preysyng, gladnesse, rest and prosperite
Rygth good newyere with all felicite
Be to yow with all myn hert yovyn.
As yow best list euer wele ye levyn.
By your seruant and sugett and euer more will be.

* * *

---

369 I.e. noblesse.
370 Meaning 'intractability', 'lack of compliancy'. I must thank Professor Helen Cooper for her help
   in reading this word.

To yow that be my soueraigne and maistresse, I recommonde me wyth all
    myn hert and spirit, with on assent euer to love yow best with all my
    besinesse be my trougth my will holy ment.
And here vp on God knowyth myn entent
How I haue fully vouyd in my mende
To love yow best and neuer to repent
Suffre me nougth I beseche yowr gentilnesse
From youre presence be leng absent
But certifieth me of youre benyngne hert, gracious and patient
A tyme of youre plesaunce
To your presence whan I may atteign
Sithyn yow to serue I may nougth ne will me refreine
Besechyng God that honour, joie and reuerence
Encres of love, vertu in dignite
Richesse, wysdom, grace, hele and prudence
Preisyng, gladnesse, rest and prosperite
Rigth good newe yere wyth all felicite
Be to yow my lady with all myn hert yovyn
As yow best list euer whill ye levyn.
More write I not at this tyme but humbly I yow pray for hys love that vs
    bothe dere hath bougth
What my sonne haue seid or in ony wyse schul say
Myn owyn lady and sister[371] displese yow nougth
But sechith wele the treuthe yf ony faut be sougth
Yf I be as I was and youre seruant perpose euer to be
Thow no mercy fynde humblement magre.
Escrit de parte le vostre amy que vous ayme tant come luy.

       * * *

Aele que ayme sur tout rien
Of all tho that in this world beene
Corde meo durefixa
Enterement me commaunde de quere
As ye that ben to me most chere
Intra mundi climata
Ma tredouce and treschere
Of youre estate I wold fayn here
Corde delectabilia
and ie fi fame de corps
and euere yif it lyke yow therof to here

---

371 See comment on p.59.

Sit deo laus altissimo
A vous ay done mon amour
As your seruant in leall labour
Hoc corde et animo
Je fy tout vostre corps et bien
Yow to serue ouer alle that bene
Stringor amoris vinculo
Souent en vous ay faux pecche
Founde gret love that causyth me
Vos preminente[372] amare
Par ce que vostre tresdouce chere
Hath causyd love be twene vs clere
Non permittatis sessare
Gare vostre amour me prent si dure
That frein myn hert I yow ensure
Mors debet eradicare
Plus a present ne fay que dyre
But salue yow wyth hert pure
Ter vicibus quingentis
Et mon kere en loial amour
Yow sende grace ioie and honour
Vurtututi [sic] que incrementis
Sancte lees prosperite
Be to yow wyth all felicite
Cum plenitudine mentis
Et Jhesu li tout pusaunt justice
That all schal deme wyth out quest or sise
In maiestis solio
Hors de dette and male vous garde
And from all dedly synne yow warde
De demonis imperio
Et emsy vou dome ly seruere
That ye mow come to hys empiere
Qui sedet in triclinio.

* * *

Goodliest of all creatures
That beryth lyf in this world so brode
Gentillest faucone that comyth to lure
Welle of vertu spryng of womanhode

---

372 This abbreviated word has not been securely identified; it could also be 'preeminente', 'perm-
inente' or 'perennie'. I must again thank Professor Helen Cooper for her assistance.

B [*sic*] of refute to all manhode
Mesure to wedowe, mayden and wyf
Flour of all that euer man bode
Princesse of my deth and lyf
To yow that be my soueraigne blis
And all my ful hertes plesaunce
My care is leche, my sore is lysse
And my paynes alegaunce
My right wis ioie and [**m.5v**] my worldly goodnesse
Myn hele and lyues sustinance
Wyth hert and all that in me is
I comaunde wyth obeisaunce
Desiryng with all godlyhode
As your humill and trewe seruant
Wyth hert, wyth will, wyth thought and dede
Al thyng that myght be yow plesaunt
And pray to God that he yow graunt
Good hele, blisse and prosperitee
And from the infernall tyraunt yow kepe and all aduersitee
Sithe hope hath youe me hardynesse
For to discuuere myn hertes peyne
To yow in triste of summe reles
I wol it serche in euery peyne
Youe haue causyd, ryght strong cheyne
Surely fastnede to myn hert rote
To love yow best it wol me streyne
Whether it so be my bale or bote
In yow it lyth as in balaunce
Whether yow list my blisse or peyn
Myn hert is your without ony variaunce
The cheyne is feste on euery veyne
Yf ne may your love atteygne
I cast my self in peynes smert
To goddes of love I may complayne
With spere of love ye perysshe myn hert
It mevyth me oft handys to wryng
The godly loke of youre eyne twyne
And syk full sadde whan other syng
My lyf may not endure this peyne
For as a tassel ye me streyne
Suyn to the hert wyth loue talon
In loue presone I may not reigne
Deth wol smert will my rawnsumme
I wold thei were writen in youre syght

The forefull thoughtys of myn hert
And suche pyte were in yow pyght
That wold a suage my peynes smert
For greuously in to the hert
With love arwes ye thrylle my syde
Now ye that be in love expert
Takyth cure and hele my woundys wyde
I dar not come be fore your face
For to compleyne myn hertes greuance
Til it lyke yow of special grace
To assigne me a tyme of youre plesaunce
Of my lagoure [*sic*] haue remembraunce
Sygth ye me brought in maladie
Beth my sorwys allegeaunce and graciously schape remedye
More of my peyne I wold discuure
But ye beth so empressyd in my mynde
That my v wyttes I yow ensure
Beth summe what distratt out of here kynde
So that to yow my lady ende
I can not half my fore expresse
Til it like yow of grace me sende
Summe mark tokyn of gladnesse.
I pray God that grace, helth and prudence
Encres of vertu and dignite
Honour, joie and reuerence
With all maner felicite
Preysyng, gladnesse, prosperite
Encres of love, wysdome and rychesse
Rest, quiete and equite
    and all goodnesse
He graunt yow and so the vengnisse
And his furiouce felonie
With hys malyce and hys anguis
And all his tortuouse tyranny
That yt mow be to hym an noye
Honour to God, glorie and preysyng and blysse to yow perpetuelly aftyr
    youre [breaks off *sic*]

       * * *

Goodlyest of creatures
Fully replete with humilite
Gentel as faucon that comyth to lure
Enncrounyd with benyngnite

O princesse of womanhode enlymnyd with all beute
Rote of refute to all manhode
Enpressyd with perdurable pyte
Welle of vertu, spryng of goodnesse
Excellyng all other in bounte
Flour and figure of stedfestnesse
Habundant in grace and equite
To yow that be my soueraigne blisse
Begynner and causer of my gladnesse
My cares leche
My sorwys lysse and cure
Helere of my seknesse
My ryghtwos joie
Myn hertes plesaunce
Reconnciler of all myn heuynesse
My goodly lyues sustinaunce
Loser and lysser of duresse
Relever of all my peynes smert
And full erthly goodnesse
Enteerly wyth all myn hole hert
I comaunde in all maner humbesse [*sic*]
Desyryng as youre humble seruant
Effectualy with hert to here
All thyng that myght be to yow plesaunt
And comfort, solas, gladnesse or chire
Gode hele, blysse and prosperite
Pray God yow graunt of hys emprere
And kepe yow from all aduersite
And from tortuose serpentes power
Thankyng with humble hert of your graciouse and goodly answere
Not withstondyng that wounder smert
It perysshyth myn thorwe as a spere
With syghyng sad and mornyng stille
With hevy chere, with outyn reste
For love in poynt my self to spille
As man that knowyth not what hym is best
For love I dye but ye take cure
With outyn juge, dome or queste
Of feyth and trought I yow ensure
Were neuer hope my hert wold breste
Now princesse gracious of womanhode
As ye that of pyte ben rote and rynde
Let on me your mercy spryng and sprede
And out of all bytter bales me vnbynde

This is the entent of my request small
That of grace suche gladnesse ye wold me sende
That I myght onys yow see and speke wyth al
Or love me bryng to sorwfull ende
For God knowyth al myn entent
How I haue fully vowyd in my mynde to love yow best and neuer to repente
Thowe I neuer grace ne mercy fynde
I pray God that grace, helthe and prudence etc.

As for an answere whan I had notyse
Althowgh it were womanly and onest
Downe to my hert as cold as yse
Yt thyrlyd even thorwghout my brest.

    * * *

To yow that be my souerain blysse
Bygynner and causer of my gladnesse
My cares leche, my sores lesse and cure
Heler of my seknesse
My rigthwus joie, myn hertys plesaunce
Recounceler of all myn heuynesse
My goodly lyves sustenaunce
Loser and lysser of my duresse
Releser of all my peynes smerte
And my full erthly goddesse
Enterly with all myn hole hert
Here I comaunde me with all maner humblesse
Desiryng with all the besynesse
Of hert effectuely to here all thyng
That myght do yow gladnesse
Comfort, solas, plesaunce or chere
Thankyng yow wyth all lowlynesse
Myn owne souerain lady dere
Of youre bountuouse goodnesse
And wele noble vndeserued chere
I bynde me holly to youre seruice
Hert, body, strength wyth will and lust in fere
I may me in no maner wyse refreyne
I am youre man with all my full power
For I know myght be youre pore of whomanhode
Semyng to me ye ben so gentill, so goodly of chere
Ye be replet with humilite
Ye be wele womanly of countenance
Ye be souerain of all beaute

Ye be the rote of all plesaunce
Ye be full benyngnite
Ye be welle of vertu spryng of goodnesse
Ye excellyn all other in bounte
Ye be flour of stedfastnesse
Ye habounden in grace and equite.

Now glad myght he and lusty be
That of youre love myght haue plesaunce
None erthly good I say for me
Myght in this world me so auaunce
For thowgh I were wounded to the hert
Yt wold relese all my greuance
And of all my peynes smert
It were souerain allegaunce.
Myn owen lady of gentilesse
Lat me not lyve in desperaunce
But lat pete youre hert in presse
And beth my lyves sustenaunce.

For in yow lyth as in balaunce
Whether yow lyst my blisse or peyne
I put me holly in youre gouernaunce
Ye be my lady and my souerain
Whether it me ese or do greuaunce
Love hath me bounde fast in his cheyne
My hert is your wyth out variaunce
I may yt in no wyse refreyne
In byttyr balys I am y bounde
Yf I ne may your atteyne
With swerde of love for ye me wounde
To the goddesse of love I may complayne.

Oft myn hert enduryth peyne
Whan I thenke on your fresly face
For as a tarsell ye me strayne
With love talon myn hert ye trice
Whan all other ben mary and glade
Harpyn, daunce and make solace
For yow I morne and syghe wel sadde
Whan other syng I say alas
Thus love me bynt in hys presone
Fro thens to scape ther is no place

Till deth wele smert wol me ransumme.
Myn owen lady where is your grace?

I wold thei were wryten by fore your face
The noyous thoughtes of myn hert
And in yow were roted such grace
That wold asuage my peynes smert
For greuously ye makyn englyde
The dartes of love thorwghout myn hert
Wyth pyte hele my woundys wyde.
Now ye that be in love expert
So faste love bynt I most abyde
Thowe I were wyld as is an herte
Love hath yow made so syker a gyde
That from the deth I may not stert.

Now wold God that y of your hert
Pete had ye gouernaunce
And of all my paynes smert
Ye had a special remembraunce
Or ellys ye of youre special grace
Had fyned me a tyme of youre pleasuance
That I mygth come before your face
For to complayne my hertes greuaunce.
Now ye that ben cause of my maladye
Puttyth me in summe maner wey of esperaunce
And graciously schapyth remedy
Of my sorwys allegeans.

More I wold of my greuaunce
And of my ~~so~~ sore to yow expressen
But I haue yt not in remembraunce
Half for all my besynesse
So fast ye haue myn hert in hold
And surly ye yt possesse
~~And that ye myght~~ that ye me bynde
In cavys cold and my v wyttys fore ye oppresse
So that I may neuer have full mynde
To complayne half myn heuynesse
Til ye lyke yow of grace me sende
Summe maner token of gladnesse.

I pray God yow graunt of hys goodnesse
Good lyf, blysse and prosperite

Encres of love, wysdome amd rychesse
Wyth reste, quiete and equite
Preysyng, gladnesse, grace, hele and prudence
Encres of vertu and dignite
Onure, estat, ioye, reuerence
With all manere of felycite
And so yow gouerne he graunt yow grace
A monges thys wordly [*sic*] aduersyte
In heven that ye mow se hys face
There he sitt in hys mageste.

[Here there is a gap and the roll is thereafter written from the other end.]

Robert Armburgh to an unknown farmer: perhaps late 1440s or early 1450s[373]

Another letter which, despite the lacunae, is obviously demanding money from a lessee.

[m.1v] [margination illegible] Right dere and welbelouyd frende I comaunde me to you, and for . . . [?]worschipful . . . cosyn and I . . . withinne schal . . . to com [?]after retournyng I pray you yevyth credens to Will[iam] [Lento]n brynger of this letter . . . me . . . writen what day and what terme the seid Reygnold[374] receyvyd of [?]you [?]shewyng . . . vs . . . by twen . . . me [?]word ye were last at Westm that ye hadde founde a bille therof for with oute that [?]thei wolle knowlech that he hath resceyvyd hit ye most pay the . . . marc but yf ye [?]canne the beter excuse you [?]therof and I pray you [?]consideryth the greet avayll that ye toke while ye hadde my lyflode to ferme and sendith me somme money, for ye wote well there is . . . be hynde without the iiij marc and I have greet nede of money. I can no more at thys tyme but God [?]kepe you etc.

---

373 The recipient is evidently a previous farmer of some part of Armburgh's land. There is no reason to doubt that the letter belongs to the same period as the others in the sequence.
374 This must be Reynold, Robert's nephew (see above, n.144).

Robert Armburgh to Thomas Bedell of London: perhaps late 1440s or early 1450s[375]

Another threatening letter, this time promising legal action, to a debtor, who is revealed as a former lessee of part of the Armburgh estate.

To Thos Bedell [in margin] Dere and welbelouyd frende I grete you well. It is not vnknowen to you how ye sent Phillip Baron[376] to me [?]anon after John Ffowler[377] was rede to rekynne with me for money that the seid John owght me, by the which rekenyng . . . that he ought me xij li. and odde money, of the which summe with inne a while after ye cam youre selfe to Westm and payd me x li.[378] and toke dayes of the remenant tille Cristemasse after and fro Cristemasse after and fro Cristemasse to Candelmasse[379] and fro thens tille Ester and diuers dayes after and [?]ouer. Wherfore I swed an accion of dette a yenst you and Phillip Baron and hadde you at *exigent* and not withstondyng the scheref of Midd hadde gode golde of you, I myght have hadde you outlawed and I had wolde, and therfore, I counseyll you, ordeyneth therfor that I be payed of my money for I have oute a newe *exigent* a yenst you, and for asmoch as ye promysed me of ffeyth and trowth that I shulde have be payed at diuers dayes a forerehersyd and was not, I schall swe you in my lordys audience of Caunterbury.[380] And, gete you all the frendschip that ye can, thowe ye wolde spende theron xx li., ye schall paye me my money, euery peny, with costys and damagys, for your neyghbours seyn that ye resceyvyd xxx li. of John Ffowler ys dette with inne a while after hys deth, with oute that ye have resceyvyd sethyn, and also ye knowlechyd to me your self that hys bernys were ful of corne that same tyme that ye were with me. Wherfor I counseile you the same tyme that ye schulde gete a sequestracion of my lord of London and have sequestryd the seid cornys tille the dettys hadde be payed.[381]

---

375 There was a Thomas Bedell citizen and coppersmith of London, active between 1425 and 1441, who could be the same man who had a corrody in Daventry priory at the king's request in 1448 and was still alive in 1459 (*Cal. Close Rolls 1435–41*, p.477, *1447–54*, p.57, *1454–61*, p.352; *Calendar of London Letter Books*: Letter Book K, pp.43, 172). The recipient of the letter was clearly a former farmer, presumably of some part of the Armburgh property, but probably not of Mancetter, since we seem to have the full sequence of farmers there i.e. Harpour and Barbour, then Draper, then a gap, then Barbour etc. (above, pp.34–5, 68, 71). The letter cannot be dated. It may belong to the late 1440s or early 1450s, the date of most of the rest of this part of the roll, but it and the next two could be from an earlier period (see n.383, below).

376 Not identified; presumably a servant or agent of Bedell.

377 Not identified. He may have held the farm jointly with Bedell.

378 The sum is obscured but this is probably correct.

379 2 February.

380 Bedell is Fowler's executor and therefore responsible for his debts. He may be sued for these in the archbishop's court because of the archbishop's prerogative powers over certain wills (see above, n.47).

381 This is again a matter of debt. Church courts were used frequently at this time for pleas of debt, especially small debts, of all sorts. The ordering of sequestration of assets from bankrupt estates during the course of probate has been termed 'routine' in this period. The letter shows that the debt was contracted in Middlesex and therefore within the jurisdiction of the bishop of London,

Forthermore ye fette oute of my place asmoch chese and corne as drew the
walu of xij li. after my seruant hadde arestyd hit and after that ye hadde left
my ferme. Whefor I may have an accion of trespas a yenst you or do you
endyte whether me lyste. I counseill you trist not to moche to my curtesye, for
ye have yeve me no cause. I can no more at thys tyme etc.

Robert Armburgh to William Warlyng: perhaps late 1440s or early 1450s[382]

A more friendly communication with a lessee concerning arrears owed to Armburgh.

To William Warlyng [in margin] Dere and welbelouyd frende I commaunde
me to me [*sic*] and astochyng the money that ys by hynde of Ester terme, I
pray you sende it to me by Thomas Max brynger of thys letter and thys my
writyng schall be youre discharge. No more to you at thys tyme etc.

Robert Armburgh at Westminster to Richard Power of Warwickshire: 28 July, year unknown[383]

A threatening letter to the farmer of the Sumpter half of Mancetter manor, concerning the waste in the woods at Mancetter which was exercising Armburgh earlier in the document (above, p.89).

To Ric Power [in margin] Dere frende I grete you well, doyng you to wete
that I have an accion of dette a yenst you and have you at *exigent* and myght
have outlawed you many a day goon and I hadde wolde, of the which I have
sent you warnyng diuers tymes by my seruantes and diuers other. Fforthermore I may have an accion of trespasse or an accion of stryppe and wast or do
you endyten for the greet wast that ye dede on my wodys while ye were my
fermour, it schewyth well that ye dede greet wast, for my Lord Gray[384] hadde
you bounde to hym in an obligacion of xx li. for the wast that ye dede in hys

who would be asked for a sequestration to enforce payment (R.H. Helmholz, '*Assumpsit* and *Fidei Laesio*', *Canon Law and the Law of England* (London, 1987), pp.263–89, and 'Bankruptcy and Probate Jurisdiction before 1571', *ibid.*, p.295; Swanson, *Church and Society*, p.145).

382 The address is difficult to read and the recipient could be 'Wirlyng', who seems to be another uni-dentified lessee of Armburgh property.

383 See above, p.89. Power was in fact the farmer of the Sumpter part of Mancetter earlier, probably in the 1420s, but had been accused by Armburgh of waste in his woods. As Power's involvement with Armburgh antedates all the other dateable occurrences in this part of the roll, it is possible that this letter is earlier than the others which follow it, and it may be that this opening group of three letters on the dorse of the later part of the roll were copies of ones which had been written a lot earlier (see above, p.57 and n.).

384 Either Reginald Grey of Ruthin or his grandson and successor, Edmund Lord Grey of Ruthin (see refs. above in n.78 to Intro.).

parc[385] and these accions mow be swed in Midd, there the contratte was made, as in Warwyk schire, there the dede was don. And therfor I counseill you to come . . . in schort tyme. Ffor astochyng the accion of dette, I purpose me to have oute a newe *exigent* at thys Mighelmasse terme and if ye wolle come trete with me, ye schull safe come and safe goo. And yf ye wolle not, trust not to my curtesye for I wolle take the avantage that law wolle yeve me. Writyn at Westmynster the xxviij day of July.

Robert Armburgh at Westminster to Clement Draper of Atherstone, Warwickshire: 27 April [1449][386]

The letter demands full payment of the rent for the lease of Armburgh's part of Mancetter for the period up to Michaelmas 1448 and also accuses Draper of cheating Armburgh's cousin and servant, John Armburgh, in the sale of a horse and taking wood which had not been agreed in the contract between Armburgh and Draper.

To Clement Draper [in margin] Dere and welbelouyed frende I commaunde me to you. Hit is not vnknowen to you that ther was made a rekenyng by twyxt you and me at Westm the xiij day of July the xxiiij yere of Kyng Harry the vj,[387] beyng present that same tyme Reygnold Armeburgh and other certeyn persones, by the which rekenyng hit was founde, all thyngys alowed, ye owght me xiij marc v s., and after that rekenyng ye occupyed the fferme, that is to say my part of the thrydde part of the manere of Mancestr, v termes, that is to say Mighelmasse terme, Saint Mary terme and midsomer terme in the xxv yere of Kyng [*sic*] the vj and Mighelmasse terme and Saint Mary terme in the xxvj yere of the same kyng, ye which v termes drawyn to the summe of xv marc.[388] The summe of both, that is to say of debet and of the v termes, drawyn to the summe of xxviij marc v s. Of the which summe ye have payd to Reygnold Armeburgh as he hath made rekenyng to me these parcelles that folowen: the xxj day of December the xxv yere of Kyng Harry the vj,[389] xl s. The x daye of Februarii the xxvj yere of the same kyng[390] by the handes of

---

[385] This could equally well be 'part', except that the entry clearly refers to Mancetter and Grey was lord of the whole of the manor, not just part of it, while 'park' would indicate a park belonging to Grey, who had lands from his Astley wife (see above, p.14), in the vicinity of Mancetter. I have not been able to find an actual park on his property here at this time, but he had free warren at Weddington and there were enclosed pastures at Bentley (a property named 'Bentley Park'), both places lying in this part of Warwickshire, and it is not impossible that he had some sort of enclosure at Mancetter as well (Dugdale, *Warwickshire*, p.120; *VCH Warks.*, iv, pp.211–12).

[386] See above, p.34. Following the sequence of dates of payment given in the letter, it may well have been written on 27 April 1449 (see end of letter for the day and month).

[387] 1446.

[388] These terms are Michaelmas 1446, Saint Mary, midsummer and Michaelmas 1447 and Saint Mary 1448.

[389] 1446.

[390] 1448.

Thomas Perkyn at Cumecestre,[391] iiij li. On Holy Rode Day at Sterebryggefayr[392] by the handes of a strangeman the xxvij yere of the same kyng,[393] xx s.
The Tewesday next after the fest of Saint Andrew the same yere[394] a hors pretii
of xlvj s. viij d. And in money the same day xl s. The summe of these parcelles
draweth to xvij marc. So that all thyng rekenyd ye owe me clerely xj marc v s.
with oute that ye can preve that ye payed Reygnold the iiij marc which he
saith that he resceyved not. And therfore I have greet mervayll, so as ye have
take greet profyte of the ferme, that ye have made so evyl payment, for ye
wote well of the first that I resceyvyd of you I reward you xiij s. iiij d. And
afterward ye by gylyd a seruant of myn John Armeburgh my cosyn[395] and
solde hym a gray hors with ij newe fete for xl s., the which hors with inne half
a yere after, as the said John came rydyng to you ward, streenyd hys legge, so
that he left the hors with you and bought a nother. And ther as ye myght have
solde the hors for ij marc as your neyghbours canne reporte, ye wolde not but
ye put the hors to labour in your plowe and in youre carte to Sterebryggefayr
and to other fayres and markettes tille ye hadde stroyd the hors, not withstondyng this, ye withdrew xx s. of my ferme for the hors costes and forthermore,
there as by your endentur ye schulde have solde none of my wode but in one
place, and that schulde have be in ij first yerys, ye have solde the said wode
ouer and ouer in your last yere and ye have take for wode that ye solde, in on
place ix marc, in a nother place iiij marc and the iij place iij marc, which
draweth to the summe of xvj marc. Also ye kepe a parcelle of my londe in
your honde for the which other menne wolde yeve yerely xvj s. more than ye
do, and so it was lette by fore that ye hadde hit. Wherfor I wolle that ye occupye hit no lenger but I pray you to geve credens to William Leynton brynger
of thys letter and paye hym alle my money that is dewe, and astochyng the iiij
marc that is in bate by twyxt Reignold and you, sende me worde by writyng
vnder your seale whether ye have payed hit or no. And pay no money here
afterward to no man but he bryng my letter and my seale, but yf ye bryng hit
or sende hit your selfe. Wrytyn at Westm the xxvij day of Aprill.

---

391 This is Godmanchester, Hunts., a town in the neighbourhood of places associated with Robert's
brother, William (*The Place-Names of Bedfordshire and Huntingdonshire*, edd. A. Mawer and F.M.
Stenton (English Place-Name Soc., 3, 1926), p.256; above, pp.6–7). Indeed a William Armburgh
of 'Gurmecestr', Hunts. husbandman was indicted in 1429 and this may well be Robert's brother
(PRO KB9/224/59).
392 Stourbridge Fair, Cambridge.
393 Stourbridge Fair ran from St Bartholomew's day (24 August) to Michaelmas day (*VCH Cambs.*, ii
(London, 1948), pp.87–8). Accordingly, the Holy Rood Day must be September rather than May
and so the date is 14 September 1448.
394 3 December 1448.
395 This could be his brother John (see above, p.128): 'cousin' for close relatives is not unknown.
Otherwise he is probably most likely to be a son of William and therefore (probably) brother of
Reynold (see above, pp.31, 49–50 and below, p.186).

Robert Armburgh to Sir Philip Thornbury of Hertfordshire: probably 1450[396]

Thornbury is addressed as a feoffee to Joan Armburgh's will. He is informed of the Chancys' entry into the Brokholes lands in Hertforshire and Essex (see next letter) and that Armburgh has taken legal action in the name of all the feoffees and is told of Armburgh's difficulties with some of the feoffees in selling part of his wife's estate and asked to help by making a release of these lands to Armburgh.

To Sir Philip Thornbury [in margin] Worschipfull sir I commaunde me to you, certefying you that certeyn persones have entryd vpon me with force and disseisyd me of the moteis of the maneres of Brokholes other called Rooshall in Radewynhter, of Gyffardes other wyse called Stanle in Moche Sampford and Litell Sampford in the schyre of Essex and of Ouerhall in Gedelston in the schyre of Hertf, wher thei nor non of theire aunceters hadde neyther title nor right, as I may schewe by myn evydens. Wherfore I swe a writte of forcible entre vpon the statute *de anno octavo*[397] in your name and in alle theire names that ben enfeffyd with me in the seid moteis[398] a yenst the seid dissesours, prayng you yf ony persone desire you to disawowe the seid sute, that ye do it not, but that ye foche safe to a wowe the seid sute or ell I leese all the costes that I do and the seyd moteys also. Fforthermore, wher as my wyfe devysed by her last wille[399] that all the fee symple londes that sche dyed seised of schulde ben solde, and devysed by the same wille that I schulde have tho seyd londes beter chepe than eny other man by c marc and made me her executour, the which is of record, and charged me with the execucion of her testament and last wille and that I schulde dyspose the money comyng of the seid lyflode for her soule, her husbondis soulys, her aunceters soulys, her frendis soulys and for all Cristin soulys, summe of my cofeffes desiren to bye the seid londes and proferen not the thryd peny that thei ben worth and summe desiren and specially myn owne cosyn[400] that I schulde yeve hym hym [*sic*] the right and title that I haue in the said fee simple londes, and at hys request a juge of this londe spake to me for the same cause and, for asmoch as I wolde not graunte these thynges, they ben evil willed to me. And therfore I pray you, if my cofeffes or eny other labour to you for eny releese, releese ye to hem in no manere wyse, for I see by their labour that, if my wyfe is last wille be not perfourmed in my

---

396 For Thornbury, see above, p.30. For the circumstances described in the letter, see above, pp.36–8. These entries occurred in 1448/9–50 (see below, pp.174–5) and the letter probably dates from 1450. I have not been able to find a Plea Roll entry, in either King's Bench or Common Pleas, which would provide a more precise dating.

397 This refers to the Statute of Forcible Entry of 8 Henry VI c.9 (*Statutes of the Realm*, ii (London, 1816, rpt., 1963), pp.244–6). (E.P.)

398 See above, p.30.

399 Joan died in 1443 (see above, p.30).

400 Reynold (see above, pp.30, 36).

tyme, hit schall be neuer perfourmed, and I may not perfourme the seid wille
with your releese so as all the fee simple londe of my wyfe ys enheritaunce is
take fro me, for ther wolle no man bye the reuersion of the seid londes but yf
he be a grete man. And yit wolle he whan he seyth by the fyne that many be
enfeffyd with me be lothe to medle with all, and therfore yf ye be in wille that
my wyfe is last wille schall be perfourmed I most praie you to seale a releese
and yf ye wolle not I trust to God I am discharged in my consience of the perfourme of the seid wille.

Robert Armburgh at Westminster to Clement Spicer of Essex: 22 April 1450[401]

*As one of the residuary heirs to the Brokholes property, Spicer is asked to help
resist the claims of the Chancys to the lands in Hertfordshire and Essex which
they have entered. In particular, he is asked to request his lord, the duke of Buckingham, to persuade the duke of Exeter, the Chancys' lord, to allow Armburgh to
show the two dukes his evidence.*

To Clement Spyso [in margin] Worschipful sir I commaunde me to you. Hit
is not vnknowen to you how I tolde you that John Chancy the yonger[402] a
squyer of my lordis of Excestr[403] entryd more than a yere a go[404] in to the
manere of Stanle other wyse called Gyffardes in the towne of Sampford
withinne the schyre of Essex which is a parcelle of the Roos enheritaunce and
a part of the lyflode that ye and your parceners schull enherite, and also John
Chancy the elder his brother[405] a non after ye were to go to the parlement a
Fryday next a fore the makyng of this letter,[406] entryd in to the manere of
Ouerhall in Gedeliston with inne the schyre of Hertf which is a nother parcelle of the Roos enheritaunce and a part that ye and youre parceners schull
enherite also,[407] and hurlyth fowle the tenantys and strayneth hem and dry-
veth a way theyr bestis and sette a court and compellyth the tenantys to
retourne to hym and specially my fermour and drove a way xij keene and a
bole of hys and wolde not suffre hym to come nye no gode that he hadde in
the said manere wherof he myght make money to paie me my ferme. And

---

401 Clement Spicer was one of the right heirs to the lands (see above, p.37, and below, p.177). The
letter is dated 22 April (below) and the reference to parliament shows that it belongs to 1450.
402 John Chancy of Gedelston, Hertfordshire (see above, p.37).
403 Henry Holland duke of Exeter 1447–61 (*Complete Peerage*, v, pp.212–15; see above, p.37).
404 I.e. probably late 1448 or early 1449.
405 See above, p.37.
406 Spicer was an MP for Essex in the parliament of 1449–50 which was prorogued to 29 April 1450
at Leicester. This fits with the date of 17 April (Friday before this letter was written) for the entry
on Gedelston, coinciding with Spicer's departure for Leicester (Wedgwood, *Biographies*, p.788;
Handbook of Chronology, p.569).
407 See below, p.177.

forthermore, for asmoch as he knowyth well that all my wyfe is eyrs be dede[408] that ye nor non of your parceners make no clayme in the said lyflode, I am enfourmed that he purposyth hym to fayne a fals title and to entre in to the manere of Rooshall in Radewynter withinne the schyre of Essex which lyeth by the manere of Stanle, other wyse called Gyffardes a bovesaid and in to alle other partes of the Roos enheritaunce where euer he may fynde hem. And thus he schall hurle the tenantys and strayne hem and dryve hem of the grovnde, which schall turne you and your parceners and me to grete hurte many yerys after. And therfore I pray you to speke to my lord of Bokyngham which is your gode lord[409] and prayith hym to speke with my lord of Excestr and pray hym that he wolde charge bothe Chancys, which be his menne, that they lete of her handys and suffre oure fermours and tenantys sitte in peese and that they make none soche wronge entryis and that he sothe safe to charge hem also to bryng here evydences whan my lord[410] and yourys and my lord of Excestr come next to Westm by fore hem and here counseyll, and I schall bryng soche evydences as I have for your title and myne by fore hem also and grauntith hardely my lord and yourys and my lord of Excestr that who can schewe best evydences reiose the said lyflode, for I trust to Godde that I schall schewe soche evydences that they and their counseill schull well feele that neyther of the Chancys nor non of theyr antecessours hadde neuer title of right to eny parcelle of the Roos enheritaunce, which evydences I schewed to my lordys counseill of Excestr that last was, my lord ys ffader that now is[411] by hys owne comaundement. And whan they hadde seen hym my lord badde me occupye the said manere of Gyffardes and do my best with alle, and thys knowyth John Chancy the elder well i nowe. And therfore labour thys matyr for your title and your parceners as well as for myn. Writyn at Westm in greet hast on Saynt George is even.

408 The Palmers (see above, pp.30, 33).
409 Humphrey Stafford earl of Stafford and duke of Buckingham 1403–60 (*Complete Peerage*, ii, pp.388–9; see above, p.37).
410 The identity of Armburgh's lord is unknown. It may have been the duke of York, in which case he was to be sorely disappointed (see above, pp.28, 37–8, below, p.191). It could also be Buckingham, 'my lord and yours' being the same person, which would fit with the links Armburgh was establishing in Warwickshire at this time (see above, p.35) and would have proved equally disappointing (see below, p.177).
411 John Holland duke of Exeter 1444–7 (*Complete Peerage*, v, pp.205–11).

Robert Armburgh at Westminster to Hanchach: 18 April 1450[412]

The letter concerns further problems with the feoffees to Joan's estate. Both Thornbury and 'Bastard', another feoffee, are reluctant to make releases as requested and Armburgh is trying to engage the support of all the residuary heirs. Armburgh explains the legal situation with regard to the various parts of the estate, including the fact that the Chancys' feoffees for the part that they took are too powerful for him to have any chance of dealing with these.

To Hanchach [in margin] Dere and welbelouyd frende I commaunde me to you doyng you to wete that I have[413] Bastard the dede of feoffament and whan he hadde redde the sayd dede he desyryd to see my wyfe is last wille and I schewed hit hym also and I felt by certeyn wordes that he said whan he hadde redde hem both and by certeyn questions that he askyd me that he is not in wille that Sir Phillip Thornbury schulde seale my releese, for whan he hadde redde the dede of feoffament he sayd these wordes, 'Here is no thyng in descender',[414] but whan he hadde redde the wille and felt that ther wer ij fynes areryd vpon the said londes and that Sir Phillip Thornbury hadde the fee, he askyd me whethir the manere of Brokholes in Munden were taylyd or no, wherby I feele well, for asmoch as he hath weddyd Sir Phillip Thornbury nese, that he hopyth by possibilite that the said londes may descende to hys wyfe and to the eyres [m.2v] of them tweyn,[415] which was neuer my wyfe is wille nor entent, for what tyme sche made knowlech of tho ij fynes a fore Newithon cheve justise of the comyn place,[416] witnesse and recorde of many thryfty menne of the towne of Westm and of maney other present at that tyme, sche prayed me that I wolde take soche persones in the sayd ffynes with me as I supposyd wolde helpe and supporte me to perfourme her last wille, which wille ye knowe well is the condicion of both fynes. And ther vpon I namyd Sir Phillip Thornbury, for I wist that sche trust hym well, and other that ben rehersyd in the said ffynes. Fforthermore I desired that Bastard schulde haue

---

412 Hanchach may well have come from the unidentified Kedington property of that name (see above, p.90). There was a Thomas Hanchet in Suffolk in 1429 (PRO KB27/674 Coram Rege rot.22). However, the most likely candidate, Thomas Hanchet/Anchettes/Hanchirche/Hancheth, whatever his origin, was of Letchworth and was active in Hertfordshire, where in 1437 and 1449 he did business with William Walkerne (see above, p.11) and Thornbury (*Cal. Close Rolls 1429–35*, p.307, *1435–41*, pp.121, 436, 439, 470, *1447–54*, pp.28, 116; see also *Cal. Fine Rolls 1437–45*, p.163). This letter, dated 18 April, must, from the similar reference to the entry into Stanley Giffards, have been written four days before the previous one i.e. also 1450.

413 'Showed' must be missing.

414 I.e. there is nothing to give rise to claims of inheritance. (E.P.)

415 See above, p.36. This may be Richard Bastard of Bedford. His wife was Isabel, probably widow of Nicholas Rickhill; it has not been possible to identify her as a niece of Thornbury. He and his wife seem to have had lands in the right sort of places (Essex and Bedfordshire) and connections with some of the right people (Buckingham, Bourchier, Holland, Grey of Ruthin) (*Cal. Close Rolls 1429–35*, pp.187, 359; *London Plea and Memoranda Rolls 1413–37*, p.196, *1437–57*, pp.24, 25; above, pp.35, 37–8).

416 For the fines, see *Essex Feet of Fines*, iv, p.34. For Richard Newton, Chief Justice of the Common Pleas 1439–48/9, *DNB*, xl, pp.398–9.

wryte a letter to Sir Phillip Thornbury for to seale my releese and he said that
my wyfe hadde graunted me by her last wille the londes that schulde be soolde
beter chepe than to a nother by c marc and therfore he said that hit was no
reson that I schulde be both byer and seller[417] and therto I answerd and sayd
that my wyfe made me her executour and non other and gave me ful power
by vertu of her testament to mynystr and to execute the seid testament and
her last wille in alle thynges. And her vpon who [sic] departyd, and he
graunted me to haue spoke with me on the next morowe and I waytid after
hym day by day and I myght no more mete with hym. Wherfor I sende you
the copye of the wille and I pray you to oversee hit and also to feele well the
entent of thys letter thow hit be febyly made and comyn with Sir Phillip
Thornbury and enfourme hym that I desyre not hys releese in disheryson of
ony persone nor for covetyse of the londes that be in fee simple. For ye weete
well, and I pray you to telle hym so, that I have sent for Barynton, Edmund
Bendysch, Clement Spyse, Barry, Batayle and Boys, for alle these come of iiij
susters of Sir John de Roos and be next eyres to my wyfe ys enheritaunce,[418]
and enfourme hym of this mater, for my wyfe, God have mercy on her soule,
and John Palmer, her newue and her eyre, required me bothe whan thei sawe
that thei schulde dye and charged me that ther schulde no man be disherited,
pore nor ryche. And astochyng the fee symple londe,[419] John Chancy, a squyer
of the duke of Excestr, entryd in to the manere of Gyffardes in Sampford
nerehand a yere and a halfe a goo, which is beter than alle the other parte, and
enfeffyd therinne the duke of Excestr, the duke of Bokyngham, the Lord
Bow[c420] and many other so that I am neuer lyke to reiose that. And astochyng

---

417 As executor and feoffee, he was responsible for the sale.
418 For Sir John de Roos, see above, p.5. I have not been able to establish a genealogy but the men can
     all be identified with reasonable certainty. For Bendyssh and Spicer, see above, pp.10, 37. Apart
     from Bendyssh, these were all Hertfordshire/Essex families. The Barringtons were of Chigwell
     and Hatfield Broadoak; the reference is probably either to John (active 1447) or to Thomas
     (active 1451, 1466) (Morant, *Essex*, i, p.166, ii, p.504). 'Barry' is Sir John Barre of Herefordshire
     and Knebworth, Hertfordshire (Wedgwood, *Biographies*, p.44; *HP*, ii, pp.132–4). 'Batayle' could
     be either Bataill of Magdalen Laver and High Ongar, Essex, a family represented at this time by
     John, or Thomas Bataill of Stock-Hall in Matching, Essex, a London mercer, or John Bataill of
     Stanford Rivers, Essex, who was one of a large number of mainpernors for William Oldhall (see
     below, p.191) in 1452 (*Cal. Close Rolls 1441–7*, p.321, *1447–54*, pp.361, 363–4; Morant, *Essex*, i,
     pp.131, 142, ii, p.498; *London Plea and Memoranda Rolls 1437–57*, pp.41, 88, 117). 'Boys' is
     probably of the Havering atte Bower, Essex family, the more elevated family of Tolleshunt
     D'Arcy, Essex having died out earlier in the century (*HP*, ii, p.320; *Cal. Close Rolls 1447–54*,
     p.140; Morant, *Essex*, i, pp.60, 395–7; M. McIntosh, *Autonomy and Community: The Royal Manor
     of Havering 1200–1500* (Cambridge, 1986), pp.269, 272). There were extensive interconnections
     between these families (*HP*, ii, p.145; Morant, *Essex*, i, pp.230, 422, ii, pp.75, 498, 504; Chauncy,
     Hertfordshire, ii, p.121). John Barre, like some of the others in the affair, served the duke of York,
     although in his case his grant from the duke was in Herefordshire, his other county of residence
     (above, p.28; Johnson, *Richard of York*, p.228).
419 This means land held by a tenant 'to himself and his heirs for ever', as opposed to entailed land,
     which was to descend in a specified way (Baker, *Introduction to English Legal History*, pp.224,
     231).
420 Henry Bourchier earl of Eu (see above, p.38).

the tenement in Chevynton,[421] hy[422] have power to selle that by vertu of the releese that I schewed you, of the which ye see Edmund Bendysch sealen on your selfe, for what tyme these ffynes were a reryd my wyfe hadde no other astate in the seyd tenementys but terme of lyve and the remayndr was to Thomas Bendysch ffader to Edmund Bendysch[423] and to his cofeffes and that ye knowe well, for I schewed you the dede of feoffament and the last wille of Phillip Kedynton my wyfe ys first husbond and so ye mowe say to Sir Phillip Thornbury. And for asmoch as myn aduersaryes have very knowlech of all tho that ben enfeffyd with me in the ij fynes a foresaid, that is the cause that I wolde have a releese of Sir Phillip Thornbury and I wolde refeffe hym and other certeyn persones with hym, the which myn aduersaryes knewe not, for I am enfourmed that they wolle swe a formedowen[424] a yeyn vs the next terme, to hurt of me and of the ryght eyres and lettyng of my wyfe is last wille, but I trust so well to Sir Phillip Thornbury ys conscience that he wolde not suffre that. And Godde kepe you in prosperite. Writen at Westmynster the xviij day of Aprill.

The co-holders of Mancetter at the abbey of Merevale, Warwickshire to Robert Armburgh: 1 December 1451[425]

They have held a meeting with the abbot, at which Armburgh was not present, to deal with problems in distributing the money coming from the Leicestershire land exchanged for the Mancetter advowson. What Reynold took without authorisation (see above, p.00) has been laid to Armburgh's account.

To Robert Armeb by the parceners of Mancestre [in margin] Worschipfull and enterly welbelouyd cosyn we commaunde vs to you and lyke you to wete that we have assembled dyuers tymes at the abbey of Meryvale for owre mater as for oure lyflode in Litell Petlyng and Brantyngthorp in Leycester schyre,[426] the which mater at oure last bying at Myrevale a bowte the feste of Saint Martyn,[427] by the assent of vs alle, was put in ordynaunce and in rule of the worschipfull ffader the Abbot of the seid Abbey of Myrevale, William

---

[421] In Suffolk, part of the Kedington estate (see above, p.10).
[422] The word is only semi-legible: this seems to be the best reading, presumably for 'I'.
[423] See above, pp.10, 90–1.
[424] A writ used for claiming entailed property (see above, n.419) under the statute *De Donis* of 1285 (Baker, *Introduction to English Legal History*, pp.232–3). (E.P.)
[425] For the co-holders, see above, n.67. The letter relates to those above, pp.69–75. The statement at the end of the letter that the abbot has two years of income must mean that the letter dates from December 1451, since that was two years from the grant of the advowson to Merevale (see above, p.34).
[426] Peatling and Bruntingthorpe, Leicestershire (see above, p.34).
[427] 11 November.

Wysetow[428] and the parson of Wethyrley,[429] the which seyd Abbot, William and the parson have made and sette vs throwe in this wyse, that eche of vs alle schall have oure parte in the seid lordschippes of Litill Petlyng and Brantyngthorp after the quantyte and the rate that we have in the lordschip of Mancestr and that Dame Anne Pyrle, Rafe Holt and ye be restreyned of vj marc, the which by the awarde of the said Abbot, William and the parson is delyuered to Thomas Arblaster, Jonet Harpour and Clement Draper as for a reward and peese with oute trowbull to be hadde a mong vs alle, of the which vj marc Dame Anne Pyrle beryth xl s. and Rafe Holt and ye other xl s.[430] And, as for xxj s. vj d. that your newow Reynold Armeburgh[431] toke vp at the said lordschippes of Petlyng and Brantyngthorp, with oute assent of alle vs, we have thowth hit reson to recalle so moche money a geyn of that the seid Abbot hath in kepyng of youres, halfe a geyn hys wille, and departid hit a mong vs alle a cordyng to the said awarde, trustyng in you that ye wolle be resonable and a gree you to the said award and rule as alle we have doen. And also cosyn we have by the assent of vs alle grauntyd and gon thorowgh with oure styward for the holdyng of oure courtes and the ouersyght of oure seid lordschippes and with oure bayly to gadyr vp oure rentes and to serue vs of oure dute holy[432] ones in the yere, and also your seid cosyn Reynold toke vp in your name and his at one tyme iiij marc.[433] And so the [*sic*] remeyneth for you in the Abbot ys honde, all thyng rekenyd and a covntyd for ij yere, xv s. Writen in the Abbey of Meryvale the morowe after Seint Andrew day.[434]

John Ruggeley, abbot of Merevale, to Robert Armburgh: probably early to mid 1450[435]

Armburgh is warned that John Barbour's claim that, as vicar of Mancetter, he has Armburgh's full support may put the whole exchange of the Mancetter advowson in jeopardy. He is also ticked off for not giving the Mancetter lease to John Atherston (see next letter).

To Robert Arm by ye Abbot of Meryvale [in margin] Right worschipfull sir I recommaunde me to you with my herte, yeldyng thankynges of the goodnesse

428 The duke of Buckingham's treasurer of the household over many years (Rawcliffe, *Staffords*, pp.71, 197).
429 See above, n.193.
430 These are all Mancetter co-owners (see above, n.67).
431 See above, p.36.
432 Either 'duty holy' i.e. tithes or 'duty wholly'.
433 See above, p.36.
434 1 December.
435 For John Ruggeley, see above, p.34. For the circumstances of the letter, which relates to those on pp.69–72, 74–5, above, see pp.34–5, above. Like the others on this matter, it is likely to date from early to mid 1450, after the advowson had been given and before the lease of Ladyday 1450 – or at least before the abbot had certain knowledge of the lease (see above, pp.34–5).

ye schewe me at all dayes, besechyng euermore of goode contynuaunce. Yf hit plese you to wete I am enfourmed the vicar of Mancestr[436] seyth ye have graunte hym favour for the which favour he trystes schall be[437] hynderaunce to the bargeyne and to the eschaunge, the which we have made with you and your cosyns for the patronage of the chyrch of Mancestr, and ye and your cosyns have therfore to parte a monges you the lordschip of Petlyng and Brantyngthorp with the pertynaunce, the which draweth yerely withoute the courtes and all other casualtes, sise of brede and ale, wayfe and streyse, warde and mariage,[438] the hole rent by side thees cometh to xiij li., the which lordschip as writyng maketh mencyon, yf we be vexede of the patronage or of any parcell that longes to the glebe, we may entyr in the forsayd lordschip and kepe oure first astate, not withstondyng the endenturs. Whefore I besech you, as my full trust is in you, sende me a bille by the brynger of thys yf ye stonde as the vicar seyth and that I may fully tryste how ye wolle a byde and whethyr ye wolle schewe soche favour to hym, the which schall hynder you and all your cosyns[439] and me, and that I may have hit in certayne in writyng wethir ye wolle schewe to hym favour and be a geynes your selfe and me, as ever I may do thyng to your plesyre in tyme to come with the grace of Godde, which have you euermore in his gracious gouernance long to lyffe to his plesaunce.

Also worshipfull sir, I am enfourmed that John Attherston[440] schall not have the rule of youre lyflode at Mancestr and yf ye put hym from hit, tryst me trow hit wolle not be to youre a vayle and ye schull forthynke hit or to daye ij yere. And therfore I counseill you to be a vysed.

John Ruggeley, abbot of Merevale, to Robert Armburgh: about the same time as the immediately preceding letter[441]

The abbot recommends John Atherstone as lessee for Armburgh's part of Mancetter.

To Ro Arm by the abbot of Merivale [in margin] Right trusty and welbelouyd frende I grete you well with alle my herte, thankyng you euer of all goodnes ye have schewed me at alle dayes, prayng for euer of youre goode continuaunce,

---

436 Sir John Barbour alias Mountford (see above, p.35 and below, n.442).

437 'No' must be omitted here.

438 These are the lord's judicial rights associated with the manorial court. The right to hold the assizes of bread and ale was a franchise, or delegated authority from the king, to enforce regulations regarding the price at which these could be sold. It was normally associated with frankpledge, another franchisal privilege. 'Waifs and strays', or 'Estrays' are the manorial rights to goods or animals found within the manor to which no claims were made. Wardship and marriage were normally associated with lordship over free lands and presumably apply to tenants in socage i.e. free tenants, within the manor (Pollock and Maitland, *History of English Law*, i, pp.581–2; *Jowitt's Dictionary of English Law*, ed. J. Burke (2 vols., London, 1977), i, p.727, ii, p.1875; F.W. Maitland, *The Court Baron* (Selden Soc., 4 (1890)), p.95; Bolton, *Medieval English Economy*, p.20).

439 I.e. the other co-holders of Mancetter.

440 See above, p.34.

441 From the tone, this seems to antedate the immediately preceding letter.

yf hit please you to wete I am enfourmed that John Attherston desireth to have youre lyvelode of Mancestr in ferme, for the which I pray you let hym be before a nother, and yf ye stonde in doute of your payement, I wolle be on that schall be bounden for hym that he schall truely kepe the dayes of payement. And that ye wolden schowe hym the more favour at my prayer, as euer I may do thyng to your pleasour in tyme comyng with the grace of Godde which have you euermore in hys gracious gouernaunce long to lyffe to hys plesaunce.

John Barbour, vicar of Mancetter, at Mancetter, to Robert Armburgh: 30 September, probably 1450[442]

He explains why he is behind with his rent: molestation by Ralph Holt, John Atherstone and Reynold and his own financial obligations.

To Ro Arm by Sir John Barbour [in margin] Right reuerent and worschipfull sir I recommaunde me to you with alle my herte, desiryng to here of your goodly prosperite and welfare that almyghty Godde to you encreese to your hertes plesaunce, certefying you I haue consaywed your letter, knowyng well I occupied your ferme in Mancestr not undur the fourme of fferme as covenaunt was with appurtenaunce etc. *vt patet*, but as your depute, havyng grete magre[443] of Raff Holt not suffryng me to occupye no parte of the wodes, also of Reynold Armeburgh havyng strange langage a gaynes you and greet thretes a gaynes me and the tenantes, that throwgh supportacion of John Atherston and other that schulde owe you good wille, in so moche that in dyuerse partes of the ferme I resceyved neuer peny, and for your sake greet maygryff, and as I vnderstonde put oute of the ferme also, for the which I can not fulle answere tille I haue spoken with my mayster Robert Grey,[444] stondyng fermour ther. Nethelez hit schall not be longe to but I wolle come to you and wolde at midsomer last past, safe ther hath ben greet pestilence with vs a fore and sethen hedurto, and yf I schall have the ferme surely I will answere you as a fermour, or elles yf I be put fro the ferme I wolle answere to my resceyte and content eche peny, for by my faithe ther is non a lyfe that me were lother to displese. Also that ye foche safe to considr my greet chare[445] in bildyng, and at this day I stonde charged with x marc of payement with my ffaders[446] dette or

---

442 Barbour was lessee of Mancetter (see above, pp.34–6). From the contents, which refer to difficulties in collecting dues at the first Annunciation and Michaelmas terms of his farm, which he acquired at Ladyday 1450, and its dating (immediately after Michaelmas), the letter appears to belong to 1450. It is clear that, though he entered on Ladyday 1450, Barbour was still expected to produce the rent for that term (see above, p.68).

443 'Ill-will'.

444 Younger brother of Edward Grey Lord Ferrers of Groby (see above, p.35) and one of the co-holders of the Mancetter farm, with Barbour and William Barkby (see below, p.188).

445 *Sic*: either 'share' or an error for 'charge'; the latter seems the more likely.

elles he hadde gon to preson and so at this daye I most stonde charged with his kepyng also, for in faithe he hath nowght. Nethelez ye schuld have hadde at thys tyme iij li. hadde not Raynold ben, ffor in the bygynnyng of oure resceyt, which is at Annuniacion and Mighelmas, he has trowbuled the tenantes and me bothe with greet thretes, as youre seruant can more playnly certefye you, that manly has quytte hym at thys tyme and wysely bothe. And as sone as ye may lette me here fro you etc. And the Trinite kepe you and youres. Writen at Mancestr the nyght of Saint Jerome.[447]

Robert Armburgh to John Barbour: between 21 June and 29 September 1452[448]

A further demand for money.

To Sir John Barbour [in margin] Dere and welbelouyd frende I commaunde me to you. Hit is not vnknowen to you how ye and I were accordyd that I schulde be quarterly payd of xl s. tille I were content of the somme conteyned in the obligacion by twen you and me, and ye wete well the first day of payment was at mydsomer that last was and the next is now at thys Myghelmas and therfore I pray you sendyth me now bothe paymentes to gedir by William Leynton my seruant. Ye wete well I have grete[449] therof for but yf ye sende me hit I must ellys have hit of Aleyn Stratton[450] which is bounde with you and I were lothe to stryve whith hym but yf grete nede of money make hit. Ffferthermore sendyth me wretyn how moche money Reygnold my cosyn resceyvyd of my tenantes while ye hadde my lyvelode in gouernance[451] etc. *vt in aliis litteris.*

---

446 Possibly Richard Barbour, the earlier lessee (see above, p.9).

447 30 September (it is unlikely to mean the night before St Jerome, the usual meaning of 'the eve of' a festival, because that would be Michaelmas and he would surely have dated the letter by that festival).

448 The bond by Stretton and Barbour to pay Armburgh £10 is dated February 1452 (*Cat. Anc. Deeds*, iv, A9130) and so, from internal evidence, this letter must date to the period between midsummer and Michaelmas 1452. Stretton was a citizen and skinner of London (*Cal. Close Rolls 1454–61*, p.61).

449 *Sic.* 'need' missing?

450 See above, n.448.

451 This implies that Barbour had already given up the farm. The 'three half years' mentioned in the next letter as the time he had the farm would mean that he gave it up at Michaelmas 1451 and this would make sense of the date of the agreement over the payment of his debts and is indeed confirmed by an earlier letter to Barbour (see above, n.53 and pp.68–9).

John Barbour, at Mancetter, to Robert Armburgh: 5 October, probably 1452[452]

He has been very ill, his life saved by a 'gentle woman'. Again, he states his financial position regarding Armburgh and promises to pay what he conceives he owes him, and finally offers advice on the reallocation of the farm.

[m.3v] To Robert Armeburgh [in margin] Right reuerent and worschipful maister y recomaunde me to you with alle my seruice euermore, thankyng you of your gode maisterschip and grete kyndnesse to me a fore tymes schewed, prayng you of gode continuance, prayng you I may be comaunded to my maistrays your cosyn[453] as for a gentil womman that I am most holden to of alle yerthely wommen, for in my consaite God and sche saved my lyfe, what with medicynes and with her counseill to entrete to me your gode maisterschip, for and ye hadde ben rugerus to me hit wolde have ben my deth. Wherfore I purpose with in schort tyme sum what to quyte her and euer dayes of my lyfe to praye for you and her, prayng you to consayve that I occupyed not your ferme but iij half yerys, for the which I have payed a fore tymes iiij marc, and j marc ye pardon me at myne inne comyng and now j marc I have delyuered your seruant, which drawes in the hole vj marc, and that ye fochesafe at thys tyme to holde you plesed and or myne obligacion be ronnen I schall speke with you and content you your dew and all my seruice with, and the Trinite kepe you body and sovle. Writen in Mancestr the v day of October last past.

[probably postscript from same] More ouer I counsayll you not to sette your ferme to none other persone but to my Maister Gray or hisson for no mannes counsaill for your owne ease.

[in margin at right-angles to the following text, running towards the top of the page] By a feoffament of trust but yf he be a tiraunt of an ewyll concyensed man

A remembrance of the settlement made by Joan and Robert Armburgh of their part of Mancetter: [November 1443][454]

This is a statement of the settlement under which Armburgh was endeavouring to execute his wife's will (above, pp.173–8) and it explains why Reynold has no right to the exchange lands in Leicestershire.

Here is a remembraunce of a ffyne areryd by Robert Armeburgh and Johane his wyfe vpon the moyte of the iij part of the manere of Mancestr in Warwyk

---

452 If Armburgh was putting heavy pressure on Barbour in the period leading up to Michaelmas 1452, Barbour's collapse and recovery by 5 October – the date of this letter – would suggest that it also belongs to 1452.
453 See above, pp.35–6 for discussion of her identity.
454 On the fine and its terms and personnel, see above, pp.30–1, 36–7.

schyre by the which fyne the seid Robert and Johane hadde astate in the seid
moite terme of the seid Jonys lyve and after the decesse of the seid Johane the
remeyndre to the seid Robert and other ceryteyn persones for the terme of x
yere for to perfourme the wille of the said Johane, of the which persones
Johane Palmer late the wyfe of Reygnold Armeburgh was on, and after the
terme of x yere the remeyndr to John Palmer, nevu and eyr to Johane late the
wyfe of Robert Armeburgh a foresayd and to the eyrys of hym comyng, and yf
none eyrys come of hym the remeyndre to Johane Palmer his suster late the
wyfe of Reygnold Armeburgh aforeseid and to the eyrys of her body comyng,
and yf none eyrys come of her the remeyndre to Robert Armeburgh and his
cofeffes and to the eyrys of Sir Phillip Thornbury vnder certeyn condicions
which ben rehersyd in the last wille of Johane late the wyfe of Robert Armeburgh a foreseyd, of the which wylle the abbot of Meryvale hath a copye,[455]
and, there as Reygnold Armeburgh pretendyth to be parcener in Petlyng and
Brantyngthorp which cam in by eschaunge for the avoyson of the parsonage
of Mancestr, he was neuer party in the fyne a foreseid and, thow Johane his
wyfe were party in the seid fyne, sche dyed long by forn the eschaunge was
made, so that he may not cleyme in the seid londys that cam in by eschaunge,
hit makyth no matere, for the eschaunge was made by twene the seid abbot
and the parceners of Mancestr and not by twen hym and straungers that have
no part in the manere of Mancestre, and yf ony man mygth make ony clayme
to ben parcener in the manere of Mancestr and in tho landys that cam in by
eschaunge, hit schulde be tho that ben rehersyd in the fyne abovesayd and
thei make no clayme nor none wolle make for ther may no man take avayle.

[John Palmer] to his mother, Sybil Palmer: probably 1440s[456]

*He warns her that, if she comes to visit him, as she proposes, she cannot be as well
entertained as he would like because of the costs that his grandfather [Robert
Armburgh?] has had to bear since the death of his grandmother [Joan?] and suggests a later date for the visit.*

To Sibill Palmer [in margin] Right dere and welbelouyd moder I commaunde
me to you desiryng to here of your prosperite and welfare. And for asmoch as

---

455 This could show that the abbot was regarded with trust by Armburgh, but it could as well reflect
the abbot's concern to possess an authoritative statement of the ownership of the Armburgh part
of Mancetter and its advowson, in case the Armburghs' right to alienate the advowson was later
questioned.

456 For Sybil Palmer, see above, pp.31–2. This letter must be from John, unless there were any other
children, since it refers to his sister (see above, p.30). It was written while he was underage. Since
we do not know whether John was of age when he died, although he was probably married (see
above, p.67), it could have been written any time up to his death in the later 1440s (see above,
p.33). This and the next two letters give every indication of belonging to an earlier period than
the rest of this part of the roll. Despite the fact that John and Joan Palmer are elsewhere called
nephew and niece of Joan Armburgh, it seems highly probable that 'my granddame', whose estate
is being cleared up, and who is clearly married to a man who is not the writer's grandfather, were

ye sent me worde that ye wolde come in to thys contre a pilgrimage after thys
Whitsontide, that is the cause that I sende you thys letter, doyng you to
vnderstond that my grandame is housbond hath me in gouernance and he
hath lost, spendyd and payed a greet summe of goode sithen my grandame
dyed, what to the erle of Oxenford for my wardhode,[457] what in money taken
of hys tenantes by the seid erle, what in money that he alowed to hys tenantes
for the harmys that the said erle dide to hem, what in money payed to my suster[458] in party of payement for her maryage money and what in gode doen for
my grandame is sovle sith the tyme of her deth, with other certeyn costes that
he hath born in plee, in reryng of ffynes, in grene wax and to the schetour,[459]
the which thynges her rehersid I knowe well drawyn to the somme of xiij^xx
marc withoute alle the costes of hys houshold and alle oure fyndyng, with
oute alle thys he schall bere a stronge coste thys same yere in byldyng of newe
hovses and reparacion of olde hovses, the which felle doen and were
destroyed for lakke of reparacion, hangyng the plee and debate by twen the
said erle and hym,[460] the which costes with other thynges that most neyds be
don this same yere, I knowe well wolle drawe to ye somme of l marc and more
and this cost most nedys be doen or we schull have no fermours and also hit
wolde be grete hynderyng to me in tyme comyng, and for alle these causys yf
ye comyn in to this contre at thys tyme, it schall not lye in oure power to resceyve you and refresh you, neyther to your worschip nor to our worschip, but
and ye wolle tarye your comyng a litill lenger, that is to seyn tille after Mighelmasse com twelmonth, the which is litill more than a yere and a quarter, I
trust to Godde we schull be in power to resceyve you and your frendys to
your worship and our also. I can no more at this tyme but I pray God have
you euer in hys kepyng and sende you prosperite and helth of body and sovle
and I pray you al way of your blessyng.

Joan, and her husband Robert Armburgh, and, in any case, 'nephew' and 'niece' could be used as
synonyms for 'grandson' and grandaughter'. For more on these issues, together with references
and the related matter of what happened to the Kedington estate of Ashdon, which seems to be
the property of which the *post mortem* settlement is discussed in the letter, see above, pp.31–3 of
Intro. If these suppositions are correct, they would place the letter in the period c.1443–4, immediately after Joan's death. Internal evidence indicates that it was written during the summer,
which would suggest 1444, as Joan died in November 1443 (see above, p.30).

457 John, twelfth earl, 1417–62 (*Complete Peerage*, x, pp.236–8). See above p.10 and refs. in n.50 to
Intro.

458 Presumably Joan Palmer.

459 These are probably all to do with settling an estate *post mortem*: settlements and recoveries
(fines), payments to the exchequer (green wax) and dealing with the escheator, whose job it was
to do the inquisition *post mortem* and execute any subsequent royal orders concerning the inheritance and livery of the estate (see above, p.47).

460 Presumably over the earl's rights over the estate as lord.

[William] Armburgh to his brother Robert Armburgh: before Easter, no later than 1443[461]

He has repaid money that Robert lent him by sending some malt. William's sons, including Reynold, appear to be living with Robert, and Reynold is instructed to meet William at Godmanchester (Hunts.) at a later date.

To Robert Armeb [in margin] Reverent and wel belouyd brother I comaunde me to you, desyryng to here of your welfare and prosperite, thankyng you of the greet chere that ye made me, and as for the money that ye lent me, I haue sent x quarters of malt by Ric Morke and his loder Thomas Brown, to be delyuered to you or your assygnes at Westm in all haste that he may. Also I commaunde me to my suster your wyfe and I grete well my sones and I sende hem my blessyng and I praye you to haue hem in gode gouernance. Also I pray you that ye charge Reygnold my sone that he ordeyn hym an hors that he be at Cumecestr[462] with me on Monday a forn Palmesonday and that William Longe your man come also and that he may lede home Reynoldis hors a yen to London with oute that he can make other purvyaunce by the pulter, and that there of Reynold and William fayle not in no maner wyse for I most make my lawe a yen William Barre[463] atte courte of Cumecestr on Thursday a forn Palmesonday with oute ony delay.[464] No more at this tyme etc.

---

461 As the only brother known to have corresponded with Robert was William, William is probably the writer of this letter and therefore the father of Reynold. Reynold's origins (see above, p.33n.) make this identification highly likely. The letter was written, in the weeks before Easter, while Joan Armburgh was still alive (she died in 1443: above, p.30) and suggests that Reynold and William's other sons had been sent to Robert in London, which is where he seems normally to have resided (see above, p.52), to learn their trade. In Reynold's case this was the law and it can be seen in the next letter that he was already acting as agent for his uncle. He was admitted to Lincoln's Inn between Christmas and Easter 1443–4, although this does not mean that he could not have been in London with Robert before then (*Records of the Society of Lincoln's Inn, i, Admissions 1420–1799* (London, 1896), p.9).

462 See above, n.391.

463 He remains unidentified but could be a member of the Barre/Barry family of Herefordshire and Hertfordshire who were distantly connected to Robert by marriage (see above, p.177).

464 William Armburgh (if he it is) requires the presence of Reynold, and possibly also William Long, so that he can make a wager of law against William Barre, probably in a local court action for debt. The defendant would swear that he did not owe the money, and produce eleven oath-helpers or compurgators to testify to his credibility. See Baker, *Introduction to English Legal History*, pp.64–5. (E.P.)

[William]Armburgh to his brother Robert: perhaps same date as the letter immediately preceding or later[465]

The letter concerns a property, perhaps in Godmanchester, with which William and John Palmer had dealings; Reynold's help with the matter is strongly urged.

To Robert Arm [in margin] Right reuerent and worschipfull brother, herteley I commaunde me vnto you desyryng to here of your prosperite and welfar and, yf ye desire to here of myn, I was in good hele at the makyng of this letter, wherfor I write to you at this tyme, letyng you wete that I wolle no lenger dele with the letter of atourney as for Manypeny Place, for I lete you wete that Stokker is seesyd in the place and the londe and ye may not put hym therfrom, nor ye can not with outen that Reygnold Armeburgh be your gode frende and helpe you in the mater, for I lete you wete the possession that John Palmer and I toke beryth no strengh nor stondyth to non effecte vnto the tyme that Stokker be fully payed that is owyng to hym.[466] Wherfore I desyre, yf that ye wolle I dele withalle, take Reygnold of your counseill, for I lete you wete that ther is no man of oure towne that wolle do a yens his counsell, for he knowith how it is and which wey is best for you to be demenyd and therfore whan Reygnold Armeburgh comyth to London lete hym knowe your entent and acordyth with Stokker in the best maner that ye kan and than sende me writyng how ye wil it be rewled and more ouer I lete you wete that the tenantes wolle paye no money but to Stokker or to his atourney, for they seyn that he is in possesion and hath state and no man but he, and ferthermore I lete you well wete that it is trowth, for the courte rolles make mynde and record with hym etc.

---

465 This letter, probably from William, could be of the same date as the previous one or later, although it is quite likely to post-date Joan Armburgh's death, since, unlike the previous letter, there is no mention of Joan and John Palmer is an active participant (the fact that he may have been a minor for most of his adulthood – see above, n.456 – need not necessarily invalidate this point), and we must assume that it predates Reynold's attempts on the estate of c.1449 onwards (see above, pp.36, 49–50). The reference to John Palmer does not mean that he was still alive and could indeed concern business arising after his death. It was written at a time when Reynold was sufficently qualified in the law to advise Robert.

466 'Stokker' is probably a member of one of the families of London drapers, with one of which William Stonor, of the family of the Stonor Papers, became connected by marriage. Perhaps the most likely candidate, given the origins of the Armburghs, is Thomas of Eaton Socon, Bedfordshire (*Stonor Letters and Papers*, i, p.xxvii; S. Thrupp, *The Merchant Class of Medieval London* (Chicago, 1948), p.367). From the references to tenants and court rolls, the property would seem to be rural rather than urban and the reference to Reynold's influence in 'oure towne' implies Godmanchester (see above, p.7), which would suggest that it is the Eaton Socon man who is the subject of the letter. The property appears to have been mortgaged, either to raise money, or because it had simply been bought and not yet fully paid for.

Robert Armburgh at Westminster to an unknown recipient in Warwickshire: 22 February 1450 or a little after[467]

Notification that he has let his part of Mancetter to John Barbour and others: the lessees have full power to collect rents from the Leicestershire land and the arrears of the farm are to be paid to Reynold.

Trusty and welbelouyd sir I grete you well with alle herte desiryng to here of your welfare, certefying you that I haue lette to ferme to Robert Gray esquyer, Sir John Mounfford vicar of Mancestr[468] and William Barkeby[469] alle my part of Mancestr and Darsthill, with alle the appurtenaunce. Also I haue geven to hem ful power to levey my part of the rent in the counte of Leycestr which is chaunged for the patronage of Mancestr, as more playnly hit apperes by endenturs of record by twyxt the seid fermours and me made, and thei to res-ceyve the hole ferme of this Seint Mary day next comyng, and alle that is by hynde of other termes a fore to be payed to my cosyn Reygnold Armeburgh, and the Trinite kepe you. Writen in Westm in the fest of Seint Petur Cathedra last past the xxviij yere of Kyng Harry the vj.

Final concord settling the estate of Ellen and James Bellers on Thomas Pekke etc., Westminster, 9 February 1436[470]

Hec est finalis concordia facta in curia domini regis apud Westm in Octavo Purificacionis Beate Marie anno regnorum [*sic*] Henrici Regis Anglie et Fran-cie sexti a Conquestu quartodecimo[471] coram Joanne Juyn, Johanne Martyn, Jacobo Strangways, Johanne Cottesmore et Willielmo Paston justiciis.[472] Et postea in Octavo Sancte Trinitatis anno regnorum [*sic*] eiusdem Regis Hen-rici quintodecimo[473] ibidem concessa et recordata coram prefatis Johanne Juyn, Jacobo, Johanne Cottesmore et Willielmo justiciis et aliis domini regis fidelibus tunc ibi presentibus inter Thomam Pekke, Willielmum Pekke[474] et Johannem Lane[475] querentes et Jacobum Bellers[476] et Elenam uxorem eius deforcientes de medietate maneriorum de Brokholes, Ouerhall et Roos cum

---

467 The date given is 22 February 1450. The date is curiously expressed, in a way which suggests it was incorrectly copied and that the date was really a little after St Peter in Cathedra, rather than on the festival itself.

468 For these two, see above, pp.34–5.

469 Unidentified.

470 On this feoffment, see above, p.28 and n.

471 9 February 1436.

472 See above, p.105.

473 1 June 1437.

474 For the Pekkes, see above, p.138 and Wedgwood, *Biographies*, p.672.

475 An ironmonger (see below, p.190 and *London Plea and Memoranda Rolls 1413–37*, p.289, 1437–57, p.23).

476 This seems to have been shortly before his death (see above, pp.28–9).

pertinentibus in Magna Munden, Parva Munden, Gedelston et Saret in Comitatu Hertf. Et de medietate maneriorum de Roos, Stanle Gyffardes et Newehall cum pertinentibus in Radewynter, Magna Sampforde et Asshildham in comitatu Essex. Et de medietate manerii de Mancestr cum pertinentibus et de aduocatione ecclesie eiusdem manerii in comitatu Warr. Unde placitum conuencionis suum fuit inter eos in eadem curia. Scilicet quod predicti Jacobus et Elena recognovit predictas mediatates cum pertinentibus et aduocacionem esse jus ipsius Willielmi. De quibus iidem Willielmus, Thomas et Johannes habent medietates maneriorum de Brokholes, Ouerhalle, Roos in Saret, Newehalle et Mancestr cum pertinentibus et aduocacionem predictam de dono predictorum Jacobi et Elene. Et illas remiserunt et quietum clamaverunt de ipsis Jacobo et Elena et heredibus ipsius Elene predictis Thome Willielmo, Johanni et heredibus Willielmi imperpetuum. Et praeterea iidem Jacobus et Elena concesserunt pro se et heredibus ipsius Elene quod predicta medietas maneriorum de Roos in Radewynter et Stanle Gyffardes cum pertinentibus quam Thomas Bernard tenuit ad terminum vite de hereditate predicte Elene die quo hec concordia facta fuit et que post decessum ipsius Thome Bernard ad predictos Jacobum et Elenam et heredes ipsius Elene debuit reuerti post decessum ipsius Thome Bernard integre remaneat predictis Thome Pekke, Willielmo et Johanni et heredibus ipsius Willielmi tenenda simul cum predictis medietatibus et aduocacione que eis per finem istum remanent de capitalibus dominis feodi illius per seruicia que ad illam medietatem pertinent imperpetuum. Et predicti Jacobus et Elena et heredes ipsius Elene warantizabunt predictis Thome Pekke, Willielmo et Johanni et heredibus ipsius Willielmi predictas medietates cum pertinentibus et aduocacionem predictam sicut predictum est contra omnes homines imperpetuum. Et pro hac recognicione, remissione et quietaclamatione concessione warranto fine et concordia iidem Thomas Pekke, Willielmus et Johannes dederunt predictis Jacobo et Elene trescentas marcas argenti.

Indentured agreement concerning the estate of Ellen and James Bellers following on from the above final concord: 8 March 1437[477]

Thys endentur made the viij day of March by twyx John Ffrank,[478] Nicolas Wymbyssh,[479] John Stopyngton,[480] Rauff Belers and Will Russell[481] on the on partye and William Pekke, Thomas Pekke and John Lane iremonger on the other partye wittenessith that where as we the seyd John Ffrank, Nicolas, John Stopyngton, Rauff and Will ben enfeffyd in the on half part of the maners of Newhall in Asshildham in the counte of Essex and in the on half of the maners of Ouerhall in Gedleston, Brokholes in Munden Magna and Rooshall in Saret in the schyre of Hertford and in the on half of the maner of Rooshall in Mancestr with all the appertenantz with avouson of the chirch in Mancestr in the schyre of Warwyk and also in the other londys, tenementz, rentz and seruices with there appurtenantz in the sayd countes by the sayd William Pekke, Thomas Pekke and John Lane, to have to vs and to oure heires and assignes for euermore, neuer the lesse we the sayd John Ffrank, Nicolas, John Stopyngton, Rauff and William willen and graunten by thys endentur that as sone as the sayd William Russell hys heires or executours been full paied and agreed of his resonnable costez and expenses ouer xxxv li. of laufull money of the issuez, rentz and profitz growyng of the seyd maners, londys or tenementz or in other wyse be agreed and content of the somme foreseid and also more ouer be content and payed of xl marc yf there be so moche dewe to certaynes persones by Jamys Belers[482] son of Rauff Belers esquyer or Elene his wyfe, and then after dewe request made to vs by the seyd Jamys or Elene hys wyfe or of the heirs of the seyd Elene, we schall make a full astate of the sayd londys and tenementz to the sayd Jamys and Elene and to the heires of theire two bodyes begetyn. And for defaute of soche yssue the rem to the heires of the seid Elene is body begetyn. And for defaute of soche issue remayndr therof to the right heires of the seid Elene. In wittenesse of which thyng both parties a foreseyd hath sette to these presentz endentures there seales. These been the

---

[477] Dated, at bottom. On this agreement, see above, p.29.
[478] Chancery clerk and keeper of the chancery rolls in 1435 (*Cal. Close Rolls 1435–41*, p.1). For his will, and a summary of his career, see *Chichele Register*, ii, pp.591–5, 654. Wymbysh was one of the witnesses to his will (*ibid.*, p.593). As the footnotes to feoffees and witnesses make clear, this was very much a chancery-based group and a cursory examination of evidence suggests that it was a well-knit one. Interestingly, the group had already had dealings with the Chancys, who were later to claim some of the Armburgh land in Hertfordshire (*Cal. Close Rolls 1429–35*, p.253, *1435–41*, pp.40, 269; above, p.37).
[479] Clerk of the chancery, chancery master in 1435 (see above, pp.22, 29).
[480] Chancery master in 1436 (*Cal. Close Rolls 1435–41*, p.63).
[481] See above, p.29.
[482] See n.138 to Intro.

witteneses: Thomas Haseley,[483] John Selby,[484] Thomas Pakyn,[485] John Stafford[486] and John Bate.[487] Yoven and made the viij day of March the yer of the regne of Kyng Harry the vj after the Conquest the xv^e.

Petition to parliament of Robert Armburgh: 1449 or 1450[488]

This gives further detail on the Chancys' seizure of the land in Hertfordshire and Essex, including the names of their powerful protectors and feoffees, and requests help from the king because Armburgh has insufficient local influence to combat them.

[m.4v] Mekely besechith your poore suppliaunt Robert Armeburgh that wher as Jone late the wyfe of the seyd suppliaunt and her auncetours were lavfully sesyd and pesible possessyd tyme owte of mynde of the maneres of Brokholes in Radewynter, of Stanle other wyse called Giffardes in Moche Sampford in the schyre of Essex and of Ouerhall in Gedeleston within the schyre of Hertf and enfeffyd your suppliaunt with other by fyne areryd in the moyteis of the seyd maneres, John Chancy the elder and John Chancy the yonger have entryd by force and armes with grete multitude of peple in to the seyd moyteis, where they nor none of theire aunceters hadde neuer title of right and enfeffyd the duke of Yorke, the duke of Exceter, the duke of Bokyngham, the earle of Ewe, Sir William Oldehall knyght, Sir Edmund Mulso knyght with other knyghtes and squiers in the seyd moyteis and left there vij or viij persones with other certeyn persones of Thaxstede, a myle thens, assossed to hem whan they wold kalle vpon hem to kepe the seyd moyteis with strenght. Wherfor lyke hit to your ryght wyse and noble discrecions, consideryng that your suppliaunt is not of power to mayntene nor defende none assise a yenst

---

483 A chancery clerk (*Cal. Close Rolls 1429–35*, pp.39, 126). See also *Cal. Fine Rolls 1430–7*, p.214.

484 There was a Richard Selby, chancery clerk, who was associated with Wymbysh and Frank, and 'John' may well be an error, although the Close Rolls copy has the same name. Alternatively, this could be the John Selby citizen of London who may well have been Richard's brother (*Cal. Close Rolls 1429–35*, pp.35, 122, *1435–41*, p.127).

485 Probably the attorney of Salisbury (*Cal. Close Rolls 1435–41*, p.114, *1441–7*, p.280; *Cal. Pat. Rolls 1436–41*, pp.26, 443; *The Tropenell Cartulary*, ed. J.S. Davies (2 vols., Wiltshire Archaeological and Natural History Soc., 1908), i, pp.160–3, 259, 260, 321).

486 The most likely of several candidates is the London attorney and clerk of the London guildhall, who acted as witness to the will of William Caldwell, one of the several London citizens involved in the affairs of the Armburghs, their associates and their opponents (*London Plea and Memoranda Rolls 1413–37*, pp.162, 180, 196, 279; above, p.80).

487 Despite the absence of a clerical title, this is most likely to be the clerk of chancery and dean of Tamworth, a kinsman of the chancellor, Ralph Bellers' protector, Cardinal Kempe. He was brother of Thomas Bate, a rising midland lawyer who, not long after, married the widow of Sir John Cokayn, one of Armburgh's Warwickshire allies (D.A. Johnson, 'Dean Bate's Statutes for St Edith's, Tamworth, Staffordshire, 1442', *Trans. of the South Staffs. Archaeological and Historical Soc.*, 10 (1968–9), pp.55–6; Carpenter, *Locality and Polity*, pp.102, 392n.187; above, pp.8, 14).

488 The wording of this petition shows that it was addressed to parliament. For the dating, circumstances and people named, see above, pp.37–8.

so myghty princes, nor deere not offende theire grete lordschippes, to sende for the bothe Chancys by a writte *sub pena* or a preue seale chargyng hem to come by fore you with theire evydences at a day assygned in to thys hye court of thys present parliament, there to schewe by what title that they clayme the seyd moyteis and that your suppliaunt may come by fore you the same day with hys evydences, there to schewe what right he hath to the seyd moyteis, to that entent that the trowth may be knowe and that thys matyr may make soche an ende as gode feyth and conciens askyth for the love of Godde and in the wey of charyte.

Indentured agreement between John Chancy sr. and Robert Armburgh, Westminster, perhaps mid or late summer, probably 1450[489]
Robert agrees to demonstrate his right to Overhall in Gedelston, Hertfordshire, to John Chancy sr., preparatory to selling it to him on terms specified in the agreement.

Thys endentur made at the towne of Westm etc. by twyx John Chancy the elder of Gedelston etc. and Robert Armeburgh etc. wytnesseth certeyn couenantz and appointementz hadde and madde by twyx the seyd John and Robert in the maner and fourme that foloweth, that is to sey that the seyd Robert by the first day of Septembr next folowyng after the date of thys present writyng schall schewe or do schewe to the seid [*sic*] or to hys counseill alle maner of dedys, munimentz and evydentz being in his possession and kepyng of the same Robert or in kepyng of any other persone to hys vse concerning or in any wyse longyng to the lordschip and maner called Ouerhall in the towne of Gedeleston a foresaid, to the entent that the sayd John or hys counseyll schall examyn and serche the seyd evydentz to knowe what right and title the seyd Robert hath or in any wyse may pretende to have in the maner of Ouerhall a foresaid, and yf it so be that the seid John and hys counseill fynde and conceyve by the sight and examinacion of the seid dedys and munimentz that the seid Robert hath good right and title to the seid maner and that it stande in no wyse entayled, that then the seid Robert schall delyuer alle the seyd evydentz to the seid John or to his attourney by the fest of Mighelmasse next folowyng after the date of thys present wrytyng, hem to hoolde and kepe to his owne propre vse and also that the seid Robert I N etc. by their dede lavfully schall releese and quyte clayme to the seid John and to his heirs that they or any of theym have or in any wyse pretende for to have in the seid maner of Ouerhall. And for all the premisses wele and lavfully to be perfourmed and done after the maner and fourme a fore rehersyd the seid John Chancy grauntith by this present endentur to pay or do to pay to the seid Robert   in the fourme that

---

[489] For dating and background, see above, p.38. The reference to 1 September suggests a mid or late summer dating. The sums specified in the indenture are left blank.

folowith, that is to say at the seid fest of Mighelmasse   and at the fest of
Cristemasse then next folowyng   and also the seid John grauntith by this
same present writyng that he schall geete suffysshaunt men to be bounden to
the seid Robert for the somme of   yerely to be payed to the seid Robert
duryng the lyf of the seid Robert. And to these couenantz well and truly to be
perfourmed in the maner a foresaid by[490] on the part of the seid Robert, the
same Robert byndyth hym by this present writyng to the seid John Chancy in
xl li. and the seid John Chancy for these couenauntz well and truly to be perfourmed in hys part byndeth hym to the seid Robert in xl li. In witnesse
wherof etc.

Statement of Joan Armburgh's claim to the other half of the Brokholes inheritance: c. 1428–32[491]

*This tells the story of the dispute over the inheritance, from Joan's point of view,
up to c.1432, offering some hitherto unmentioned points of detail.*

. . . de . . . [in margin] Be it in mynde that Dame Elyne Brokhole of Essex
hadde issue Johane now the wyfe of Robert Armeburgh and Margery sum
tyme the wyfe of John Sumpter of Colchester, the which John Sumpter and
Margery hadde issu Cristine and Elyne, these Cristine and Elyne deyden
aboute Lammesse was viij yere, the which John Sumpter the fader dede berye
be nyght and toke ij bastarde doughters of his owne and put hem oute to his
frendys in to the contre and made the contre beleve that thei were the same
that he had by his wyfe, and whan he hadde kept hem there v or vj yere he
token hem home a yene and made hem be founde by an inquisicion takyn be
fore the eschetour mulirers and copersoners with the said Johane of alle the
londys and tenementz that Dame Elyne Brokhole a foreseid deyede seysed of,
and thus thorow the vntrowthe of the seid Sumpter the seid Robert and
Johane have be kept oute of the seid lyflode, which is worth xl li. a yere, this

---

490 'Or' appears to be omitted.
491 The *terminus ad quem* for this statement is set by the mention of the fact that John Sumpter senior
is still alive and it is unlikely therefore to date from much after early 1432 (see above, p.61). There
is also the allegation that the true Sumpter daughters had died at about Lammas (August) eight
years before and that, after their deaths, the false ones had been hidden away for five or six years.
This would not have had any point until John the younger had died, an event which occurred in
July 1420 (see above, p.6). If the girls died, or were thought to have died, about the same time
(possibly from the same illness), the five or six years' concealment would fit with the greatly
delayed IPMs for John the younger, which established the girls' identity, the first of which was
held in October 1426. As we learn that all this had led to the Armburghs' exclusion from the property for eight and a half years, which presumably means from the deaths of the girls, the date of the
petition could be very early 1429, or possibly early 1430. If, as has been surmised (above, p.92n.),
the petition was used to secure the support of Lady Ferrers of Chartley, it could even date to February 1428, when an approach to her was first made (see above, p.92), for the chronology allows
for the girls to have died in summer 1420. But it could also have been a ploy to secure continued
assistance during the period after this (see above, p.27).

viij yere and a half. The somme therof that schulde have falle to the seid Robert and Johane in the mene tyme drawyth to v^c marc and x, the whiche somme to have my lordes good lordschip in alle here maters and specially in this thei will yeve to my lady [breaks off]

Also be it in mynde that Thomas Aspall sum tyme husbonde to Johane now the wyfe of Robert Armeburgh and John Langham of Essex squier[492] were bounde in an obligacion of v c mark to enfeffe Johane the wyfe of Robert Armeburgh in xx li. worth londe in Essex which was neuer perfourmed, so that the bonde stant in strenght and the executours of John Langham be sufficeant to answere to the somme, the which bonde William Notyngham[493] executour to Dame Elyne Brokhole of Essex, moder to the seid Johane, hath in kepyng, the which the seid Robert and Johane will yeve to my lady to have my lordes good lordschip in alle here materes.

Also be it in mynde that John Sumpter of Essex and Johane the wyfe of Robert Armeburgh while sche was wydue were bounde eche to other in an obligacion of an c li. to stonde to the awarde of certeyn persones of all maner debates hangyng by twene hem for the maner of Sampford in Essex and the maner of Gedeleston in Hertfordschyre, in the which maners William Notyngham and Symond Mate[494] with other were enfeffyd by Dame Elyn Brokhole of Essex moder to the seid Johane for the entent to perfourme here last will, the which arbitrours awardyd the xxx day of Janyvere the vij yere of Kyng Harry the fyfte[495] that the seid John Sumpter schulde do the seid feffes make a state to the seid Johane Armeburgh in the moyte of bothe thoo maners by midsomer next folowyng this awarde. And also to delyuer her alle the evydentz touching her enheritaunce by the fest of Ester next after this award, the which perfourmed was neither in the astate yevyng, neither in delyuering of the seid evydentz. Wherfor the obligacion stont in strenght and the seid John Sumpter is a lyve and sufficeaunt to answere to the somme, the which obligacion thei will yeve my lady also to have my lordes good lordschip in alle here maters, with that condicion that the seid Robert and Johane be saved harmeles thorow my lordes good lordschip of the obligacion of c li. that John Sumpter hath of the seid Johane.

---

[492] For Langham, see *Cal. Close Rolls 1399–1401*, p.26 (a transaction involving Sumpter), *1405–09*, p.277, *1409–13*, p.192.
[493] See above, p.9.
[494] See above, p.9.
[495] 1420.

Petition of Alison Beek: c.1450–2[496]

This petition, made by a servant of Robert Armburgh, concerns the fate of Thomas Beek, a cleric, who lent money to the wife of one Thomas Moore. According to the petition, Moore's wife, to prevent Beek claiming his money, alleged that the latter had raped her. Armburgh became involved as Alison's employer, and Alison herself when she tried to speak up for her brother. Most of the document recounts the complicated procedure on the case in the eccclesiastical courts.

Mekely bescheth your poore suppliaunt Alison Beek that where as Sir Thomas Beek[497] her brother for askyng of his owne money which he lent by the prokering[498] and by the hondes of on Sir Thomas Hulle[499] to Johane the wyfe of Thomas Moore,[500] was sommonnd to come by fore the Ordinary of Westm[501] and whan he came there, for to forbarre hym of the seid money, thei bare hym onhonde that he wolde have ravysschyd More his wyfe and there was More hym selfe with xiiij or xv persones with hym by the waye of mayntenance and there thei pullyd of Sir Thomas Beek is hode and beete hym with her fystys a boute the hede and not withstondyng that, for asmoche as Sir Thomas Beek wolde not bryng iiij mene to be bounde for hym for suerte

---

496 This case, on which there is a chancery petition from More, which gives us both an approximate date and a rather different version of events (PRO C1/19/35), belongs to Kempe's second period as chancellor, in the period before he became archbishop of Canterbury, that is January 1450 to July 1452 (*Handbook of Chronology*, pp.87, 234). The only connection with Armburgh is the fact that Alison Beek, the petitioner and sister of the accused priest, was employed by Armburgh and that Beek was briefly given by the Ordinary into Armburgh's custody, at an early stage in the case. It is more than likely that Armburgh wrote the petition for Alison. As it is the last entry on the later part of the roll, it is probable that it was entered to fill up the roll.

497 There is a Thomas Beek chaplain in a Lincolnshire–Nottinghamshire deed of 1439 and a Thomas Beke late of Boxwell, Gloucestershire, clerk, who was allegedly involved in thefts at Boxwell in 1439–40 (*Cal. Pat. Rolls 1436–41*, p.546). There is also Thomas Bak alias Beke who escaped from the Marshalsea in c.1447, although he is not designated cleric (*Cal. Close Rolls 1441–7*, p.484) and a Thomas Beke chaplain who appeared before the commissary general of the chancellor of Oxford in 1449 (*Registrum Cancellarii Oxoniensis 1434–1469*, ed. H.E. Salter (2 vols., Oxford Hist. Soc. 93–4 (1932), i, p.186).

498 The last three letters are obscure.

499 There was a Thomas Hulle chaplain who was presented to Slapton church, in the diocese of Lincoln, in 1433. The benefice was in the gift of the abbot of Barking, a possible connection with Thomas Aspall and Armburgh (see above, n.93) but this may be too far-fetched (*Cal. Pat. Rolls 1429–36*, p.249).

500 There was a Thomas More gentleman of London, a Thomas More citizen and possibly leatherseller of London, a Thomas More gentleman of Rochester, Kent and a Thomas More of Buckinghamshire. Either of the last two could also be the gentleman of London, since that was a designation often used for people who resided part of the time in London, usually lawyers, but it is unlikely that the London citizen overlaps with any of the other three (*Cal. Close Rolls 1447–54*, p.97, *1454–61*, pp.183, 195, 206, 253, 281, 383; *Cal. Pat. Rolls 1429–36*, p.397; *Cal. Fine Rolls 1445–52*, p.241, *1461–71*, p.201; *London Plea and Memoranda Rolls 1437–57*, pp.182, 184).

501 George Norwich, archdeacon of Westminster (PRO C1/19/35). It was the abbot who was normally referred to as 'the ordinary' within this liberty (Pugh, *Imprisonment in Medieval England*, p.137), although this was a title normally reserved for the bishop, meaning the possessor of ordinary jurisdiction within the diocese (A.H. Thompson, *The English Clergy and their Organization in the Later Middle Ages* (Oxford, 1947), p.51).

of peese to the Ordinary of Westm, a yens the libertees of that holy plase and a yens the kynges prerogatiue and his lawes,[502] the seid Ordinary put hym in preson and kept hym there iiij or v dayes and afterward the seid Ordinary made Robert pray his scribe to take the seid Sir Thomas owtt of preson and bryng hym to the hovse of Robert Armeburgh mayster to your seid suppliaunt, and forthwith by collision of the ordinary and his scribe there came v or vj persones with stavys, glevys and axis rennyng in at the seid Robert Armeburgh is gatys and thredyn the seid Sir Thomas Beek to sle yf thei myght come by hym and theruppon a none came the Ordinary hym selfe and fette the seid Sir Thomas Beek from Armeburgh is house and put hym a gayne in to the seid preson and bare hym onhonde that he dyd hit for his saluacion which was not trewe, and that schewe welle, for he kept hym there stille in preson in to the tyme that the seid Sir Thomas was fayne to be bounde in a symple obligacion of c marc to abyde the awarde of certeyn persones the which obligacion the seid Ordinary toke into his owne honde to kepe as in a mene honde and rehersyd the condicion by mowthe which condicion was, but yf the arbitrours myght acorde that the obligacion scholde be delyuerd a yen and the parties stonde at large and not withstondyng that the abritrours and vmpeers which were chosyn myght not acorde, the seid Ordinary wolde not delyuer the seid obligacion but bare onhonde that hit was made vnder that condicion that the seid Sir Thomas scholde not appeele to the court of Rome from his iurisdiccion.[503] And theruppon the seid Sir Thomas by avyse of his counseill appeelid to the court of Rome and hadde an inhibicion owte of the Archis and inhibit the Ordinary[504] and made a procuracy vnder an instrument to certeyn persones to answere for hym in his absence[505] and went forth to the court of Rome to sve his appeele. And none,[506] after that he was gone, the Ordinary and his scribe sette a citacion vpon the abbey doore to that entent that he scholde appeere a fore hem the next court day and so purposed hem to have

---

502 The jurisdictions referred to here are those of the abbot within the liberty of Westminster (G. Rosser, 'London and Westminster: The Suburb in the Urban Economy in the Later Middle Ages', *Towns and Townspeople in the Fifteenth Century*, ed. J.A.F. Thomson (Gloucester, 1988), pp.50–1), here acting in place of the king, and of the royal jurisdiction, which would normally allow the accused to be bailed on production of sufficient security (*Proceedings Before the Justices of the Peace in the Fourteenth and Fifteenth Centuries*, ed. B.H. Putnam (The Ames Foundation, 1938), pp.cvii–cviii).

503 I.e. Beek was persuaded to give the Ordinary an obligation to accept an arbitration between himself and the Moores, a common means of resolving disputes and the normal mechanism for binding the parties to accept the award and to keep the peace in the mean time (see E. Powell, 'Arbitration and the Law in England in the Later Middle Ages', *Trans. Royal Hist. Soc.*, 5th ser., 33 (1983), pp.49–67), but then found that his obligation allegedly included a promise not to appeal to Rome.

504 For inhibition, see above, n.159. This is another instance where the inhibiting provincial authority is that of Canterbury.

505 That is, appointed proctors as his sworn representatives to answer for him in his absence; the clerical equivalent of an attorney in a lay court (Woodcock, *Medieval Ecclesiastical Courts*, p.52).

506 *Sic*: presumably 'anon.' is meant.

hadde hym in a contempt and denuncyd hym a cursed,[507] hadde not Thomas Chopyn[508] come in to the court and notefyed to the Ordinary that Sir Thomas Beek hadde take his jornay to the court of Rome and schewed an instrument theruppon and yit the Ordinary and his scribe wolde not sese ther by but sette vp a nother citacion a pon the same dore to that entent that the seid Sir Thomas scholde appeere by fore the seid Ordinary the next court day after that and there they hadde ordeyned that on scholde have brought in an instrument at that day recordyng that the seid Sir Thomas was seyn with in the jurisdiction of Westm after the daye that Thomas Chopyn hadde notefied to the seid Ordinary that the seid Sir Thomas hadde take his jornay and to verifye theire seiyng they made a Rome Renner[509] come in to the abbey of Westmynster and to telle to dyuers persones that he sawe Sir Thomas Beek at Calyse[510] with in ij dayes after that day hit was assigned in the instrument that the seid Sir Thomas was seyn with in the jurisdiction of Westm, and so thei purposyd hem to have hadde hym in a contempt and denuncyd acirsed, hadde not Thomas Chopyn come a gayn at the next court day to the ordinary and to his scribe and offerd hym selfe to repreue that instrument and made hem to sese so of her malyce and, within a while after that the seid Sir Thomas was come from the court of Rome, he was sommonnd to come by fore the Ordinary of Westm at the next court day and whan he came there there was Moore and his wyfe with xl or l persones with hym by way of mayntenance and there Moore his wyfe by fore the Ordinary pulled of Sir Thomas Beek his hode and beete hym a boute the hede with her fyste. Wherfor the Ordinary pronuncyed her in a contempt and denuncyed her a cursed. And the next court that the Ordinary helde he helde hit in Saynt Margaret[511] is chirch porche, where as he helde neuer none by fore that tyme, and the chirch doore I schitte and dide so calle Sir Thomas Beek and purposyd hem fully yf he hadde aperyd that he schulde have be take with strenght and have be bore oute at the yates and so have be delyuered to his enemyes and, not withstondyng that Moore is wyfe stode acursed for leying hondes vpon Sir Thomas Beek and was neuer acordyd with hym, the Ordinary assygned her to come in the next court day to make her purgacion of avowtry in generall[512] and for asmoche as Alyson Beek your suppliaunt laboured for Sir Thomas Beek her

---

507 Effectively a summons to attend the court. Failure to do so without good cause could result first in public suspension of the defendant for contumacy and ultimately in excommunication, and these are apparently the two fates alluded to here (Woodcock, *Medieval Ecclesiastical Courts*, pp.50–1, 93–5).

508 There was a Thomas Chopyn active in London in 1448 and 1459 (*Cal. Close Rolls 1447–54*, p.61, *1454–61*, p.434).

509 There is no doubt about the reading of this word and there seems no other explanation than that this is a runner i.e. messenger to or from Rome.

510 This must be Calais.

511 St Margaret's, the parish church of Westminster (G. Rosser, *Medieval Westminster 1200–1540* (Oxford, 1989), p.253).

512 By 'avowtry' is meant compurgation, the normal method by which the defendant cleared himself

brother and spake for hym, the Ordinary made the paryssh prest sommon the seid Alison and her brother the Sonday next folowyng opynly in the pulpit to be by fore the Ordinary the same day that was assygned to Moore is wyfe, to make her purgacion and to telle the cause why sche scholde not make her purgacion of avowtry in generall. Wherfor your suppliaunt by avyse of her counseill, seing how the Ordinary purposyd hym to have her in a contempt and to denunce her acursed and to do her paye Moore is wyfe is costis and so to put her to a grete rebuke, sche appeeled from his jurisdiction to the court of Rome and to the court of the Archys and hadde out an inhibicion and inhibit the Ordinary and sommonnd Moore is wyfe to appere the v lavfull day after the fest of Saint Hillary[513] and, not withstondyng that the Ordinary was inhibit at the next court day, whan Moore is wyfe came in to make her purgacion, the seid Ordinary dide do calle your suppliaunt to telle the cause why that the seid Moore ys wyfe scholde not make her purgacion.[514] Wherfor your seid suppliaunt came in by fore the Ordinary with her counseill vnder protestacion that they wolde knowe hym for theire Ordinary in that case and withsayden the purgacion and offerd hem to put in matyr of preve and so the purgacion was lette as for that day, and in the mene tyme your suppliaunt is counseill made a matyr a yens Moore is wyfe is purgacion of avowtry in generall. And after, thei serched the regester and founde that the matyr was alteryd and chaunged, for there as your suppliaunt was sommonnd to come by fore the Ordinary to telle the cause why Moore is wyfe scholde not make her purgacion of avowytry in generall, hit was entryd in the regester that sche scholde telle the cause why that sche scholde not make her purgacion of avowtry doen with Sir Thomas Beek your suppliaunt is brother in speciall.[515] Wherfor your suppliaunt is counseill made a bille of addicion answeryng to that matyr to put in with the other bille at the next court day. And therupon your suppliaunt with her counseill whan the next court day was come and Moore is wyfe [m.5v] was come in to make her purgacion came in by fore the Ordinary and there they founde so grete multitude of pepull with Moore and

in ecclesiastical proceedings. Since Mrs Moore had apparently been excommunicated for her assault on Beek, she could not simply purge herself with the help of other oath-takers, but would need to be absolved (Woodcock, *Medieval Ecclesiastical Courts*, pp.57–8, 97–101; Swanson, *Church and Society*, pp.175–7, 179–81).

513 St Hilary was on 13 January; this presumably means on the fifth day on which sessions were held after that; counting St Hilary as the first day, in the manner of the secular law terms, would make this 17 January, or, if the fifth day after was meant literally, the date would be 18 January. According to a fourteenth-century schedule for the Court of the Arches, if it really does mean the fifth day on which pleas could be held after St Hilary, then the date is 18 January, as the first session was on 14 January (Cheney, *Handbook of Dates*, p.73).

514 I.e. the Ordinary was continuing with the case in the court of Westminster, when the appeal to Rome with its accompanying inhibition should have ended all activity in the lower courts (see above, n.159).

515 This is presumably a distinction in canon law between compurgation of a general nature and compurgation for a particular offence, but I have not been able to discover either the nature or the force of the distinction.

his wyfe by waye of mayntenaunce that they myght not come to the barre, but as thei put theire billes over mennys schulders in to the Ordinary, and not withstondyng that bothe the billes were redde by fore the Ordinary and indictyd in the regester and not withstondyng that Moore is wife stode acursed, the Ordinary admitted her to her purgacion with compurgatrices, money of hem vnlavfull and suspecte. And therfor for these grevys and wrongys and money other a fore rehersyd your suppliaunt by the avyse of her counseill appeeled from his jurisdiccion to the court of Rome and to the court of the Archys, and Sir Thomas Beek your suppliauntes brother for wronges and grevys doen to him which ben rehersyd in this bille, he appeeled also from his jurisdiccion to the court of Rome, and for feere of dyuers thyngys which were coniectyd a yens hym in Westmynster he went to Saint Martyns[516] and from thens he toke his way to the court of Rome. And after that he was owt of the jurisdiction of Westm the Ordinary called hym in a contempt on Saint Hillari[517] is even and in the morne after he made the morwe masse prest to denunce hym a cursed at the morwe masse by candel lyght.

---

[516] Almost certainly St Martin-in-the-Fields, the next parish to St Margaret's, which had been carved out of the latter: there he was out of the Westminster jurisdiction, one which was exempt from all authority save the pope's (Rosser, *Medieval Westminster*, pp.230, 252). Alternatively, it could be St Martin-le-Grand in the City, where Beke would have been completely secure from any judicial process (Rosser, 'London and Westminster', p.50).

[517] 12 January.

199

BIBLIOGRAPHY

Bibliography of printed works used in this edition

Printed Sources

A Calendar of the Feet of Fines for Suffolk, ed. W. Rye (Ipswich, 1900)

Calendar of Close Rolls Preserved in the Public Record Office 1396–1509 (19 vols., London, HMSO, 1927–63)

Calendar of Fine Rolls Preserved in the Public Record Office 1399–1509 (11 vols., London, HMSO, 1931–62)

Calendar of Inquisitions Post Mortem . . . Preserved in the Public Record Office (20 vols., London, HMSO, 1904–   )

Calendar of Inquisitions Post Mortem . . . Preserved in the Public Record Office, Hen.VII (3 vols., London, HMSO, 1898–1955)

Calendar of Letter Books of the City of London, ed. R.R. Sharpe (11 vols., London, 1899–1912)

Calendar of Patent Rolls Preserved in the Public Record Office 1399–1509 (17 vols., London, HMSO, 1903–16)

Calendar of Select Plea and Memoranda Rolls of the City of London, edd. A.H. Thomas and P.E. Jones (6 vols., Cambridge, 1926–61)

Calendar of the Signet Letters of Henry IV and Henry V, ed. J.L. Kirby (London, 1978)

Calendar of Wills . . . in the Court of Husting, London 1258–1688, ed. R.R. Sharpe (2 vols., London, 1889–90)

Calendarium Inquisitionum Post Mortem sive Escaetarum, iv, Hen.V – Ric.III (Record Commissioners, London, 1828)

Calendars of the Proceedings in Chancery under Elizabeth I, to which are Prefixed Examples of Earlier Proceedings in that Court (2 vols., Record Commissioners, London, 1827)

Cartae et Alia Munimenta quae ad Dominium de Glamorgancie Pertinent, ed. G.T. Clark, rev. G.L. Clark (6 vols., Cardiff, 1910)

The Cartulary of the Augustinian Friars of Clare, ed. C. Harper-Bill, Suffolk Records Soc., Suffolk Charters, 11 (Woodbridge, 1991)

The Cely Papers 1472–1488, ed. A. Hanham (Early English Text Soc., 273, 1975)

Class List of Chancery Files, List and Index Soc., 130 (1976)

Collections for a History of Staffordshire, ed. by the William Salt Archaeological Soc. (1890–   )

M.M. Condon, 'A Wiltshire Sheriff's Notebook 1464–5', *Medieval Legal Records Edited in Memory of C.A.F. Meekings*, edd. R.F. Hunnisett and J.B. Post (London, 1978), pp.410–28

The Coventry Leet Book, ed. M.D. Harris (4 vols. in one, EETS, o.s., 134,135,138,146, 1907–13)

A Descriptive Catalogue of Ancient Deeds in the Public Record Office (6 vols., London, HMSO, 1890–1915)

Early English Lyrics, edd. E.K. Chambers and F. Sidgwick (rpt. London, 1947)

English Historical Documents, iii, 1189–1327, ed. H. Rothwell (London, 1975)

'Exul', 'Cases from the Early Chancery Proceedings', *The Ancestor*, 8 (1904), pp.167–201

Feet of Fines for the County of Somerset 12 Edward III–20 Richard II, ed. E. Green (Somerset Rec. Soc., 17, 1902)

Feet of Fines for the County of Somerset Henry V to Henry VI, ed. E. Green (Somerset Rec. Soc., 22, 1906)

Feet of Fines for Essex, iv, 1423–1547, edd. P.H. Reaney and M. Fitch (Essex Archaeological Soc., 1964)

Feudal Documents of the Abbey of Bury St Edmunds, ed. D.C. Douglas (British Academy, London, 1932)

Sir John Fortescue, *De Laudibus Legum Angliae*, ed. S.B. Chrimes (Cambridge, 1942)

The Grey of Ruthin Valor, ed. R.I. Jack (Sydney, 1965)

Historical Manuscripts Commission, Hastings Manuscripts, i (1928)

Inquisitions and Assessments Relating to Feudal Aids . . . Preserved in the Public Record Office (6 vols., London, HMSO, 1899–1920)

F.W. Maitland, *The Court Baron* (Selden Soc., 4, 1890)

Medieval English Lyrics, ed. R.T. Davies (London, 1963)

Paston Letters and Papers of the Fifteenth Century, ed. N. Davis (2 vols., Oxford, 1971–6)

The Paston Letters, ed. J.G. Gairdner (6 vols., London, 1904, rpt. in 1 vol., Gloucester, 1983)

Plumpton Correspondence, ed. T. Stapleton (Camden Soc., 1839, rpt. Gloucester, 1990)

Proceedings Before the Justices of the Peace in the Fourteenth and Fifteenth Centuries, ed. B.H. Putnam (The Ames Foundation, 1938)

Records of the Society of Lincoln's Inn, i, Admissions 1420–1799 (London, 1896)

The Red Book of Colchester, ed. W.G. Benham (Colchester, 1902)

The Register of the Gild of the Holy Cross . . . of Stratford-upon-Avon, ed. J.H. Bloom (London, 1907)

The Register of Henry Chichele Archbishop of Canterbury 1414–43, ed. E.F. Jacob (4 vols., Oxford, 1938–43)

Registrum Cancellarii Oxoniensis 1434–1469, ed. H.E. Salter (2 vols., Oxford Hist. Soc., 93–4, 1932)

Reliquae Antiquae, edd. T. Wright and J.O. Halliwell, i (London, 1845)

Rotuli Parliamentorum, 1377–1503 (4 vols., London, 1783)

J. Rous, *Historia Regum Angliae*, ed. T. Hearne (Oxford, 1716)

Select Cases in the Court of King's Bench, ed. G.O. Sayles, vii, Selden Soc., 88 (1971)

The Statutes of the Realm, i–ii (London, 1810–15, rpt. 1963)

The Stonor Letters and Papers 1290–1483, ed. C.L. Kingsford, (3 vols., Camden Soc., 3rd ser., 29,30,34, 1919–24, rpt., ed. C. Carpenter, Cambridge, 1996)

The Tropenell Cartulary, ed. J.S. Davies (2 vols., Wiltshire Archaeological and Natural History Soc., 1908)

The Visitations of Essex, ed. W.C. Metcalfe (2 vols., Harleian Soc., 13, 1878)

Warwickshire Feet of Fines, iii, ed. L. Drucker (Dugdale Soc. Publs., 18, 1943)

Secondary Works

A. Acheson, *A Gentry Community: Leicestershire in the Fifteenth Century c.1422–c.1485* (Cambridge, 1992)

C. Allmand, *Lancastrian Normandy, 1415–1450* (Oxford, 1983)

J.H. Baker, *An Introduction to Legal History* (2nd ed., London, 1979)

J.H. Baker, *The Order of Serjeants at Law*, Selden Soc., Supplementary Series, 5 (London, 1984)

J.L. Bolton, *The Medieval English Economy 1150–1500* (London, 1980)

A.L. Brown, *The Governance of Late Medieval England 1272–1461* (London, 1989)

J. Brownbill, 'St John of Bletsoe', *Genealogists' Magazine*, v (1929–31), pp.355–9

C. Carpenter, 'Gentry and Community in Medieval England', *Journal of British Studies*, 33 (1994), pp.340–80.

C. Carpenter, 'Law, Justice and Landowners in Late-Medieval England', *Law and History Review*, 1 (1983), pp.205–37

C. Carpenter, *Locality and Polity: a Study of Warwickshire Landed Society, 1401–1499* (Cambridge, 1992)

C. Carpenter, 'Political and Constitutional History: before and after McFarlane', *The McFarlane Legacy*, ed. R.H. Britnell and A.J. Pollard (Stroud, 1995), pp.175–206

H. Chauncey, *The Historical Antiquities of Hertfordshire* (2 vols., 2nd ed., Bishops Stortford, 1826, rpt. Dorking, 1975)

C.R. Cheney, *Handbook of Dates for Students of English History* (2nd ed., London, Royal Historical Soc., 1970)

G.T. Clark, *Limbus Patrum Morganiae et Glamorganiae* (London, 1886)

J.S. Cockburn, *A History of English Assizes 1558–1714* (Cambridge, 1972)

J. Collinson and E. Rack, *The History and Antiquities of the County of Somerset* (3 vols., Bath, 1791)

The Complete Peerage, edd. V. Gibbs, H.A. Doubleday *et al.* (13 vols., London, 1910–40)

W. Cooper, *Wootton Wawen: its History and Records* (Leeds, 1936)

J.S. Corbett, *Glamorgan: Papers and Notes on the Lordship and its Members*, ed. D.R. Paterson (Cardiff, 1925)

M. Creighton, *A History of the Popes from the Great Schism to the Sack of Rome* (2nd ed., 6 vols., London, 1897)

Dictionary of National Biography, ed. L. Stephen *et al.* (53 vols. with 6 supplementary vols., 1885–1912)

E. Duffy, *The Stripping of the Altars: Traditional Religion in England c.1400–c.1580* (Yale, 1992)

William Dugdale, *The Antiquities of Warwickshire* (2 vols., London, 1730, rpt. Manchester, n.d.)

C. Dyer, *Warwickshire Farming c.1349–1520* (Dugdale Soc. Occasional Papers, 27, 1981)

A.B. Emden, *A Biographical Register of the University of Cambridge to 1500* (Cambridge, 1963)

A.B. Emden, *A Biographical Register of the University of Oxford to A.D. 1500* (3 vols., Oxford, 1957–9)

H. Fishwick, *The History of the Parish of Rochdale* (Rochdale and London, 1889)

E. Foss, *A Biographical Dictionary of the Judges of England 1066–1870* (London, 1870)

F. Gastrell, *Notitia Cestriensis*, ii I (Chetham Soc., 1849)

Thomas Gerard, *The Particular Description of the County of Somerset*, ed. E.H. Bates (Somerset Rec. Soc., 15, 1900)

R.A. Griffiths, *The Reign of King Henry VI* (London, 1981)

Handbook of British Chronology, edd. E.B. Fryde, D.E. Greenway, S. Porter and I. Roy (3rd ed., London, Royal Historical Soc., 1986)

A. Harding, *The Law Courts of Medieval England* (London, 1973)

G.L. Harriss, 'Introduction' to *England in the Fifteenth Century: Collected Essays of K.B. McFarlane* (London, 1981)

I.M.W. Harvey, *Jack Cade's Rebellion of 1450* (Oxford, 1991)

M. Harvey, 'England and the Council of Pisa: Some New Information', *Annuarium Historiae Conciliorum*, 2 (1970), pp.263–83

M. Harvey, *England, Rome and the Papacy, 1417–1464* (Manchester, 1993)

F. Haslewood, 'The Ancient Families of Suffolk', *Proceedings of the Suffolk Institute of Archaeology and Natural History*, 8 (1884), pp.121–214

M. Hastings, *The Court of Common Pleas in Fifteenth Century England* (Ithaca, N.Y., 1947)

P. Heath, *Church and Realm 1272–1461* (London, 1988)

R.H. Helmholz, 'Assumpsit and Fidei Laesio', *Canon Law and the Law of England* (London, 1987), pp.263–89

R.H. Helmholz, 'Bankruptcy and Probate Jurisdiction before 1571', *ibid.*, pp.291–305

The History of Parliament: The House of Commons 1386–1421, edd. J.S. Roskell, L. Clark and C. Rawcliffe (4 vols., Stroud, 1993)

R.F. Hunnisett, *The Medieval Coroner* (Cambridge, 1961)

M. Innes, *Hare Sitting Up* (Harmondsworth, Penguin Books, 1964)

E.W. Ives, *The Common Lawyers of Pre-Reformation England* (Cambridge, 1983)

E.F. Jacob, 'To and From the Court of Rome in the early Fifteenth Century', *Essays in Later Medieval History* (Manchester and New York, 1968), pp.58–78

D.A. Johnson, 'Dean Bate's Statutes for St Edith's, Tamworth, Staffordshire, 1442', *Trans. of the South Staffs. Archaeological and Historical Soc.*, 10 (1968–9), pp.55–62

P.A. Johnson, *Duke Richard of York 1411–1460* (Oxford, 1988)

W.J. Jones, *The Elizabethan Court of Chancery* (Oxford, 1967)

Jowitt's Dictionary of English Law, ed. J. Burke (2 vols., London, 1977)

F. Klingender, edd. E. Antal and J. Harthan, *Animals in Art and Thought to the End of the Middle Ages* (London, 1971)

D.H. Lawrence, *Women in Love*, edd. D. Farmer, L. Vasey and J. Worthen (Cambridge, 1957)

John le Neve, comp. B. Jones, *Fasti Ecclesiae Anglicanae 1300–1541, xi, The Welsh Dioceses* (London, 1965)

List of Sheriffs for England and Wales, ed. A. Hughes (PRO Lists and Indexes, main series, 9, London, HMSO, 1898, rpt. New York, 1963)

F. McCulloch, *Medieval Latin and French Bestiaries* (2nd ed., Chapel Hill, 1962)

A. Macfarlane, *The Origins of English Individualism* (Oxford, 1978)

K.B. McFarlane, *England in the Fifteenth Century: Collected Essays* (London, 1981)

M. McIntosh, *Autonomy and Community: the Royal Manor of Havering 1200–1500* (Cambridge, 1986)

P. Morant, *The History and Antiquities of . . . Colchester* (2 vols., London, 1748, rpt. East Ardsley, 1970)

P. Morant, *The History and Antiquities of the County of Essex* (2 vols., London, 1768)

C. Moreton, *The Townshends and their World: Gentry, Law, and Land in Norfolk c.1450–1551* (Oxford, 1992)

T. Nicholas, *The History and Antiquities of Glamorganshire and its Families* (London, 1874)

J.G. Nichols, *The History and Antiquities of the County of Leicester* (4 vols., London, 1795–1811, rpt. Wakefield, 1971)

R.C. Palmer, *The Whilton Dispute 1264–1380* (Princeton, 1984)

S.J. Payling, *Political Society in Lancastrian England: The Greater Gentry of Nottinghamshire* (Oxford, 1991)

The Place-Names of Bedfordshire and Huntingdonshire, edd. A. Mawer and F.M. Stenton (English Place-Name Soc., 3, 1926)

The Place-Names of Essex, ed. P.H. Reaney (English Place-Name Soc., 12, 1935)

A.J. Pollard, *North-Eastern England During the Wars of the Roses* (Oxford, 1990)

F. Pollock and F.W. Maitland, *The History of English Law Before the Time of Edward I* (2nd ed., 2 vols., Cambridge, 1898)

L. Poos, *A Rural Society after the Black Death: Essex 1350–1525* (Cambridge, 1991)

E. Powell, 'After "After McFarlane": The Poverty of Patronage and the Case for Constitutional History', *Trade, Devotion and Governance: Papers in Later Medieval History*, edd. D.J. Clayton, R.G. Davies and P. McNiven (Stroud, 1994), pp.1–16

E. Powell, 'Arbitration and the Law in England in the Later Middle Ages', *Trans. Royal Hist. Soc.*, 5th ser., 33 (1983), pp.49–67

Bibliography

E. Powell, *Kingship, Law, and Society: Criminal Justice in the Reign of Henry V* (Oxford, 1989)

R.B. Pugh, *Imprisonment in Medieval England* (Cambridge, 1968)

C. Rawcliffe, 'The Staffords, Earls of Stafford and Dukes of Buckingham 1394–1521' (unpubl. Sheffield Univ. Ph.D. thesis, 1974)

C. Rawcliffe, *The Staffords, Earls of Stafford and Dukes of Buckingham 1394–1521* (Cambridge, 1978)

M. Richardson, 'Early Equity Judges: Keepers of the Rolls of Chancery, 1415–47', *American Journal of Legal History*, 36 (1992), pp.441–65

C. Richmond, *John Hopton: A Fifteenth-Century Suffolk Gentleman* (Cambridge, 1981)

C. Richmond, *The Paston Family in the Fifteenth Century: The First Phase* (Cambridge, 1990)

J.E.T. Rogers, *A History of Agriculture and Prices in England* (7 vols. in 8, Oxford, 1866–1902)

J.T. Rosenthal, 'The Estates and Finances of Richard, Duke of York', *Studies in Medieval and Renaissance History*, 2 (1965), pp.115–204

G. Rosser, 'London and Westminster: The Suburb in the Urban Economy in the Later Middle Ages', *Towns and Townspeople in the Fifteenth Century*, ed. J.A.F. Thomson (Gloucester, 1988), pp.45–61

G. Rosser, *Medieval Westminster 1200–1540* (Oxford, 1989)

B. Rowland, *Animals with Human Faces* (London, 1974)

I.J. Sanders, *English Baronies: A Study of their Origin and Descent 1086–1327* (Oxford, 1960)

Walter Scott, *Guy Mannering* (3 vols., Edinburgh, 1815)

R.L. Storey, *The End of the House of Lancaster* (London, 1966)

P. Styles, *Sir Simon Archer*, Dugdale Soc. Occasional Papers, 6 (1946)

R. Swanson, *Church and Society in Late Medieval England* (Oxford, 1989)

H.J. Thomas, 'Castle, Church and Village: Medieval Barry', *Barry: The Centenary Book*, ed. D. Moore (Barry Island, 1984), pp.57–100

A.H. Thompson, *The English Clergy and their Organization in the Later Middle Ages* (Oxford, 1947)

S. Thrupp, *The Merchant Class of Medieval London* (Chicago, 1948)

A. Tuck, *Crown and Nobility 1272–1461* (London, 1985)

Victoria County Histories:
  Cambridgeshire, ii (London, 1948), v (London, 1973)
  Hertfordshire, ii, (London, 1908), iii (London, 1912)
  Huntingdonshire, iii (London, 1936)
  Lancashire, v (London, 1911)
  Leicestershire, v (London, 1964)
  Northamptonshire, iv (London, 1937)
  Warwickshire, ii (London, 1908), iv (London, 1947), vi (London, 1951)

R. Virgoe, 'Aspects of the County Community in the Fifteenth Century', *Profit, Piety and the Professions*, ed. M.A. Hicks (Gloucester, 1990), pp.1–13

J.L. Watts, *Henry VI and the Politics of Kingship* (Cambridge, 1996)

J.C. Wedgwood, *History of Parliament: Biographies of Members of the Commons House 1439–1539* (London, 1936)

W.O. Wehrle, *The Macaronic Hymn Tradition in Medieval English Literature* (Washington, D.C., 1933)

T.H. White, *The Bestiary: A Book of Beasts, Being a Translation from a Latin Bestiary of the Twelfth Century* (London, 1954)

B.P. Wolffe, *Henry VI* (London, 1981)

Bibliography

A.C. Wood, *Typescript List of Escheators for England and Wales*, in the PRO (List and Index Soc., 72, 1971)

B.L. Woodcock, *Medieval Ecclesiastical Courts in the Diocese of Canterbury* (OUP, London, 1952)

S. Wright, *The Derbyshire Gentry in the Fifteenth Century* (Derbyshire Rec. Soc., 1983)

INDEX

Advowson, 9; of Mancetter, 21–4, 34–5, 36, 57, 66–7, 68–73, 145, 147n, 178–80, 184, 188

Agriculture (*see also under* woods), 169–70, 172; at Mancetter, 77, 117, 179; at Over Hall in Gedelston, 174–5; at Radwinter, 121,123; at Roos Hall in Sarratt, Herts., 113–14

Alberti family, bankers, 101n, 102

Ale(y)n, Clement of Atherstone, Warks., 34n

Alvecote, Warks., 111n

Andrews, John of King's Ripton, Hunts., 96n

Arbitration/settlement: 5, 37, 38–9, 51–2, 83, 97, 117, 130–1, 153, 170–1, 192–3, 194, 196

Arblaster, Thomas of Staffs., co-owner of Mancetter, 22, 35n, 145, 179; wife, Alice, 22n

Arbury, Warks., 111n

Archer family of Warwickshire, 3; Sir Simon, 3

Armburgh family, 1–2, 8, 12n, 13, 17–18, 20–4, 26–7, 29, 39n, 41–3, 45–7, 50, 52–4, 58, 62n, 78n, 98, 107n, 110n, 113, 119, 124n, 134n, 140, 142, 184n, 187n, 190n, 191n, 193n; John, citizen and girdler of London, 49, 128–9, 171–2; Reynold/Reginald, nephew of Robert, 7, 29–30, 31n, 33, 36, 38–9, 43, 49–50, 59, 68, 70–5, 77, 102n, 111–13, 168, 171–3, 178–9, 181–4, 186–8, wife, Joan (see Joan Palmer); Robert, 1–2, 6–21, 23n, 25–8, 29n, 30–46, 48–59, 61, 63–6, 67n, 68–74, 75n, 76–7, 79–81, 82n, 83, 86–7, 89, 92–4, 95n, 96, 98n, 102–4, 106, 107n, 110–12, 114–15, 118–19, 120n, 123–4, 126–34, 135n, 138, 139n, 140, 141n, 142, 144–9, 151–2, 154, 168–71, 172n, 173–4, 175n, 176, 178–84, 185n, 186–8, 191–6, wife, Joan (see Joan Brokholes); William of Godmanchester, Hunts., 6, 7n, 31, 33, 36, 49–50, 59, 102, 110, 127–8, 172n, 186–7

Armburgh, John, 32n

Arms, law of, 75–6

Ashdon, Essex, 9–10, 31–3, 39n, 96n, 123n, 185n

Asheldham, Essex, 30, 39

Aspall, Thomas of Essex, 5, 6n, 9, 48, 56, 75, 77–8, 79n, 80–6, 194, 195n; wife, Joan (see Joan Brokholes)

Astley, Lord William, of Astley, Warks. and estate, 14–19, 26, 35, 41, 74n, 108n, 171n

Atherstone, John, 34–5, 49, 70–3, 74n, 75–6, 179–81

Atherstone, Warks., 9, 11, 34, 53, 104, 126

Babyngton, William, CJCP, 105

Bak, Thomas, alias Beke, 195n

Bakepuys, William of Derbyshire, 63n

Bakepuz, William, 63

Barbour, John of Mancetter, alias Mountford, priest, 9n , 34–6, 43–4, 49, 68, 69n, 71–2, 76–7, 169n, 179–83, 188

Barbour, Richard, yeoman of Atherstone, 3, 9, 11, 17, 24–25, 28, 35n, 49, 68n, 89, 104, 106, 111, 112n, 114–16, 124, 129, 132, 134, 135n, 138–9, 145, 148, 169n, 182n

Barkby, William, 35, 181n, 188

Barking, Essex, 86; abbey, 79n; abbot, 195n

Baron, Phillip, 169

Barre family of Herefordshire and Knebworth, Herts., 186n; John, 177

Barre, William, 186

Barrington family of Chigwell and Hatfield Broadoak, Essex, 177n; John, 177n; Thomas, 177n

'Bastard', 36, 176

Bastard, Richard of Bedford, 36, 176n; wife, Isabel (see Isabel Rickhill)

Bataill family of Magdalen Laver and High Ongar, Essex, 177n; John, 177n

Bataill, John of Stanford Rivers, Essex, 177n

Bataill, Thomas of Stock-Hall in Matching, Essex, mercer of London, 17n

Bate, John, chancery clerk and dean of Tamworth, 191

Bate, Thomas [of Warks. And Staffs.], 191n

Baynard, Richard of Messing, Essex, 12n, 16, 37n, 61n, 62–3

Beauchamp family of Warwick: Richard, Lord Despenser and earl of Worcester, 98n; Richard, 5th earl of Warwick, 14–15, 17–19, 21, 23n, 26–7, 41–2, 52, 62n, 89n, 98n, 107n, 125, 149–50; Thomas, 4th earl of Warwick, 62n; William Lord Bergavenny, 15–16, 42, 62n, 89n, wife/widow, Joan, 15–19, 26, 42, 62, 63n

Beauchamp, Ralph, vicar of 'Scharnyffeld', Leics., 9, 42, 59, 93–4, 133–4

Bedell, Thomas citizen and coppersmith of London, 169

Bedford, John, duke of, 34, 104n

Bedfordshire, 29, 176n

Beek, Alison, servant of Robert Armburgh, 195, 197–8

Beek, Sir Thomas, cleric, 56–7, 195–9

Beke, Thomas, chaplain, 195n

Beke, Thomas, of Boxwell, Gloucs., clerk, 195n

Bellers family of Leicestershire and Brownsover, Warwickshire, 16n, 22–23, 28, 34, 57, 151n;

Index